STATELESSNESS

STATELESSNESS

A Modern History

MIRA L. SIEGELBERG

Harvard University Press

Cambridge, Massachusetts
London, England
2020

Interior design by Dean Bornstein

Library of Congress Cataloging-in-Publication Data

Names: Siegelberg, Mira L., 1983- author.
Title: Statelessness : a modern history / Mira L. Siegelberg.
Identifiers: LCCN 2019055654 | ISBN 9780674976313 (cloth)
Subjects: LCSH: Statelessness. | Stateless persons.
Classification: LCC K7128.S7 .S54 2020 | DDC 342.08/3—dc23
LC record available at https://lccn.loc.gov/2019055654

For my parents, Florence and Alan Siegelberg, with all my love

CONTENTS

STATELESSNESS

Introduction

IN A 1930 LETTER, the German artist Kurt Schwitters described the impetus for his *Merzbilder*, a style of painted collage that he had invented at the end of the First World War. "Everything was wrecked anyway," he explained, "and new things had to be made from the fragments."[1] Schwitters's collages from the 1920s decontextualize the detritus of modern life, turning everyday trash—old tickets, buttons, train schedules, bus routes, bits of newspaper—into grid-like compositions of abstract shape, color, and line. Re-formed into something else altogether, the reconfigured fragments convey, in certain moments, rigid lines separating distinct territories, while at other moments they show how the territories overlap and blur together.

Like many of the individuals discussed in this book, Schwitters became a stateless person as a result of the political upheavals of the twentieth century. In Schwitters's case this meant that he lost the security of his German citizenship when he fled Nazi Germany in 1937, eventually finding refuge in West London, though not before facing internment as an enemy national on the Isle of Man. Schwitters's *Merz* paintings from the 1920s are an apt place to begin this study of statelessness—not primarily for reasons of biography but rather because his works from this period powerfully evoke the way in which the First World War unsettled the basic concepts that defined political reality. The map of the world, it seemed, would need to be remade entirely. The *Merz* collages date from the decade reconstructed in the first half of this study, an era of imperial breakdown and state creation following World War I, when mass numbers of people defined by their exclusion from any political community entered international politics and became the object of intensive debate about the foundations of political order.

Intuitively, the concept of statelessness relates to a broad set of issues surrounding the political organization of humanity. The term brings to mind contentious conflicts over when and how communities that seek to govern

1

themselves gain recognition as independent and autonomous agents. It equally suggests the plight of the more than seventy million people who are currently forcibly displaced around the world. When applied to the growing numbers of those whose countries are sinking beneath the waves of the Pacific Ocean, "statelessness" exposes the limits of how statehood and political membership have been defined in international law, as climate change has begun to reshape the territorial basis of sovereignty. In short, statelessness is a concept that encompasses some of the most destabilizing developments of modern politics.[2]

Despite the explosive, and various, political implications of the concept in its broadest sense, it is the international agreements created in the aftermath of the Second World War that define what it means to be a stateless person and set the basic rules for living outside the boundaries of states and seeking entry into them. These agreements demarcate limited exceptions to the general presumption that states possess a fundamental right to determine who counts as a member and to exercise control over who crosses their borders.[3] Governments in turn legislate the basis for nationality in two main ways: according to descent, and according to birth within a particular territory or jurisdiction. They also stipulate a variety of conditions for naturalization. In the narrower meaning defined by the Convention Relating to the Status of Stateless Persons adopted by the United Nations General Assembly in 1954, a "stateless person" is anyone "who is not considered as a national by any State under the operation of its law," which today means that a person does not possess the primary legal affiliation that defines formal membership in any one of the world's 195 recognized states. A refugee, by contrast, according to the 1951 Refugee Convention, is someone who retains their formal legal connection to a state but is "unable or unwilling to return to their country of origin owing to a well-founded fear of being persecuted for reasons of race, religion, nationality, membership of a particular social group, or political opinion."[4]

Until recently, legal statelessness has been treated as a comparatively marginal issue, gaining prominence only in the past few years among legal scholars and political theorists and within humanitarian agencies.[5] In her 1991 work on American citizenship, the political philosopher Judith Shklar felt compelled to remind readers that legal membership within a state was "not trivial" and that "to be a stateless individual is one of the most dreadful political fates that can befall anyone in the modern world."[6] Yet what now seems like a small part of the broader crisis of mass homelessness and global migration has a history that clarifies how expectations about the legitimate boundaries of political life were forged in the first place. Despite the fact that not all countries have signed on to such agreements, and not all signatories abide by their provisions, the conventions that set the terms of international inclusion and exclusion are one of the critical ways that the world was carved up into its constituent political parts.

The central aim of this book is, therefore, to reconstruct and clarify the arguments that shaped the eventual stabilization of shared understandings of citizenship and noncitizenship in the decades following the Second World War.[7] I explore the origins of the legal frameworks that govern the relationship between states and their nationals, and the roles of ideas, arguments, and ideological justification in their creation. To do so, this book investigates how the problem of statelessness informed theories of rights, sovereignty, international legal order, and cosmopolitan justice, theories developed when the conceptual and political contours of the modern interstate order were being worked out, against the background of some of the most violent and catastrophic events in modern history.

The emergence of the modern legal category of statelessness has most often been portrayed by historians as a consequence of the triumph of nationalism in the twentieth century and the collapse of more fluid forms of political identification and protection characteristic of expansive empires. According to these narratives, in the name of national cohesion, and often in defense of democracy and popular sovereignty, national states claimed the right to define their communities in more exclusive ways, while the rise of fascism and violence against minority groups produced unprecedented flows of refugees by the mid-twentieth century. The nearly forty-year crisis of mass displacement and political homelessness precipitated by the two world wars and the end of empire culminated, on this account, in the creation of the modern international legal frameworks that define those excluded in one way or another from the security of citizenship. These histories in turn tend to trace the rise of modern regimes of rights and governance, from incipient efforts at the League of Nations to provide legal protection to select groups of refugees, to the creation of more universal legal frameworks at the United Nations, its postwar successor. They describe exclusion from the

3

privileges of citizenship as the dark side of democracy, sovereignty, and national self-determination—deficiencies that international organizations and international law have tried to address by legalizing the rights of individuals who do not benefit from the protection of states.[8]

This book tells a different story, one that is more responsive to the fact that the conceptual, legal, and political architecture that defines modern international order has in recent years emerged as the urgent object of historical and theoretical investigation. Historians have shown that it was not until the 1960s that alternative forms of political organization—city-states, princedoms, federations, protectorates, dominions, extraterritorial enclaves, and complex polities—gave way to a more homogenized political map of the world. Both historians and political theorists have likewise begun to recover how ideas of collective self-determination, sovereignty, political representation, and democratic self-rule were conceptualized in a range of ways, often compatible with greater integration with imperial polities. The retrieval of such alternative visions of collective political life generates new pressure to explain how the modern state became the dominant form of political organization in the period after the Second World War. It also raises new questions about the role played by international law and international organizations in the formation of the modern international order, an order that is premised on the formal equality of states but which contains persistent hierarchies and asymmetries of power and privilege. In other words, once we appreciate that the nation state as the sole postimperial claimant to international legitimacy is a more recent phenomenon than previously understood, we have reason to investigate how the international categories defining noncitizenship contributed to the formation and legitimation of the boundaries of interstate order.[9]

The dynamics of Great Power politics governed the postwar settlement in myriad ways, but so did ideas and expectations about interstate order, and it is those ideas that this book seeks to elucidate. To provide a comprehensive account of the evolving significance of statelessness in international thought and international politics, I investigate the history of critical reflection on the meaning of statelessness from the parallel perspectives of the international agencies that directly addressed the crisis of citizenship and sovereignty and the legal scholars who related this crisis to wider debates in legal and political thought. To recover the major conceptual and argumentative terms,

I read the archives of international history in the context of more theoretical discussions about law and political order and survey a variety of legal and literary sources including court cases and novels. Writing such a history therefore means bringing international legal sources within the same frame as more canonical figures in the history of political and legal thought, and reading their systematic and critical reflections together with more traditional archival sources of international and diplomatic history. Both constitute the intellectual and legal context in which the problem of statelessness was conceptualized, debated, and eventually codified into international law.[10]

Nationality has most commonly been defined as the legal or international side of citizenship. In the historian Patrick Weil's recent formulation, "The legal dimension of citizenship reflects the formal linkage of each individual to the nation-state. It is manifested in the passports and national identification documents that confer the official status of national citizens on roughly 99 percent of all human beings. Legal citizenship exists independently of an individual's sense of belonging or degree of participation in national and patriotic institutions."[11] But how should we understand the history of the idea of nationality as the legal or formal side of citizenship? It has mainly been social theorists who have taken up the broader transition in legal thought in the twentieth century—often described by the term "deformalization"— away from assumptions about the rational foundations of law and the autonomy of the domain of law from that of politics.[12] This book links ideas about law, and about the fate of the rule of law, to the representation of the relationship between individuals and states. I explore the impact of a wider transformation of legal consciousness on conceptions of citizenship, noncitizenship, and the significance of statelessness for international politics.

The chapters that follow trace the evolution of debates about the meaning of statelessness from the first period of sustained reflection in the decade after World War I through the expansion of the European refugee crisis in the 1930s, which culminated in the creation of a permanent regime of international definition and protection of refugees and stateless persons after the Second World War. Together they tell a story of critical thought on statelessness that itself offers a new way of comprehending how a world based on hierarchical forms of political order was transformed into one based on the formal equality of states and peoples. In reconstructing the ideological struggles that resulted in the grounding of rights in national citizenship, this book also helps make sense of the process by which the national territorial state emerged as the sole legitimate organizing unit of global politics, and what that has meant for people placed beyond its borders. By documenting a pivotal transformation in how the problem of statelessness was conceptualized from the end of the First World War through the postwar era it shows how the post-1945 political settlement shaped the conceptual and legal boundaries of international politics that we continue to live with today.

~:~

The war that began in 1914 was global in its scale, drawing in soldiers from across Europe, America, and the British and French imperial worlds. At the start of the conflict, there were just over fifty internationally recognized states, mostly found in Europe and the Americas. When it ended, the German, Habsburg, Russian, and Ottoman Empires lay in ruins; millions of combatants had been slaughtered or left carrying the brutal scars of industrial artillery or poison gas; and the future of the formal empires of Britain, France, Japan, and the United States remained the object of Great Power dispute and anticolonial politics. A revolutionary political regime, Bolshevism, established control over the former Russian Empire, while the victors of the war carved up the former imperial holdings of the Ottoman and German Empires, transforming imperial politics through the establishment of the League of Nations. New states that succeeded the Russian, Ottoman, and Austro-Hungarian monarchies included Poland, Austria, Hungary, Czechoslovakia, Yugoslavia, Bulgaria, Lithuania, Latvia, Estonia, and the Greek and Turkish republics.

Revolution and the dissolution of empire left millions without the security of national identification. During World War I, governments began to insist that migrants and travelers carry passports if they wished to cross a border or remain legally within a territory. A subset of people actively pursued recognition as persons without a nationality in order to avoid the punitive consequences of identification with an enemy nation. Over a million émigrés crowded into British-controlled Egypt, Constantinople, Prague, Vienna, Berlin, and Paris after fleeing the Russian Revolution. Thousands more claimed to have become stateless as the successor states to the Austro-Hungarian and Ottoman Empires imposed more restrictive requirements for citizenship. Refugees fleeing violence in the Eastern Front during the war found themselves in the capital cities of the new states of Central Europe

6

without a claim to citizenship, while former imperial subjects who had remained in their homes during the war discovered that they were unable to provide the necessary documentation to obtain national identification.

But what did it mean to be stateless? Historians have tended to assume that until after the Second World War anyone without a nationality qualified as a legal anomaly because, according to orthodox legal doctrine, individuals entered into international society only through their national status. However, the entry of mass numbers of people without a claim to national identification into international politics began to inspire reflections on the foundations of law and rights in a period when the futures of empire, nation, sovereignty, the state, and international law all appeared in question. Older sources of political legitimacy, including dynastic rule, for the most part did not survive the conflict, and the boundaries of political order and international politics became the object of intense political and intellectual contestation. In this context, the deprivation implied by the absence of national status represented the flip side of its revolutionary implications for the future of international legal order.

The status of individuals without a connection to any sovereign government had been uniquely bound up with debates at the heart of political and international thought for several centuries. In the era of early modern imperial competition, the seventeenth-century Dutch jurist and theorist of natural rights Hugo Grotius argued that an eclectic array of agents, including corporations, individuals, and states, represented the subjects of the law of nations. In his 1625 work *The Rights of War and Peace*, Grotius asserted that individuals, states, and corporations were all equally subject to rules governing contract and exchange, and that the state represented one agent among others in international society.[13] By contrast, the dominant theory of international law at the turn of the twentieth century, a theory developed in the context of Western state building and imperial expansion, argued that individuals become part of international legal order only through their status as nationals of particular states. Legal treatises documenting customary state practice insisted that only states represented the "subjects" of international law and that all other entities—individuals, corporations, and nonstate groups—were the "objects" of international law without independent agency. In this view, only states counted as "persons" in international society, while nonstate groups and individuals accessed international law only derivatively through their national status.[14] From the perspective of international law, nationality implied that the more concrete connections that link individuals to the state—through family, history, affinity, affection, ethnicity, race, and religion—were not relevant when it came to whether the state is obliged to recognize and protect someone who bears this legal identification. "Nationality" designated the legal side of political belonging, distinguishing the subjects of one political community from foreign outsiders. It was an identification that defined an interstate category of membership while "citizenship" denoted the relationship of individuals to a particular political society. For more privileged legal subjects, nationality provided a formal status ensuring security as individuals moved around the world, safe in the knowledge that their private property and contractual agreements would be respected. Meanwhile, the legal category of nationality furnished imperial powers with a legal apparatus that allowed them to claim to rule over imperial subjects without granting them the full political rights of citizens.[15]

Though nationality had become a more significant source of identification by the end of the First World War, the governing expectations about interstate order—how new sovereign states emerged, how political membership was determined, and how conflicts that arose between political communities over national status were worked out—all represented sources of instability and radical innovation in the decade that followed. Even as the stateless began to represent a new object of humanitarian attention, they symbolized the possibility of legal and political identification beyond the jurisdictional boundaries of states. The growing number of people after the war that began to claim this status represented a particularly destabilizing development from the perspective of officials at the League of Nations, who tried to regulate how new states entered the international system and to contain the conflicts and disorder that arose from the creation of new sovereignties and new forms of international authority. For the same reasons, theorists drew on the novel scale of statelessness and its more widespread recognition as a critical resource for comprehending international legal order, the foundations of sovereignty, and the possibility of rights and self-governance beyond the boundaries of the state in the decade following the conflict.[16] The concept of legal personality became the intellectual battleground for debates about the nature of the state, public authority, and nonstate legal order. In interwar legal thought, the status of individuals, corporations, and groups depended on a determination of whether such persons possessed agency in the eyes of the law, and on how to explain the nature of that agency. Legal treatises on statelessness from this period argued that if stateless people were able to benefit from legal institutions and the rule of law as claimants in civil suits or before international courts, then they possessed agency in the eyes of the law. The possession of such qualities in turn challenged the prevailing theory of agency and personality in international thought.[17]

The story is framed by a generation of jurists and international legal publicists from the former Russian Empire and the former Habsburg Empire who responded to the collapse of empire and the rise of mass statelessness through juridical analysis and legal advocacy. These figures and their writings illuminate how the grounds of argument about the meaning of statelessness and the relationship between national and international spheres of authority evolved over the twentieth century. This group included Marc Vishniak, Boris Mirkine-Guetzevitch, Andre Mandelstam, Hans Kelsen, Josef Kunz, Hersch Lauterpacht, Maximilian Koessler, and Paul Weis. Each contributed to the development of international law and to the legal architecture of international protection for refugees and stateless persons. From an ideological standpoint, the Jewish background of these jurists meant that they had much to lose from the dissolution of the age of capital, empire, and liberalism in the twentieth century. All faced the challenges of statelessness, exile, and emigration.[18] As the Moscow-born émigré Vishniak recalled in his 1933 lecture on the legal status of statelessness, "it is very natural that the question of regulating the juridical situation of the stateless has been, in numerous cases, taken up by those who have suffered most from the absence of rights."[19] Yet this is only one piece of a larger story that is not limited to the theorist' personal histories. The initial intellectual response to mass statelessness captured a legalistic understanding of international politics, constitutionalism, and social relations that governed international and imperial politics in the nineteenth and early twentieth centuries. Legal and conceptual innovations sharpened in the late nineteenth century were brought to bear on a range of debates and political controversies that dominated political thought after the First World War. In this context, statelessness represented a phenomenon intrinsically bound up with debates about the fundamental nature of law, politics, and modern statehood.

The meaning of statelessness was transformed further as the European crisis accelerated and was followed by the even larger crisis of displacement and flight after the Second World War. Beginning in the late 1930s, mass numbers of displaced people in Asia as a result of the policies of imperial Japan joined the millions uprooted in Europe by total war, Nazi occupation, and the Holocaust. This book follows these thinkers from the postimperial moment after the First World War through the decades following the Second World War, when most of them found new political and institutional homes in the postwar United States. As the book pivots from Europe to the United States, from the League of Nations to the United Nations, the establishment of more permanent international agencies devoted to refugee identification and relief is examined alongside debates about the nature of law and its relationship to international politics. Tracing the evolution of critical reflection on statelessness illuminates how the legal scholars associated with the development of human rights in the postwar period endorsed state authority on new pragmatic foundations. Rather than searching for the source of international legal authority beyond the state, legal scholars sympathetic to the project of international law laid the groundwork for creating international legal norms on the foundations of state agreement and customary practice.[20]

Without question, Hannah Arendt is the most widely studied figure in the history of political thought to reflect on the meaning of statelessness. In a series of articles in the late 1940s and then most famously in *The Origins of Totalitarianism*, published in 1951, Arendt explored the origins of mass statelessness and its implication for global order in the aftermath of the Second World War. Her account traced the rise of mass numbers of people without a political home after the First World War back to the later nineteenth century, when European imperialism, capitalism, and pan-national movements undermined the Enlightenment-era ideals of citizenship and equality under the law. As she surveyed efforts at the United Nations to elaborate the meaning of human rights in the context of the ongoing European refugee crisis, Arendt concluded that the experience of the modern homeless had decisively shown that rights derive only from membership in a particular community. Arendt articulated the tension between the aspiration to make all human beings the bearers of rights and the fact that in reality rights depend on membership in particular states. The complete political organization of humanity into discrete sovereignties with full control over membership meant that anyone without political status was effectively devoid of rights. The only meaningful right would be a "right to have rights," or a right to belong that could ensure a place in some political community.[21]

Set in the longer history of international thought and empire, Arendt's interventions reveal an unappreciated dimension of the creation of the legal frameworks that govern international politics. The question taken up in the second half of this study is how the wider assault on legalistic approaches to politics transformed the terms of argument and debate about the significance of statelessness and ultimately shaped the creation of the legal frameworks governing non-citizenship. In diverse institutional settings—from the United Nations to the International Court of Justice and the US Supreme Court—nationality began to be defined as something more robust and entrenched than the formal link between an individual and a sovereign government, a mere condition of protection. As empires faced the end of their dominion over far flung territories and peoples, they also sought to reshape legal nationality to suit a legal framework that reflected more substantial ties linking individuals to the national state.

The task for the latter part of the book is, therefore, to explain how the successful assault on the legalist approach to political and international legal order shaped approaches to statelessness and the international legal categories of noncitizenship. International law and international organizations acknowledged the limits of formal inclusion, but the result was a general marginalization of the premise that legal statelessness intrinsically represented a crisis of international order. This study therefore shows how the postwar international settlement domesticated the foundations of political and legal membership—bracketing reflection and contestation over the fundamental boundaries of international politics.[22] I propose that the question we should be asking is not why the postwar arrangements to define and regulate the displaced did not live up to their original promise, or how they were thwarted by sovereignty and politics, but what they did accomplish in the creation of the postwar international settlement and in the domestication of the questions entertained in the interwar era about the foundations of political community and the basis for membership in it.

1

From a Subject of Fiction to a Legal Reality

Statelessness did not begin with the First World War, but the war and its aftermath transformed its significance for international politics. When Max Stoeck first arrived in London after leaving his native Prussia in 1896, he gave little thought to naturalizing as a legal subject of the British Crown. In London he advanced to the position of managing director of the Concordia Elektrizitäts-Aktiengesellschaft (CEAG), a German-based corporation that designed and marketed electric lamps for industrial use. While he worked to establish a CEAG branch in the UK, Stoeck maintained his connection to other German speakers through the German Gymnastic Society in St. Pancras and traveled frequently between England and Germany to strengthen ties between the two firms.[1]

These easy crossings came to an end in September 1914. When war broke out in Europe, nationality already defined the international legal dimension of citizenship, formally linking individuals to particular governments, though the laws determining how someone became a legal subject or citizen (or lost this connection altogether) varied considerably from place to place. Within a few weeks of the declaration of war, Stoeck tried to naturalize as a British subject, but by the time that he submitted his application, it was already too late. In the years that followed, Stoeck's status evolved from cosmopolitan business agent to enemy alien—a relatively novel identification forged in the course of the war—and finally to stateless person. In *Stoeck v. Public Trustee*, a suit that he brought before the Chancery Division of the High Court in England in 1921, a British judge affirmed Stoeck's claim that he had lost his legal connection to the German Reich years earlier and, since he had never been naturalized in Britain, was therefore a person of "no nationality." According to the judgment, "statelessness" represented a legal identification distinct from the ordinary division between nationals protected by a government's civil law and foreigners protected by their governments from abroad.[2]

Stoeck's life was transformed as a result of the war and the nationalization of borders, but his case is not the typical way we generally understand statelessness in the twentieth century. A manager of a multinational corporation, Stoeck pursued recognition as a person with no national status in order to recover the property seized by the British government due to his identification as a foreigner from an enemy country. He faced the upheaval of internment, the confiscation of his property, and the dissolution of his marriage, all as a direct result of his identification during the war as the legal subject of an enemy nation. Yet becoming stateless in legal terms represented a strategic identification for Stoeck, a way of freeing himself from the constraints placed on nationals from enemy countries and on private economic actors during the First World War. His case therefore does not fully capture the novel scale of vulnerability in the twentieth century resulting from political revolution, the nationalization of boundaries, and exclusionary political movements. From the perspective of these wider revolutions of modern politics, the court's recognition of the fact that Stoeck had no nationality appears to be merely a symptom, a by-product of a much deeper shift toward more exclusive forms of legal and political identification.[3]

However, *Stoeck v. Public Trustee* is a significant event in the history of statelessness because it provides an altogether different picture of the category's mainstream emergence after World War I. The question of whether to acknowledge statelessness in law prompted explicit reflection and argument about the conventions governing interstate order and the broader significance of the court's acknowledgment of this legal status. Stoeck's case underscores the fundamental ambiguities surrounding the meaning of statehood and sovereignty as the war came to a close. The arguments produced in the course of the suit, and the reception of the judge's decision to recognize Stoeck as a stateless person, establish why statelessness became so significant intellectually in the years that followed. Moreover, as we will see, the judgment itself directly shaped the international response to the growing number of people without a nationality in the decade after the First World War.[4]

At first glance, the rise of statelessness as a mass phenomenon in the interwar period reflects the sharpened divide between domestic and international relations. Indeed, the *Stoeck* decision did affirm that the ultimate power to determine the legal bond between an individual and a state lay within the sovereign power of that government. However, the recognition that stateless people existed within the boundaries of the Western state system reveals a key dimension of the reordering of diplomatic relations after the war because it challenged an earlier premise in Western political thought that statelessness was an unrecognized status within the boundary of civilized states. Governments had been reluctant to acknowledge that an individual could be stateless, without a legal connection to any government that could provide protection and identification. The acceptance of claims to statelessness therefore broke with earlier patterns of imperial and interstate relations, when empires and states tussled over questions of imperial subjecthood, protection, and national identification. Statelessness transformed from a "subject of fiction"—a status confined mainly to works of literature—to an acknowledged political reality. Once we understand the meaning of the decision in the context of prior legal history and the history of international thought we can appreciate why the legal recognition of statelessness threw the future of political order within and without the frontiers of nations and empires into question.

This chapter and the two that follow establish how the category of statelessness entered into international society and international law. All three seek to show the uncertainty surrounding the meaning of sovereignty and the basic principles of interstate political order after World War I. As we will see, recognition of the category generated expectations about the future of international law and legal order. For those who envisioned the expansion of international law's jurisdiction, the recognition of statelessness presented new possibilities for legal authority beyond the confines of the state. And in order to understand why, it is necessary to comprehend the argumentative terms of the case and its wider reception.

I

One could certainly appreciate the details of Stoeck's biography in terms of a broader historical transformation: from a period of intense economic and technological globalization during the mid-nineteenth century to one of policed borders during the First World War. Born in 1872 in the Rhine region of Prussia, one year after the unification of the German Empire, Stoeck left Germany for Belgium at the age of twenty-three. Once there, he applied to the imperial German government to grant him discharge papers relieving him of his rights and responsibilities as a German national. Stoeck was already beyond the years of military service, so German officials handed over the document confirming that he no longer remained a legal subject of the empire. From Belgium, Stoeck moved to London in 1896, though he never saw the need to naturalize as a British subject. That ease of movement across borders would continue, until it came to a sudden stop.[5]

Stoeck moved to London in a period when many countries, including Britain, had begun turning against unrestricted immigration. A few decades earlier, cross-border movement had been easier for all social classes, but by the 1890s the laboring poor faced increasing restrictions on migration. However, businessmen like Stoeck generally managed to stay above all the paperwork. Their lives exemplified how capitalism nurtured the connection between world citizenship and commerce. In Britain, they were prevented from owning land but were otherwise free to live and conduct business as legal residents.[6] From the perspective of the entrepreneur pursuing opportunity and profit, borders and nationality hindered global sociability and commerce. Throughout the nineteenth century, the expansion of legal and bureaucratic mechanisms to control migration developed in tandem with the liberal argument that progress depended on the capacity of individuals and capital to flow freely around the world.[7]

By relinquishing his legal ties to the Reich, Stoeck found himself in the company of some better-known subjects of the German Empire who wished to pursue their own interests without the burden of national attachment. In the name of personal freedom and convenience, individuals could avoid the growing demands on the subjects of industrializing and militarizing European states of the later nineteenth century. In his letters, the philosopher Friedrich Nietzsche expressed an eminently practical attitude toward this voluntary loss of nationality, presenting the obligations of citizenship as an administrative annoyance. Nietzsche wrote, "From 1869 until 1879 I was at Basel; I had to give up my German citizenship, because as an officer (mounted artillery) I would have been drafted too frequently and disturbed my academic duties."[8]

The great technological breakthroughs of the nineteenth century, including railroads, steamships, and electronic communication, conquered the challenges of distance; new ideas about space and time buttressed the internationalist spirit of the *fin de siècle*.[9] Internationalist movements in Europe, the United States, and Latin America nurtured the growth of political and social interdependence through new economic institutions and legal innovations. For example, in the later decades of the nineteenth century, jurists worked to systematize and rationalize private international law, the field governing cross-border legal relationships around a commercially connected globe. Unlike public law, which defined the field covering topics such as sovereignty and the boundaries of the state's authority, private law designated a legal arena responsible for the enforcement of contracts between individuals and corporations as private agents regardless of national status.[10] Between 1900 and 1909, 119 international organizations were established, and an additional 112 were formed in the five-year period just before the war.[11]

Stoeck's company, CEAG, exemplified the economic internationalism of the era of liberal capitalist ascendency, with shares divided equally between German and British nationals. The company's technological contributions to the mining industry were celebrated in 1912 when the British Home Office awarded the CEAG lamp—designed by a German engineer—first prize in an international competition for the best electric miner's safety lamp.[12] Stoeck remained loyal to the company over his entire career as an inventor and corporate manager. Following the competition, Stoeck traveled to British mining districts exhibiting the prize-winning lamp. He also oversaw the expansion of the company from its base in Dortmund, Germany, to a new factory in Barnsley, England.[13]

Change came suddenly. War intensified the distinction between nationals and aliens or foreigners who belonged in a formal legal sense to other sovereign nations. When the war broke out in August 1914, retired British military and naval officers taking the waters at German health resorts found that they had become enemies in the eyes of the German government. Within weeks of declaring war, Western liberal democracies such as France, the United Kingdom, and the United States introduced restrictions on the ability of their citizens to travel abroad in order to preserve military manpower and to prevent the movement of politically suspect individuals.[14] Those who had enjoyed the relative ease of cross-border movement and residence faced the consequences of the nationalization of people and of industry. Outside of Europe, foreigners who had enjoyed extraterritorial legal privileges as they conducted business in the Ottoman Empire in previous decades were granted forty-eight hours to renounce their foreign citizenship once the Ottoman Empire allied with the German and Habsburg Empires. Only a week after entering the conflict, Sultan Mehmed V signed an official declaration abolishing the system of legal rights that had ensured that Westerners were not subject to the jurisdiction of Ottoman law in the second half of the nineteenth century.[15]

It became paramount for individuals and corporations to label themselves clearly as national security took priority over private industry. CEAG divested from its German shareholders and reconstituted as a purely "English" limited liability company.[16] As a non-British national originally from an enemy country, Stoeck quickly realized the imperative to naturalize as a British subject. Britain had already begun to make life more difficult for legal residents before the formal outbreak of hostilities through the 1914 Aliens Restrictions Bill, which authorized the roundup of aliens suspected of espionage. As a result, thousands of suspected aliens began lining up daily outside of police headquarters in London to register their status as legal aliens after the August 1914 British Nationality and the Status of Aliens Act, which placed the burden of proof on the suspected party.[17] Stoeck's application to naturalize as a British subject from August 12, 1914, submitted a few days after the passage of the Nationality and Status of Aliens Act, indicates how he tried to affirm the national status of his company, CEAG, and to argue for its vital importance to the British economy and war effort. Stoeck described himself as a "merchant and managing director of an English Limited Liability Company," which produced safety lamps for English mining companies.[18] Corporations, whose stockholders and employees had been multinational, nationalized as well once warring governments began to investigate who really owned the companies registered in their countries. Despite a great deal of litigation, contracts between British subjects and nationals from enemy countries were eventually suspended during the war.[19] Great Britain was among the countries, including France, Austria, Italy, Germany, and the Netherlands, to implement legislation allowing for emergency powers, including the power to seize property such as railways for the public defense. Coal mines in Britain, owned before the war by 1,500 different companies, were brought under the control of the Board of Trade by 1916 as the British state became more involved in regulating industry to ensure that it could meet wartime demands.[20]

Though his naturalization request was denied, Stoeck continued to hold out hope that his position within CEAG would allow him to avoid the difficulties facing anyone defined as an enemy alien. The creation of the enemy alien category entailed considerable invention on the part of legislators and state bureaucrats since before World War I governments generally avoided formal measures against enemy subjects residing in their territory during times of war.[21] Stoeck argued in letters to the Home Office, the British ministry responsible for immigration and naturalization, that his safety lamps were vital for the war effort and the general mining interests in Britain.[22] Indeed, officials fretted over the decision to designate Stoeck as an enemy alien since CEAG was the main producer of safety lamps for mines across the British Empire, and held exclusive contracts with the War Department to produce lamps for use in sapping and trench warfare. Deliberations over Stoeck's status indicate the level of detail that went into such bureaucratic decisions and the indeterminacy of the new categorization. Designating him as an enemy alien was hardly an exercise in rubber-stamping; officials at the Home Office interviewed employees at the Barnsley factory to determine Stoeck's importance for daily operations.[23]

As he faced the possibility of internment as an alien enemy, Stoeck relied on the London-based law firm of Cruesemann and Rouse to advocate on his behalf. His lawyers initially succeeded in keeping him out of internment by arguing that Stoeck was too important to the English mining industry to lock up.[24] His application was ultimately denied, and on May 24, 1916, nearly two years after he applied for naturalization, the Home Office determined that Stoeck was an enemy alien and dispatched a letter to the commissioner of police stating that he should be interned.[25] Cruesemann and Rouse did not abandon their client, and continued to argue for leniency so that he could attend board meetings outside of the internment camp at Alexandra Palace. They also represented him when he appealed to the courts to declare that he was not an enemy alien. Stoeck and others in a similar position faced the difficulty of internment as well as the loss of their property and personal possessions once legislation early in the war granted a new agency called the Public Trustee custodianship over enemy property. The suit filed by Cruesemann and Rouse to free Stoeck from the enemy alien label was not successful, but the Public Trustee designated the proceeds from his shares of CEAG for his bank account though Stoeck himself remained interned.

Any flexibility that Stoeck had enjoyed as an internee came to an end once he was sent to Holland as a civilian prisoner in March 1918 and from there to Germany. Stoeck's return to Germany authorized the Board of Trade to consider him an enemy under the terms of the 1914 "Trading with the Enemy Act," which in turn allowed the Public Trustee to seize the proceeds from the sale of Stoeck's CEAG shares.[26] When the war was over, the peace treaty between Britain, its allies, and the German Empire, which was signed at the French palace of Versailles and came into force in January 1920, granted the German government use of the property of its nationals to pay off its war debt and permitted the British government to automatically appropriate the property of German nationals living in the British Empire. After the years of internment, the seizure of his property, and personal turmoil resulting from his status as an enemy alien, Stoeck asked for a declaration from the court validating that he was not a German national but a person of no nationality, a stateless person.

II

It may appear to be merely a matter of logical necessity that when no country recognizes you as a citizen, you are a person of no nationality. Yet when the case came before Francis Xavier Joseph Russell, a judge on the Chancery Division of the High Court of Justice, thousands who claimed they had been mislabeled as enemy aliens waited on the judgment to see whether they would be recognized as stateless persons. In the years immediately following the war, individuals not just in Britain but across Europe sought recognition from the courts that they did not possess any national status.[27]

After the victors of World War I set out the punitive terms of the Versailles Peace Treaty, there was an even greater clamor among former subjects of enemy powers—including Germany, Austria, and Hungary—residing in the British Empire to be formally recognized as stateless in order to avoid the Versailles penalties. Many in the British Empire also hoped to hasten their naturalization as British subjects since the 1914 British Nationality and Status of Aliens Act stipulated that naturalization requests by anyone from an enemy country automatically required a ten-year waiting period. As one article reporting on *Stoeck v. Public Trustee* in the *Times Law Reports* detailed, the case depended on whether "English law recognized the condition of a 'stateless man' i.e. a man of no nationality."[28] As we will see in more detail later on, wartime cases indicated that, from the perspective of the British courts, it could be assumed that a person who had never sought a new nationality could never fully relinquish their prior legal connection to an enemy state. Now, the outcome of the Stoeck decision presented an opportunity to revisit previous wartime legal pronouncements refusing to acknowledge that a person could have no nationality. Home Office officials charged with reviewing naturalization applications meanwhile waited on the judgment to determine whether they could begin processing requests from stateless people who did not face the same restrictions as those who had been properly identified as enemy nationals.[29]

Questions of order from around the empire and areas of military occupation after the war drove the urgency of the legal decision. Yet understanding the decision itself and its reception requires a reconstruction of the more refined terms of argument mobilized in the course of the proceedings. The case is therefore significant for two reasons. First, it was received by a wider legal public in Europe and across the Atlantic in the United States as a significant development in the legal conception of nationality, since municipal courts had not acknowledged statelessness up to this point. Second, the case is important because it provoked explicit reflection on the nature of international order, and the arguments over whether Stoeck was indeed a person of no nationality, and whether English law recognized such a status, illuminate the wider international and political stakes of the judgment. Stoeck's case shows how debate about the principles governing interstate order—at least at the level of regulatory expectations, if not practice—manifested in the justification for the recognition of statelessness as a real status within the boundaries of international society, and how the risks of such acknowledgment were understood.

The arguments each side presented depended not on the fine points of law but rather on contending visions of international society and the principles that govern the system of sovereign states. Two competing visions of interstate order were articulated in the course of the suit. For the advocates from the office of the Public Trustee arguing that the judge should not validate Stoeck's claim that he was a person of no nationality, the case rested on the foundations of international order. They argued that by accepting statelessness as a legal category in Britain, the court would be rejecting a prior moral commitment to excluding the possibility of statelessness from interstate order. As the Public Trustee representatives insisted, it was within the power of a British court to determine whether an individual remained the national of a different state even if their own government had stripped them of their prior national connection. They cited the outcry from the British and American publics a few decades earlier when Jewish subjects had been refused citizenship in Romania after the country obtained independence in 1878. It followed, they argued, that the court could reject the claim by another sovereign that a subject no longer remained a national of that country.[30] By pointing to political precedents in which statelessness was not recognized out of moral and political conviction, the solicitors tried to show that it was the prerogative of the British judge to determine the status of a person's nationality and hence the legitimacy of nationality law in other states.[31] The judge would be within his rights not to recognize Stoeck as a stateless person because it would create a situation analogous to that in Romania, which had become the object of moral derision by the British public. As the lawyers presented the central issue of the case, accepting statelessness into the European state system thus implied the end of a guiding sense of moral purpose. Upholding a moral vision of international order in which no person lacked the state's protection meant placing limits on the sovereign capability of any government to fully determine the boundaries of membership.[32]

In their efforts to prove the opposite, that Stoeck had in fact severed his prior membership to the German Empire, and that therefore he must be acknowledged as a stateless person, Stoeck's lawyers emphasized that the acceptance of the Prussian government's decision was the significant element of the case. They justified the recognition of statelessness in English law by arguing that the mutual recognition of the nationality legislation of another country, and the formal equality of sovereign states in matters relating to nationality, represented defining features of international society. Their argument was simple: Stoeck had received a document from the Prussian government releasing him from his nationality, and since he had never succeeded in becoming naturalized as a subject of the British Empire, he was necessarily stateless. Stoeck should be acknowledged as stateless because the court should accept Prussia's sovereign decision to dissolve a legal bond with one of their former subjects, and the Home Office file on Stoeck already included a translation into English of the document from Prussia certifying that he had been discharged of his nationality.[33]

The arguments articulated by Stoeck's solicitors to persuade the judge to acknowledge Stoeck as a person of "no nationality" touched on the dilemma at the heart of the case. Stoeck himself seemed to have been more than happy to live in London under the conditions of bourgeois freedom, which allowed him to reside, work, and travel without the need for national identification. His lawyers, however, acknowledged the danger of recognizing statelessness as a distinct category, because it introduced the possibility that a person could live untethered from the law altogether.[34]

The Public Trustee had invoked the episode of public criticism of Romania's treatment of its Jewish subjects in order to prove that ordinary diplomatic relations between states, and respect for a country's sovereignty, did not preclude the refusal to acknowledge that subjects of another sovereign government had no legal ties to the political community to which they ostensibly belonged, especially if such a person did not have legal membership anywhere else. To counter this objection, Stoeck's lawyers cited international legal treatises detailing how stateless persons could be treated as foreigners under the law, and thus retain the same rights as any non (enemy) British subject within the territory of the British Empire. To acknowledge Stoeck as a stateless person, in other words, did not imply that the court would become complicit in the creation of pockets of lawlessness, leaving some unlucky individuals without rights or access to legal remedy. Despite the fact that a person without a national status technically had no country of their own, they could still claim the essential rights and remedies ordinarily guaranteed only to subjects and foreigners.

The stronger, and more carefully argued point that Stoeck's lawyers put forward, however, rested on the epistemic priority of each state to set—and interpret—the rules governing naturalization and denaturalization. Like the Public Trustee representatives, who argued that the central issue of the case concerned the nature of interstate order, Stoeck's lawyers likewise presented a vision of the guiding principles governing one of the most fundamental ways that states relate to the jurisdictional authority of another country. They hired prominent jurists from Germany to testify to the laws of the German Empire showing that Stoeck had in fact been released from his prior attachment to Germany.[35] After arranging visas for the two witnesses, they successfully brought Dr. Siegfried Goldschmidt of Berlin and Dr. Eduard Baerwald of Frankfurt to testify to the fact that Stoeck had lost any prior legal connection to Germany in accordance with the rules governing nationality elaborated in the German civil code. In their testimony, the witnesses asserted that the "plaintiff had absolutely lost his German nationality and according to German law was a stateless person."[36] By calling on expert witnesses from the country whose laws were in question, Stoeck's lawyers asserted that only those representatives from the legal system under consideration could explain the true meaning of the nationality legislation. Only they could prove the validity of their interpretation of Prussian law. Their appearance as expert witnesses thus served a double function: they testified about the proper interpretation of German law, undercutting the claim that courts or bureaucrats are within their rights to interpret the laws of another country when they sought to determine the national status of a foreign subject, and their presence showed how such legal exchanges were part of the normal intercourse between states. Indeed, during the war, the German legal experts would not have been permitted to travel to London to appear before the court.

After listening to the opposing arguments, Judge Russell issued his ruling. Russell recognized the condition of statelessness, validating Stoeck's claim that he had lost his status as a national of the German Empire well before World War I. In his decision Russell described statelessness as an entirely new category in English law, separate from that of the alien and that of the citizen. Until this point, he reflected in his judgment, modern conceptions of citizenship had centered on the distinction between citizens and foreigners. By recognizing Stoeck as a stateless person, therefore, he would be validating a third category that represented a departure from the standard legal distinction. In an earlier period, Russell stated, it was sufficient for the "ordinary purposes" of the common law to distinguish between subjects and aliens, and the stateless person would have been legally synonymous with an alien who possessed rights under the law.[37]

The justification for acknowledging this novel category in a legal sense rested largely on the arguments presented by Stoeck's lawyers, who insisted that it was beyond the jurisdictional scope of an English court to interpret whether, according to German law, Stoeck had lost his prior connection to Germany. In the course of their arguments, both parties had cited treatises written by authorities on international law from the late nineteenth and early twentieth century. However, as Russell concluded, such treatises contained enough ambiguity, and conflicting opinion, that international law could be invoked to support both sides of the argument.

The emerging body of doctrinal writings on international law produced by legal treatise writers in the decades before the war held little sway compared with the vision of interstate order portrayed by Stoeck's advocates. Against the authority of international legal doctrine, Russell referenced the common sense basis for his decision, citing the fact that the recognition of statelessness had become conventional across Europe, and that the category had entered into everyday speech and acts of government. A treaty between Germany and Denmark, for example, listed the term "staatenlos," and Stoeck's identity paper issued by the German police had applied the same term.[38] Russell concluded, "whether a person was a national of any country must be decided by the municipal law of that country. It might be said that a person was to be 'deemed to be' or 'treated as' a national of another country but he could not be made such a national. By German law the plaintiff was not a German national and he could not be made one by English law."[39] The idea that a British judge could not make a determination about the legitimacy of another state's nationality laws affirmed a vision of international order defined by equally sovereign entities that each demanded respect for their legal decisions. Russell did not have the power to interrogate the nationality laws of another country, in this case Prussia's voluntary dismissal of Stoeck's national status. The court could only accept the testimony of experts representing the foreign legal system in question. It did not matter whether people had lost their nationality as a result of denaturalization or had sought to sever the legal bond between themselves and their government. Russell thus articulated a principle about the nature of nationality and its relation to wider diplomatic and international relations.[40]

Stoeck v. Public Trustee staged a clash between the idea of sovereign equality—the idea that each state is sovereign in matters of naturalization—and an imperial right to reject the absolute authority of other sovereigns to label their subjects. As the representatives of the Public Trustee asserted, the judge would need to consider the place of public order in the conventional understanding of interstate relations. By contrast, Stoeck's lawyers insisted on epistemic humility in the evaluation of foreign law as the relevant foundational principle.[41] The legal question of whether Stoeck should be acknowledged as a stateless person "according to English law" touched on the broader ambiguity surrounding the relationship between sovereignty and nationality. The rules of the game ordering relations between states when subjects moved across political borders, and how to characterize the basic principles of order, emerged as the most pressing issue at stake in the judgment.

As a result of the ruling, Stoeck was able to regain a small balance in the bank and some furniture. But far more important is the fact that Stoeck became the first person in the British Empire to bear the formal title of "stateless person."[42] Even as *Stoeck v. Public Trustee* affirmed that statelessness had become an increasingly acknowledged status across Europe, the ruling itself had profound practical implications for the thousands whose lives depended on whether they could claim this identification. The decision also had significant ramifications for theories of international law, rights, and legal personality, as the contours of imperial and international order began to take shape in the years after World War I. In order to comprehend the fundamental shift created by Judge Russell's ruling, we must look backward to the preceding two centuries to appreciate how the recognition of statelessness as a political and legal status broke from earlier conceptions of statelessness in international thought, and from earlier conventions and practices of global legal order.

III

By the late eighteenth century, statelessness had become conceptually and rhetorically linked to the idea that individuals are the bearers of rights and duties by virtue of their status as human beings rather than as subjects of particular political communities. At the same time, beginning in this period, theorists began insisting that such a figure—a human being that possessed natural rights without the protection and guarantees that derived from political membership—could only exist in the realm of the imagination rather than real-world politics. The political theorist and parliamentarian Edmund Burke described the plight facing anyone without a government to call upon in a moment of need in a 1781 speech to the British Parliament in which he invoked the law of nations as a potential source of protection for people without the security of a political community. The occasion for Burke's intervention was a parliamentary debate over imperial governance and the regulation of the British military, a discussion precipitated by the actions of

British commanders governing the island of St. Eustatius in the Caribbean during the American Revolutionary War. Military commanders had summarily banished the Jewish residents of the island who were accused of illegally trading with the American colonists, and had seized their property and sold it off through public auction. As Burke eloquently argued, without a country, the Jews of the island had no source of redress. "If Dutchmen are injured and attacked, the Dutch have a nation, a government, and armies to redress or avenge their cause. If Britons are injured, Britons have armies and laws, the laws of nations (or at least they once had the laws of nations) to fly to for protection and justice. But the Jews have no such power, and no such friend to depend on. Humanity then must become their protector and ally."[43] Burke seized on the idea that the law of nations provided at least theoretical protection for individuals as members of the human race, drawing on the influential writings on this subject by the eighteenth-century Swiss jurist Emmerich de Vattel, though this idea had deeper sources in Roman legal thought. The speech thus tied the condition of statelessness—of not having a sovereign government to back up legal claims, or to intervene more directly in moments of insecurity and danger—to the concept of a common humanity, but simultaneously indicated the fundamental danger of relying on international law or membership in common humanity to ensure personal safety. In his famous critique of the idea of natural right in *Reflections on the Revolution in France* from 1789, Burke articulated the related idea that rights depend on membership within a collectivity, and derive from history and prescriptive precedent.[44]

As nationality consolidated as the central category of legal identification linking individuals to states in the late eighteenth-century Atlantic world, courts denied that "no nationality" represented a plausible, recognizable status. For example, in *Talbot v. Janson* from 1795, a case involving a man who renounced his allegiance to the state of Virginia, the US Supreme Court considered the possibility that such a figure might exist. The court reasoned that the claimant remained a citizen of the United States since the "citizen of the world" was a "creature of the imagination" and did not exist in the real world governed by various jurisdictional authorities. Theoretical and legal debate about nationality in the context of the late eighteenth century revolutionary Atlantic world affirmed the deep connection between freedom from national status and ideas about cosmopolitanism and humanity that had been circulating in Enlightenment thought in previous decades. Yet the question of whether to recognize an individual with such a status (or the absence of one) ultimately led the court to reject the possibility that such cosmopolitans existed in the real world.[45]

By the mid-nineteenth century one could find legislation in Europe that addressed the legal standing of individuals without a national status. Switzerland was the first European state to define a legal approach to people claiming that they did not possess any nationality. In the nineteenth century the country had become linked to political homelessness by providing a base for anyone without a country seeking to establish an independent nation or to develop international movements for socialist revolution. The 1848 Swiss constitution listed the *heimatlos*, or homeless person, as a distinctive status within the constitutional order. Federal legislation in Switzerland periodically addressed the question of which canton, or member state of the Swiss confederation, should claim responsibility for providing social welfare to people without a national status. Conflicts over jurisdictional responsibility for vagabonds evolved into the national question of local obligations toward the *heimatlos*. By legislating local jurisdictional responsibility for a person without national status, the Swiss called attention to the larger question of legal responsibility for a person with no connection to any government.[46]

However, despite some recognition of individual statelessness in the nineteenth century, popular narratives tended to reinforce the idea that a person without a nationality belonged to the realm of fiction. The American writer Edward Everett Hale's short story "The Man without a Country," published in *The Atlantic* in 1863, underscored new controversies surrounding nationality and allegiance as states strengthened their hold over citizens and subjects in the mid-nineteenth century. In the story, an American army lieutenant, Philip Nolan, is tried for treason and spends the remainder of his life at sea after renouncing his allegiance to the United States. The story delineated the attributes of a modern state by describing what it meant to lose its recognition. Nolan's deprivation—his disconnection from land, from companionship, his lack of a proper uniform with identifying buttons—illustrated what it meant to be part of the nation.

"The Man without a Country" conveyed the extent to which states had begun to claim more territorial and bureaucratic control as they increasingly relied on large citizen standing armies and more expansive forms of taxation.

STATELESSNESS: A MODERN HISTORY

The story of a former soldier who unwittingly banished himself in a moment of passion is full of the symbols of nationhood and patriotic loyalty that began to designate national identification in this period. In the United States, naturalization, which previously had been granted state by state, came under the purview of federal courts after the American Civil War. The Lieber Code, the rules of military conduct formulated during the American Civil War, stressed the importance of a regulation army uniform since the laws of war applied only to enemy soldiers who wore the proper regimentals. In keeping with this presumption, the other sailors on Nolan's ship call him "Plain-Buttons" because he wears a regulation army uniform but is not permitted to wear the army button, since it bears the insignia of the country he disavowed.[47] As a student at Harvard, Hale had entertained ideas about the future of world government and the establishment of a world court. However, his story articulated a message similar to the one expressed in Burke's parliamentary speech. To be deprived of a country threatened your humanity. Part of Nolan's punishment is that he is forbidden from speaking of home, and he loses the capacity for companionship and speech. The idea of the open sea, a space free from sovereign control and competition at the center of the law of nations, appeared as a cruel joke in Hale's morality tale. Nolan was free to exist in the middle of the ocean, but he lost the qualities that define what it is to be a human being along the way.[48]

In the succeeding decades, the idea of the "man without a country" would generally be invoked as a subject of fiction rather than as an international reality, though by the later nineteenth century wars of national consolidation and expansion introduced the real threat of mass numbers of people with no national attachment. In the diplomatic relations of the nineteenth century, a tension developed between the imperative to recognize the documentary proof issued by another state and the sovereign right to evaluate how the law—even the law issued by a foreign state—applied to individuals residing within one's own territory. Even if someone did lose their legal connection to any government through expatriation and migration, countries reserved the right to determine the national status of any migrant.[49]

One reason, therefore, why statelessness was not acknowledged as a reality was that governments generally retained the right to interpret the nationality laws of other states when it came to determining the status of potential newcomers. Russell's decision to defer to German law when evaluating the national status of noncitizens who originally held German nationality represented a break from how European empires had conducted international diplomacy before the First World War. It represented an innovation seen against the background of an earlier history in which government bureaucrats, immigration officials, and courts did not make the same presumption. The notion that a legal authority like the High Court should simply accept that another power—in Stoeck's case, the Prussian government—had allowed him to lose his Prussian nationality represented a new understanding of the presumptive norms of the international society of states.

By contrast, in earlier decades when an individual migrated to a new country, the determination about whether a migrant had lost her prior legal connection to her home state depended on how the receiving country decided to interpret foreign law. The creation of common procedures for border control in the mid-nineteenth century helped standardize the state form. However, Western imperial powers claimed the right to evaluate how other sovereign states determined the status of their subjects. Consulates and immigration authorities retained the authority to evaluate an emigrant's national status when they sought to cross the border or obtain legal residence. No country had ultimate sovereignty in matters of naturalization and denaturalization since other states could reject a country's right to eschew responsibility for a person who could not claim a legal status elsewhere.[50]

This feature of modern nationality law—the rules legislated by governments to regulate naturalization and denaturalization—evolved in response to concerns that residents would be able claim protection from other governments, and countries developed nationality laws in response to claims made by other countries on their subjects. Nationality legislation around the world rested primarily on an individual's inherited rights to citizenship (*jus sanguinis*) or the legal right to membership that arose from being born in a particular territory (*jus soli*), or acquired through naturalization. The Ottoman Empire developed the most comprehensive legislation on the nationality of their subjects in 1869 in response to the actions of foreign powers such as Russia, France, and Britain that claimed the right to protect foreigners living under a separate jurisdiction within the boundaries of the empire. In response to these incursions, the Ottoman bey asserted the power to evaluate the status of all residents and visitors to the empire and issue the final judgment on naturalization and expatriation.[51] In European countries facing the mass migration of people to North America, officials worried that immigrants would avoid conscription by absconding to the United States and then return to their home countries with the protection of their American nationality.[52] Explicit membership rules specifying who was to count as a member of a state were delineated for the first time in bilateral and multilateral treaties, yet the ultimate authority to determine the terms of the treaties and to interpret foreign law remained within the power of officials at the border.[53]

Russell's determination that a British judge could not interpret another country's laws when it came to evaluating a claimant's national status therefore broke with earlier conventional international practice. However, in order to appreciate the significance of Russell's ruling, and of the formal entry of the stateless into law, we must delve into the rhetorical and legal status of statelessness in the context of the emerging debates about nationality and global cooperation in the later nineteenth century. To do so, we must turn to the history of international law. The field of international law that developed from the late eighteenth century through the nineteenth century defined the juridical relations between states, and generally portrayed states, rather than any other kind of moral agent, as the subjects of this legal order. In the decades following the Congress of Vienna, the growth of a more professionalized class of international lawyers facilitated the development of normative criteria for statehood. As recent scholarship has emphasized, by establishing the sovereign state as the basic unit of governance, international lawyers obscured the diversity of polities and peoples that interacted with each other and exercised domination over one another within the global imperial system.[54]

Treatises on international law produced by European legal publicists thus contributed to a particular vision of interstate order. These treatises were written in the context of the territorial expansion of national states with empowered central governments that also sought to expand their share of the world market through formal imperialism. An earlier separation in European political thought between law governing relations between states from law regulating relations between "peoples" or nonstate groups (consisting of tribes, would-be political nations, and recognized sovereign countries) buttressed the claim that only proper states possessed moral personality, or agency, in the international arena. The term *nation* rather than *state* was at times applied to distinguish polities that had achieved a certain level of development. And such developed political communities could not admit that anyone within their borders did not possess a nationality. The German jurist Ludwig von Bar, who published an influential treatise on international private law, provided an alternative but equally normative definition of statehood. According to von Bar, "a nation in that sense, by which we understand a body of human beings held together by means of certain common characteristics and a common civilization, has as such no law of its own. International law only recognizes the existence of true legal communities, or constituted states; it does not recognize communities which may some day become legal communities, or in times past were so, or may again become so."[55] The separation of nationality from citizenship in international law at the turn of the twentieth century was facilitated therefore by the already established distinction in Western legal thought between the formal structures of the state and the organization of social power and civil society. Nineteenth-century treatises on the state and legal theory distinguished between the state as a legal creation and the idea of a community based on social allegiances. Such a division allowed states to consolidate their authority even as they constituted the groups they claimed to neutrally referee. In addition, the distinction developed in such texts between legal statehood and national groups served to reaffirm the civilizational hierarchy between European-style states and groups that had not yet achieved such legal qualifications.[56]

Over the course of the century, European and American jurists began to develop a body of jurisprudence addressing legal questions arising from individuals conducting business across national boundaries. These works did not merely document the range of emergent clashes and questions at the ground level of national and imperial bureaucracies. The authors of the major treatises on international law sought to elaborate the governing norms of international conduct. In the nineteenth century, Western domination over much of the rest of the globe was accompanied by the emergence of international society as a distinctive sphere of political and legal engagement. Above all, it indicated a concerned public that reached beyond any given political boundary, a public concerned about issues defined as "international"—including the making and unmaking of imperial or national borders—although what counted as an international matter remained up for dispute.

The men who in 1873 founded the Institut de Droit International, an international scientific organization for scholars of international law, constituted themselves as a community of experts on international legal matters. By elaborating a set of facts about international order, these texts created normative depictions of an international system. Legal concepts and frameworks helped lawyers and jurists impose an order on international and imperial politics. The first generation of professional international lawyers could generally be described as liberal nationalists who also developed the legal architecture of formal imperialism. The Institut de Droit Internation-al promoted the idea that international law was not based on the will of the state but rather arose from a common European consciousness that the trained jurist could assess, elaborate, and codify. It was a movement to humanize relations between civilized states while at the same time removing impediments to ruling over groups outside of Europe.[57]

The notion that individuals like Nolan, devoid of national connection, represented a "subject of fiction" rather than a reality of interstate order in turn figured prominently in the major treatises on international law written in the later nineteenth century. Members of the professional association of international lawyers in Europe and the United States approached the subject of statelessness in their legal treatises by way of larger discussions about international law and the nature of interstate order. What are the "rules" governing (and constituting) international society? Who gets to decide what the rules are? How do individuals fit into international society? As theorists consolidated the concepts that define international society, statelessness carried two main implications. The combined effect of the legal treatises produced by European and American legal scholars was to introduce a fundamental ambiguity about the significance and meaning of statelessness in relation to international law. To acknowledge that an individual might be stateless within the boundaries of a "civilized" state risked effacing the markers established in international thought for distinguishing between the community of equal, civilized states and the territories of the world that could not develop, or had not yet developed, into fully self-governing polities. However, the treatises introduced the possibility of comprehending statelessness in terms of the sovereignty and agency of individuals within international legal order.

Legal publicists promoted the idea that statelessness did not represent a plausible condition within the confines of the modern state system in an ideological context in which they were also promoting a world-making picture of how to characterize such an order. The American legal codifier David Dudley Field's *Outline of an International Code* from 1876, for instance, identified the existing rule as "who has ceased to be a member of a nation without acquiring another national character is nevertheless deemed to be a member of the nation to which he last belonged."[58] The authors of these works ratified a hierarchical vision of the world, excluding the possibility of statelessness from within the boundaries of legal states. A "standard of civilization" established a hierarchy separating communities capable of full independence from those in a permanent state of subjection and those capable of gaining entry into international society in terms set by the European powers.[59]

As we have seen, in *Stoeck v. Public Trustee* both sides had touched on the nature of international order in the course of presenting their arguments. What is the "international system"? Is it anarchical? Or is it based on conventions of sociability and order? The lawyers representing the Public Trustee argued that there remained an overriding moral reason to deny Stoeck's claim to statelessness. They referenced an earlier moment in European diplomatic history when Britain had refused to recognize that another state had denationalized their Jewish subjects. As the solicitors explained, "When Roumania [sic] some years ago denationalized her Jewish citizens, it did not involve that English municipal law must recognize that a denationalized Roumanian Jew was not a Roumanian national."[60] The circumstances of Romanian independence exemplified Great Power influence over European affairs in the nineteenth century. Romania had denied Jewish residents civil and political rights on the basis that they were aliens in the country, though they remained subject to conscription. Once Romania gained its independence from Ottoman rule after the Congress of Berlin, both Britain and the United States insisted that Romanian statehood remain contingent on the standards of civilization. Along similar conditional lines, the Great Powers recognized the independence of Serbia, Montenegro, and Bulgaria, and established treaties guaranteeing religious, civil, and political rights to Jews and other minorities in the Balkans under international law. The lawyers from the Public Trustee thus referenced an earlier moment in which Britain had taken an interest in the Jews of Romania when it, along with the other Great Powers, became the protectors of semi-independent Romania at the end of the Crimean War.[61]

Indeed, as the Public Trustee had argued, in the writings of liberal theorists of international law, the idea that the "civilized" countries of the western hemisphere—compared by these authors to the parts of the world subject to imperial rule—would tolerate the existence of people disconnected from any political community appeared as a moral failing and a legal impossibility. The writings of the Swiss jurist Johann Kaspar Bluntschli (1808–1881) clarify how the theorists of international law in the late nineteenth century portrayed the problem of statelessness in relation to the profession's portrayal of the qualities of statehood. Bluntschli's writings brought together international law's disciplining of the meaning of statehood and its rejection of the status of statelessness. A professor of constitutional law at Heidelberg, Bluntschli had also served as a member of the Baden parliament in Switzerland and was one of the founding members of the Institut de Droit International. His treatise *Theory of the State* was a widely used political theory textbook, and he became well known as a publicist of international law. Bluntschli's theoretical reconstruction of the foundations of liberal constitutionalism and of international law defined the modern international system in such a way as to exclude nonstate entities, such as national groups or individuals, as the subjects of international order. In his state theory, he argued that the modern state unified the *volk* politically. The state, rather than the people, is sovereign. Like many of the founding generation of professional international lawyers, he endorsed the expansion of state power and the necessity of militarization, and envisioned international law as a civilizing, mitigating force checking sovereign authority just as constitutional rights placed limits on state power in domestic contexts. International cooperation coincided with, and reinforced, nation-building. For bourgeois lawyers and administrators, international cooperation reinforced a social order that could resist revolutionary movements—of either socialist or nationalist varieties.[62] In his comments on the international public law status of the Jews in Romania, Bluntschli insisted that even if Romanian Jews were precluded from political citizenship, "they can only be regarded as Roumanian, since they belong to Roumania and are not connected with any other foreign state." The stakes were high. If, as he argued, Romanian Jews were not recognized as at least Romanian nationals, then Europe would exhibit the same reprehensible conditions as the extra-European colonial world, in which dispossessed peoples did not belong to any state. He wrote, "The

European law of civilized nations admits of no tribes dispossessed of country or home but it allocates them to the state or country with which they are connected by descent or domicile."[63] Dispossession was an acceptable state, Bluntschli argued, outside the boundaries of "civilization" but should not be allowed to press into Europe.[64]

Yet by the 1880s one could find examples of international legal authorities tentatively addressing the plausibility of statelessness and articulating a competing impulse: the possibility of international law regulating the disorder produced by mass migration in the later nineteenth century. International legal publicists sought to order the international system made more complex by mass migration and the increasing regulation of borders, and began to embrace the practical questions provoked by migration and the growing demand by enfranchised citizens to protect labor markets. They conceptualized the problem of statelessness in the context of a rules-based approach to interstate relations that marked the boundaries of the world in particular ways, between civilized and uncivilized, state and nonstate, national and international, state and empire.[65] One of the treatises on international law cited by Stoeck's lawyers, by William Edward Hall, first published in 1880, acknowledged that as a result of the peculiarities of different naturalization and denaturalization regimes, a person may not be able to claim any nationality. However, the existence of such persons represented an "embarrassment" that states could solve through agreements such as the one signed by the Swiss cantons and the German states that anyone found to be stateless should be considered a subject of the state in which he or she was living. Franz von Holtzendorff's *Handbuch des Volkerrechts* from 1885, another treatise introduced into evidence by Stoeck's lawyers, offered the clearest assertion that statelessness must be recognized as a possibility in municipal and international law. Holtzendorff, who was a member of the Institut de Droit International and a professor of law at the University of Munich, wrote, "if no state exists according to the municipal law of which a given individual is its national, it is difficult to see to what state he can belong, how he can be other than a stateless person, or why an international lawyer or anyone else should close his eyes to such a possibility."[66]

In the context of mass migration, jurists sought to develop legal principles to regulate the movement of people across oceans and into new polities.

In the 1880s and 1890s, the Institut de Droit International codified standards for the treatment or removal of refugees and for the power of the state to determine entry and exit.[67] The group put forward a set of recommendations to mitigate the harsh consequences of mass migration and the conflict of nationality laws, recommending that states refrain from forbidding entrance to those without a national status and condemning mass expulsion of minority groups. In 1896 the Institut laid down the following principle: "Denationalization can never be imposed as a punishment." Treatises on international private law from this period addressed the question of whether states were obligated to accept people who would otherwise have nowhere else to go.[68] The arguments rested, however, on claims about the governing principles of interstate order rather than on moral principles per se. Legal theorists justified their claims by citing state practice and by the idea of civilized order itself.

The limits of the legalist approach to the dilemmas produced by mass migration encouraged the turn toward more rigorous methods of ethical theory. Contemporaries weighed the efficacy of legalistic approaches to the political and moral quandaries produced by mass migration, particularly as unprecedented numbers of people from eastern and southern Europe made their way across the Atlantic to the United States and South America. In 1891, Henry Sidgwick introduced his new approach to ethics and political philosophy by reference to the alien question in Britain, at the same time that the British Parliament began entertaining legislative proposals to limit immigration from Russia and created more bureaucratic mechanisms for distinguishing "deserving" refugees from undesirable foreigners. As opposed to analyzing mass migration from the perspective of interstate order, Sidgwick emphasized the moral issues the British government would have to weigh as large numbers of poor migrants sought entry to Britain. Sidgwick in turn defended immigration restrictions by arguing for their relative utility in the maintenance of a domestic society. Though foreigners seeking entry had some moral claim on the country, the needs of domestic society ultimately outweighed this moral consideration. By contrast, the jurists of the Institut de Droit International approached the dilemmas introduced by accelerated migration from the perspective of international order, and the danger to the international system that large numbers of people without the protection of nationality introduced.[69]

Although international legal treatises from the late nineteenth century had begun to acknowledge that mass migration had produced novel problems for interstate order and to discuss the problem of statelessness created by the contradictions between naturalization regimes, nonrecognition of statelessness remained an essential part of imperial legal thought. The idea that stateless individuals remained outside the realm of legal possibility within the boundaries of civilized states proved to be a key principle as lawyers elaborated the legal order of late imperialism. In *United States v. Wong Kim Ark*, a 1897 US Supreme Court case that enshrined the constitutional principle of birthright citizenship, the court determined that the "man without a country is not recognized in law." The court's reasoning rested in part on the idea that a person born within the territorial boundaries of the United States must be considered a citizen, or else he would be a person of no nationality. This is not to suggest that this reasoning determined the outcome of the case; however, it indicates the significant justificatory role that statelessness—or the norm that states should not acknowledge this identification—played in the legal formation of American national membership.[70]

The idea that the "man without a country" remained a subject of fiction rather than a legal reality likewise played an important role in the conceptual justification of American empire in the early twentieth century. After the American acquisition of former Spanish colonies in the Pacific, the US Supreme Court designated new subject people as a third legal category between citizens and foreigners. In a series of opinions that came to be known as the "Insular Cases," the court determined that overseas islands could be "foreign to the United States in a domestic sense," indicating that subjects would share allegiance and nationality with other Americans but were not full citizens.[71] The cases led to impassioned debate in the United States over the relationship between areas controlled by the United States and the status of inhabitants, and touched on long-standing constitutional ambiguities on the nature of American citizenship. It fell to Frederic Coudert, a partner in the first international law firm in the United States, to articulate the conceptual and legal issues at stake in the case, and his reasoning demonstrated the significance of the person of no nationality in international legal argument. How could the court, he asked, accept the term *American alien* when doing so implied that the "man without a country is thus transferred from the realm of poetry into that of politics"?[72] In presenting the case for the validity of the category of "American national," Coudert invoked the idea that the transformation of the man without a country from a subject of fiction to an acknowledged legal personage violated an essential feature of international order.

Regardless of the particular history of citizenship and nationality in the United States, what matters here is how Coudert invoked the governing principles of international relations, and how his argument demonstrated the power of the comparative imperial legal imagination. He called attention to the way that the legal category of nationality—in contrast to citizenship—provided an important way to characterize the legal status of subject peoples. He drew on case law from France on the legal character of the Algerian population to analyze the concept of the American national and to demonstrate that it did not represent an "anomaly" in domestic and international law. Native subjects of the French state were defined as "French nationals" but did not possess the rights of citizenship. Coudert likewise drew an analogy with common-law jurisprudence, in which one could be a "subject" rather than a citizen of a particular jurisdiction. Other examples from Great Britain likewise revealed that "such tribes or peoples living under a different law and civilization, possessing a complete organization of their own, should be treated as nationals of the sovereignty of which they were really subject, but should be in their private relations governed by their tribal law." As he argued, the recent legal treatment of indigenous peoples in the United States demonstrated the turn to such logic. He wrote, "It is settled doctrine that there are to be found under the flag of the United States not only American citizens but American 'nationals' or persons owing allegiance to the United States but without those privileges that go only with citizenship."[73]

By the turn of the century, however, theorists began to increasingly integrate statelessness into the picture of international law and international society represented in their legal treatises. Lassa Oppenheim's 1905 treatise on international law developed a doctrinal approach to statelessness that would become the most influential legal source on the subject before the First World War. In his work, Oppenheim established the broader significance of recognizing "no nationality" as a distinct legal status. Born and educated in imperial Germany, Oppenheim began teaching and writing on international law after emigrating to Britain in 1895. The publication of the first edition of his study of international law led to a placement as the Whewell Professor of International Law at Cambridge and established him as the leading expert on international legal positivism—the doctrine that only agreements between states, and not natural law, defined international law.[74]

Oppenheim sought to build a sustainable theory of international law based on positivist foundations. Whereas natural law implied that there is law that inheres in human communities and is subject to rational exploration, positive law was based on the idea that communities create the law that binds them. Law is thus a set of rules whose content can be determined without resort to moral argument. As the discipline of international law expanded and became an important feature of imperial diplomacy, jurists faced more pressure to explain the basis of international law in the absence of a coercive sovereign. They faced the issue of defining what made international law "law" in any real sense.[75]

The publication of his treatise in 1905 enhanced Oppenheim's reputation in England and abroad.[76] Faced with an increasing number of cases in which individuals and groups of people could not claim national identification, Oppenheim proposed that a stateless person is best understood as a "legal anomaly" in the context of international legal order. He based this argument on the fact that according to regularly observed maritime rules, ships flying under the flag of a particular state were "at every point considered as though they were floating parts of their home state"; ships flying without a flag lacked the legal connection to any state and therefore to international law. Territorial jurisdiction extended into the sea by virtue of the ship's formal connection to a home state, and by analogy, a stateless person could be understood as a ship flying without a flag, bearing no connection to any government.[77] Oppenheim's formulation of the essential legal condition of statelessness in light of legal positivism established the terms of the debate to follow on the status of individuals in international law. Individuals who did not possess a nationality should be acknowledged within international law, according to Oppenheim; however, they revealed that an individual's legal status derived from their membership in a state.

Did statelessness represent the sovereign power of individuals, or their fundamental dependence on membership within particular political communities? Real-world examples further supported the doctrine, Oppenheim argued, that only states possessed rights and legal personality. Meditating on the political fate of the Jews of Romania, he concluded that international law clearly could not guarantee the rights of humanity. Rights derived only from the state's protection.[78] Indeed, if one read outside of the legal literature, stories recounted in the press at the turn of the century of displaced people who could not lay claim anywhere emphasized a clear opposition: there were those that belonged to civil society, and then there were others, outsiders who were doomed to wander the oceans in a state of lawlessness. Individuals who ended up spending the remainder of their lives, like Philip Nolan, living on board ships at the discretion of steamship companies became notorious "men without countries." In these accounts lives spent on board ships at sea with no hope of resting on shore played on archaic ideas of the sea as a sphere defined by its lawlessness.[79]

As a countervailing trend, private actors and corporations acquired new capabilities and independence in the context of late imperialism in the nineteenth century, and from this perspective statelessness held out the promise of nonstate forms of political authority. In Sir Francis Taylor Piggott's 1906 treatise on English naturalization law on the high seas, for instance, he described statelessness as "the state in which a man is cast adrift upon the world, and from which many curious consequences may flow: ranging from the commission of murder with impunity and to the acquisition of uninhabited islands in his own right of sovereignty."[80] Such works by international legal authorities served as important resources for consular officials at the turn of the century who were called on to evaluate the status of people seeking entry into a particular territory or naturalization. Consular authorities turned to treatises on international law written in the later decades of the nineteenth century to adjudicate questions of national identification, dual nationality, and at times the absence of national status. The conflict of laws had certainly been important sources for statelessness and dual nationality in the nineteenth century. But these sources are tentative when it comes to evaluating the status of statelessness in law, an ambiguity that border officials could exploit in their patchwork, discretionary approach to making determinations about nationality.[81]

The lack of consensus over whether the law, both domestic and international, recognized the status of statelessness began to seem like more of a problem on the eve of the war. It had become far more difficult to deny the presence of people without nationality living on the social margins across

Europe. As one Swiss jurist noted, urban police forces had become increasingly cognizant of stateless people within their patrol zones. The German Civil Code of 1900 empowered local German police to issue identity passes to stateless persons or foreigners. In Hamburg around the turn of the century, police began carrying a publication containing all the laws of European nations on the acquisition and loss of citizenship.[82] Outside of Europe, statelessness also began to achieve greater recognition as a distinctive phenomenon demanding legislative scrutiny, particularly in countries with large immigrant populations.[83] The Argentine jurist Estanislao Zeballos, who also served as minister of foreign affairs, reported that the "hundreds of thousands of our immigrants are no longer Italians, Spanish, French, or Germans. Legally, they are no longer foreigners ... these are people without country, and who belong to the universal human group, those who qualify as *heimatlosen*."[84]

Do the stateless prove that rights depend on national protection? Or do they represent the possibility that rights do not depend on the state? As we will see in more detail in Chapter 3, the reality of statelessness—the fact that a person free from nationality no longer represented a subject of fiction—lent credibility to the vision of the unconstrained individual of classical liberal political philosophy.[85] Jurists considering the nature of rights framed the implication of courts "admitting" that a person could indeed possess no nationality in terms of the ultimate determination of what it meant to be a rights-bearing subject. In *The Diplomatic Protection of Citizens Abroad* from 1915, Edwin Borchard proposed that "the person without any nationality, or heimatlos" did indeed exist as a legal possibility, insisting that the idea that a person always has some kind of nationality "can hardly be considered a recognized rule of international law." Borchard, an American lawyer born in Germany who was a founder of the American Civil Liberties Union and a law professor at Yale, wrote one of the most widely cited legal texts on citizenship and nationality after World War I. His book cited disagreement among legal writers on whether nationality is a condition that precedes the enjoyment of rights. Borchard explained that constitutions provided the "rights of man" enjoyed by citizens. However, an older idea of natural rights that did not depend on the state was also influential among the treatise writers who insisted that the *heimatlos* could be the subject of international rights and duties. As Borchard explained, such a conception of natural rights had been "positivized" in light of the reality of statelessness.[86]

Yet wartime cases that appeared before the courts in the years before Stoeck brought his suit affirmed the idea that statelessness represented the mere subject of fiction, not a real status that required recognition by a British court. The most well-known case on statelessness before *Stoeck*, *Ex Parte Weber* in 1915, reinforced the idea that English law did not recognize anyone without a nationality. In the 1915 case brought before the British High Court, Antonius Charles Frederick Weber claimed that he had lost his German nationality through his absence from the Reich since the 1890s. He argued that a law passed in 1879 meant that Germans who left the territory of the confederation and lived uninterruptedly abroad for ten years had lost their nationality. During the war Weber was interned on the Isle of Man as an enemy alien but sought a writ of habeas corpus, claiming that he in fact had no nationality whatsoever. Despite evidence presented at the trial by an available expert on German law that Weber had indeed lost his previous legal connection to Germany, Lord Justice Phillimore, the judge presiding over the case, argued that it would be "going a step further to say any country has recognized that a man can shake off his position as a national of the country in which he was born without acquiring the duties and responsibilities of a national of some other country."[87]

It proved expedient in the midst of the conflict to presume that individuals who appeared to come from an enemy state retained their nationality. In *Ex Parte Weber*, the presiding judge relied on the presumption that judicial discretion could determine the legitimacy of another national legal system claiming that a person had in fact relinquished his or her legal nationality.[88] The judge drew on the debates in the House of Lords discussing the laws of German nationality to argue that Weber and others requesting habeas corpus on the basis of being stateless could not have lost their German nationality. In other words, the interpretation of German law by British legislators was sufficient justification for a particular reading of the legislation.[89] In November 1915, for example, the British War Office in Cairo asked the Foreign Office to determine whether individuals taken off ships near Egypt carrying the same certificate that Stoeck would later offer as evidence of his statelessness—the Entlassungs-Urkunde, a document provided by Prussian authorities releasing subjects who wished to emigrate from their legal obligations—were in fact free from their prior status. Drawing on the available international legal literature, the War Office responded that there was "considerable doubt as to whether Germans do in fact lose their nationality under any condition."[90]

Such cases were not unique to the British Empire. Similar justifications for denying the status of statelessness also appeared in a 1915 court case in France, in which a former Austrian subject residing in France at the start of the war sued for recognition as a person of no nationality in order to retrieve his property seized by the French state. As in *Ex Parte Weber*, the French court determined that the loss of Austrian nationality could not be proven. Altogether, the wartime judgments on whether individuals were stateless from a legal perspective indicated the unwillingness to acknowledge statelessness as a recognized status. One legal publicist writing in the United States concluded that the decisions "tend to show a decided indisposition to admit a status of 'statelessness' at least with respect to the circumstances of these cases."[91]

Despite the fact that some authorities presented statelessness as a reality of international order that should be acknowledged in international law, the conclusions offered by the major treatises were hardly definitive. By the time that Stoeck brought his claim before the High Court, it was possible to find supporting evidence for the recognition of statelessness in international law and for the argument that modern, civilized states did not acknowledge the plausibility of such a status. When Russell offered his ruling on Stoeck, he seized on the ambivalence expressed in these sources. In his analysis of the international legal sources offered during the proceedings, Russell stated that it was impossible to draw any definitive conclusions. By the turn of the twentieth century, treatises on international law affirmed the doctrine that sovereignty was the governing principle of international legal order. Yet the meaning of sovereignty, at the level of theory, in a world of mutually recognizing states, when it came to the determination of the national status of individuals, remained fundamentally ambiguous. The fact that the judgment did not rest on the authority of such texts would become crucially important in subsequent debates over the significance of statelessness in relation to the expansion of international law's authority. When Russell decided that the norms governing the interaction of states reflected the vision presented by Cruesemann and Rouse—that judges and other legal authorities should defer to the way legal experts from other countries interpreted their own law—he affirmed a normative expectation about the boundaries of international society.

IV

It is important to appreciate what was fundamentally new about statelessness as national courts began to adjudicate the terms of peace. As Russell had elaborated in his ruling, the principle of honoring another state's decision to denationalize its subjects became the overriding justification for recognizing statelessness after the 1921 decision. Courts enacted the transition from wartime to peacetime by endorsing the validity of a classification that had not been an acceptable form of identification during the war, when national security dictated that residents be clearly marked as friend or foe. The decision established that states depend on what other states tell them about their nationals rather than relying on their own judgments in interpreting the nationality legislation of a foreign government. Russell's ruling determined that statelessness represented a new category in English law and that its recognition depended on an understanding of the norms of international order.[92]

The ruling transformed how officials across the British Empire evaluated claims of statelessness. Administrators cited *Stoeck* as the reason they would need to accept individual claims to statelessness as peoples across the empire sought to regain the property they had lost after being designated enemy aliens. After their victory in *Stoeck*, Cruesemann and Rouse became known as the expert litigators for nationality questions and in the coming decade would represent a number of clients in the same position as Stoeck. In 1922 they represented the estate of Hugo Hoffmann, arguing that Hoffman was stateless according to the German embassy and that the seizure of his property in Trinidad by the Scottish custodian of enemy property had not been a legitimate application of the Versailles Treaty.[93] The Colonial Office, the British ministry charged with overseeing the British Empire's vast colonial territories, agreed that once Russell's decision had established that *Staatenlosigkeit* was a recognized category under British law, there was no choice but to give Hoffman the proceeds from his liquidated property on the basis of the ruling.[94] As one civil servant in the British Board of Trade wrote after ruefully deciding to relinquish the case against a wine merchant accused of falsely identifying himself as a person of no nationality, "it seems that the effect of the decision of the Stoeck case is that English law now recognizes that a person may be "stateless."[95]

Stoeck v. Public Trustee affirmed that states possessed the ultimate power to decide whether a person who had a prior legal connection to that government remained a national according to the laws of that country. However, as new states emerged from old empires, and new states faced revolution, it was not always clear who was sovereign at the critical moment of decision. One year after Stoeck, a case appeared before Judge Russell in which a plaintiff asked the court for a declaration that he was not a national of the former kingdom of Hungary. Like Stoeck, the subject of the suit sought to avoid the punitive terms of the Versailles Treaty through recognition as a person of "no nationality." The representatives of the Public Trustee argued that the document the petitioner had provided to prove that he had relinquished his prior national status was invalid on the grounds that the revolutionary Hungarian government which had issued the document was not in fact sovereign. Russell decided against the arguments of the Public Trustee, because he did not wish to interrogate the status of the Hungarian government at the time when the document was issued. As he wrote in his decision, "he was really asked by the defendant to overrule the executive act and to restore to the ranks of the nationals of Hungary a person who had been dismissed therefrom in accordance with the executive practice of that country. That he felt wholly unable to do."[96] As we will see in more detail later, the legal nature of state formation in Central Europe after the end of the Habsburg Empire became critical to larger debates in the post–World War I period about the meaning of sovereignty.

However, even as Russell sought to avoid the knotty problem of adjudicating the sovereign status of another government, the fact that courts were now called upon to evaluate the nature of sovereignty in cases involving potentially stateless individuals indicated how statelessness as a more general phenomenon could not be kept separate from the political and constitutional subjects that defined the domain of public law.[97] Though we will consider the reception of statelessness in international thought in more detail later on, it is important to note that *Stoeck* was immediately taken to have wider implications for international law. Debates about *Stoeck v. Public Trustee* among jurists in Europe and the United States reveal a tension between the view that recognition by states of the legal validity of statelessness was a victory for the authority of international law and the rights of the individual against the state, and one that adopted a more pragmatic, socially oriented view of the stateless person as a new and particularly vulnerable victim within the international order. One commentator distinguished between the significance of the case from the perspective of "abstract legal theory" and its social consequences. "Aside from the injustice resulting to individuals in a condition of practical international outlawry, it would seem to be in the interest of organized society to admit of no person being without a political status."[98] Professional legal organizations in other national contexts likewise looked at the *Stoeck* decision with great interest. In a speech delivered in 1926 to the legal society in Cologne, Germany, a solicitor from London spoke to German lawyers about the Stoeck case and its implications for the possibility that a person could hold dual citizenship or no citizenship at all.[99]

The court's acknowledgment of statelessness was also seen to bear on discriminatory immigration regulations. According to Taraknath Das, a professor of political science at Columbia University who had previously founded an anarchist group in India, the legal recognition of statelessness represented a positive step toward addressing the increasingly restrictive and racially discriminatory naturalization regime in the United States. In a speech delivered to the American Society of International Law in 1925, in which he discussed the Stoeck decision, Das insisted that it would be better if countries began recognizing the reality of statelessness. Only two years earlier, the US Supreme Court had made immigrants from South Asia ineligible to become US citizens, and Das, and his American-born wife Mary, had been denationalized as a result. Das explained in his speech how revoking the citizenship of Hindus in the United States had left them stateless persons. To name the problem, Das suggested, by recognizing statelessness as a distinct status, might be a way to begin to combat this novel form of vulnerability.[100]

As national states expanded and consolidated their power in the nineteenth century, Edward Hale's popular story about "The Man without A Country" supported the claim that statelessness represented the subject of fiction rather than a reality of interstate order. In a twist, however, the most poignant accounts of the vulnerability of living without the security of nationality and identifying documents like a passport began to appear in interwar works of fiction. By the 1920s, fiction most accurately portrayed the reality of statelessness for new numbers of people, introducing the real plight of people without the protection of national status into wider popular consciousness. In *Das Totenschiff (The Death Ship)*, a novel written by the mysterious anarchist author B. Traven in 1926, an American sailor loses his identity papers in Europe and is doomed to wander the seas without hope for rest on solid ground. The hero of the story is an outcast, part of the mass of paperless people dumped into neighboring states under cover of night by border police. His fate is to find work only on a "death ship," a vessel bound for calculated shipwreck so that the owners can collect the insurance money. The sailor's story echoed the real accounts reported during World War I of people condemned to a life on the sea because they were refused entry at every border. Traven's novel portrayed the dehumanizing consequences of political dispossession and the implicit violence of modern bureaucracy and police power. The protagonist of *The Death Ship* shared a common fate with the hero of "The Man without a Country," but Traven's protagonist becomes stateless wholly without choice, without the act of denying his country that precipitated Nolan's fate. A bestseller in Germany upon publication, *Das Totenschiff* found similar success in Britain and the United States after its translation into English in 1934.[101]

Stoeck's biography did not echo the fate of the sailor featured in *The Death Ship*. After the uncertainty of his wartime status, Stoeck ultimately accepted renaturalization as a German citizen and continued to patent his industrial inventions.[102] Yet what is so striking about the suit and its reception is the way it created a setting for direct reflection on the governing norms of international order and how statelessness fit into those assumptions. Two conclusions follow from this observation: first, that acknowledging statelessness as a reality rather than as the subject of fiction carried important intellectual implications for doctrinal theories of international law and the nature of rights; second, that ideas about international order matter because they provide the justifications that underwrite judicial and bureaucratic decision-making. Though statelessness implied exclusion from any legal order, the implications of its entry into the landscape of international life from the perspective of international thought remained far from clear, and as it emerged as the explicit subject of debate and international politics, the conventions and norms of an interstate system remained in flux. Evidence that individuals possessed legal standing before a court did not indicate whether a person was the bearer of political rights. In fact, the legal status of imperial subjects marked incorporation into a hierarchical system of governance and domination. In the decade following the *Stoeck* decision, a range of new international legal subjects would gain international recognition to challenge the doctrine that only states possess agency from the perspective of international law. However, as we will see in Chapter 2, unlike other new forms of international identification that emerged in the interwar period, statelessness was not seen as a creation of international legal order. Through its formal legal recognition, it would become a powerful theoretical resource for legal scholars in search of support for the ultimate authority of international law over domestic legal regimes. As the stateless gained international visibility, they became the paradigmatic victims of circumstance and the symbols of a coming order in which legal status did not depend on national belonging.

We will return to taking up the implications of statelessness for international thought and debates about the boundaries of international society. However, in Chapter 2, we need to examine how the problem was addressed at the League of Nations, the organization established in the wake of World War I that contributed to the creation of a defined public sphere for addressing problems at international and global scales, and for debating the boundaries of international order. From the perspective of the League, statelessness threatened the fragile boundaries that the organization sought to establish between international and national spheres of authority. Rather than marking the ultimate triumph of the modern state, statelessness became an acknowledged reality as the boundaries of sovereignty and political agency in international society became the object of global political and conceptual contestation.

2

Postimperial States of Statelessness

IN THE FALL OF 1921—the same year that Max Stoeck appeared before the British High Court—the League of Nations received a letter from Jakob Sinnwell, a machinist from the industrial center of the Saar coal basin, a region in what is today southwest Germany. Sinnwell began by identifying himself as a person of "Saarbrucken origins, with Prussian parents," and then described how French gendarmes had taken him handcuffed from his home, brought him to the border, and expelled him. Despite a "colorful youth," Sinnwell wrote, where he had occasional run-ins with the police, he could not discern a reason for his expulsion. He therefore appealed to the governing authority in the region in the hope of returning home, or at least of discovering the official justification for his exile. He implored the Governing Commission, "If it cannot annul my expulsion at least to inform me why I have received this terrible treatment from a nation against which I have never done the slightest thing, nor even thought of it."[1]

A long-contested, resource-rich swathe of forested lands crossed by the Saar River, the Saarland had been granted to France on a fifteen-year lease in the course of peace negotiations at the end of World War I. Germany held control of the territory before the war, but the region had come under British and French occupation in the course of the conflict. In need of access to coal and fearing German rearmament, France made sovereignty over the Saar a condition of the peace agreement with Germany. The treaty, however, deferred the question of which power possessed ultimate control to some future date, when the region's inhabitants could opt for German or French nationality in a plebiscite to determine which country would claim legitimate political authority. Sinnwell's expulsion highlights the more local consequences of the national conflict over territory—by expelling him the French army had seized an opportunity to rid themselves of a local who could eventually vote for German rule. Unlike Max Stoeck, the majority of people who would begin to define themselves as stateless in the interwar era faced the insecurity of their legal and political status as a result of the breakdown of imperial orders, the formation of national states, and conflicts over national sovereignty. B. Traven's portrayal in *The Death Ship* of sailors living without the security of a legal status facing expulsion, or being pushed over a border by the police under cover of night, more accurately conveys Sinnwell's predicament.

Yet the fact that Sinnwell wrote to the League for assistance also indicates the emergence of a novel sphere of political authority to which people without the protection of their own governments could appeal. Established in 1919 as the first international organization devoted to collective security, the League of Nations introduced a distinctive arena for managing problems on a grand political scale. Individuals began looking to new international authorities to adjudicate their national status or for direct protection and legal recognition. Governance over the Saar was a case in point. According to the terms of the treaty establishing the League's authority over the region, until sovereignty could be determined, an international body called the Saar Basin Governing Commission would be charged with the administration of the territory. The treaty that established the commission furnished an internationalist solution to national political conflict by granting the Council of the League, the League of Nations' central governing body, the authority to appoint the five members of the commission: one seat was designated for a French representative, another for representatives of the Saar inhabitants, and the other seats designated for commissioners loyal to the League of Nations. The commission itself had the authority to function like a civil government by administering public infrastructure, levying taxes, and setting standards for labor and civil rights. It also had the right to exercise jurisdiction when the existing courts were not deemed competent and had the final say in the interpretation of the treaty applying to the Saar. The Saar Basin Governing Commission constituted, as one of its contemporaries commented, "the first experiment in international administration under the League of Nations."[2]

The scale of international governance transformed in the decade after the war. The crises of the post–World War I period—including swelling refugee populations, displaced prisoners of war in need of repatriation, disabled veterans requiring medical care, a rising number of people without the protection of national membership, and mass starvation—stretched throughout the European continent and across European empires. The League provided a centralized locus for international organizations like the International Committee of the Red Cross, which was established in the nineteenth century to provide medical care and sanitation for soldiers on the battlefield but had evolved by the end of World War I into a more expansive humanitarian association. Separate international legal institutions and organizations also took shape under the League's umbrella, including the Permanent Court of Justice and the International Labor Organization, whose mission involved creating common international standards for working conditions.

In order to grasp the unique significance of the entry of the legal category of statelessness into international law and international politics after World War I, it is necessary to establish how officials within the League conceptualized this phenomenon. Recent research on the history of the organization has emphasized its role in the reconfiguration of imperial power after the First World War, the rise of global governance, and the expansion of the international society of states. As the gateway between the world of nineteenth-century imperialism and the twentieth-century nation-state, the League was far reaching in its ambitions and in its effects on international order, ultimately embodying the transformation from a world of imperial governance to one in which the bounded territorial state became the organizing unit of global order.[3] The League and its associated international institutions introduced a novel approach to the stabilization of Europe and empire after the war, playing an outsized role in the re-establishment of the political settlement relative to its rather small budget. One method of stabilization involved establishing new collectivities as subjects of internationally defined rights, including minorities, the subjects of the mandatory powers, and to a more limited extent, refugees and stateless persons. The system of mandatory rule overseen by the League, the Minority Protection Treaties, and the High Commission for Refugees represented innovative responses to the reconfiguration of imperial authority, the ongoing violence of the postwar years, and rising demands for political independence and self-government.[4]

However, understanding the League's approach to the problem of statelessness in particular illuminates its significance for international politics in an era when the nature of sovereignty both practically and conceptually remained fundamentally contested. The stateless did not represent a novel constituency recognized by the League because their recognition would have challenged the organization's efforts to facilitate the re-establishment of international order and the terms of the peace set out by the victors. As the Stoeck case demonstrated, the entry of statelessness into law after the First World War had direct implications for some of the dominant ideas about international order, particularly about the status of individuals in international law. The League's approach to the stateless amid the uncertainties about the future of global political order reveals how the growing numbers of people without citizenship in the years after the war threatened its attempt to set the boundary of international authority. By analyzing how officials responded to the problem of statelessness as it evolved over the course of the 1920s, we can grasp its fundamental importance for key debates about the governing norms of international politics. In the course of this chapter, I identify and foreshadow the importance of two main groups of stateless people in the interwar era: Russian émigrés who obtained a protected international status and the *heimatlosen* of the central European successor states who could not claim similar international protection. The records of the League read together with the published and unpublished sources on these two main groups offer a unique perspective on the argumentative context in which the problem of statelessness entered, and upended, the boundaries of international politics.

I

It is important to appreciate the suddenness of the global political changes wrought by the First World War to understand the role of the League of Nations in the stabilization of the postwar settlement. The Habsburg, Romanov, Ottoman, and Prussian dynasties did not survive the conflict, yet their demise was not a foregone conclusion. In the midst of the fighting, and then in the tumultuous years of enacting a peace settlement, the underlying norms and expectations about international order remained far from clear. In 1915, the polymath American intellectual and activist W. E. B. Dubois asserted that the prospects for peace and democracy for peoples subjected to European colonial exploitation depended on the extension of the principle of "home rule" to "groups, nations, and races."[5] During the war, military mobilization accelerated demands for political representation, but imperial governments proposed revisions to the constitutional structure of their empires that would accommodate demands for self-government without dissolving imperial orders altogether. Subjects of the Ottoman Empire, for example, did not anticipate the end of the empire and envisioned achieving national autonomy without separating from the ultimate sovereignty of the Ottoman bey.[6] And in the Habsburg case, while war raged on, the Austrian emperor promised to reorganize the empire into a federal state in which constituent nationalities would acquire more political independence though remain subject to the ultimate authority of the imperial government. Bolshevik revolutionaries overthrew the Czarist government in Russia in 1917, but a civil war between revolutionary and counterrevolutionary forces to determine ultimate control over the territories of the Russian Empire continued through 1921. Military conflict continued long after the standard chronological endpoint of the war and the shape of the world that would ultimately replace the vast continental empires—the kinds of political communities and social organizations that would succeed them—remained in question and the object of long-standing contestation.[7]

During the conflict the American president, Woodrow Wilson, and the Bolshevik leader, Vladimir Lenin, both rejected dynastic rule as illegitimate. Self-determination, a concept originally invoked during the Enlightenment in the name of the individual's power to determine the shape of his or her own life, became associated with collective emancipation in the mid-nineteenth century. But what exactly did national self-determination imply? Wilson presented the war as a global crusade for democracy, though his emphasis on the liberal subject as the basis for democratic government left ample room for the continuation of empire. Lenin's vision for the postwar order was oriented, meanwhile, against the liberal, capitalist, imperialist states of Britain, France, and the United States. The implications of the principle of self-determination for the political map of the world remained far from certain as the conflict drew to a close. Robert Lansing, the American Secretary of State who accompanied Wilson to Paris as a legal advisor, worried, "When the president talks of 'self-determination' what unit has he in mind? Does he mean a race, a territorial area, or a community?" Who possessed the right to insist on self-determination? And who rightfully stood in the position to recognize such a claim?[8]

It quickly became apparent that the establishment of the League of Nations created a new public sphere for recognizing political independence, or, as the case may be, for publicly denying the legitimacy of the cause. International society began to more clearly signify a zone in which groups formerly placed beyond the pale of international law could be brought into its orbit. Germany signed the armistice agreement on November 11, 1918, and three weeks later Woodrow Wilson left New York for Paris to establish the foundations for a new international order. For the next six months, Wilson along with representatives from the victorious European powers pieced together a settlement for the postwar world. The imposition of peace terms reflected a broader cross section of the globe than previous settlements in which European sovereigns set the terms of international order. The decision to manage international relations through an international organization after World War I in turn represented an innovative break from the system established by the Great Powers at the Congress of Vienna in 1815 following the Napoleonic Wars. Wilson envisioned the League of Nations, the organization of states that would stand at the center of this new order, as a new approach to collective security: an international institution that represented a dynamic improvement on the secret covenants that had governed Great Power relations in the previous century. Its purpose would be to reconcile divergent interests and to promote international co-operation to address problems that affected the world at large. The new organization would reflect an era in which public opinion and the voice of the people mattered above all.[9]

Political representatives from around the world converged on Paris and then Geneva to present the case for political independence. Ho Chi Minh is one of the most famous figures to have pressed the case for the independence of Indochina from French rule at Versailles. Deskanah, a Cayuga chief from Ontario, visited the League in 1923 to advocate for recognition of the Iroquois as a nation with treaty rights under international law, though he never received a hearing by the League General Assembly.[10] By fashioning itself as the site for bringing individuals and groups into international legal order, the League of Nations established a way of controlling the process of obtaining political independence, setting the terms of independence and creating new subjects of international governance. The organization worked to minimize the harsh implications of popular sovereignty even as it facilitated the creation of new states with the power to create new constituencies and exclude people.[11]

For example, rather than risking the outbreak of new hostilities as a result of the victorious powers competing over former colonial and territorial holdings of the German and Ottoman Empires, the Council of the League established the mandates system. The League would serve as a trustee over the governance of these territories until the people themselves were deemed ready for full political independence and statehood. The Covenant of 1919 establishing the League provided for a Permanent Mandates Commission to advise the council and receive reports from the fifteen mandated territories. The technical language of international law in turn allowed the League secretariat to carve out a distinctive institutional role in the stabilization of international order after the war. Sovereignty would emanate not from the League but rather from the authority of the mandated power. Settlers were given the nationality of the mandatory power and local inhabitants were called "protected persons." Administrators who led the commission hoped to demonstrate the power of the League's protective role in the administration of a gentle form of imperial rule. The League served as a buffer zone, transforming the diplomacy of the Great Powers by filtering their interactions and conflicts through a separate bureaucracy and compelling the public articulation of domestic events and complaints. Debating the legality of a particular action, or adjudicating the legal issues at stake in a dispute between imperial powers or complaints from mandatory subjects, transformed how empires conducted diplomacy.[12]

As we have already seen in the case of the Saar, in particularly contested European territories the League sought to establish direct international governance. Whereas earlier "international cities" like Cracow and Shanghai had been placed under a consortium of Great Power administration, the League inaugurated direct jurisdiction over contentious territories. The League directly administered the Free City of Danzig through a League-appointed high commissioner; it was also granted specific responsibilities over the Saar and Upper Silesia. The League's government of the Saar promised eventual self-government in the territory by figuring the people as the goal of the legal order rather than its point of origin. Rather than states acquiring territory through conquest, with the population compelled to change their allegiance, the people themselves could determine the jurisdiction in which they resided. Plebiscites were held in northern Schleswig, where people could choose to live under German or Danish rule, and in Upper Silesia, where inhabitants decided between German and Polish rule.[13] The existence of the international bureaucracy significantly informed the outcome of major disputes and set the stage for how new political communities could gain entry into the international community while preserving the stability of the system overall.[14] British officials discussing a proposed treaty between Poland and Danzig in 1920 distinguished between Poland, "an ordered government recognized by the powers," and the Danzigers, who existed "by the will of the Powers." As the officials explained, referencing Danzig's distinctive status, the Great Powers and the League of Nations were "within their rights in imposing the conditions of existence on a child of their own creation."[15]

The organization of the League's internal bureaucracy contributed to the impression that it had established a distinctive source of political authority, separate from the constituent independent states that composed the organization's main deliberative body. Sir Eric Drummond, an Oxford-educated civil servant, became the organization's first secretary-general. He and others built on their considerable experience working for the British civil service as overseas imperial administrators to develop the League's governing apparatus. Drummond broke with expectation by organizing the secretariat according to function rather than national affiliation, devolving its central functions into categories such as the Legal Section, the Economic and Financial Section, and the mandates section. His organizational creativity allowed international civil servants to claim loyalty to the institution and its missions rather than to their countries of origin.[16] In addition to regulating the procedure for gaining recognition as a state, the League brought together experts and imperial servants with a mandate for the first time to investigate, and at times intervene, in social and economic matters at a global scale. Their work established precedents for global regimes of economic, health, labor, and energy policy as well as refugee relief.[17]

Yet as we shall see, the League's approach to statelessness, and its reluctance to name it as a more general phenomenon, points to the conceptual and political significance of the category in the context of the League's efforts to facilitate the political reordering of continental Europe and the wider imperial world. As the walls of national sovereignty rose up, many placed their hope in an organization that promised to respond to problems at a novel scale of political organization and action, and appeared to some as the realization of dreams to establish a perpetual peace, which European publicists had been writing about since the eighteenth century. Many rallied around the League because it seemed to enshrine solidarity beyond the boundaries of the ever more demanding state. In light of these aspirations, the members of the League's bureaucracy sought to police the dreams of peace and freedom, and in particular of world government, generated by its establishment. M. J. Landa, a journalist who covered developments at the League, recalled that there "was a morbid fear that the League, as if it were an entity with a corporeal existence and a soul of its own, might materialize as a super-state."[18] The question, then, is what exactly about the generalization of the problem of statelessness in the interwar years threatened the international order that officials in the organization sought to establish and maintain.

II

The threat of mass numbers of people without a national status loomed over the breakup of the Habsburg Empire into independent successor states and presented a major challenge for those who sought to restore continental order after the war. At the turn of the twentieth century, the Habsburg Empire was a dual monarchy with a total population of fifty-three million, made up of more than fifteen nationalities. After Prussia defeated Austria in 1866, the empire was divided through the compromise of 1867, which remained the constitutional basis of the multinational empire until its dissolution in 1918. A single imperial citizenship was created in 1867 that guaranteed the same civil rights to all subjects, regardless of religious status. The two parts of the empire had separate parliaments and a significant degree of autonomy, even though foreign affairs, defense, and finance were designated areas of common concern. Like the Russian and Ottoman Empires, Austria-Hungary was an inherited monarchy that deployed a variety of measures to accommodate mass politics and demands for national autonomy.[19] Demands for greater national representation engendered new legal and constitutional theories according a degree of public authority to the members of national groups with extraterritorial autonomy. The legal recognition of groups in the Austro-Hungarian Empire after the 1860s threatened to turn a matter of constitutional structure—how the empire was composed—into a matter of international law, with politically independent groups interacting through this legal framework. National autonomy had already been introduced in the late nineteenth and early twentieth centuries in the Habsburg Empire to devolve a degree of public authority to nonterritorially organized groups, and Austrian jurists produced a range of creative works on minority protection and the legal recognition of national groups from 1897 to 1910.[20] Imperial administrators implemented a range of constitutional alterations to hold the empire together, including converting the Austrian side of the dual monarchy into a federation of national member states.[21] The Russian Jewish Labor Bund in 1905 and the Mensheviks in 1912 had proposed a similar plan for group autonomy within the Russian Empire.[22] In the decades before the war, the Habsburg Empire's eleven officially recognized nationalities—Germans, Hungarians, Czechs, Slovaks, Slovenes, Croats, Serbs, Romanians, Ruthenians, Poles, and Italians—struggled over their national rights. As recent research on the Habsburg Empire has shown, agitation for imperial recognition of national groups represented a form of imperial politics rather than revolutionary movements to dissolve empires into discrete sovereign states—national autonomy generally did not indicate an ultimate goal of sovereign independence. According to this view, the Austrian imperial constitution was flexible and innovative rather than hopelessly sclerotic.[23] Constitutionalism in the nineteenth century provided legal solutions to growing demand for political emancipation and national representation.[24]

Before the meaning of self-determination could be sorted out at the end of World War I, new countries began declaring their independence and asserting their status as independent sovereign communities. Wilson did not initially endorse full independence for the nationalities of Central Europe, suggesting self-government within the Habsburg Empire along the lines proposed by the emperor. At issue was the question of whether nationalist demands could be satisfied through constitutional measures or international guarantees without the creation of an independent, territorially distinct state. Once Austria-Hungary was pronounced legally dead in 1918, some national groups claimed to recover the sovereignty they had lost centuries before (Poland, Lithuania, Estonia, and Latvia) while others established the sovereignty of groups struggling to emerge as recognized independent political collectivities (Yugoslavia and Czechoslovakia). Czechoslovakia became the first government of the successor states to withdraw from the Habsburg monarchy and made the "Declaration of Independence of the Czechoslovak Nation" in October 1918 in Washington, DC.[25]

The collapse of a world that had seemed to possess perpetual life left enormous uncertainty in its wake, particularly for imperial subjects who faced exclusion on the basis of their national identification. For the Viennese satirist Karl Kraus, the dissolution of the Habsburg Empire was an apocalyptic event analogous to the end of days.[26] Lucien Wolf, a leader in the diplomatic wing of the Board of Deputies of British Jews, who would become one of the architects of international minority protection, initially saw European peace and Jewish survival as contingent on the preservation of empire.[27] Without the protection of imperial citizenship, individuals identified with certain national groups or religious minorities would be left stranded within the boundaries of the new states, and as the war drew to a close women's groups, socialists, and pacifists took up the idea of international protection by law for minorities. In 1919, a group called the Committee of New States, dominated by British and American members, drafted model minority treaties, first for Poland, then Czechoslovakia, Yugoslavia, Greece, and Romania. Support for legal minority protection expanded as reports of massacres targeting Jews reached the Versailles deliberations.

Internationalism as an approach to controlling the entry of new states into the international community, and minimizing the potential for mass disenfranchisement as a result of the dissolution of diverse empires into national states, took the form of an international minority protection regime in the Habsburg successor states. The treaties at the Paris Peace Conference gave sixty million people their own state, but left around twenty-five million "minorities" outside their national states. According to the treaties signed by the successor states and the Allied powers, Austria, Hungary, Poland, Czechoslovakia, Yugoslavia, and Romania undertook stipulations as to nationality and other provisions for the protection of minorities. The Treaty of Saint-Germain, signed in July 1920, and the Treaty of Trianon, signed in July 1921, left the basis for nationality in the successor states uncertain—allowing each country to refer either to domicile or residence or the "native" (*indigenat*) status of the person in question.

These treaties in turn established a system in which an international authority defined and defended the rights of minorities rather than a separate sovereign state that could use the minority group as a pretense for territorial revision—a marked difference from the nineteenth century, when the Great Powers had agreed to protect vulnerable minorities at the Congress of Vienna and later at the Congress of Berlin. The League could refer cases to the Permanent Court of International Justice, though minorities could not petition the court directly. The Minorities Section, a division within the League Secretariat, consulted with governments, collected information locally, and heard from petitioners, who had no formal role in the investigative process. The system granted linguistic rights to individual members of collective groups, guaranteeing, for example, non-Hungarian speakers in the Hungarian part of the empire the right to use and cultivate their own language and culture.[28]

For some, the treaties ratified a solution to contestation over group rights and national political representation that had become central to the constitutional politics of the empire in the years before the war by affirming that nonstate groups had become the subjects of international law. International oversight replaced the constitutional efforts to regulate relations among the peoples of the empire. These agreements built on late imperial proposals to grant national groups greater local autonomy within the empire: such proposals envisioned political allegiance to a wider state and personal allegiance to one's group, which would govern institutions vital for the preservation and fulfillment of its cultural and social life. They went beyond the protection of religious freedom assured in earlier international treaties by promising protection of civil and political rights, as well as certain cultural rights, to individuals as members of recognized collective entities.[29]

According to more contemporary histories of human rights law, the minority protection treaties represented the first time that individuals and groups gained independent standing in international law. As we will see in more detail in Chapter 3, both the members of recognized minority groups and individuals without citizenship prompted similar reflection on the subjects of international law, and on the concept of legal personality. The agreements and the system of international oversight established by the League failed to prevent the rise of a new class identified generally as the *heimatlosen*, individuals without a national status living in the Habsburg successor states. Both the stateless and minorities carried important implications for long-standing debates in legal and political thought about the nature of entities acknowledged to have legal personality. Did they exist merely at the discretion of some more substantial source of authority with the capacity to represent them and transform their fictive presence into real action and agency?

If we return briefly to the legal condition of deported individuals in Roman law, the loss of civil status in favor of a status under the law of nations defined the nature of the punishment itself. Along similar lines, looking back on the post–World War I era, Hannah Arendt called minorities and the stateless "cousins-germane" because both represented the fundamental breakdown of the nineteenth-century ideal of civic emancipation. Dependence on an international organization such as the League of Nations, or the Permanent Court of International Justice, left minorities and the stateless—categories that often blended together in practice—in a position of fundamental vulnerability. The category of the minority in practice created a permanent state of exclusion for anyone who qualified as a member of a designated minority group. For Arendt, both kinds of persons, regardless of how they were identified by the League, represented a violation of the ideal of citizenship and civil equality.

Yet as we shall see, officials at the League *did* differentiate the mandate to intervene and hear matters relating to minority rights, from the general phenomenon of statelessness. Whereas minority protection remained within the ambit of its internationalist approach to governance and political order, statelessness as a general category of identification threatened the boundary they sought to define between national and international spheres of authority.[30]

III

League-directed internationalist approaches to reconfiguring political order after the war only indirectly addressed the potential for the breakdown of empires and the creation of new independent states to produce mass numbers of people who did not belong anywhere. However, the organization's involvement in the creation of international arrangements to assist refugees from the Russian Empire directly took on the question of how to define statelessness, though ambivalently and in a highly selective manner.

Russian citizens from the professional and intellectual classes had begun to leave Russia in mass numbers in 1918, following the czar's abdication after the Russian Revolution. Many landed in Constantinople; others made their way to military outposts in China and Bulgaria. The exiles included White Russian officers and their families as well as civilians, many of whom were civil servants from the former imperial court and administration.[31] Wartime saw a variety of ad hoc local and imperial measures for assisting people flee-ing from conflict. Administrators from the British Foreign Office and private philanthropic organizations oversaw the evacuation of thousands of Russian imperial subjects fleeing the Bolshevik Revolution. With the help of human-itarian organizations, individual civilians began to leave Constantinople for Western and Central Europe.

The transfer of responsibility for refugees from the former Russian Em-pire to the League of Nations from the wartime armies signified the end of formal struggles as militaries began to disband across Europe and the former Ottoman Empire.[32] The arrival of Russian refugees in the Central European successor states and in the territories of the former Ottoman Empire in 1921 marked the end of the Russian Civil War and the begin-ning of a new era in international refugee identification and management. The League appointed Fridtjof Nansen, a world-famous Norwegian polar explorer, to organize relief efforts and to repatriate war refugees from camps around Constantinople and Gallipoli to other countries in Europe. Nansen had been part of the great race to map and colonize the earth's surface in the final decades of the nineteenth century, and his association with the spir-it of scientific internationalism made him an ideal candidate for the posi-tion. He was officially appointed high commissioner at the League's second assembly in September 1921, where he was given a mandate to assist "any person of Russian origin who does not enjoy or who no longer enjoys the protection of the government of the USSR, and who has not acquired an-other nationality." An intergovernmental conference held in Geneva in 1921 led to the creation of an international agreement for the protection of Rus-sian and Armenian refugees that eventually provided an international travel document—generally known as the "Nansen passport."[33]

The foundation of the High Commission for Refugees was a critical turning point in the long aftermath of the war because it was the first for-mal acknowledgement of international responsibility for refugees. However, the national status of former Russian imperial subjects remained ambigu-ous until December 15, 1921, when the Bolshevik government formally re-voked the citizenship of the expatriates.[34] Defining the Russian refugees as stateless was a highly politicized decision. Consular officials who recognized the one million Russian subjects scattered across port cities as "stateless per-sons" indicated European states' acceptance of the Bolshevik government by acknowledging the government's right to denationalize its citizens. French courts initially refused to give effect to the Russian decrees denationalizing Russian émigrés as "measures violating the law of nations" and treated the Russian émigrés who had settled in France as Russian nationals.[35] The journalist Landa recalled in horror how it seemed that the League "was actually asked, and indeed was being driven, to make people homeless and stateless by law!"[36]

The intrinsically political nature of the international refugee arrangements resulted, therefore, not only from the challenge of establishing diplomatic relations with the Bolshevik government, but also due to the League's role in recognizing statelessness as a novel feature of the international landscape. In response to these worries, Nansen emphasized that the arrangement to assist refugees should be understood as humanitarian and therefore politically neutral, a particularly important claim in light of the acceleration of ideological conflict since the Bolshevik Revolution.[37] Separating an arena of technical administration from the messier world of politics represented a method of imposing order. Claiming technical, neutral, expertise would become a hallmark of the bureaucrats, lawyers, and economists at the League. Nansen's vision for stabilizing the continent involved finding overseas states willing to take in refugee populations and providing these countries with assistance to develop their agricultural capabilities so that refugees could find work once they arrived.[38] Officials were intent on resettling or repatriating dispossessed people in an effort to stabilize the social and economic order. As Nansen detailed in a letter to a civil society organization in Vienna established to support the work of the League of Nations, the repatriation of prisoners of war living "as refugees in countries foreign to them," would mean "the removal of a great and dangerous evil" that would help secure the settlement of Europe.[39]

Reports and images of refugee suffering lent credibility to the vision of the High Commission for Refugees as a purely humanitarian agency that stood apart from politics.[40] In the cities where they had found momentary refuge, the refugees faced disease and starvation, especially in places that had not recovered from the devastation of the war and its aftermath. One member of the International Labor Organization's Overseas Settlement Committee tasked with facilitating the resettlement of the refugees, wrote to the British government in 1921 that "Russian Refugees are an almost hopeless problem, and as they are dying by scores from starvation in Salonica . . . we are naturally anxious not to miss an opportunity for disposing of them."[41] The rate of mortality among the refugees as a result of famine, typhus, and sanitary conditions reached a peak in 1922, though in that same year many of the refugees had begun to secure more permanent settlement. By 1922, more than a quarter of all Russian refugees had settled in Germany, with 360,000 in Berlin, while one-fifth sought new lives in Poland, France, and China. France drew Russian émigrés who had been living in temporary settlements from Constantinople, the Balkans, and Poland with the promise of employment. In March 1922, at the Council of the League of Nations, Nansen proposed issuing a "Nansen passport" that would allow the refugees to travel and protect them from deportation.[42]

Nansen's speech at the Nobel Peace Prize ceremony in 1922, where he was awarded the prize for his humanitarian leadership, underlined his perspective on the vital neutrality of his internationalist work. The League, he stated, had "already in its short active life, settled many controversial questions which would otherwise had led, if not to war, then at least to severe disturbances." He listed assistance to destitute Russian refugees as part of a list of successful stabilizations, including fighting the spread of epidemics and arranging an international loan to Austria.[43] Humanitarian undertakings, as Nansen emphasized in his speech, contributed to solving intractable political disputes because of their remove from politics. The alleviation of suffering stood apart from politics, though as Lenin pointedly noted, Nansen's nonpolitical commission had been "mixed up with others with political purposes" since in the context of the Great Powers' efforts to contain the threat of Bolshevism, claims about the neutrality of humanitarian relief became highly politicized.[44]

Lawyers and jurists from the former Russian Empire who designed the legal infrastructure of the fledgling international regime likewise resisted the idea that the measures introduced to regularize the legal status of the refugees were merely humanitarian, though for different reasons. Russian legal scholars, who had played a pivotal role in Russian imperial foreign policy and legal diplomacy before the First World War, led the initiative to create an international legal status for former citizens of the Russian Empire. A community of people trained to theorize and argue about law beyond the confines of states, and who were compelled to live outside the security of citizenship after the

Bolshevik revolution, emerged as critical theorists and advocates for the state-less in general, but the Russian émigré community in particular.[45]

Representing those who did not wish to have their nationality restored, or to return to the Soviet Union, the jurists advocated for the recognition of Russians divested of their nationality by the Soviet regime as stateless persons under international law.[46] For many of these jurists, their perspective on the possibility of nonstate forms of political representation had developed years earlier in the context of efforts to achieve liberal reforms in the Russian Empire. The revolution of 1905 had introduced academics and political writers to new forms of political representation. Now, in the post–World War I setting, intellectuals coordinated with existing representative groups to form ad hoc electoral bodies called zemstvos.[47] In 1923, the Russian zemstvos in Paris and London in turn called on the League to replace Nansen with someone more sympathetic to the ideals of the refugees. Émigré representatives expressed concern about falling under the "tyranny of the international," where stateless people would become a "mandate" of the League—connecting their situation as wards of the High Commission to the dependent legal status of former colonial subjects now under the legal authority of the League of Nations. A representative of the Nansen office meanwhile offered the exasperated response, "They live only with the hope of a complete restoration of the former Russian Empire."[48] The goal of re-establishing continental and imperial order was thus seen to conflict with the needs and aspirations of those who sought to establish a new kind of political identification and form of political representation.

IV

In the first few years of its existence, then, the League of Nations did not address statelessness as a general phenomenon that impacted a range of people in the new international order. As an international legal category, it belonged only to people who had formerly possessed Russian imperial citizenship but had lost their national status when the Bolshevik regime declared that they were no longer recognized as Russian citizens. Yet the scale of the crisis in the post-Habsburg successor states generated a counter movement to expand international recognition and protection for the people who were unable to acquire citizenship in the postimperial states. In the course of the upheaval of war and military occupation across Habsburg territory, large numbers of imperial refugees from Galicia and Bukovina had fled occupying armies into the relative security of Vienna and into the regions of Bohemia and Moravia. By 1915, 285,645 refugees resided in Vienna. By the end of the war, 400,000 people from the border regions of the empire had moved to postimperial Hungary. Unable to return to their homes, many hoped to acquire citizenship in the states that succeeded the Austro-Hungarian Empire. While some of the successor states were anxious to acquire new citizens and extended membership to any refugee who could prove residence at the time of the ratification of the peace treaties, others limited the right to opt for citizenship. For example, Poland extended citizenship only to those who could prove that they descended from someone who had fought for Polish independence in the nineteenth century.[49] Austria, Czechoslovakia, and Hungary, also excluded the refugees who poured into urban centers from the imperial periphery during World War I on the grounds of both their nationality and their religious identification. According to the Treaty of Saint-Germain, the 1919 agreement between the victors and the Austrian republic, former imperial citizens could opt for citizenship in any successor state in which they identified according to "race and language" with the majority of the state's population. However, the agreement required proof of German education, which many of the wartime refugees from the outskirts of the Habsburg Empire did not possess.[50]

Legal precedents drawn from imperial law furnished the successor states with a framework for exclusionary naturalization policy. In the Habsburg lands before World War I, legal identity was primarily based on the relationship between the subject and the province or town within the empire, or *Heimatsrecht*, where one had the right to live and to draw on social services. Anyone living within the right jurisdiction could be counted as a subject of the government. Over the course of the nineteenth century, the gap between the legal rights of citizens and those of foreigners in Austria had gradually widened. Identification as a foreigner meant, among other things, exclusion from poor relief, which was available only to citizens and provided by the municipality to which a person officially belonged even if the person did not reside there.[51] Introducing *Heimatsrecht* into the citizenship legislation of the successor states allowed governments to exclude war refugees from the ranks of their citizens. In Austria, a 1918 citizenship law passed by the national assembly excluded the seventy thousand Jewish refugees from Galicia who had remained in Vienna after the war but could not claim indigenous land rights. In Czechoslovakia, the right to claim Czechoslovak citizenship depended on proof of residency. Former legal subjects of the Habsburg lands who had been granted residency in Czechoslovak territories after 1910 could apply for citizenship; however, the offer could be refused to those who were not "Czechoslovak by language and race." In Hungary, thousands of inhabitants of the former Hungarian half of the monarchy where formal proof of residence was rarely given, including poor Ruthenians and Hungarian speakers, had no papers proving legal residency, which prevented them from obtaining Hungarian citizenship.[52]

As the consequences of exclusionary policies became more evident, individuals began sending letters to the Permanent Court of International Justice and to the League of Nations claiming that they did not possess a nationality, petitioning these authorities to intervene on their behalf or to furnish them with documents validating their identity and allowing them to cross international borders. Joseph Reich, for example, who wrote the League in December 1923, requested that the League provide a passport for him. As he explained in his letter, he had an Austrian passport until 1918 and now, residing in Polish territory, had become a "Staatenloser."[53] One petitioner who wrote to the Permanent Court at The Hague in 1923 referred to the court as the "protector of the rights of persons without nationality" and asked that officials provide him with a document that would allow him to travel across borders.[54]

After receiving a number of such letters, Ake Hammarskjöld, the League's representative at the Permanent Court of International Justice, wrote to officials in the League's legal section in November 1923 to ask whether it would be possible to develop an international arrangement to regulate the status of the *heimatlosen*. He wrote, "I cannot help feeling a great pity for the persons concerned, who, more often than not by no fault of their own, are deprived of their essential rights."[55] Hammarskjöld did not elaborate on how such a generalized legal status would work, but he looked to the League as a potential source of rights and protection for people who could not claim the security of political membership in their own states.

V

Hammarskjöld's proposal to create an international arrangement that would provide those without citizenship in the Habsburg successor states with a legal status prompted discussion among legal officials at the League on what role, if any, the organization could play in addressing the condition of the *heimatlosen*. The question of what kind of authority the League possessed to adjudicate disputes over nationality directly confronted the interstate foundations of the organization. These reflections were recorded in a 1923 memo written by an unknown official labeled "The Case of Persons without Nationality." The memo is significant mainly because of how it clearly sets out the way officials sought to avoid naming statelessness as a more general feature of postwar disorder, and how the codification of international law emerged as a neutral substitute for a more expansive regime of international oversight. The memo listed the various types of people who broadly fit into the classification of statelessness—those facing "hardships" as a result of the peace treaties between the victors and the Habsburg successor states, Russians divested of their nationality by the Soviet regime, and people like Max Stoeck who had their property seized after the war because they had been identified as German nationals but claimed to have lost their national connection to Germany. The memo therefore acknowledged the range of constituencies who could claim to be stateless since the war (though the author of the memo was careful to preface his use of the term *Staatenlos* with the phrase *so-called*). However, the memo proceeded to explain why the League should not officially acknowledge the "case of persons without nationality" as a general or widespread problem, since the absence of nationality "does not seem to be either a very wide spread evil or one which causes any general inconvenience to governments or even to individuals."[56] Those living without a national status as a result of the peace treaties in Central Europe presented a particularly "delicate matter," the memo continued, due to the complexity of the political situation in the post Habsburg successor states. In any case, the memo concluded, the organization could not appeal to any rule of international law preventing states from depriving a person of their national status, even if they had not acquired another nationality, or one creating an obligation for states to grant nationality to someone living without one. Despite the fact, as the memo noted, that the Stoeck decision had shown the emerging legal significance of statelessness, general recognition of statelessness threatened the boundary that officials at the League sought to conserve between matters defined as "international," and within the remit of the organization and its associated institutions, and those beyond it. The document, passed back and forth among the legal experts and civil servants within the organization, their notes scribbled along the margins, throws into relief how statelessness as a generalizable category posed a threat to the particular boundaries of international political order that the League's internationalist and legalist innovations were designed to contain.[57]

One less radical way, the unknown official suggested, for the League to address the "case of persons with no nationality" would instead be to present the problem as a defect of private law, an anomalous occurrence that nineteenth century treatises on international private law had established as largely the result of individual emigration, evasion of military duties, or acceptance of service with foreign governments. By coordinating the nationality legislation of countries around the world, the League could initiate the creation of international agreements in which states "surrender their existent sovereign right of deciding for themselves the condition under which their nationality is automatically or may voluntarily be acquired or lost."[58] League officials therefore pressed for an international convention on the conflict of nationality laws to bring the increasingly byzantine and divergent laws defining national membership into common order in the name of smoothing relations between countries. They argued that experts should formulate a code covering all conflicts and eventually produce a multilateral convention in which states agreed upon shared or compatible laws for naturalization and denaturalization. By limiting the scope of the problem of statelessness to the project of transnational legal unification, the League promoted a vision of mankind's slow progress toward the elimination of this anomalous occurrence through coordinated legislation. These plans fit with a style of thought associated with the domain of private law. In nineteenth century legal thought, public law did not have to be systematically coherent since the law could be presumed to derive from the command of a sovereign. Private law, by contrast, preceded sovereign command and could transcend states. The more internally rational and coherent it seemed, the less subject to national discretion it would become—hence the impulse to systematize the rules and make the system as comprehensive as possible. Presenting nationality as part of the mechanics of internationalism shifted attention away from restrictive regimes of citizenship, locating blame with the shiftless individuals who did not remain in any place long enough to acquire a nationality and were away from their original site of nationality long enough to lose a prior legal connection. These reflections reveal how international officials resisted the proliferation of ideas and practices surrounding nonstate forms of political order.[59]

But the proposal to include nationality in upcoming international legal codification plans rested on the fiction that a world of exclusive, sovereign states already existed. In fact, codification evaded the more contentious issues surrounding the nature of sovereignty that the problem of statelessness provoked. The project to systematize the multiplicity of nationality legislation that had sprung up across different nations and empires did hold some promise, but it was the complexity of political sovereignty that was at the heart of the citizenship crisis. Many of the letters that the League received from individuals requesting assistance in determining their national status, or requesting a Nansen pass, came from former subjects of the Ottoman Empire. Norman Bentwich, the Jewish attorney general of Mandate Palestine, commented on the multiplicity of nationality regimes in former Ottoman territories: "No less than five new nationality systems have been created, each with its distinctive features as to acquisition, retention, and loss. There has been no such multiplicity of national civitas in this part of the Orient since the extinction of the Herodian Kingdoms."[60] Such conflicts existed not only between states recognized as sovereign and independent but also across postimperial territories poised between nation and empire. Individuals who had Ottoman nationality under the 1869 law were not considered automatic Palestinian citizens under new nationality legislation after 1925. The British mandatory power placed local Arab authorities in charge of nationality legislation in Iraq and Transjordan. In Britain's African mandates, inhabitants remained British protected persons. In Syria and Lebanon, the French gave mandatory representative bodies the power to enact nationality legislation.[61] Meanwhile, individual subjects of the mandatory powers required documentation to find work. Some pursued their claims before the Egyptian Mixed Court, the judicial institution founded in the 1870s to hear legal cases involving foreigners, and disputes over nationality claims were among the most numerous cases brought before the court. Workers who had previously held Ottoman citizenship petitioned the court to adjudicate their national status, as they required documentation to work in mandate territories. International legal codification, then, could provide principles that guided states in a way that promoted the general rationalization of nationality legislation; however, it evaded the more profound political questions about sovereignty and empire that the League helped to keep in suspension.[62]

The project to gather information on the variety of nationality laws across the world in turn brought together a range of international legal experts to participate in the ambitious project to collect information on how countries legislated the rules governing national membership—who counted as a legal citizen and how individuals gained or lost such status. A transatlantic group of law professors and jurists led by Manley Hudson, an American from the Midwest who taught international law at Harvard, began meeting periodically after 1924 to consolidate their research in preparation for the third Codification Conference to be held at The Hague. The team of international lawyers led by Hudson sought to produce a common record of each country's legislation on nationality. In preparation, they sent questionnaires to member and non-member nations to survey levels of interest in proposed subjects for international codification, including nationality and the regulation of territorial waters. They then compiled an exhaustive list of the nationality laws of every country to be used during the Codification Conference.[63] The committee proposed several treaties whose ultimate purpose would be to require states to adopt a common criterion for the conferral of nationality. It was expected that this codification would eradicate statelessness at least to the extent that it arose from the conflict of domestic laws. The role of the legal codifiers would not be to dictate rules from above, setting the terms of how governments defined membership. Instead, legal scholars sympathetic to the aims of the League undertook the work of gathering the material, and organizing it in a way that facilitated coordinated national efforts to refine how countries legislated naturalization and denaturalization. The enclosure of national communities through nationality law produced new sources of international dispute as conflicting regimes of naturalization and denaturalization left migrants and state bureaucracies uncertain of their status. According to the vision of international legal codification, clarification of the norms regulating nationality—how someone acquired it or lost it—was vital to the preservation of peaceful relations.[64]

VI

However, as codification plans progressed, the crisis of post-imperial citizenship persisted. After 1924, the League faced more pressure from civil society associations and other international organizations to acknowledge stateless-ness as a more general problem, and to consider expanding the jurisdictional remit of the High Commissioner for Refugees. The implications of the new forms of international administration became vivid and concrete in Central Europe. The Nansen passport did not provide carriers with access to the growing number of social protections that states provided for their citizens or prevent arbitrary expulsion and deportation. Nevertheless, stateless refugees who carried the international passport benefited from international recognition and from their unique status as "Nansen refugees."[65]

For those who obtained the protected status as Nansen passport carriers, international legal authority became tangibly real. The passport determined the juridical status of stateless persons and allowed an international agency to act as a steward for those without regular legal standing.[66] Though Austria recognized the Nansen passport, the high commissioner's delegation in Vienna battled with the Austrian government over the boundaries of their respective authorities. Correspondence between the Austrian delegation to the League of Nations and the High Commission office in Vienna testifies to the tension between the government and the representatives of the international office, who congratulated themselves for successfully claiming the right to grant identity certificates for the Russian refugees rather than the Austrian authorities. Austria in fact tried to implement a *Staatenlosepasse*, a form of identification that would allow noncitizens to live and travel freely. The High Commission worked to maintain the Nansen regime for the refugees rather than institute the *Staatenlosepasse* for persons without nationality resident in Austria so that it could act as a distinct jurisdictional authority for the refugees.[67] As the Austrian state worked to establish its authority, the question of who possessed jurisdiction over the refugees in Vienna initiated a clash between different forms of governance in the city, building on fears that Austria had been reduced to a colonial territory as a result of the League's intervention in the Austrian economy.[68] Through the High Commission's efforts, Russian refugees preserved their distinctive status as subjects of the consular regime emanating from Geneva, enjoying rights normally only granted to foreigners on the condition of reciprocity.[69]

Within a few years of the empires' collapse, thousands of former imperial subjects found themselves without citizenship in any of the successor states.

After receiving numerous petitions from the *heimatlosen* requesting assistance in acquiring a definite nationality for themselves, the Red Cross wrote to the League to advocate for further internationalization of the problem of statelessness. The letter sent from the Red Cross to the League explained that the peace treaties and the minority protection treaties did not "cover the entire ground" and left numerous people adrift. The problem of the *heimatlosen*, the letter continued, had for some time engaged the attention of jurists but "it has assumed such proportions during the past few years that international action seems to be necessary."[70]

In March 1926, a commission of jurists from the International Union of Associations for the League of Nations met in Geneva to inaugurate a project to regulate the status of the stateless in the successor states of the former Habsburg Empire.[71] Walter Napier, a member of the British League of Nations Union, concluded that the only way to ameliorate the situation of the stateless would be to borrow the practices applied to the Russian and Armenian refugees. As he stated, "It is enough to compare the unfortunate situation of other stateless who don't have the protection of the High Commissioner to appreciate the high value of this international action."[72] Napier turned from a legal analysis of the problem in terms of the nature of sovereign authority and the boundaries of citizenship in the new states to more concrete considerations about how to alleviate the situation of those who found themselves without citizenship.[73]

Denunciations of the Russian refugees' unfair advantages often accompanied complaints about the severe limitations of the minority protection regime to ensure citizenship or access to state goods. Commentators reinforced the contrast by emphasizing the particular poverty and deprivation specific to the experience of the *heimatlosen*. In an article written on the International Committee of the Red Cross and its work on behalf of the *heimatlosen*, one author referred to the Russian refugees as the most numerous but "least characteristic" of the several categories of *heimatlos* since they were in a "more satisfying condition than other *apatrides*." Those not in this group were the "unfortunates," or *ces gens malheureux*, who first addressed various charitable organizations and asked the Red Cross to intervene through intermediaries from other philanthropic organizations.[74]

The nature of the organizations that stepped in to advocate for the *heimatlosen* lent credence to the claim that assistance to those who professed

to be stateless in the postimperial successor states could only be comprehended in terms of charitable giving rather than more radical innovations
in international political representation. Since many of the *heimatlosen* were
of Jewish descent, organizations established to assist Jewish migrants before
the First World War stepped in to provide assistance. The major Jewish networks of advocacy and protection developed out of the great demographic
redistribution of Jewish people from the East to the West in the wake of
successive pogroms and poverty in Russia and Eastern Europe between 1881
and 1914.[75] In addition to the request from the Red Cross, the League of
Nations High Commissioner for Refugees also received appeals on behalf of
the *Staatenlosen* from the Comité Unifié Juif and the Congrès de la Fédéra-
tion des Ligues des Droits de l'Homme.[76] The British-based Jewish Board
of Deputies petitioned the League to expand their work on behalf of refugees and the stateless. International Jewish relief organizations, including the
Jewish Board of Deputies and the Alliance Israélite Universelle, wrote to the
League in September 1926 to call attention to the numerous letters they had
received from people in the successor states who claimed to have lost legal
connection to any state.[77]

The League's response to the request by the Red Cross to expand the
purview of their responsibility for stateless people hinged on the limited jurisdictional and legal capabilities of the organization. After the appeal from
the Red Cross, the Vienna office of the High Commission for Refugees considered whether to extend the measures taken to assist Russian and Armenian refugees to "other analogous categories of refugees." The administrators
managing the Vienna office of the High Commission tried to preserve the
status for the Russian and Armenian refugees alone. In response to an inquiry from the central office about the number of these "analogous categories," the Austrian office reported back to headquarters that after conferring
with the chief of police in Vienna, he was "assured" that the federal authorities did not have any statistics on the people claiming not to possess citizenship.[78] But how to justify the League's position on this matter? The lawyer
in the League's legal section tasked with responding to the 1926 Red Cross
letter argued that although on the surface the situation of the *heimatlosen*
was comparable to that of the Russian refugees in 1921, in fact the Red Cross
admitted that "the present question is not one which comes within its sphere
of action" and that they therefore did not have the right to bring the issue

before the council. Since the Red Cross had determined that any initiative on behalf of the *heimatlosen* was beyond their remit, they could not similarly bring the case of this group before the League council.[79]

Another way of handling requests to intervene in cases where an individual's national status remained ambiguous was to turn the case over to one of the offices established at the League to administer issues around postimperial identification and governance. One year after the memo, in 1927, the legal department picked over a letter from a former Ottoman subject. In November of that year, the League received a letter from B. S. Nicolas, a man who described himself as an "Assyrian of Christian faith, native of Kurdistan." Nicolas wrote that he had fled from his country due to the "Turkish atrocities and massacres taking place." As he explained in his letter, he fought with the Allies against the Ottomans in Baghdad. His family left Iraq in 1925 for France with an Iraqi certificate of identity and had resided in Marseilles since then. They had repeatedly requested British protection but were denied, and had since applied for recognition as Turkish subjects. Nicholas stated that he had documents in his possession that would show definitively that the three nations had refused protection, or to confer nationality to him and his family, and "as such, our nationality is undetermined."[80] The chief of the mandates section responded that the "League of Nations has no general authority to determine the nationality of individuals or to grant nationality to them." Nicolas was advised to present a petition in which he would elaborate the obligations assumed by Iraqi and British officials according to the terms of the mandate.[81]

Mackinnon Wood, a senior member of the legal section of the secretariat, assessed the legal implications of the request, reasoning through the available categories and institutions established to manage the crises generated by the creation of states after the war. Wood reasoned that the secretariat did not have the authority to interfere regarding French or Turkish nationality or to intercede with the French authorities in Marseilles. Nor could they assist Nicolas in obtaining Greek citizenship since Greece did not have mandatory status or a treaty protecting particular minorities. Wood concluded that since Nicolas possessed an Iraqi certificate of identity, the petitioner had a claim to receive protection from the British mandatory power.[82] A further memo attempted to analyze whether Nicolas qualified for Iraqi citizenship in accordance with Iraqi nationality law from 1924. It depended, the author concluded, on whether the Iraqi authorities considered refugees subject to the rules of domicile or "whether or not they consider refugees to have their 'usual place of residence' in Iraq or to be merely sojourning there in a very precarious and temporary way." He suggested that the matter be sent to the refugee section of the International Labor Organization for further clarification.[83] Finally, another lawyer reviewing the claim concluded that based on Nicolas's own story, he had been legitimately denied Iraqi, French, or Turkish nationality and that "this is a case of statelessness, which can only be immediately remedied through a considerate and generous action on the part of the Iraq authorities."[84] Determining whether someone was stateless depended on reasoning through a shifting international landscape.

The growing number of people, like Nicolas, acknowledged as stateless by national courts and international authorities further fueled the campaign to expand the Nansen regime after 1928. As one study of statelessness from that year explained, the number of stateless persons had grown substantially since the war, but the causes and their legal character varied considerably.[85] As a common consciousness of the problem of statelessness emerged, activists rhetorically linked this community to the concept of world citizenship. Walter Furgler established Homeless: World Committee for the Defense of the Interests of People without a Recognized Nationality in July 1928. The aim of the organization was to "procure all the *sans-patrie* a legal paper like the Nansenpass which would permit them to go to all states, without being cast out."[86] The passport possessed a concrete practical significance and a more symbolic one. Assuming border control recognized the document as valid, possession of the Nansen passport allowed individuals to obtain work or to cross borders. However, in the context of internationalist idealism after World War I, anyone without a national identity represented the possibility of postnational cosmopolitanism. Much like the proletariat in Marxism, the people with no nationality represented a third estate on which hopes for the future could rest. At a gathering of the stateless and organizations advocating on their behalf in Geneva, the pacifist author Romain Rolland told the crowd that "statelessness" was an honorable term that denoted European and world citizenship.[87] Carriers of the Nansen passport in turn appeared as the glamorous embodiment of world citizenship. In 1928 Shell Oil and the Ariel Motorworks company sponsored I. S. K. Soboleff's around-the-world motorcycle trip, in which the cyclist carried only a Nansen passport for identification. In his memoir, *Nansen Passport: Round the World on a Motorcycle*, Soboleff, a Russian aristocrat exiled during the Russian Revolution, described himself as the embodiment of the Russian diaspora. According to Soboleff, "all over the world I can always find others who speak my own language and who carry the Nansen passport, issued by the League of Nations to those who have no longer any country of their own."[88]

Still, the Nansen passport reaffirmed the normativity of the state's ultimate control over borders, and it rarely guaranteed security. A separate agreement signed in Geneva on June 30, 1928, sought to further shore up the legal status of Russian and Armenian refugees. However, many found that the passport did not provide protection from police harassment or from deportation. Holders of the passport could obtain a visa to enter another country to seek employment but if they failed to find work they often discovered that they had no place to return.[89] Some passport carriers bitterly recollected the years when they relied on nothing else but a Nansen pass. Vladimir Nabokov, who was a stateless Nansen refugee living in Berlin in the interwar years, later wrote that the passport was a "dreary hell that had been devised by European bureaucrats."[90] Yet it also symbolized the way that many had already begun to experience the reality of living in a nonstate political community. The lives of Russian refugees in China particularly illuminates how many anticipated that international institutions would supplant the loss of imperial privileges. In Chinese courts, Russian refugees endeavored to preserve the extraterritorial legal status they had previously been afforded as subjects of the Russian Empire. Even when they did not succeed in this endeavor, the community carried on as though they had brought their world with them. One stateless member of the Russian diaspora, who was part of the migration during the war from Russian territory to China, recalled how the sound of Russian and the smell of street kiosks serving comforting bowls of beef stroganoff filled the city of Harbin.[91]

While League officials resisted the idea that the stateless symbolized the future of international politics, non-western political thinkers and leaders observing the movement to characterize the stateless as a distinct group viewed the phenomenon in precisely these radical terms. The implications of mass statelessness, as well as the emergence of a novel international legal status for a defined group of stateless persons, for wider debates about empire, sovereignty, and the future of global order could not be ignored.

Indeed, the plight of the European stateless resonated particularly with non-western political actors considering the future of postcolonial statehood. M.K. Gandhi learned about the movement to publicize the condition of the European stateless from an issue of *Pax International*, the monthly journal published in Geneva by the Women's International League for Peace and Freedom, a pacifist organization founded during World War I. In his weekly paper, *Young India*, Gandhi cited the growing numbers of the stateless in Europe as evidence for the decline of European civilization and the model of statehood that it had established. The proliferation of people disconnected from any political community demonstrated, he argued, that when it came to European forms of governance, "all that glitters is not gold." Gandhi in turn pointed to the rise of a movement to protect the stateless as an indication that "a large number of the westerns are awakened to a sense of this very grave limitation of their civilization and are making a serious effort to overcome it."[92]

As he published these comments, Gandhi was locked in struggle with other leaders of the Indian National Congress over when to press the case for independence from Britain, whether to seek dominion status, and what the future legal and constitutional organization of the independent political community would be. In the context of these debates over the future of independent India and its postimperial political formation, Gandhi viewed statelessness as a sign of Europe's decadence and degeneration, and a clear warning to those who saw the European state as a model of future independence. For the European and American international lawyers who contemplated the significance of statelessness in the decade after the war, the search for alternatives to the state did not necessarily consist in the return to vernacular communities and local custom. For Gandhi, an anti-state political theory meant eschewing the institutions and hierarchies that had come to define "modernity" in favor of village communities that represented a different kind of self-governing political association.[93]

However, in the more direct context of confrontation over the legal status of refugees and the implications of international governance, the émigré jurists from the Russian Empire presented the strongest case for the notion that the stateless embodied the future of nonstate political order. To present the case for the independent political standing of nonstate legal subjects, the representatives of the Russian imperial diaspora sought to distance the political questions facing their community from earlier precedents of philanthropic relief for migrants. Their emphasis on legal innovation and extraterritorial identification in part reflected their attempt to retain a separate identity from that of Eastern European refugees and economic migrants, who had been the source of much debate in Western countries, including England, France, and the United States.[94] A memorandum presented by the committee of experts of Russian and Armenian jurists on the legal status of Russian and Armenian refugees in 1928 demonstrates their attempt to draw a clear line between problems of a humanitarian nature and a juridical conception of right. The jurists stated that whereas initially the problem of Russian and Armenian refugees was humanitarian, the League of Nations and the International Labor Organization had successfully resolved the crisis. Their status, the memo argued, nevertheless remained precarious because they remained without a national status and did not for the most part want to acquire a new one.[95] The report therefore highlighted the sui generis character of the Russian and Armenian refugees and turned to the idea of right to describe their situation. By claiming that the crisis had ceased to be a humanitarian disaster and was now a question of politics, Russian jurists sought to place their predicament at the center of international affairs rather than relegating it to a part of the League bureaucracy designed to manage problems of a social or technical nature.[96] As we will see in more detail in Chapter 3, Russian émigré jurists turned to the language of international human rights to transform the terms of Russian statelessness, and provided the intellectual force behind the creation of the Institut de Droit International's Declaration of International Rights in 1929. They sought to distinguish the movement to promote international legal identification for the stateless from the wider humanitarian response to the war and subsequent continental upheaval. The context of the 1929 declaration therefore illuminates a universe of political debate in the interwar period around questions of governance and political representation on an international scale. Concerns about domination, paternalism, and depoliticization developed alongside the rise of ideas and practices around new forms of victimhood in the twentieth century.

The idea that stateless people represented the future of rights and legal personality beyond the confines of the state struck some advocates as a dangerous proposition in light of the alternative goal to ensure that all people gained the rights of citizenship. From 1921 until his death in 1930, Lucien

Wolf was involved in the coordination of two major international initiatives of the interwar era: the creation of the High Commission for Refugees and a system of minority protection for postimperial successor states in Eastern Europe. In both ventures, he sought to standardize international protection for Jewish and non-Jewish subjects. Wolf saw Jewish survival in Eastern Europe as contingent on the basic rights of citizenship and equal protection under the law. In his work on behalf of the stateless, Wolf promoted enforcement of the terms of the minority treaties promising civic inclusion to the members of particular minority groups rather than the extension of the Nansen passport. Wolf argued that the goal of the international minority protection regime was emancipation and emphasized international institutional means of getting there. Minority protection was a means to an end. Expanding the Nansen regime to those owed citizenship represented a further exclusion, and he instead sought to ensure that new states fulfilled the promise of the treaties by recognizing the citizenship of minorities within their borders. In his personal notes on the stateless problem, he wrote, "Proposals to extend refugee arrangements to *staatenlose* will perpetuate existence of large unassimilated and political restricted element in states concerned. This is not desirable."[97]

The conflict between nonstate legal order and civic emancipation recapitulated the battles over the meaning of international minority protection, and the dilemmas of Jewish emancipation resurfaced in a new international key after World War I in debates over minority rights and refugee relief. During his tenure managing the relief effort for Jewish refugees from the Russian Empire from 1921 to 1923, Wolf clashed with the members of the Jewish World Relief Conference who petitioned the Nansen office for a separate Jewish section of the High Commission for Refugees, as a way to acknowledge the distinctive goals of Jewish and non-Jewish refugees. By contrast, Wolf argued that the broader crisis was inseparable from the plight of Jewish refugees and insisted that attempts to solve them separately would lead to failure.[98]

Wolf's minority and refugee diplomacy placed him at odds with other actors in Geneva who presented the growing population of stateless people as the vanguard of world citizenship. He contended not only against the unwillingness of national governments to grant citizenship to people living in their territory, but also against jurists promoting the extraterritorial legal status of the wider group of *apatrides*. When the Polish government argued that the stateless residing in Poland were mostly refugees from the Russian Civil War, Wolf stated that the population was in fact "habitually resident" at the time of the Treaty of Riga in 1919 and therefore should have been deemed Polish nationals under the treaty. He insisted, "This is a class quite distinct from refugees possessing a temporary domicile" and that it would not be "proper to give them Nansen passports."[99] By contrast, Boris Mirkine-Guetzevitch, a Russian émigré political scientist and constitutional legal scholar living in Paris who served as legal counsel for refugees in France, argued that Jews from Poland were part of the broader population of the postwar stateless and the harbingers of a new regime of international rights.[100] Wolf thus articulated a broader concern about the danger of exceptional legal statuses. By insisting on preserving the territorial authority of the state and relying on international institutions that could help pressure states to adhere to their promises, he promoted a statist cosmopolitanism that returned after World War II as a more widespread response to the problem of statelessness.

From the beginning of his days advocating for British imperial intervention to defend the rights of Jewish subjects in the Russian Empire, Wolf had mainly sought to expand emancipation and civil rights. However, the association promoted by the Russian jurists between international human rights and the stateless threatened, as he saw it, the larger goal of civil emancipation and political enfranchisement. The pressure exerted by imperial, and later international, powers to compel wayward governments to adhere to their agreements to respect the rights of all inhabitants served as a means to an end. Like many political actors operating in the sphere of the League at this time, Wolf did not comprehend internationalism as a challenge to the centrality of the state for international politics.

VII

In the decade after the end of the First World War, the term "statelessness" generally referred to a diverse group—refugees, political exiles, denaturalized citizens, those who never regained a national status after the war and the post-imperial political settlements. This chapter has presented an argument about the meaning of statelessness in relation to the novel experiments in international governance introduced in the decade after the war. Russian jurists campaigned to create statelessness as an international legal status. However, as officials at the League feared, the category threatened to over-extend the organization's claim to oversee and regulate the sovereign capacities of the states. As the war and the dissolution of the continental empires opened up the Pandora's box of sovereignty, lawyers and civil servants within the League of Nations saw the expansion of international oversight to cover the many different kinds of "statelessness" as a particular threat to the boundaries it sought to institute between national and international spheres of political authority and legal jurisdiction. Instead, the League framed the question of statelessness in terms of the standardization of nationality law and the limits of the international regimes to ensure the rights of citizenship, or at least of nationals, to anyone designated within their administrative purview. Extending the Nansen passport only to individuals who were part of certain protected groups also represented a method of containment. Reflections on the concept of statelessness within the League illuminate what was so significant and distinctive about its entry into international politics and international thought. Read together with sources outside the League, we get a sharper sense of how the introduction of statelessness into international law and politics in a new way and at a new scale had significant implications for the foundational questions about politics and boundaries taken up in Chapter 3. In the interwar era the League's administrative goals were not the final word on the meaning of mass statelessness. The formal recognition of the status in national courts and at the League reverberated in unexpected ways. No longer a story told in works of fiction, or a curious anomaly, the stateless person provided a new conceptual point of reference as the world made by the war took shape.

3

Postimperial Foundations of Political Order

In a 1933 lecture delivered at The Hague Academy of International Law on the international legal status of the stateless person, Mark Vishniak, a Russian Jewish jurist who had fled to Paris in 1918, proposed that statelessness was as ancient as the expulsion of Adam and Eve from Eden. According to Vishniak, the figure of the *apatridie*, the French term for a person without citizenship, stretched back to the very first human experience of migration and exile. Vishniak spoke in The Hague as an expert on international law and as one of the leaders of the community of former subjects of the Russian Empire scattered across Europe since the revolution. A professor of public law before fleeing Moscow, he had been a leading figure of the non-Bolshevik left in Russia, serving as the secretary of the Constituent Assembly that briefly controlled the government in 1918 before the Bolsheviks seized power. In Paris he became the force behind the quarterly journal of the emigration, *Sovremennye zapiski* (Contemporary Notes), as well as an energetic participant in the international conferences to confer legal protection to the Russian diaspora, detailed in the previous chapter.[1]

A different study on the legal status of the stateless, published a few years later by a legal academic from Italy, I. G. Lipovano, countered that Vishniak had failed to appreciate the fundamental novelty of the phenomenon since the war. Lipovano insisted that the appearance of new terms to describe people without legal connection to any state marked the emergence of a wholly novel legal and political concept: in Italian, *apolide*; in French, *apatride*; in English, *stateless*; and in German, the designation *staatenlos* to replace the older term *heimatlos*, or "homeless." The word *heimatlos* remained in use, as we have seen, but was largely eclipsed by a vocabulary that more precisely denoted the absence of any legal connection to a political community.

"The discussions on terminology," Lipovano explained, "are not without interest. They prove that the facts and the conceptions which are behind these
words have changed: it is that new facts have appeared, and a new conception
has substituted for the old."[2] What new conceptions motivated the birth of
a novel vocabulary to denote individuals without nationality? As Lipovano
argued, the scale of statelessness fundamentally challenged the doctrine of
legal positivism that individuals only possess rights and duties through their
national status. The entry of the stateless into the landscape of international
politics provided new information critical to what in the previous decades
had become the "question of questions" for theorists of international law: is
the state the only subject of international law? Do individuals have rights
and duties that do not depend on their membership in a state?[3]

Despite disagreement over the novelty of statelessness, Vishniak and
Lipovano both portrayed the rise of mass numbers of people without a
national status as critically important for grasping foundational political
concepts. Vishniak, for example, concluded his lecture by stating that statelessness since the war provided essential insight into the nature of rights
and sovereignty: "just as disease is very precious as an instrument of methodological verification of the study of physiology, so too the study of the
problem of statelessness has contributed to a better understanding of the
question of nationality, and the essential problems of the doctrine of right
and of the state."[4] In their respective studies on the legal status of stateless
persons, Vishniak and Lipovano both argued that the analysis of the "problem of statelessness" could clarify core political and legal concepts such as
rights, statehood, and sovereignty. Their interventions, therefore, illustrate
the important links forged in this era between philosophical and legal reflection on political concepts such as the state and international law, and the
material conditions facing stateless people.

The question, however, is how and why the concept of statelessness became so bound up with the foundational questions of international politics
in the interwar years. As we saw in Chapter 2, League officials portrayed the
general recognition of statelessness as uniquely destabilizing in the context
of their introduction of novel internationalist approaches to the problems
of postwar political order. The task for this chapter is to develop a more
in-depth understanding of the radical implications of statelessness from the
perspective of political and legal thought. The first section examines why the

entry of statelessness into law and legal thought carried particular meaning for theorists concerned with the status of individuals within international society, legal personality, and the source of political foundation and political community. The second half of the chapter focuses on the postimperial setting of Central Europe—particularly interwar Vienna—where the predicament of individuals without citizenship in the successor states to the Habsburg Empire challenged legal theorists to consider the capacity of law to bring order to social life and to set the boundaries of political order. This section focuses on the Austrian jurist Hans Kelsen and his students because Kelsen was the legal theorist associated with the idea that the boundaries of the state are ultimately legal, and thus subject to the authority of international law as the constituting source of its sovereignty. In the decades that followed, Kelsen's approach to the problem of statelessness would provide a pivotal intellectual touchstone for legal theorists and international civil servants shaping the post-Second World War legal frameworks that define what it means to be a refugee or a stateless person in international legal terms.

The theoretical approach to statelessness in the post-World War I era in turn reveals a broader appreciation of the role of law in shaping the terms of political and social conflict. Jurists confronted the problem of statelessness through the lens of urgent but long-standing disciplinary questions and debates: what is law? What is the relationship between international law and the state? To what extent is it plausible to claim a legal identification beyond a territorially bounded political community? Examining the boundaries of political and legal membership through the lens of legal interpretation and jurisprudence increasingly came under attack in the 1930s as a failure to confront reality, a fantastical and ultimately powerless response by liberal cosmopolitans to the irrational passions of mass politics. The deeper question this chapter explores, however, is why debates about legal theory were seen to directly inform questions about the nature of public power and how political communities establish the boundaries of nationality and citizenship.

I

The Great War vividly and brutally demonstrated the unprecedented organizational and military power of the countries that went to fight in 1914. By war's end, amid the chaos and destruction brought by the fighting, it became clear to some theorists that the modern state was a unique and ultimately inevitable form of political organization in the modern world. In a lecture delivered on January 28, 1919, at the University of Munich on the subject of "Politics as a Vocation," the German sociologist Max Weber developed what has become one of the most influential definitions of the state. In the past, Weber argued, a diverse array of political organizations had the ability to create laws and to command allegiance. However, after the war and a revolution in Germany, the state's capacity to legitimately coerce an entire population under threat of violence had been successfully wrested from other forms of collective identification. In his words, the state defined the only "human community which (successfully) lays claim to the monopoly of legitimate physical violence within a certain territory." More than a modern Moloch with the power to devour the young, the state had become the only organization recognized as a legitimate source of authority and power. Politics, he concluded, represented an activity defined by the striving for power among various states or among the groups of people contained within a single state.[5]

Yet even as the awesome power of the empire-states that went to fight in 1914 seemed beyond question, the legitimacy and authority that such entities possessed remained the source of urgent debate and political conflict. Though couched as a general description of political authority in the modern world, Weber's speech represented a defense of national sovereignty as an answer to the disorder of the war and the resulting civil upheaval. The end of the war did not herald the ultimate triumph of this form of political organization due to the persistence of imperial rule, conflicts among groups that claimed rights to the same territory, and ideological disagreement about the future of political community at a global scale.[6] In Chapter 1, we saw how the Stoeck case affirmed that recognized states were sovereign when it came to determining national membership. But what counted as a state, and the relation between international law and the establishment of statehood, only became more perplexing in the years following the Great War. For this reason, as Chapter 2 described, officials at the League of Nations viewed the problem of statelessness as a challenge to their efforts to set the limits of international forms of political authority. Though the organization oversaw innovative experiments in nonstate forms of political governance, including the High Commission for Refugees, it defined the limits of its authority in terms of its inability to prevent any state from setting the terms of naturalization and denaturalization.

However, in the decade after the war, commentators on both sides of the Atlantic questioned the value and validity of the state as the central organizing unit of human life. The discourse of state-skepticism encompassed a range of figures from across the political spectrum. Herbert Croly, a leader of the progressive movement in the United States, insisted a few months after the United States joined World War I that "states must, as a result of the war, consent to a diminution and a redistribution of authority as the one indispensable condition of an increase in grace."[7] The rhetorical questioning of the status and future of the state persisted throughout the interwar era. In his preface to *State and Revolution* from 1917, Vladimir Lenin began with the observation, "The question of the state is now acquiring particular importance both in theory and in practical politics."[8] In 1932, the political philosopher Leo Strauss took it as a matter of known fact that "in the present age the state had become more questionable than it [had] been for centuries or more."[9]

It is against the general conceptual and political uncertainty around the concept and future of the state that statelessness became so significant for political and international legal thought. The introduction of statelessness as a recognized legal category by national courts, as well as in a more limited fashion by the League of Nations, established statelessness as a critical factor in the major theoretical debates of the era about the nature of international law, sovereignty, and how the boundaries of political order are established. In European legal treatises on statelessness, as well as in more general works on international law, theorists portrayed the reality of statelessness as a significant new fact that recast fundamental debates of political and legal theory. Once statelessness became a recognized fact of international life it served as an ideal case that could yield to greater generalizations about the future of international politics and political order. Rather than compelling a stricter definition of statehood, the stateless represented the possibility of life beyond the state when a wide array of publics began to rethink the possibilities for political organization.[10]

The prospects for the expansion of the authority of international law after World War I were directly tied to broader preoccupations of Western legal thought, especially the question of whether individuals could ever be considered the direct subjects of international legal order. As we saw in Chapter 1, turn-of-the-century treatise writers speculated about whether individuals could be the bearers of "international rights." According to natural law theory, individuals have rights prepolitically, before entering society. What, however, is the status of individuals without citizenship according to positivist theories of international law, which for the most part sought to exclude reasoning on the basis of natural law or natural right? Oppenheim and other positivist theorists of international law argued that individuals only possess rights and legal status derivatively, through their nationality. Building on the logic of this argument, theorists speculated about whether the expansion of the authority and institutional reality of international law meant that individuals could claim legal recognition directly through international law. They would represent the "subjects" rather than the "objects" of international legal order. And so in the decade after World War I, the legal status of stateless persons therefore became conceptually linked to the ambition to expand the authority of international law.

As we have seen, organizations and individuals who advocated on behalf of the wider population of stateless people in interwar Europe challenged efforts by League officials to ensure that the category remained limited to the select groups—particularly the Russian émigré diaspora—who received Nansen passports and consular representation from the High Commission for Refugees. At least in theory, carriers of the Nansen passport possessed a legal status that derived from the legal authority of the High Commission for Refugees and the League of Nations, conferred by international agreements. Statelessness, however, represented a status already recognized by more established sources of legal and political authority. Its entry into the terrain of law and politics served as important evidence in established debates about the nature of rights, agency, and political authority. One legal scholar, Jean Spiropoulos, noted in a 1929 lecture that the problem of the position of the individual in international legal life was the most discussed one in the profession. If individuals could directly address international society, he argued, then even the stateless person would have status and legal standing.[11]

In other words, from the perspective of due process and legal equality, if it could be shown that some legal authority possessed the power to ensure the right to appear in court for civil matters, the right to protect property, and the right to reside even in the absence of citizenship, then other political rights associated with citizenship seemed less significant. According to the same logic, the capacity of international legal authorities to provide stateless people with access to the rule of law furnished real-world evidence that international law constituted a body of norms that transcended individual state agreement. One study on the legal status of statelessness by Herbert Glücksmann, published in 1930, succinctly summarized the interdependent logic governing the legal personality of a person without a nationality and the prospects of international law. Glücksmann, a doctoral student at the University of Breslau, argued that the legal status of the stateless person represented the "crux" of international law. The nature of international law depended on determining whether the stateless possessed an independent legal standing. Statelessness, Glücksmann argued, represented a "third term" distinct from that of nationals or foreigners. Nationals participated in legal proceedings as the subjects of a particular jurisdiction; foreigners in modern states were also subject to territorial jurisdiction. If stateless persons represented a "third term," which jurisdiction did they belong to? Glücksmann surmised that perhaps it could be shown that they were subject to the jurisdiction of international law. The nature of international law depended, he argued, on an analysis of the legal agency of stateless people. A stateless person who successfully participated in civil law effectively overcame the need for national status to enjoy the protections and rights of international law or civil procedure.[12]

The presumption, affirmed in the positivist treatise on international law by Lassa Oppenheim, that rights and legal status depend on national membership, and that countries reciprocally recognize the legal rights of foreigners, faced a fundamental challenge if it could be shown that stateless persons benefited from equality under the law, and enjoyed the rights of free economic subjects. The ideal of formal legal equality—an ideal implicit it Glücksmann's analysis—had been subject to sustained criticism from the left for concealing the real conditions of social inequality and domination, a critique that gained more adherents in the succeeding decades. The significant point here, however, is that Glucksmann's work demonstrates how the meaning of statelessness hinged on the nature and future of international law; and by the same logic, how the legal personhood of stateless persons carried important implications for the dominant theory of international law.

II

Before turning to the significance of statelessness for international legal thought, it is necessary to consider the status of international law at the end of World War I. By the end of the war the profession of international law appeared beset by crisis. Since the founding of a professional organization of international lawyers in 1873, jurists had been integral to the conception and implementation of internationalist solutions to questions of imperial rule and interimperial conflict. International lawyers provided the legal arguments and justifications that supported new forms of territorial acquisition and violence against colonial subjects, and, before 1914, many served as advisors in foreign ministries or became foreign ministers themselves.[13] Signs of the diminished reputation of the profession when the war ended, however, could be seen in the antilegalist foundation of the League of Nations and in the reorganization of foreign ministries. Pamphlets, books, and articles spoke of the failure of international law to prevent the war or to preserve the cosmopolitan spirit that defined the original establishment of the Institut de Droit International, the professional organization of international lawyers founded in 1873. In the United States, meanwhile, the legalist approach to foreign policy, which had become an important feature of American diplomacy and the establishment of a formal American empire in the decades before the war, lost much of its force after World War I. In postwar Germany, the widespread condemnation of the Versailles settlement likewise weakened the position of international law as a regular feature of diplomacy. Lawyers who defended the League were pushed into alignment with the pacifist movement or abandoned their ideological commitment to internationalism in order to stay involved in policy making.[14]

The career of Lassa Oppenheim, the jurist who promoted the doctrine that only states are the subjects of international law, illustrates the collapse of the careful balance maintained by the members of the Institut de Droit International between liberal nationalism and cosmopolitanism. Until the outbreak of the First World War, Oppenheim had co-edited with Josef Kohler the *Zeitschrift für Völkerrecht*, the journal that Kohler established in 1906 as the first German publication devoted to international law. In defining the role of international law in modern diplomacy, Oppenheim designed a research agenda for international lawyers who sought to oversee more peaceful international relations. Lawyers would clarify existing rules and promote codification to standardize legal practice around the world. By establishing journals and academic institutions devoted to international law, practitioners created the field by building up the body of source material and fashioning themselves as the experts who not only navigated the field but actually represented it through their professional conduct. The nationalization of the community of European international lawyers following the outbreak of war therefore appeared as a tragic blow to the legal and moral ambitions of the profession. Oppenheim made a public declaration of loyalty to Britain, denouncing Germany's attack on Belgium as the "greatest international crime since Napoleon I." Kohler meanwhile turned away from his prior commitment to pacifism to offer legal arguments to defend Germany's wartime actions.[15]

Yet we would be remiss if we were to take the transformation that the profession underwent in the course of World War I as indicative of what international law signified for the future of international politics, and for what it meant to be a stateless person, in the decade that followed. The importance placed on international law in how the war was fought, in adjudicating how blame was doled out, and after 1919 in how it was applied to redraw the boundaries of Europe, demonstrated the significance of this specialized field and its practitioners beyond aspirations for a more peaceful world.[16] Hersch Lauterpacht's intellectual and professional trajectory points to the evolving practical significance of international law during and after the First World War. Lauterpacht is one of the most celebrated international lawyers of the twentieth century, and his reflections on the problem of statelessness will be discussed in more detail later on in this chapter, as well as in the second half of this book. It is important to briefly consider here, however, the significance of his initial decision to study international law, and his important contributions to reshaping it as a discipline and professional practice. Born in 1897 to a Jewish family in Zolkiew, a city in Galicia that at that time was part of the Austro-Hungarian Empire, Lauterpacht moved with his family to the imperial city of Lemberg (known as Lviv in Polish) in 1914, at that time occupied by the Russian army. Lauterpacht was conscripted into the Austrian army in 1915, though he did not ultimately experience combat. In the fall of 1915, he enrolled at the law faculty of Lemberg University, where he studied Roman law and German public law, among other subjects. For those who viewed the law as a means to negotiating a political future, the need to learn the law was more certain than the outcome of the conflict. Since the 1870s, legal training across the civil and common law worlds emphasized abstracting principles from legal cases or legislative codes and relating new cases and problems to established concepts and precedents. Such training, initiates hoped, would allow them to formulate their political aspirations, and to devise innovative political settlements.[17] David Ben Gurion, the future first prime minister of Israel, traveled from Ottoman Palestine in 1915 to Salonika and then Constantinople to study Ottoman Turkish and to enroll as a law student, anticipating that at the end of the war Jewish nationalists would need to negotiate with the Ottoman Empire for greater autonomy.[18]

Lauterpacht's turn to the study of international law took place against the backdrop of the fragile political situation in the contested borderland region between the new Polish state and the nascent Ukrainian state. During the war, Polish nationalists navigated the complex political scene in London to negotiate Polish independence in anticipation of the collapse of the Austro-Hungarian Empire and Czarist Russia. In 1916, the Central Powers agreed to proclaim a self-governing Polish constitutional kingdom, bound by military convention with Austria and Germany, and with its economic affairs placed under Austro-German condominium.[19] In November 1918, Ukrainians took control of Lviv, declaring it the capital of the West Ukrainian People's Republic. In the context of the ensuing violence, particularly against the Jewish population in Lviv, Lauterpacht began to move away from the study of Austrian private law and took his first course on international law in the autumn of 1918 with Dr. Jozef Buzek, a jurist who had served in the State Council in Vienna before the war and wrote about the statistical study of nationalities in the empire. In the summer of 1919, Lauterpacht left Lviv to participate in the redrawing of the map of Europe, where he provided translation assistance to the Intergovernmental Commission on Polish Affairs tasked with defining Poland's eastern boundary.[20]

Lauterpacht went on after his stint at Versailles to write a doctoral thesis on the League of Nations at the University of Vienna. After moving to London in 1923, he acquired a third doctoral degree under the supervision of Arnold McNair, a British legal scholar, on "Private Law Sources and Analogies of International Law," a work that traced the influence of national rules on the development of international law. Together, Lauterpacht and McNair shifted the focus of international legal scholarship away from diplomacy and statesmanship toward the application and interpretation of international rules by lawyers and courts. They insisted that international law was not a profession in decline; rather, the Great War had set the stage for the elaboration of doctrine and technical expertise and for the establishment of a legal system institutionally grounded in courts and jurists. In fact, legal practitioners had been called on to handle problems of international law for the first time during the war. Lauterpacht and McNair began publishing the first collection of international case law in 1929 to begin the process of establishing international law as a technical field analogous to domestic law. Their joint project brought to life an argument that Lauterpacht had presented in his British doctorate, *Private Law Sources*, which had argued that international law represented the analogue of domestic law: treaties were just contracts; the law of territory was the law of property. According to Lauterpacht, the growth of international organizations implied that laws regulating the relations between states and the institutions of the international community would evolve to mirror constitutional and administrative law operative within states.[21] Institutions established in the wake of the war, such as the Permanent Court of International Justice, began to generate the content of international legal doctrine. Claims commissions and arbitrations provided international lawyers with volumes of case law richer than anything they had previously seen. International legal scholars contributed to the making of international law by analyzing the emergent practices of international politics and establishing its reality through their classifications and evocative descriptions. Though the more far-reaching agendas in the field of international criminal law and experiments in international governance had a particularly European provenance, American legal academics nevertheless also participated in the transatlantic analysis of the new world order. For example, Philip Jessup, an international legal scholar in the United States and a supporter of the League of Nations, wrote to Edwin Borchard in 1926 that he hoped to find cases that demonstrated "the ultimate victory of international law over national law."[22]

For the legal scholars who sought to marshal evidence for the displacement of the state as the central subject of international politics, the more one looked, the more evident it seemed that states were not the only actors on the international scene. The fact remained that one could find confederacies, federations, protectorates, spheres of influence, suzerainties, and self-governing dominions, all of which flew in the face of the orthodox theory that all territory in the world resides under the exclusive sovereignty of some sovereign state.[23] In *Mandates under the League of Nations*, published in 1930, Quincy Wright, an American political scientist, argued that the mandates system indicated a shift in the nature of sovereignty—especially in its traditional ties to territoriality. The existence of vast territories that did not lie under the sovereignty of any one state proved that the future lay beyond exclusive political control over a bounded territory.[24] The establishment of a free city in Danzig administered as a mandate of the League of Nations, the formation of internationally mixed nationality courts in Upper Silesia to adjudicate nationality disputes, and the new power of international administrators to influence state practice in Central Europe also served as positive signs for those looking to dethrone the centrality of the state in political and legal thought. In his doctoral dissertation, Schulim Segal, a law student at the University of Paris, analogized the condition of the stateless in Europe to the subjects of the mandates. Segal argued that, like the stateless, residents in the mandates were not citizens but could nonetheless appeal directly to the international organ charged with their protection. And just as the mandates had created certain rights for individuals, stateless people could appeal to international institutions. In this way, according to Segal, individuals had already, de facto, become subjects of international law.[25]

The problem of statelessness therefore became a central point of reference for a broader inquiry into the nature of international law in the world created by the war. The establishment of new forms of international administration after World War I lent credence to the idea that nonstate entities, including individuals, could be the direct subjects of international law. Institutions like the international tribunal in Upper Silesia—the court to which Jacob Sinwell sent his petition—allowed residents alleging a violation of their right of domicile, in spite of losing their nationality or not acquiring a new one, to appeal to the tribunal to adjudicate on their behalf against states. Legal commentators later argued that the tribunal represented the first realization in practice of individuals as subjects of the law of nations.[26] Lauterpacht recollected that the question of who counted as a subject of international law "occurred incessantly" in the period after World War I. An entry in the *Encyclopedia of the Social Sciences* from 1932 by Edwin Borchard is exemplary on this point. Borchard explained, "The word international would indicate that the rules govern nations. But individuals, pirates, recognized revolutionists, minorities, shippers of contraband, mandated territories, administrative unions, the League of Nations—all these are also the subjects of rights and duties declared by what is called international law."[27] Clyde Eagleton, an American international lawyer, asked Manley Hudson to place him on the committee on piracy at an upcoming conference, "not because it is romantic, but because of its connection with a subject which attracts me. How an individual can violate international law, and all that."[28] Even Oppenheim, the jurist who provided the most influential doctrine on the incommensurability of states and individuals within international society, speculated after the establishment of the League of Nations that individuals had begun to acquire a new status in international law. The significance of statelessness in this context therefore depended on the political salience of the tradition of international legal expertise in the reconstitution of European interstate order, and on the liberal internationalist ambition to expand the authority of international law in the years after World War I.[29]

III

Apart from the status and future of international law, the problem of statelessness in the interwar period remained entangled with fundamental debates in political and social theory, particularly those that hinged on the concept of legal personality. In its broadest sense, the concept of legal personality indicates which actors or entities have the capacity to engage in legal relations and are the bearers of rights and obligations. According to the theory of natural right, individuals are the bearers of rights before their entry into the political state. Applied to the stateless, the theory implies that without legal membership, individuals revert to the pre-political state of possessing the rights of nature. Hannah Arendt would later argue that the real plight of the stateless in interwar Europe revealed the emptiness of appealing to the ideal of natural rights when it was clear that only membership in a political community is a guarantee of basic security and moral personhood. However, in interwar legal and political thought, examples of the legal standing of stateless persons, such as their capacity to perform as legal agents, particularly in domains associated in the nineteenth century with "private law" like contract and torts, provided crucial evidence that could be deployed in ongoing debates about the nature of legal, and corporate, personality and its implications for political order beyond the state, and the concept of the state itself.[30]

It is important to note here that, on the surface, the nature of corporate personality stands in direct opposition to the legal status of natural persons since it is the nature of corporations as *collective* agents that requires explanation and justification. It is their fictional representation as entities with agency and will that demanded the contortions of legal argument. However, the debates over the political and legal theory of corporate personality that took hold across the Atlantic around 1890 resonated with the intellectual reflections about the status of stateless persons in the years following the First World War. Before the war, the German jurist and historian Otto von Gierke provided the most influential philosophical inquiry into the nature of group identity and the legal status of non-state groups. In his theory of associations, or *Genossenschaftsrecht*, from 1881, Gierke sought to explain how the identity of groups (such as corporations, guilds, churches) did not depend on the recognition by the state. According to the "concession theory" derived from Roman law, corporations, guilds, and religious communities are fictitious legal entities that only acquire their form by grant from a higher authority. Gierke argued, however, that groups counted as real persons because though they were the subjects of rights, they were not the creations of law. They were not, in other words, contingent legal arrangements. To describe the legal personality of a group as a "fiction" implied that its identity as a group depended on the creative power of those responsible for the law. The social integrity of groups creates the condition for their rights and independence from the power of the modern bureaucratic state. Gierke's theory of associations, in turn, had potentially radical implications for the origins of statehood at a moment when many groups clamored for recognition as independent states, since the theory directly addressed whether moral communities existed prior to the legal orders that defined and categorized such groupings. Corporation theory generated further political and philosophical considerations about whether constitutions reflect an already existing community, or whether the legal structure of the state constitutes and creates the boundaries of membership. Gierke posed the following question: Does the state evolve out of the organic unit of the people? Or are the people constituted by the government and administration of the state? If the state devolves from an original unity forged by history and tradition, then the rights of the people are not dependent on the apparatus of government or statehood. The people possess an independent existence apart from the recognition of state-created law.[31]

Gierke was particularly keen to distinguish between the law's creation of "certain fictitious, artificial, or juristic persons" such as the corporation, and a "group person," which signified a living being apart from the galvanizing properties of legal fictions, such as a trust. However, his theory of associations was pivotal for debates about corporate personality, and the nature of state personality, following the rise of the business corporation in the later nineteenth century. The transformation of the legal personality of corporations in US law freed the corporation from prior constraints and introduced one of the signal developments in the rise of modern capitalism from this period. Incorporation no longer depended on receiving a charter, and corporations could live on in perpetuity. The new status of corporations in modern life, and the analogies drawn between the capacities of natural persons and that of corporations, in turn generated further reflection on the meaning of legal personality. This led to the inquiry: What is a corporate person—is it an aggregate of individuals? Or an entity separate from the individuals that compose it? Are the rights of corporations reducible to the civil rights of shareholders? Do collective actors really exist such that they are not reducible to the individuals composing them? In the United States, the country that exemplified the future of global capitalism in the decades before World War I, the Supreme Court attributed certain "core rights" to corporations, including the capacity to sue and be sued, to own and transfer property, and thereby to claim certain constitutional rights. In the eyes of the law, these non-natural persons looked and acted like natural persons. Outside the United States, the rise of big firms like Siemens and Krupp from 1870 to 1914 involved the replacement of real persons owning and managing enterprises with juridical persons such as business corporations owned by shareholders.[32]

The origins and nature of political order—and the possibility of nonstate political order—became a central theme in the writings of the British legal theorist Frederic Maitland, who translated Gierke's theory for an English-speaking audience. In his essays from the turn of the century, Maitland—drawing on Gierke—investigated the sources of communal political life, and the mechanisms by which communities project themselves through time. Of particular significance for our purposes is how he reflected on the relationship between legal forms and political reality, and on the unique capacity of juridical expertise to shape political reality through the creation of such legal forms. Maitland was particularly interested in the legal concepts and modes of reasoning that animated economic and political entities seemingly independent from a centralized state authority. The expansive, territorial, and sovereign independent state clearly represented a distinctive kind of political entity; yet corporations like the Massachusetts Bay Colony and the East India Company that populated early modern Europe behaved like states, and eventually turned into states. Borrowing a metaphor from evolutionary theory, Maitland remarked that on close inspection, it was difficult to distinguish the natural history of the state from other kinds of group formations. Corporate entities, in other words, might begin their lives as mere creatures of the law, animated only by an original act or charter, but they could evolve into autonomous agents with independent life.[33]

Maitland described the power of legal fictions and juridical fictions to shape political reality but also marveled at their absurdity. The surprising practical and picayune origins of a legal concept or practice could not account for the way such a concept could facilitate political transformation on a grand scale. It took the nimble imaginations of jurists to transform obscure legal concepts such as the "corporation sole" into working political theories. The legal idea of a trust was just one example of a device developed at a particular time for a particular purpose that had a surprising and expansive afterlife. In the second half of the nineteenth century trust law transformed from a subsidiary of property law to an autonomous legal category, and assumed a more expansive political significance when it was applied to matters of governance and empire. In his essay "Trust and Corporation" from 1906, Maitland described how legal concepts shaped economic and political reality since new ways of owning stock and shares evolved from the concept of "trust," and clubs and associations began to define their independent legal existence in the terms borrowed from the law of trusts. The history of the concept of trust operated in accordance with the theory of evolution; a contingent mutation allowed for adaptations unrelated to the original point of transformation. In the minds of jurists, Maitland argued, trust represented an "elastic form of thought in which all manner of materials can be brought."[34] Maitland went on in this essay to suggest that this style of thought had become even more politically significant with the proliferation of internationalist solutions to the perplexities of group life under law. The Americans, he noted, explained their sovereignty in Cuba after the Spanish-American war through the language of "trust"—a term inherited from Roman law. "Trust," as Maitland argued, was nothing more than a metaphor. But it possessed real power to stabilize a political settlement, though he speculated whether the application of ideas native to the system of private law to a proliferating range of international and economic entities—from American imperial territories to the imperial parliament in South Africa—had reached the end of its plausibility. "Some would perhaps say," he wrote, "that the time for this sort of thing has gone by."[35] However, at the turn of the twentieth century, arguments for the independent political life of national and social groups—everything from ethnic groups to religious organizations to labor unions—depended on claims about legal personality and personhood in general.

Maitland's writings on legal personality, however, inspired the political theory of a group of British political writers known as the "Pluralists," who at the turn of the century envisioned democratic alternatives to the coercive, centralized state in the context of industrial society. The Pluralists—a group which included J. N. Figgis, G. D. H. Cole, Harold Laski, and Ernest Barker—developed an alternative to the Hobbesian juristic theory of the state. From the perspective of strict sovereignty, associations like churches, joint stock companies and trade unions derived from state recognition. Pluralism sought to dethrone the state as the ultimate "person" in international society by ascribing reality to groups and associations that did not constitute states in the doctrinal sense. The empirical existence of nonstate groups—from corporations, to nationalities—provided an alternative vision of political order, and the entities that populated that order. The Pluralists conceptualized political and legal association as distinct from the sovereign territorial state, investigating a range of corporate forms and associations that existed independently from the sovereign territorial state such as religious bodies, guilds, neighborhood associations, and trade unions. The real or fictitious nature of legal entities, their dependence on state recognition, and the nature of their rights and obligations, cut in different political directions. Personality could be the basis for liability; the independent life of trade unions seemed to accord labor a power that it did not have when dependent on the state in the increasingly violent labor disputes of the early twentieth century. One of the essential features of the social state was the rise of corporate groups deriving from industry, labor, or special interests that each represented a juridical subject. By the time that World War I broke out in 1914, pluralism was already identifiable as a strand of political thought—not just associated with the British thinkers, but also French legal theorists like Léon Duguit.[36]

The First World War powerfully challenged the theories of nonstate political order popularized in the decade before the war. When war broke out the pluralists had ready arguments for attacking the outsized power and supremacy of the modern state, but the power of the state evident in the government's ability to call upon its citizens and imperial subjects to fight, to marshal vast resources, and to imprison foreigners undermined the empirical dimensions of the theory. In the face of these undeniable facts, Cole and Laski eventually abandoned their antistatism in favor of using the power of the state to bring about real political and social change in the world.[37]

Yet the question of how the law ascribes agency remained a significant feature of international thought after World War I. Debates in political theory about the administrative state and the legal status of corporations demanded continued reflection on the power of legal fictions and the nature of the agency ascribed to them. When the war began, a growing number of legal commentators across the Atlantic argued that concepts such as legal personality, or fictional persons, generated confusion in constitutional theory and in international law. At the start of the conflict, Josef Kohler published an essay intervening in the debate in which he asserted, "the question whether the juristic person is real or imaginary should never have been seriously advanced. It is a reality in the law like every reality created by the law. It is not a human being of flesh and blood. Old and new absurdities that testify to the failure to comprehend this need not be considered."[38] In attempting to clarify what it meant to possess personality in legal terms, Kohler distinguished between the impulse to imbue nonnatural persons with metaphysical properties, and the more plausible claim that law constitutes reality, even if it does not create "real" beings in the sense implied by Gierke.

Legal cases involving nonnatural persons seized the imagination of a wider public because of the way such conflicts touched on the central preoccupations of political thought. For example, a 1925 case on the legal status of Hindu idols in India generated a great deal of attention in Europe and the

United States. Observers interpreted the outcome of the case in terms of standing controversies about the nature of legal agency and the capacity of a legal system to bestow personality on non-natural persons, and the real or fictitious nature of juristic personality.[39] When he commented on the case in a landmark essay from that same year, the American pragmatist philosopher John Dewey attributed the widespread curiosity about the legal personality of the idol to growing resistance to the idea that the state is the "sole or even supreme person."[40] In commenting on the problem of the ontological approach to corporations and legal entities in general, Dewey highlighted the political importance of such reflections. From a normative standpoint, Dewey argued, it was absurd to portray the artificial creations of law as meaningfully equivalent to natural persons. Conceived as either quasi-public entities created by state power or legal persons, Dewey suggested that the scope of corporate power was a political question rather than a matter of legal ontology. Bringing corporations in line with democracy meant asserting political control over what corporations do, not what they are. And yet he pointed out the power of such creations—the same observation that Maitland had made a decade earlier. In his 1927 lectures "The Public and its Problems," Dewey proposed that what seemed like pointless metaphysical speculation about the nature of objects that the law ascribed with agency filtered into the concrete decisions made by judges. "Theories are held and applied by legislators in Congress and by judges on the bench, and make a difference in the subsequent facts themselves," he explained.[41] The English literary critic and poet William Empson expressed a similar mixture of frustration and wonder at the power of legal forms to shape social reality in his 1928 poem, "Legal Fiction," which begins with the line, "Law makes long spokes of the short stakes of men." More than a general statement about legalism, Empson's inspiration for the poem derived from his observation of contemporary debates in the common law world over how property rights applied to the novel realm of airspace.[42]

Dewey would have had to look no further than wartime judgments about the distinction between a corporation's shareholders, who retained their national affiliations, and the legal entity of the corporation, which could remain aloof from the conflicts of nations, for confirmation of the real world consequences of legal theory. During the war the argument that corporations remained uncorrupted by ties to an enemy nationality solved an eminently practical problem. On the subject of corporate legal personality, Max Radin, a professor of law at Berkeley, wrote, "there are few subjects which seem more thoroughly theoretical, but surely no subject can be so termed which is declared by courts to be the basis of their decisions and upon which rights in valuable property have been determined and enormous sums of money distributed."[43] The significance of the subject rested, according to Radin, on how judges applied the concept of legal personality to reason about cases with immediate practical implications. Pointing out the scholastic nature of corporate personality theory did not change the fact that the arguments shaped judicial analysis and decision.

Legal personality captivated jurists as well as a wider public because unlocking the mysteries of how law ascribes agency to natural and nonnatural persons seemed to many like the key to explaining the nature of collective life. In his 1921 collection of essays, *The Foundations of Sovereignty*, Harold Laski insisted, "Nothing is today more greatly needed than clarity upon ancient notions. Sovereignty, liberty, authority, personality—these are the words of which we want alike the history and the definition; or rather, we want the history because its substance is in fact the definition."[44] Laski thus articulated the idea that philosophical investigation into the nature of the fundamental concepts of modern politics—their semantics—carried real world implications. He described a perspective shared by many of those who wrote about the problem of statelessness in the years after the war: that philosophical reflection on the nature of the state as a legal and moral agent entailed real-world political consequences. They connect because both relate to the question of whether the state is the sole, or supreme, person and to the power of legal form to shape social reality. Indeed, though legal writing on corporate personhood in Europe and across the Atlantic in the United States seemed to have run its course by 1930, interwar treatises on the legal status of stateless persons demonstrate how the legal condition of individuals without a nationality had direct implications for critical debates in political theory.

At the same time that the emergence of statelessness as an acknowledged reality from the perspective of legal thought informed ongoing debate in the decade after the war about the foundations of political and legal order, legal and political theory could be brought to bear to analyze what it meant to be a stateless person in legal terms. Indeed, for some legal writers the task became proving through legal reasoning and analogy that the stateless possessed standing within the law. The dominant doctrinal theory of international law, as we have seen, defined a person without a national status as a lawless anomaly. Yet Stoeck, and others like him, who successfully regained property after the war through their recognition as stateless persons by the courts, challenged this foundational doctrine. In his *fin de siècle* study of public law, Georg Jellinek, a German legal scholar who developed an influential theory of the modern state, had claimed that from the point of view of international law, citizenship meant simply "belonging to a certain jurisprudence."[45] The formal separation between nationality as a concept within international law and political citizenship in turn invited analogies with imperial forms of belonging, where subjects possessed a formal legal tie to a larger imperial order without possessing the same rights as citizens of the metropole. This flexible conception of legal membership had, as we have seen, furnished imperial and international legal thought with resources for conceptualizing common membership within an empire. Contemporary commentators also reflected on the imperial legal sources for post–World War I ideas about the status of individuals under international law. From his perch at Yale Law School, Edwin Borchard observed in 1930 that the popular proposal to provide individuals, including stateless people, access to international courts relied on colonial precedents such as the mixed court in Egypt, which granted special protections and rights to "non native" residents beginning in 1876.[46] The colonial implications of internationalist proposals to provide the stateless with legal rights appeared strikingly in discussions over a 1926 resolution put forward by the Federation of the International League for the Rights of Man recommending that the League, rather than national governments, protect the political émigrés by providing consular services.[47] Roger Picard, a French legal scholar, endorsed the proposal to have the stateless adopted by the League of Nations, which would serve, in his words, as their "protector and guardian."[48] Picard proposed that League representatives could serve as chancellors or ambassadors on behalf of the stateless, and suggested that with the League as the protector of the stateless, "those whom an unjust constraint would have stripped of their county would find one more generous, also more ideal. Thus the stateless transformed themselves—but without looking back or having regrets—into its true super patriots."[49]

For theorists trying to establish what it meant to be stateless from the perspective of legal thought, Roman law made sense of a world in which people related to one another through the law. In a study of Italian émigrés living in France, who had been denationalized by the Fascist government in Italy in 1926, the jurist Giuseppe Nitti compared the émigrés to Roman slaves living in a state of civil death because they do not possess rights in the state where they reside.[50] Such reflections registered the basic tension embedded in the application of the dominant categories of legal thought to comprehend the phenomenon of statelessness. If, according to the traditional doctrine, individuals without a nationality were defined as "lawless," then evidence of their legal capacities carried significant implications for the orthodox, positivist theory of international law. However, legal subjecthood or legal personality in the tradition of Roman law and in international law in the nineteenth century often implied relations of subjection and domination. In Roman law, the law of persons delineated legal status, which in turn depended on the possession of legal personality. Slaves possessed legal personality but were relegated to the realm of things, or items of property. By contrast, to possess citizenship meant that a person could freely take part in legal procedures and economic transactions.[51] The historian of political thought J. G. A. Pocock captures the allure—and the limits—of this juristic model of citizenship. According to Pocock, the concept of citizenship articulated by the Roman jurists imagined the citizen as a legal being who related to the world of persons and things through "litigation, prosecution, appropriation." The idea of citizenship derived from Roman law allowed for the infinite extension of rights and personality, while relationships to other people were mediated through law and the mask of legal personhood.[52]

The introduction of statelessness into international politics—and particularly its recognition as a legal status in Western countries—clarified the political implications of the juridical conception of nationality that Jellinek had articulated. Statelessness thus made a number of theoretical questions quite concrete: what does it mean to be ruled or to rule oneself? What are the implications of legal membership without full citizenship? The intimate relationship between theorizing about statelessness and the experience of people defined by this category becomes clear in the interwar writings of émigré jurists from the Russian Empire, who calculated the risks of assuming a legal identification that promised certain protections without the full political rights of citizenship. As these jurists understood, in the late nineteenth century, international lawyers had characterized polities subordinate to imperial rule as entities with international personality, granting them limited capacity to act as agents in conducting international relations.

Alexandre Gorovtsev, a Russian émigré jurist based in Paris, demonstrates how theorists applied legal insights to explain—and mitigate—the problem of statelessness. In Russia he had been a professor of legal philosophy and international law. His expertise had led him into imperial legal diplomacy, and he had been a member of the Russian delegation to the Treaty of Portsmouth that concluded the Russo-Japanese war in 1905. He left the Soviet Union in 1921 and tried to reestablish himself as a professor of legal philosophy and international law in Paris. Gorovtsev's biography reveals the desperate struggle to find employment for former subjects of the Russian Empire. In the late 1920s, Gorovtsev contacted the prominent American jurist Roscoe Pound at Harvard in the hope of securing a position in the United States. Gorovtsev explained that he had tried to continue his "scientific activity in Paris notwithstanding the very difficult conditions in which I find myself." Gorovtsev described his work on the legal theory of property, proclaiming his commitment to developing a "formal science" of law that would keep the analyst on the "hard road of reality" in the investigation of the "phenomenon of right."[53] After failing to find steady work, he committed suicide in Paris in 1933.[54]

Like other jurists in this period, Gorovtsev presented the emergence of statelessness as a significant new fact relevant for debates within legal thought in writings produced during his exile in Paris. He analyzed statelessness drawing on the intellectual tools he had honed as a jurist and international lawyer in the Russian Empire. In Gorovtsev's legal scholarship, the stateless person could be seen to bear the status and rights of citizenship if it could be shown that he or she had gained access to the legal marks of citizenship—that is, the ability to relate to other people through the institutions of the law. Gorovtsev's understanding of what it meant to be an agent in a legal sense in turn informed his resistance to the more expansive vision of international administration. For instance, he balked at the 1926 proposal put forward by the Federation for the International Rights of Man to place the stateless under the guardianship of the League. An exchange between Picard and Gorovtsev in *La Paix par la Droit*, the journal of the French pacifist organization Association de la Paix par le Droit (APD), over the proposal recommending a more expansive role for the League in representing and protecting the stateless reveals the politics of expanding international protection. Gorovtsev's response tracks two of the more significant features of the debates over the meaning of statelessness in this period. He resisted the idea that the stateless possessed a legal status comparable to imperial subjects and he drew on his own juristic training and expertise to assess the importation of Roman legal concepts to comprehend the novel legal categories of the world created by the war. His legal training provided the resources for conceptualizing a more robust political status for stateless persons. Against the suggestion that the stateless could become "super-patriots" under the tutelage of the League, Gorovtsev recommended an international commission in which representatives would act on behalf of refugee and stateless populations. Stateless people would also represent themselves in this scheme and would assume leadership of autonomous local organizations and set the course for their own internal affairs.[55]

As we have seen in Chapter 2, other émigré Russian jurists likewise put forward a more robust vision for political status outside the boundaries of state recognition. Like Gorovtsev, Mark Vishniak described how throughout his life he used legal analysis to engage with contemporary social crisis.[56] And in the same spirit as Gorovtsev's writings on the stateless, Vishniak asserted a vision of deterritorialized politics that did not place populations outside the state in a position of moral or political tutelage. His perspective on the possibility of nonstate forms of political representation had developed years earlier in the context of efforts to achieve democratic reforms in the Russian Empire, when the revolution of 1905 had introduced academics and political writers to new forms of political representation. Vishniak described the minority protection treaties as a manifestation of the revolutionary character of the postwar order. In a pamphlet on the protection of the rights of minorities published in 1921, Vishniak portrayed the new independent legal existence of minorities as the creation of a "new species of moral persons" now "in the public law."[57] Vishniak presented the League of Nations not as the instrument merely for defending the rights of others but as a platform or parliament in which minorities could defend themselves and their interests. The rise of "minority congresses" that brought together such groups indicated a shared sense of political interest and fate.[58] Vishniak put forward a similar claim about how the stateless had become a distinct legal group in international public law.[59] Like Gorovstev, then, Vishniak articulated a broader faith in the relationship between legal theory and political reality. The problem of statelessness, Vishniak proposed, contributed to juridical knowledge about the development of international public law, and he expressed faith in the capacity of jurists, and legal forms of reasoning, to set the terms of political activity.[60]

IV

In the postimperial context of Central Europe the crisis of citizenship was bound up with ongoing debate about independent statehood and sovereignty, and the role of juridical interpretation and analysis in the creation of the boundaries of membership. The problem of statelessness depended on the status of new states under international law, the nature of state succession, and the meaning of legal sovereignty. Walter Napier, a member of the British League of Nations Union, traveled around Central Europe in 1926 gathering information about the treatment of minorities in the successor states and the emerging problem of statelessness. In his report, Napier described the problem as fundamentally juridical in the sense that determining the national status of individuals who claimed to have no citizenship would depend on how legal experts interpreted the relationship between the successor states and the former empire, and the international obligations established by the minority protection treaties.[61] Napier noted some of the questions that would need to be answered in order to determine the cause and scope of the problem: "If Austria is a continuation of the former state, former nationals can retain their nationality . . . if however the former Austria ceased to exist as an international entity, these former nationals would have ipso facto lost their nationality."[62]

As we saw earlier, during the 1920s a growing number of people pleaded for intervention to adjudicate their national status in the Central European successor states. Internationalist associations petitioned the League of Nations to expand the jurisdiction of the Office of the High Commission for Refugees to include former imperial subjects without national citizenship. These individuals and associations appealed to the League as an international authority that could resolve the ambiguous or absent national status of former imperial subjects by determining each individual's rightful nationality. Napier proposed submitting the issue to the Permanent Court of International Justice, and putting "the whole question of nationality within the successor states to a commission largely consisting of jurists among whom should be one or more qualified to deal with questions of Austrian and Hungarian law." They would constitute a "tribunal of an international character which shall be charged with assigning an appropriate nationality to any person finding himself without a nationality, or in possession of a nationality which he considered has been improperly allocated to him."[63]

Napier's proposed solution would mean giving a separate, international, body the authority to determine national status—an approach that the League avoided except in defined, circumscribed cases, to evade the charge of violating the sovereign right to determine nationality. However, Napier hit on the fact that the situation in Central Europe meant that the problem of statelessness, its nature and scope, remained wrapped up in ongoing controversy over how to comprehend the end of the empire. The plight of the *heimatlosen* depended on a set of unresolved legal and constitutional questions about state succession and the emergence of new states in international law. Evaluating the status of former imperial subjects depended on more than the new states adhering to the minority treaties and ensuring the civil rights of individuals as the members of minority groups. The nature of the problem of mass statelessness in Central Europe rested on fundamental political and constitutional questions about the status of the new states under international law and about the legal relationship between the successor states and the empire they succeeded.

The heaven of legal theory thus met the reality of humanitarian disaster in the capital cities of Vienna, Prague, and Budapest. Statelessness in the territories of the former Habsburg Empire represented a critical test of one of the dominant theoretical approaches to law and the state in Central Europe. The Vienna School of Law, a group that coalesced around the legal philosopher Hans Kelsen, brought together the theoretical questions about law and the state with activism on behalf of the statelessness in Central Europe. Vienna, the capital of the truncated Austrian state, contained both a large number of stateless people—though the numbers remained subject to dispute—who were former subjects of the Habsburg Empire, and refugees from the former Russian Empire. In addition to the thousands of Galician refugees who fled to the capital from the Eastern Front during the war, the republic received thousands of displaced former imperial civil servants and military officers from across the former Habsburg Empire. The already overstretched and impoverished capital also accommodated Russian refugees moving out of refugee camps set up during the war.[64]

Rather than searching for evidence that individuals enjoyed a legal status beyond the limits of national identification, the Vienna School analyzed the legal boundaries of the state to confront the crisis of statelessness. Their approach highlights how the meaning of statelessness depended on the shifting legal definitions of annexation, conquest, succession, state birth, and state death. As opposed to invoking moral arguments about the boundaries of political community, the jurists referred to the transcendental presuppositions that made meaningful identification of law and the state possible in order to make sense of the citizenship crisis in the successor states. Though the Vienna School of Law did not cite the stateless as the exemplary subjects of international legal order, they characterized the question of whether an individual could claim to be stateless as fundamentally dependent on the formal boundaries of the state, rather than on any affective ties that substantively linked individuals to a political community.

However, before turning to the application of the Vienna School's legal theory to comprehend the problem of statelessness in the successor states, it is necessary to outline the contours of Kelsen's interwar thought and the intellectual and political context of its reception. When the stateless emerged as a mass problem in interwar Central Europe, Kelsen had already spent much of his legal training thinking about nonstate legal order. Born into a Jewish Viennese family in 1881, he graduated as a doctor of law in Vienna in 1906 and became a *Privatdozent* in 1911, an associate professor in 1918, and a full professor of public and administrative law in 1919. Kelsen's academic supervisor, Leo Strisower, an Austrian Jewish jurist, argued against the more prominent doctrine that the direct subjects of international law are not states but rather individuals. Strisower advocated a vision of private law that transcended the legal boundaries of states. The question at the heart of Kelsen's own doctoral dissertation, completed in 1905, was closer to the research of another supervisor, the jurist Edmund Bernatzik, a professor of constitutional law and an authority on nationality legislation in the dual monarchy. Kelsen considered the possibility of a space of politics between and beyond states in his study of the state theory of Dante Alighieri, the medieval Italian poet and politician who proposed that a single ruling power was capable of ordering the will of humanity. Kelsen investigated how Dante portrayed the relationship of monarchy to subordinate kingdoms, in the context of contemporary debate over Habsburg imperial constitutional reform.[65]

More significant, however, is the fact that Kelsen's theory in this period began to address the basis for membership in a state. In the quiet years before the outbreak of the First World War, from the center of the Habsburg Empire, Kelsen argued that the central question of whether an individual belongs to a state is a matter of law rather than psychology. Kelsen focused on the grounds of interpretation and recognition of concepts such as statehood and legal personality, becoming the leading continental theorist of positivism, the theory that law consists of a set of rules that can be determined without≈resort to moral or political argument. His legalist perspective depended on an understanding of legal analysis as a scientific practice, with a domain of validity separate from the sphere of politics. This abstract approach developed in the face of growing awareness of the multiplicity of values within any given society and the absence of a common ground to evaluate political and moral claims. Kelsen's theory of law and the state attempted to find a value-free way of evaluating the nature of positive law by creating a system in which it was possible to ask about the qualities of the law rather than a normative question about justice.[66]

As we saw in Chapter 2, the end of World War I sharpened and radicalized the question of how political communities constitute themselves and how membership within a political community is determined. The principle of national self-determination, invoked by Woodrow Wilson and Vladimir Lenin, placed a spotlight on the origins of constituent power. A political community based on popular sovereignty raises the question of whether "the people" exist prior to the constitution of the state. And if so, how were the people constituted in the first place? Kelsen had a prominent position in the imperial wartime bureaucracy from which to contemplate these questions. He served in the imperial central command during the war, first as part of the war office, and then in the department of justice within the ministry of war. Kelsen later recalled that he was contacted by the minister in the middle of the night after Wilson announced that the imperial state must agree to the principle of national self-determination. In response to the minister's prompt, he composed a memo arguing that the emperor should establish a commission, composed of advisors representing the various nationalities of the empire, to arrange for the orderly transition of one extended commonwealth into distinct sovereign states.[67] In 1918, Karl Renner, the chancellor of the provisional Austrian government, asked Kelsen to formally contribute to the legal preparations of the federal constitution. Kelsen's constitution, according to the celebrated historian of the Habsburg Empire Robert Kann, successfully offered a "common denominator ... for the whole people of the state."[68] The Austrian Constitution of 1920 that Kelsen authored also granted a Supreme Constitutional Court jurisdiction over constitutional rulings, establishing a model for judicial review.[69]

By the 1920s, Kelsen was widely acknowledged as the premier legal scholar of his generation. Kelsen became associated with the idea that what we think of as the "state" is in fact a way of representing the legal order that constitutes a defined political community. He envisioned a legal order as a hierarchy of norms, based around a single rule establishing the nature of the rules themselves. For Kelsen, only a norm could warrant that which was taken as fact. In his theory, Kelsen raised the question of how one might recognize a distinctive political community in the first place. What are the rules that determine what counts as a state? Who or what authority sets the terms for this determination? Even the territory of a state rested on "legal cognition" rather than empirical observation.[70]

To his critics, Kelsen's legal theory evaded the essential problem of accounting for how a normative order is generated in the first place. According to the interwar critique of legal positivism, Kelsen was unable to recognize the dependence of the liberal constitutional state on a collective substance. The state was more than a legal fiction; it was a collectivity bound by a set of value commitments. In *Constitutional Theory* from 1928, the German jurist Carl Schmitt characterized Kelsen's legal theory as the direct product of the "bourgeois *rechstsstaat*," the imagined political entity that came of age in the seventeenth and eighteenth centuries and that defined the state as a legal order based on concepts of private property, personal freedom, and equality before an impersonal law. Schmitt claimed that despite Kelsen's insistence on developing a neutral scientific method for analyzing what counted as a valid legal statement, his theory also sought to "repress the political, to limit all expressions of state life through a series of normative frameworks."[71] The supposedly logical basis for Kelsen's theory of legal order in fact, according to Schmitt, concealed his faith in scientific progress and the ability of enlightened specialists to govern according to scientific principles. Hermann Heller, a legal philosopher active in the Social Democratic Party in the Weimar

Republic, targeted Kelsen's legalism in his 1927 book on sovereignty. Kelsen's idealization of a state regulated by prior laws, Heller argued, blinded him to law's foundation in power and in historical and cultural practices rather than in logic or formal principles.[72]

Kelsen posited the logical necessity of a foundational norm from which other norms are generated but left the question of its original creation as a logical premise rather than as a matter of historical investigation or object of political theory. For Kelsen, the act of foundation is thus a matter of politics and power, beyond the scope of legal science. He adopted a view of law as a system of norms authorized by some founding norm whose authority must be presupposed rather than proven as a matter of fact. A proper science of law, or a "pure theory," by contrast, assesses the domain of law and its validity from the internal criteria established by the legal order in which norms or commands are articulated.[73]

However, urgent political questions of the day—about national borders and citizenship—depended on how one understood the status of law and the nature of legal order. As the legal theorist David Dyzenhaus has argued, the difficulty with Schmitt's theory of sovereignty is that it fails to account for the fact that the people who author the law must first exist as a distinct agent, and that such agency must first be identifiable through available legal forms. In his major treatise from 1925, *The General Theory of Law and State*, Kelsen turned to the examples of the French Revolution in the eighteenth century and the Russian Revolution in the twentieth to show that courts, referencing the relevant doctrine, had determined in both cases that the acts of revolutionary governments were not legal acts. "Whether a state is a state or a gang of robbers is a normative fact because it is decided by courts rather than by one state recognizing another, which is politics and diplomacy."[74] In other words, a fact has legal significance only insofar as it has meaning within a normative system.[75]

Controversy over the sources of legal authority echoed a broader intellectual conflict that characterized late imperial thought in the Habsburg Empire. Earlier in the century, the distinction between constitutional formalism and the reality of social existence generated novel theories of law that mirrored two dominant responses to the perception of a problematic gap between appearance and reality. The Free Law Movement founded by Eugen Ehrlich rejected the formal constructions of law altogether, advocating more creative approaches to legal interpretation. Real law, the law that governed marriage, family life, contracts, and so on, was something different from the rules artificially laid down by jurists. Life exceeded the boundaries of arid legal form, and truth lay beneath the surface of appearances.[76] Ehrlich captured the intellectual importance of this division perfectly—his version of sociological jurisprudence sought to uncover the laws of life that governed the peripheries of the Habsburg Empire. The state did not govern real life in the empire; instead, communities organized by customs, habits, and particular forms of life existed side by side.[77] Property rights, labor disputes, and family law revealed the structures underlying social existence. Ehrlich emphasized the division between a constitutional order in which one must structure one's legal status, formal career, and public activities and the "real life" of falling in love and making money. Until recently, histories of the empire supported the characterization of a sharp break between constitutional form and political reality.[78] However, Kelsen and Ehrlich represented distinct approaches to the problem of legal authority. Authority could be rooted in myths about the past, the original founding act of a sovereign people, or custom linked to particular charismatic rulers. Alternatively, one could seek the fundamental principles underlying all systems of law.[79]

Imperial law in the Habsburg Empire informed Kelsen's theory of the basic norm required to make logical sense of the legal system. Kelsen reflected on the historical conditions and context of his theory and characterized his conception of positive law as a reflection on the constitutional law of the Austrian Republic.[80] The complex empire, with its patchworks of jurisdictions, demanded the flexible mind of the jurist who could think historically and across contingent variation. The crown reserved rights over the empire overall, but provincial constitutions were maintained through the nineteenth century, especially as "historical rights" in the Kingdom of Hungary and in Bohemia. The Czech lands, for example, were part of Austria, whereas Slovakia was part of Hungary, each subject to distinct sets of laws.[81] The field of jurisprudence bridged the philosophical, the technical, and the practical. Rights to control territory depended on historical claims and arguments framed in legal terms. Professors of law attained a unique status since their efforts to explicate the jurisdictional complexity of the empire served a significant administrative function.[82] Jurists translated political debate and controversy into juridical and constitutional terms. The statesmen and politicians determined what counted as the realm of the state or that of the national, but the jurist established the terms of dispute.[83] Kelsen implied that sociological or psychoanalytic theories of the state failed on the grounds that the Habsburg state did persist in spite of the variety of subjectivities that coexisted within its legal boundaries. The multiplicity of jurisdictions in the empire led to legal conflicts that generated the need for some basic rules that created the foundation for a legal whole to bring each jurisdiction into common regulatory understanding.[84]

Philosophical assumptions drawn from Neo-Kantian philosophy about the relationship between philosophical understanding and scientific discovery likewise informed Kelsen's thought.[85] One of Kelsen's essays on the neo-Kantian theorist Hans Vaihinger illuminates his perspective on the relationship between legal concepts and social reality. In this essay, Kelsen tried to puzzle through the dual function of legal fictions, the fact that they represented a heuristic resource for analyzing reality and that they created reality. Law, like reason in Kantian philosophy, establishes categories that allow the world to be rationally known. Practices and institutions associated with law are recognizably legal because we possess a prior understanding of what law means. Kelsen distinguished between legal fictions, which serve a ruling function and enable the practice and application of law, and fictions that elucidate the nature of law itself. Legal fictions, Kelsen argued, are concepts whose aim is to comprehend something about the law and legal order. The "person" in the legal sense was established as an "aid to thinking"—as a framework for grasping the legal order. Judicial decisions often relied on fictional, or legalistic, ways of reasoning; deciding that someone is dead within the meaning of the law does not imply a failure to grasp the distinction between natural death and legal death. The law does not claim that an adopted son is the same as a natural son. Instead, it posits that for the purposes of law they are the same. Kelsen acknowledged the similarity, though, between the use of law to regulate and create social reality and the idea that categories could be applied intellectually to make the world legible. He wrote, "Of course, there is a deep connection between the intellect which orders the world by employing categories and which thus creates the world as ordered unity, on the one hand, and the law that regulates and thus creates the world, on the other." A legal person is a fiction; so is the law of property. Yet as Kelsen pointed out they have the power to shape social reality.[86]

114

Arguing against those who would present the identity of a group of people as "real," Kelsen insisted that the unity of a state's population derived only from the fact that their behavior was regulated by the same legal order.[87] In contrast to the theories that drew on earlier debates about group agency and collective identity, Kelsen argued, "There is, at any rate at first, no more fellowship in the fact that a number of people wish, feel or think alike than is occasioned theoretically by the conception of a common physical character."[88] He applied his rationalist and legalist approach to the question that occupied theorists across the social sciences: what is the nature of collective politics? Does the combined force of a group add up to something greater than the sum of its parts? How can one explain the existence of a group beyond the natural, biological limits of its constituent members?

Kelsen carefully distinguished between the power of legal institutions to determine facts and the "reality" of juristic persons. The assumption that the interaction of a number of individuals could produce a superindividual being that could be assessed as though it were an inert objective for scientific analysis led social theorists to attribute a meaningful reality to the state and to society. Kelsen tried to counteract this misapprehension first by demonstrating that, from a purely logical perspective, the state had to be distinguished from other forms of communal organization such as the nation or a religious community. If the fact that people associated with one another was enough to delimit the boundaries of the state, the state could not be distinguished from other groups that were also based on a basic association and interaction among individuals. "The family, the nation, the working class, the religious community would all be unities bound together by reciprocal reactions," Kelsen wrote, "and if they are to be distinguished from one another and contrasted with the social unity of the state, then a conception of these unities that is entirely beyond the scope of sociology or of psychology would have to be presumed."[89] In other words, the logical possibility of identifying the state as a distinct kind of authority depended on the separation between the study of empirical facts—for example, about society, or psychology, or power and domination—and an appreciation of the normative foundations of law.

A great deal seemed to rest on Kelsen's claims about the nature of political order, and his popularity as a supervisor and teacher in Vienna indicates how he embodied one side of a debate about the nature of the state and law with life and death implications. Kelsen's student Helen Silving, one of only six women in the political science faculty, called Kelsen the "superstar" of the faculty of law and political science at the University of Vienna. Young disciples at the University of Vienna formed a "Kelsen Circle" to discuss Kelsen's teachings, and students filled the seats of his lectures.[90] Other professors at the University of Vienna clashed with Kelsen over the nature of the state's legal order, and as Silving recalled in her memoir, students viewed these conflicts in political terms.

> Kelsen taught that the state is but a "personification of the national legal order." Or, if we dispense with the metaphor, law itself. Schwind had published a pamphlet in which he laid down what he apparently believed to be the true, living definition of the nature of the state. He said that it was indeed ridiculous to equate the state with the law. "Take, for instance, the Italian state, he elaborated, if it is to be nothing but the Italian law, where are the sunny skies, the blue sea, the red cardinals, so characteristic of Italy?" . . . we, the young students, sided with the professor of our choice. We were young and excitable and the professorial fights were a source of tremendous elation to us.[91]

As this quotation suggests, the academic dispute between Kelsen and Schwind staged a clash between two opposing perspectives on the foundations of statehood, a subject that had significant implications for the citizenship crisis in the Habsburg successor states.

The legal origins of the postimperial republics in turn lent credibility to the idea that the boundaries of membership did not depend on legislative democratic will. Determining who counted as a citizen in one of the new states plausibly rested on its legal relationship to the former empire. Looking back on the breakup of the Habsburg Empire, Josef Redlich—an Austrian constitutional lawyer and politician—wrote, "History will not see it as a mean achievement that . . . the dissolution of the Habsburg Empire took place in a legal fashion, that there were no internal conflicts, no civil wars or war, and that the new states, suddenly called into being, found themselves at once supplied with state governments and the indispensable administrative machinery for carrying them on by the one effective available instrument— the national civil service of the empire that had passed away." This vision of legal regulation remained an important part of Austro-Marxism and was central to various political projects in the Austrian republic. National states were established under the authority of the emperor; the dissolution of the old Austrian state was his last act.[92] Nationalist politicians preserved key features of the imperial legal and administrative systems in the new independent states.[93] Despite their nominal independence, successor states maintained imperial laws and bureaucratic structures and personnel, and governed minority populations in ways continuous with the empire they replaced.[94]

The Vienna School of Law saw legal theory as bearing directly on the real lives of individuals excluded from the national state in postimperial central Europe. In 1929, Kelsen published an article on the birth of Czechoslovakia and the implications of statehood for the nationality of its resident subjects. The article reads more like a legal brief litigating on behalf of those excluded as nationals of Czechoslovakia and Austria than abstract legal theory. Kelsen assessed whether the peace treaties that set the territorial settlement of the dissolved empire were responsible for the startling number of people living without nationality in the successor states. In the Austrian case, Kelsen targeted the Treaty of Saint-Germain, signed in 1919 between the Allies and Austria, which mandated significant territorial losses for the Austrian state. Kelsen dismissed the treaties by arguing that they had nothing to do with the legal birth of the state. Anyone who possessed domicile on the territory, or anyone who had domicile there with respect to the formerly valid order, counted as a national according to the terms of the treaty.[95] The *Prager Tagblatt* echoed Kelsen's argument when the newspaper demanded that the government grant Czechoslovak nationality to everyone "regularly domiciled in Czechoslovakia before the revolution."[96]

Ensuring the status and rights of everyone residing in the successor states depended on the outcomes of such legal analysis, especially since Kelsen denied that individuals have rights against the state. In the preface he wrote to Heinrich Englander's study on the situation of the *heimatlosen* in the successor states, *Die Staatenlosen* (1930), Kelsen asserted that whoever does not belong to a state as a citizen is an "outlaw" from the standpoint of international law.[97] The legal identity of states, how they persisted through time or disappeared from the international map, therefore preoccupied Kelsen. He encouraged his students to take up the question of how states are born, and how they could die, as a model case for the international legal regulation of political disputes. Kelsen and his students produced the major work on the criteria for statehood in international law. The language of "birth" and "death" implied that the state was an organic entity, a premise associated with nineteenth-century nationalism. However, the idea that what counted as state birth or death could be comprehended only through international recognition provided support for the priority of international law. What did the end of old monarchies mean? What was the new source of legitimacy? If a new order was birthed within the old, did legitimacy transfer? Or was the ground still radically contingent?[98] The death of a state—for instance, the Polish commonwealth devoured at the end of the nineteenth century by Austria, Prussia, and Russia—represented an instance of pure power politics and will. The determination of what it meant for a state to live, die, and face future resurrection remained subject to juridical regulation. Did the successor state take over sovereignty, like the passage of property rights from one owner to another? Or was the successor state free from any legal tie to the former regime? Kelsen's first doctoral student at the University of Cologne, Hans Herz, wrote his dissertation on the question of state identity at Kelsen's urging. He recalled that his choice of dissertation topic was typical for Kelsen's students. "When Kelsen was in Cologne, I went to meet him. I became his first Cologne doctoral student. As topic of my dissertation I suggested the problem of the 'identity' (i.e., legal continuity) of a state in case of revolution or change in territorial jurisdiction. . . . It also touched upon the theoretical question of what 'state' meant, of its relation to international law, all of these being problems that had been discussed within the Vienna School in often conflicting fashion."[99]

Kelsen's students worked simultaneously to conceptualize the nature of sovereignty in the new states and to advocate for the stateless of Central Europe. Josef Kunz, one of the more avid promoters of Kelsen's approach to law, became directly involved in publicizing the plight of and advocating on behalf of the stateless in Central Europe.[100] He studied law and political science at the University of Vienna, and by the late 1920s, he was a lecturer on international law at the University and the legal director of the Austrian League of Nations Society.[101] Along with Adolf Merkl and Alfred Verdross, Kunz actively promoted the scientific perspective that unified those who adhered to Kelsen's theory. Kunz described the linkage between the adherents of the Vienna School of Law as "a bond of common theoretical thinking and a common methodological approach."[102] The Vienna School of Law addressed statelessness because many of them were affected personally by the citizenship crisis and because the concept directly related to the range of legal and political questions at the center of their intellectual inquiry.

A great many intellectuals left the trenches critical of liberalism and its promise of progress and the rule of law. Kunz, however, remained committed to the progressive promise of legal science. Before the war he had studied in Paris, attending lectures by Louis Renault and studying the work of the French vitalist philosopher Henri Bergson. When the Austrian army began to mobilize in July 1914, he returned to Austria to join a dragoon regiment leaving for the Russian border. In a handwritten memoir, Kunz reflected that many of the questions he would work on after the war, including the legality of the use of gas in warfare, arose from his practical experience of the battlefield as part of the cavalry in the imperial army.[103] He later devoted some of his work to the laws of war because of his experience on the front. After the war he was active in the League of Nations Union and held a post as a lecturer at the University of Vienna from 1930 to 1932.[104]

Because nationality implies a legal relationship between individuals and states, it remained subject to legal interpretation. In his legal writing from the 1920s, as well as his advocacy for the *heimatlosen* of the Central European successor states, Kunz portrayed national membership as a formal legal status. Nationals could claim the rights of citizenship, but determining who counted as a member of a national community did not necessarily depend on an individual's deeper historical, social, or affective ties to a particular country. Kunz argued that the boundaries of national membership in the states that succeeded the Habsburg Empire depended on the terms of international treaties. His most well-known work analyzed the capacity of inhabitants of a particular territory to opt for a different nationality in accordance with the terms of the post–World War I peace treaties. Kunz's study on the peace treaties and their effects on the nationality of inhabitants described the difficulties faced by former imperial citizens attempting to regain citizenship due to their inability to navigate, or pay to overcome, bureaucratic hurdles.[105] An American reviewer of one of Kunz's massive tomes on international law from this period linked Kunz's theoretical claims about international law and sovereignty with new developments in international politics. The reviewer stated, "The shifting theories of sovereignty in the last two decades, the birth of new states and dependencies, imperial conference, The League of Nations, the Mandate System, and other new forms of control, give this work an importance which commends it to the student of international relations, and especially the student of political theory and the modern state."[106]

Hersch Lauterpacht took a different approach to the same problem. Rather than dismissing the treaties as the basis for the state and its subjects, he argued that they had been misinterpreted. A proper legal analysis of the treaties would demonstrate that many of the people who could not claim citizenship in the new states in fact belonged within their legal boundaries. In 1928, Lauterpacht was invited by the editor of the Polish periodical *Glos Prawa* to respond to the decision of the Polish Supreme Court on the Polish state's responsibility for former contracts, debts, and property belonging to the Habsburg Empire. At issue was the legal relationship between the successor states and the empire from which they emerged.[107] Lauterpacht argued that the new state was a legal successor but only took on prior burdens and debts insofar as it explicitly accepted them. Austrian courts, for instance, did not consider Austria to be the universal successor to the former Austrian Empire and recognized only those obligations provided for in the Treaty of Saint-Germain (which included, for example, paying the pensions of former soldiers and administrators of the imperial railways). The treaty, however, provided that Austria represented a continuation of the former Austria in terms of certain matters, particularly on the issue of the state's responsibility to former citizens of the empire.[108] Lauterpacht worked around the tricky language of Article 80 of the Treaty of Saint-Germain, which stated that a claimant seeking citizenship in the Austrian republic would have to show "tangible evidence" of connection to the broader citizenry.[109]

Together, Kelsen, Kunz, and Lauterpacht interrogated the conceptual boundaries of states to promote maximal inclusion, though Kelsen carefully avoided reference to the normative implications of such arguments. A different student of Kelsen's from the University of Vienna, Benjamin Akzin, called attention to the tension between the idea of equality under the law and substantive equality. He suggested reconsidering the status of legal subjects within the boundaries of the state in light of status hierarchy. In an article titled, "The Subjects of International Law" from 1929, Akzin connected his discussion of rights and legal personality to the concrete problem of stateless people. His article acknowledged how important the stateless had become for the debate over the nature of international law. He argued that regardless of the answer to the major theoretical question of who were the true subjects of international legal order, preserving the diverse forms of legal personality within the state would be beneficial. According to Akzin, even in the interior of a single state the formal qualities of "personality" were diverse and varied according to age, sex, health, education, wealth, and race. Akzin thus retreated to the perceived security of hierarchy, in which differences could be explained through distinctions of rank. The problem, in Akzin's view, remained access to the law and equality within it. Recognizing the internal diversity within the state counterintuitively offered the possibility of equal access to the law.[110]

<h1 style="text-align:center">V</h1>

For Kelsen and his students and associates in the Habsburg successor states, the citizenship status of former imperial subjects presented an essential test case for their theoretical assumptions about the nature of law and the state. The division between the juridical and the sociological—a critical distinction at the core of Kelsen's legal theory—would in turn shape subsequent debate over the international legal conception of national citizenship. However, as we saw in the previous chapter, jurists from the Russian Empire who represented the political interests of the broader Russian refugee community portrayed the emergence of statelessness as an acknowledged legal reality in terms of the concept of rights, especially the idea of international human rights. André Mandelstam, Mark Vishniak, Josef Kunz, and Walter Napier belonged to the Association of League of Nations Societies Legal Commission, which met a few times a year to discuss the international protection of minorities. In this shared institutional setting, it is difficult to separate philosophically rooted disagreements from the fact that the Austrian and Russian jurists represented different constituencies. The Vienna School theorists clashed with the Russian émigré legal scholars over the latter's insistence on linking the broader phenomenon of statelessness to the idea of individual rights guaranteed by international society rather than through citizenship. As we have seen earlier, Russian jurists sought to distinguish the project to create an international legal status of stateless former Russian imperial subjects from the humanitarian efforts to provide relief to various victim groups after World War I.[111]

At one meeting of the Legal Commission in April 1924 at the Foreign Office in Vienna, in which Kunz presented his report on the status of Russian refugees, Kunz criticized a proposal put forward by one of the Russian jurists for a "new international Magna Carta." He reported that he felt that "none of the projects had any juridical value and offered no effective means of developing international law."[112] Based on the report, the Legal Commission voted to reject the Magna Carta proposal because "the terms of the project do not seem to recognize the fact that juridical protection is already everywhere accorded to Russian Emigrants" and that the "drafting and adoption of a Magna Carta of the rights and obligations of peoples does not respond to the scientific method in use today as regards international public law."[113] When the committee met again two months later in Lyon, an outright clash developed between Kunz and Mandelstam. Mandelstam pressed for further discussion on the legal status of the Russians. Kunz pushed the item off the agenda. The criticism of the orthodox doctrine of sovereignty articulated by both groups reflected substantially different assumptions, and varying philosophical commitments justified the expansive visions of international legal authority. Philosophical disagreements about the concept of rights and the foundations of international law played out during the tense debates over the extension of the Nansen passport. In the course of their meetings, Kunz clashed with the representative Russian jurists both over the status of Russian refugees as the exemplary victims in Europe and over the role of international law in protecting vulnerable populations.

Mandelstam, Vishniak, and Boris Mirkine-Guetzevitch, another prominent émigré lawyer who wrote about human rights, belonged to a democratic and liberal intellectual Jewish elite who saw the solution to the Jewish question in Russia in the ideal of the rule of law and a liberal "legal" revolution.[114] Mandelstam and Vishniak both trained in St. Petersburg under the jurist Fedor Martens, the most prominent expert on international law in the Russian Empire.[115] Mandelstam had already recommended universalizing the Nansen passport in a 1921 memo on the "Legal Position of the Russian Refugees."[116] The Institut de Droit International's 1929 Declaration of the International Rights of Man that Mandelstam did so much to support aspired to generalize a common legal status for all people, regardless of citizenship. In his lecture in The Hague in 1931, Mandelstam contrasted the protection of minorities with the rights of humanity, which "have not had the same ardent champions." "L'homme tout court," he stated, was not protected by the treaties in certain countries, but "the hour of the generalization of the rights of man is approaching."[117] He tried to draw the attention of international legal scholars toward the international protection of the rights of humanity, which was "a question intimately tied to the grave problem of the protection of minorities" but would "interest not only portions of the populations of certain states, but every population of the earth without distinction."[118] He understood the 1929 Declaration of Rights as an assertion of the rights-bearing character of nonstate entities. In an earlier piece, "Das Menschenrecht der Heimatlosen" from 1930, Mirkine-Guetzevitch wrote optimistically about the rise of a legal awareness since the war of "international human rights" and the transfer of the protection of those rights to the area of international law.[119]

The undercurrent of competition between international activists, and the developing distinction between politics and humanitarianism, appeared vividly in Mark Vishniak's 1933 course on statelessness in The Hague. Vishniak stated critically that the Austrian League of Nations Society, the organization led by Josef Kunz, approached the problem of Central European statelessness as a "humanitarian" dilemma. Vishniak set his own proposal for an international statute to regulate the legal status of stateless people against the work of the association, claiming, "The legal, political, and administrative situation of the stateless does not interest the Union as much as the social dimension of unemployment, or the purely humanitarian dimensions of the problem."[120]

The Russian émigré jurists argued that the orthodox conception of sovereignty could not properly convey the extent to which states and individuals were not autonomous but interdependent. This is not to say that they based the idea of international rights on natural right; rather, they argued that international rights derived from the fact that a certain level of global solidarity had already been achieved. A global community united by social solidarity could ensure rights for all people, regardless of their national status, as legal consciousness evolved.[121] Kelsen and his students, by contrast, appealed to a "logical systematic" objection to the state's capacity to set its own rules.[122] Though the Declaration's main proponents portrayed it as an attempt to move beyond the categories and differentiations imposed by international regimes, its significance in its own time must be understood within the context of controversies over the stateless and legal theory during the 1920s.

In retrospect, the use of legal theory to confront the exclusionary practices of new states in Central Europe appears naive and idealistic, dangerously divorced from the reality of politics and social conflict, and therefore subject to the criticism of liberalism that achieved prominence after the war.[123] Helen Silving's memories of Kelsen's lectures indicate how she later came to see Kelsen as an emblem of the futility of liberal order against the irrationality of mass politics. In her recollection, Kelsen epitomized the rational ego idealized by liberals, grasping onto legal constitutionalism in the face of mass democracy and the longing for chaos. Kelsen wanted to explain the normative and regulative role of legal order in complete analytical isolation but he remained immersed in his own volatile times. Attending classes at the university, Silving wrote in her memoir, required courage. As students entered their classroom, advocates of Greater Germany yelled, "Jews, get out." "I sat there tense and distracted," she wrote.[124]

In the following decades, Kelsen faced growing criticism for claiming that legal analysis could be purified of the concrete struggle of politics as he and his family were compelled to leave their homes and find security elsewhere. Kelsen was dismissed as a judge in the Austrian Constitutional Court in 1930 and left Austria after securing a position as a professor of international law at the University of Cologne in Germany. He was then forced to leave this post in April 1933 following the passage of the so-called "Law for the Restoration of the Professional Civil Service" in Nazi Germany. At this point, Kelsen left for Geneva, where he accepted a position to teach international law at the *Institut Universitaire des Hautes Etudes Internationales* (University Institute of Advanced International Studies), a university opened in 1927 by Paul Mantoux, the first director of the political section of the League of Nations. In 1936, he moved to accept a position at the German University of Prague. At his first lecture at the University of Prague, fascist students forced everyone but Jews and communists to leave and then beat up the remaining students.[125]

Kelsen's approach to the political conflicts of the era, including the exclusionary citizenship regimes in the new states, indeed appears vulnerable to the mordant satire of the dysfunctional Habsburg Empire in Robert Musil's postimperial 1921 novel *The Man without Qualities*. Musil produced a highly influential and resilient account of the peculiar philosophical and political predicaments that arose in the Habsburg and post-Habsburg context. The novel elaborates a critical distinction between law's fictions and what Musil described in the novel as real life. The narrator distinguishes between the "petrified formality" of the empire and the teeming forms of life, the "cultural chaos," that simmered beneath the surface. "On paper it was called the Austro-Hungarian monarchy, but in conversation it was called Austria, a name solemnly abjured officially while stubbornly retained emotionally. Just to show that feelings are quite as important as constitutional law and that regulations are one thing but real life is something else entirely."[126] In the chapter "Kakania," the narrator describes the maddening disjuncture between how things were named and how things actually were. Living within such a schizophrenic society, the novel suggested, spurred one to be either heedlessly utopian about the future or utterly apathetic.

A similar conceptual dichotomy framed criticism of Kelsen's theory. Critics charged him with concealing the liberal political commitments that lay hidden beneath his abstract theory of law and state and with retreating to the formal abstraction of legal theory as an escape from the real struggles of politics. Though he converted to Catholicism in 1905, Kelsen's efforts to distance the law from the facts of sociology or psychology belonged to a broader culture of Viennese Jewry in which individuals promoted the Enlightenment ideal of a "pure humanity" divorced from particular characteristics. His turn to theorizing about international law and international relations was, according to the historian of Austrian intellectual history William Johnston, fundamentally ideological because through international society Kelsen sought to rediscover Austria's pre-1914 "world of security."[127] He was guilty, then, of failing to honestly confront his own political convictions, and what he presented as a scientific analysis of law as a matter of logic and epistemology in fact concealed his own political faith in liberalism. The separation of law from power, and law from morality, had contributed to a dangerous delusion. This assessment of Kelsen resonates with how historians of Austrian liberalism have conventionally linked liberal faith in the rule of law to the pathologies of Austrian modernism, as an escape into form and a failure to confront reality.[128] As we will see in more detail in Chapter 4, by the mid-1930s Kelsen began to symbolize an approach to law and politics particularly out of step with political reality and with the weakness of the liberal democratic state. Even more so than the debates over the Weimar Constitution, self-proclaimed "realist" approaches to international politics turned Kelsen into the representative of a hopelessly out-of-date legalism that failed to confront the fundamentally combative and violent nature of politics. In the ex post facto canon of realist thought invented by later twentieth century theorists of international relations, which included Machiavelli, Hobbes, and Clausewitz, law and morality would always be marginal relative to considerations of power.[129]

However, in order to appreciate the significance of statelessness in interwar legal and international thought, it is necessary to look beyond the standard debates about the status of liberalism in the context of mass politics and moments of emergency. The perspective articulated by the Vienna School of Law on the meaning and significance of statelessness hinged on particular ideas and assumptions about the relationship between legal theory and practical politics—and thus about what membership in a particular political community really depends on at a moment of breakdown and creation. Though the critics were surely correct that the pure theory of law could not ultimately be separated from a particular vision of liberalism in the history of the Habsburg Empire, Kelsen and his students offered a rich framework for theorizing the boundaries of political order that made the problem of statelessness central to such reflection. For these theorists, the comprehension of those outside of legal and political order depended on foundational principles of law, politics, and constitutionalism. In contrast to the idea that international law does not begin to take up the plight of the stateless until after the Second World War, this chapter has shown how statelessness represented a distinctive and important cognitive resource after the First World War when debates about how to characterize and define the boundaries of international order flourished across a range of contexts and geographic settings, and has sought to clarify the particular intellectual and ideological conditions in which these debates took place.

4

The Real Boundaries of Membership

In a measured and pragmatic letter to the League in 1934—addressed to the nonexistent "Department of Stateless People"—Oskar Brandstaedter wrote that he needed a permit to start a business in London, where he had been living for the past three years without legal identification.[1] A year later, having received no response, he wrote to the League again, but from a new address in Vienna. This time, his letter communicates profound fear and hopelessness, revealing the escalating despair of those without a passport. Brandstaedter explained that he faced imminent expulsion from Austria. For a stateless person, he wrote, there was no way out, other than to commit suicide. By the time he received their response, he might already be dead.[2]

Between January 1933 and September 1939, roughly 1.2 million people were compelled to leave their home countries in search of refuge. Of these, 420,000 were Jewish refugees from Germany and annexed areas. Those fleeing the violence of the Spanish Civil War and persecution in the Middle East contributed to the vast numbers seeking entry into safer countries. Once Japanese troops invaded China in 1937, thousands sought sanctuary in Shanghai, which remained an internationalized port city, and millions more fled into the interior of China. Getting out required a visa, and most countries stopped granting refugees this lifesaving document.[3] A remarkable reference book published in 1938 for the thousands of German Jews desperately seeking to leave Germany after Kristalnacht highlights how the geography of escape created a new global topography defined by safe travel routes and sites of refuge. The book lists the offices in European capitals that would provide passports and visa documents, as well as the countries taking people in, and the climate and jobs that might await new entrants.[4]

The grim reality portrayed in works of popular fiction offers a comple-
mentary perspective to the more theoretical debates about law, rights, and
the boundaries of political membership discussed in Chapter 3. In the 1930s
pulp thrillers encouraged a wider public to consider the lives of people without the security of citizenship. The budding genre of noir fiction, with stories of detectives and spies moving surreptitiously across borders, resonated
with readers and writers absorbed by the legal predicament of the stateless.[5]
Eric Ambler's bestselling 1938 detective story *Epitaph for a Spy* features a
language teacher named Joseph Vadassy, a former subject of the Habsburg
Empire who never recovers his citizenship after the war. Ambler's stories often featured clandestine people who shape-shift across imperial and national
identifications, staying one step ahead of the detectives and police in pursuit
of their locations and identities. Written from Vadassy's point of view, the
account indicated how the problem of statelessness had sunk into a wider
popular consciousness, and compelled readers to grapple with the particular
experience of the *heimatlosen*. Living in a state of melancholic uncertainty in
the French port city of Marseilles on a false Yugoslavian passport, Ambler's
protagonist describes in detail the consequences of living without a nationality in a world of policed borders. "If France expelled me," Vadassy states in
the novel, "there was nowhere left for me to go." He faces arrest in Yugoslavia,
joblessness in England, and illegality in America. Traveling to China requires
a passport and an entry visa. It might be possible to gain entry into South
America, Vadassy speculates, but such a scheme requires mountains of loose
cash. Every jurisdiction, across the globe, closes before him. The worldwide
economic depression has made the predicament of the stateless more severe,
as Vadassy describes in concrete terms: "There would be nowhere I could go,
nowhere. After all, what did it matter? What happened to an insignificant
teacher of languages without national status was of no interest to anyone.
No consul would intervene on his behalf; no Parliament, no Congress, no
Chamber of Deputies would inquire into his fate. Officially he did not exist;
he was an abstraction, a ghost. All he could decently and logically do was
destroy himself."[6]

The idea that statelessness belonged to the province of fiction had served
an important ideological function in transatlantic international thought since
the late eighteenth century. However, interwar fiction, such as the works by
Ambler but also B. Traven's *The Death Ship*, discussed in Chapter 1, provided

strikingly accurate, almost journalistic, descriptions of what it was like to live without the security of national belonging. Without the right papers, Vadassy was unable to get a job or migrate somewhere else where he might be able to find employment. Though he was willing to travel across the world for a semblance of security, governments had made it nearly impossible to cross freely into their territory. National status meant that some recognized political and legal authority—an official representing a consulate or a politician holding political office—had be to be concerned about Vadassy's fate even in a minimal way. The absence of such legal recognition made him vulnerable to expulsion or even total extinction.

As we will see later, the tension between the value of strong states with the greater capacity to improve the lives of their citizens, and the urgent needs of those who could not claim the protection of citizenship, would become an increasingly important feature of debate about the meaning of statelessness. With the passage of the racially motivated exclusionary National Origins Act in 1924, the United States had already limited the number of people allowed to enter the country. The liberal argument for greater national control over migration likewise gained adherents as a result of the success of Keynsian justifications for a bordered world. In the wake of the Great Depression, the Cambridge economist John Maynard Keynes argued that global financial collapse created an opportunity to reconsider a set of flawed political and economic assumptions. The crisis of capitalism demanded that governments begin to "shuffle out of the mental habits of the prewar nineteenth century world" by assuming greater control over national economies. They had to reimagine the meaning of wealth to include the robust welfare of citizens and acknowledge that economic internationalism had failed to prevent the outbreak of the Great War. For Keynes, it was the work of civilization to transform the state from an organization modeled on a joint stock company, concerned with revenues and balanced books, to one with a far greater public function and purpose.[7]

Yet focusing on the history of exclusion and expulsion and on the restrictive immigration and asylum policies presupposes that the boundary between statehood and international legal order was already determined and that the only issue of political significance after the onset of the refugee crises of the 1930s was whether countries would be willing to grant asylum to refugees and what rights they held before regaining citizenship. However, debate about the boundaries of membership and the role of law in the construction of those borders persisted, especially in light of the practical questions about the norms governing nationality that the accelerating refugee crisis of the late 1930s introduced.[8] At the moment when the precarious lives of people living without the protection of citizenship began to puncture popular consciousness, nationality and statelessness began to recede as touchstones in debates over the future of international legal order.

The evolution of the legal thinking on statelessness might seem like an inevitable response to the rise of fascism and the collapse of the League of Nations. In the first decade after the war, internationalization had fit harmoniously with Great Power interest. By the 1930s this alignment gave way to skepticism about international solutions to international problems, especially after the combined shocks of the Japanese invasion of Manchuria, the dramatic exit of the Germans from the League, the subsequent rearmament of the Rhineland, and the evident failure of international minority protection. In response to these events, the vision of international society connected to the discussions around statelessness gave way to greater focus on facilitating migration and liberalizing immigration legislation.

The growing numbers of people in search of asylum provoked a new set of controversies, for both national governments and international lawyers, over the limits of the state's legal authority in matters relating to nationality. Rather than affirming what had always been within the sovereign power of states—control over membership—the crisis of the 1930s called further attention to the lack of common consensus about what nationality meant and how it functioned internationally. As opposed to viewing mass statelessness in terms of the future of legal order beyond the boundaries of any particular political community, the task for legal scholars became determining the role of international law in the regulation of nationality.

This chapter first explains how mass statelessness was and was not internationalized in the mid- to late 1930s. It argues that The Hague Codification Conference and the refugee relief arrangements created after 1933 shifted how international lawyers approached the issue. As we will see, theorists and publicists adapted their thinking in light of the lackluster results of the League-organized international conference to systematize nationality law in 1930. Refugees from Europe seeking asylum in the 1930s transformed the significance of international legal authority without discrediting it as a distinctive sphere of political and legal order. In order to comprehend how the crisis of the 1930s reframed the significance of statelessness, it is necessary to consider the wider context of the transformation of legal thought in the 1930s and a broader intellectual assault on legal formalism and abstraction. The second part of the chapter weighs the challenge to legal formalism, especially to Hans Kelsen's legal theory, and explores its effect on how statelessness was conceptualized in relation to international order.

I

As we have seen, legal experts at the League identified international codification as a more limited way of addressing the growing number of petitions they received from people who claimed to be stateless since the war. They identified the problem of statelessness within the domain of the conflict of laws and avoided addressing it as a wider international or humanitarian crisis resulting from mass denationalization or exclusionary national legislation. Infringing on nationality law would directly threaten the delicate boundary the League had created between new forms of international authority and the sovereign right of states. The conference eventually held in The Hague from March 13 to April 12 1930 brought together representatives from state governments to discuss nationality law, the international rules governing territorial waters, and the responsibility of states for damage caused in their territory to the person or property of foreigners. In attendance were delegates from member and non-member states of the League of Nations, including Australia, Austria, Brazil, Bulgaria, Canada, Chile, China, Colombia, Cuba, Czechoslovakia, the Free City of Danzig, Denmark, Egypt, Estonia, Finland, France, Germany, Great Britain, Hungary, Iceland, India, Ireland, Italy, Japan, Latvia, Luxemburg, Mexico, the Netherlands, Nicaragua, Norway, Persia, Peru, Poland, Portugal, Romania, Salvador, the Union of South Africa, Spain, Sweden, Switzerland, Turkey, the United States of America, Uruguay, and Yugoslavia. The Soviet Union sent representatives as observers only.[9] The task for the representatives of these nations, as the opening speech by the Minister for Foreign Affairs from the Netherlands asserted, would be nothing less than the "framing of the rules of international law."[10]

Though League officials viewed the conference as a contained way to address the problem of statelessness, discussions during the meeting worried national representatives who did not wish to relinquish control over how they determined the boundaries of membership. During the conference delegates offered widely differing opinions on the validity of denaturalization and denationalization, though many agreed that states should be prohibited from expelling people with no nationality because there was nowhere for them to go, and they might encroach on countries trying to police their borders. Once government representatives began to sense that the conference might infringe on the sovereign capacity to dictate nationality law, representatives became more skittish. The American minister to The Hague, a former Republican congressman from Michigan named Gerrit J. Diekema, reported to the US secretary of state that the questions explored at the conference on nationality and the territorial sea "have been found to have been more real than was supposed when the governments agreed on this conference." For this reason, the minister wrote, the conference would ultimately be a "set back to the whole idea of the codification of international law."[11]

The conference's success in promoting the cause of international legal codification depended on its minimalist approach to addressing the global problems it was ostensibly designed to contain. Writing from The Hague, David Hunter Miller, an American lawyer who had advised the American delegation at the Paris Peace Conference, assured the readers of *Foreign Affairs* that statelessness was "only a problem for the individual" and had few consequences for state officials charged with adjudicating nationality and immigration questions.[12] In April 1930, Miller sent a telegram to the concerned US State Department stating, "The discussions here have shown that world sentiment on the whole question of nationality is in a state of flux and that the trend is our way despite the fact that at this time various countries have other views which are based particularly on social and economic conditions and partly on religion."[13] Miller meant that the representatives from other countries who met in The Hague to discuss the possibility of a common code to regulate nationality shared the same interests as the United States in seeking to minimize international infringement on how governments legislated nationality. From the perspective of internationalists who believed that the project of international codification served the cause of peace, the conference was a failure. Edwin Borchard, who attended the conference as a legal advisor for the US delegation, argued that disappointment in the conference was so extreme that it put to rest the great hope internationalists had placed in codification.[14]

Though considered in its own time a failure as a means of resolving international conflict, the Codification Conference reshaped the legal possibilities for regulating nationality law by confirming the limits of attempts to regulate nationality through an international organization. As states elaborated the rules governing naturalization and legal membership, they looked to formal international meetings like the Codification Conference and to the practices of other states. The failure to mark out nationality as part of the purview of international law served as an acknowledgment of the overriding sovereignty of individual states in matters of naturalization and denaturalization. During the conference, denaturalization had been placed under scrutiny. Yet the fact that it met with little disapproval affirmed that governments stripping former nationals of their national status did not violate interstate order. Regardless of the moral questions surrounding the creation of statelessness, it was the prerogative of the state to determine who was and was not a national.

The codification project was internationalist in the sense that it asked states to acknowledge the large-scale consequences of their nationality legislation—loss of nationality after entering foreign military service, entering the civil service, or accepting public office. Perhaps if governments could see how each country's legislation created innumerable complications, they would reflect on their laws in more internationalist terms. Members of the League secretariat resisted the argument that their involvement in the regulation of nationality had larger implications for debates about the nature of sovereign authority. When Manley Hudson, the American law professor who led the project to codify laws of nationality from around the world, proposed that the Codification Conference could also address the legal status of nonstate legal subjects, including that of pirates, Mackinnon Wood sneered at the suggestion and commented that Hudson was only "stirring up dead bones" by introducing the status of individuals under international law to the conference agenda.[15]

Feminists placed great hopes in the Codification Conference, seeing it as a test case for the use of international law to advance the status of women. By the turn of the twentieth century, the eighty or so states with delineated laws of nationality all stipulated that a woman's nationality depended on that of her husband, and she could lose her nationality according to her marital status and her husband's citizenship. Some states, such as France and Venezuela, went against the grain by legislating nationality laws late in the nineteenth century that prevented women from losing all citizenship. In interwar Czechoslovakia, the importance of family unity dictated citizenship law, which affirmed that a woman's citizenship was determined by her husband's state of allegiance. As of 1918, most other nations in the world upheld the same principle in accordance with the doctrine of family unity.[16]

An international women's movement for independent citizenship coalesced in the years before The Hague conference of 1930 as the campaign for equal nationality rights for married women gained full support across different women's organizations.[17] The International Council of Women, the Women's International League for Peace and Freedom, and the International Alliance for Women's Suffrage—later renamed the International Alliance for Women's Suffrage and Equal Citizenship—campaigned for national legislative reform. Between 1918 and 1929, eighteen nations enacted protection against a married woman's involuntary loss of citizenship. Women's organizations saw the creation of international standards for naturalization as a way to incorporate equal citizenship into state law and to prevent women who married foreigners from becoming stateless. They envisioned achieving citizenship reforms via an international treaty that would require its signatories to give women complete control over their own citizenship regardless of marital status. In arguing the case for equality, they claimed that "the right of citizenship is the most fundamental political right" and, as such, women should not be deprived of this right on marriage. The agreement produced at the conference ultimately did not stipulate that national legislation should separate a women's national status from that of her husband. Instead, the conference draft recommended that states "study whether it would not be possible to introduce into their law the principle of the equality of the sexes in matters of nationality."[18]

The conference at The Hague failed to generate consensus—even rhetorically—on the status of denationalization. For the Americans, who did not wish to be encumbered by an international arrangement that placed restrictions on nationality legislation, the conference was a success because it affirmed that no such constraining norm existed, and established consensus around a critical issue that distinguished domestic political matters from international ones. By the late 1930s, the US Congress had codified all its provisions relating to nationality. This legislation culminated in the Nationality Act of October 1940, which stipulated an automatic loss of citizenship for naturalized citizens residing three years in a foreign state.[19]

One of the major legal studies of statelessness written by an American legal scholar in 1934 reinforced the idea that internationally codifying the laws of nationality was not ultimately a promising way forward to prevent statelessness. In her study, Catherine Seckler-Hudson focused on the problems created by the conflict of laws rather than on the implications of mass statelessness for the expansion of international authority or the boundaries of statehood. Her book portrayed statelessness as a phenomenon that arose for different reasons; she divided the study between statelessness arising from marriage, statelessness of minors, and statelessness of adults not resulting from marriage. The latter group reflected the over two million former Russian nationals and the growing number of refugees from Germany. She concluded that though a universal agreement would be the optimal solution to limiting the number of stateless persons worldwide, unilateral municipal solutions represented the most reasonable option, though it would certainly leave some number of stateless people without the assurance of national recognition.[20]

By contrast, British representatives left the 1930 conference greatly disappointed in the failure to internationalize the regulation of nationality legislation. For the British, the conference represented a missed opportunity to ratify a new settlement regarding the nationality law of the empire and its dominion territories. From 1839 to 1931, the British colonies of Canada, Australia, New Zealand, and South Africa pressed for greater autonomy and eventually became independent states, though they retained constitutional links with the British crown. British officials hoped that the public setting would help stabilize and legitimize a revised imperial constitutional settlement. One question they hoped to resolve was whether to preserve an empire-wide nationality. The officers strategized that it would be important to ensure the recognition in international law "of a system peculiar to the unique conditions of the British commonwealth under which two nationalities are recognized viz. Dominion nationality for certain purposes, and the 'common status' of British subjects for certain other

purposes."[21] Obtaining international recognition was particularly important because of the complex nature of the settlement. As one official wrote,
"it is not even clear whether the British Commonwealth should be regarded as co-extensive with the British Empire or exclusive of the non-self governing parts of the empire. But however this may be, the commonwealth is
not and presumably never will be a state in the ordinary sense of a single
political and international entity, since its component parts are already for
many international purposes separate political entities."[22] An international
forum like the Codification Conference in turn seemed like an opportunity
to ratify the settlement reestablishing the political boundaries of membership in the empire.

The Codification Conference matters, therefore, in ways that more traditional international and diplomatic histories of interwar internationalism
have not appreciated. International conferences, far from failures, proved
successful in establishing common standards to define the legal boundaries of international politics. For example, after a decade of vigorous debate
about the meaning of statehood, national representatives agreed to a common definition at the international conference in Uruguay that produced the
Montevideo Convention on the Rights and Duties of States in December
1933. Jurists from Latin America had pursued formal codification of the attributes of statehood in the hope that laying down formal rules would prevent intervention into the affairs of Latin American states. The convention
ultimately established four criteria for statehood: a permanent population,
a clearly defined territory, effective government over the territory, and the
capacity to engage in international relations. This agreement established that
international legal personality depended on states achieving a set of concrete
criteria rather than on recognition by other states. The convention did not
mean that the question of how to define statehood in international law had
been permanently settled, but it indicates how an international forum could
successfully minimize the uncertainty surrounding the criteria for statehood
and sovereignty that had taken on new urgency in global politics since the
First World War.[23]

II

The entry of statelessness into international life (as a reality acknowledged
by national courts and in a more limited way by the League) touched directly

on foundational questions entertained in the decade after the war about the nature of sovereignty, statehood, and international legal order. Fascism and discrimination against minorities had contributed significantly to the creation of statelessness as a mass phenomenon—a fact that the League had avoided acknowledging. However, the League could not avoid addressing the new crisis precipitated by Nazi policy, which led thousands to seek entry into other countries. After 1933 the League directed its attention toward the growing number of people fleeing fascist dictatorships. The refugee agreements of the 1930s in turn reinforced the idea that nationality did not lie within the domain of international regulation. There were several attempts to solve the crisis through international agreements. The first was the establishment of a High Commissioner of the League of Nations for Refugees (Jewish and others) Coming from Germany in 1933. The League's participation in refugee relief beginning in 1933 represented a qualitative leap from its earlier involvement with refugees. Refugees from Germany were not entitled to Nansen passports, and separate treaties provided for a distinct identity certificate. The October 28, 1933 Convention Relating to the International Status of Refugees was designed to be legally binding for signatories and to deal with a broad range of concerns. It granted refugees the enjoyment of civil rights, free access to courts of law, security and stability in their settlement and employment, and admission to schools and universities and specified the right not to be expelled.

The League's attempts to limit how directly it intervened in the definition and protection of people without the protection of their governments put the organization at odds with those interested in a wider and more sustained international approach to statelessness as a general phenomenon, one that affected a range of people for different reasons but who all shared a common insecurity. In deliberations, participants had raised the question of whether the convention should provide more coverage to include the post–World War I stateless. Should advocates push for an international form of protection by expanding the new refugee convention such that it covered all forms of statelessness, or should the stateless be assimilated to the legal status of foreigners? In April 1934 the League of Nations Union wrote to the British Foreign Office urging them to submit to the League council a proposal for an international agreement extending the convention from October 1933 to cover all stateless refugees. The proposal represented a final attempt to place those without the protection of any state, whether they had formally lost all connection to their prior nationality or not, in a single analytic category. In the memo included with the letter, the author explained that the problem of statelessness had been aggravated by the action of various states—including Russia, Turkey, Italy, and Germany—in depriving their former citizens of nationality on political or racial grounds. This class of stateless persons, the memo stated, was being steadily increased, and it was the responsibility of international society to account for them and provide for their status, their right to work, and their liberty of movement. In addition to an international passport, stateless persons required "some international basis for civil rights so that they might not be the helpless flotsam and jetsam of society."[24] The proposal by the League of Nations Union thus continued the line of argument put forward by liberal internationalists throughout the 1920s that international law should assure the rights of noncitizens. In response, the Foreign Office wrote that the problem of statelessness was dwindling. The desire to internationalize the problem was a scheme "inspired and pressed by countries who would be too glad to dispose of their refugees elsewhere."[25] Major Johnson of the Nansen Office pointed out the limits of such an argument because the British would have to deal with the problem of stateless Assyrians since the independence of Iraq, and on this basis they should participate in the creation of a general convention that provided protection for all those undefended by any particular state.[26]

The League's High Commission for Refugees reinforced the conceptualization of the refugee in statist terms and consolidated a particular image of the state as the agent responsible for representation and protection. The Intergovernmental Advisory Commission for Refugees, for example, focused on stopping arbitrary expulsions from host states.[27] The 1933 convention provided assistance not with a view to correcting an anomaly in the international legal system but to ensuring the refugees' bodily well-being. Over four hundred thousand refugees fled the Nazis between 1933 and the outbreak of the Second World War. The refugee agreements adopted between 1935 and 1939 redefined the refugee condition in largely social rather than juridical terms. After 1936, refugees from the Spanish Civil War became the largest group of refugees in Europe.

The Evian Conference in July 1938 was the last attempt before World War II to find an international solution to the refugee crisis. Franklin Roosevelt deliberately called for a conference outside the formal framework of the League of Nations "for the primary purpose of facilitated involuntary emigration from Germany (including Austria)."[28] This resulted in a definition of refugees as any person affected by certain social or political events with the emphasis placed on ensuring safety and well-being rather than legal identification.[29] In the 1938 Convention concerning the Status of Refugees from Germany, refugees were defined as "any person who has settled in that country, who does not possess any nationality other than German nationality, and does not enjoy the protection of the Government of the Reich."[30] At the conference, representatives established the Intergovernmental Committee on Refugees, an agency that would be responsible for refugees from Germany and Austria forced to emigrate on account of political opinion, religious beliefs, or racial origin, as well as individuals from this group who had not found permanent settlement elsewhere. A separate convention adopted in Geneva in 1938 conferred on stateless persons the right to equal treatment with friendly aliens.[31] Yet there remained an important difference between governments agreeing to treat stateless people as if they are foreigners, with the same civil rights as legal visitors, and the idea that an international organization would act independently to protect and validate the identity of stateless people.

III

More significant, however, than the statist character of the refugee relief agencies established in the late 1930s, is how the legal scholars who sought to develop arguments against Nazi policy were hampered by the results of the Codification Conference. After the lackluster Hague Conference, legal scholars clashed over the question of whether depriving Jewish nationals of citizenship, leaving them with national status but without political rights, violated international law. Denationalization in Germany was originally envisaged as a case-by-case measure to punish emigrants accused of spreading propaganda against the Nazi regime. The Nazi party followed the script of previous revolutions by identifying enemies of the state, particularly émigrés, and then stripping them of citizenship. In July 1933 the Nazi Ministry of the Interior drafted proposals for a law to exclude Jews from citizenship rights. The result was a new status called *Reichsbürgerschaft*, excluding Jews from full citizenship rights and banning marriages or sexual relationships between Jews and non-Jews. This legislation transformed Jews in Germany into "subjects" rather than "citizens," deliberately undoing the history of civic emancipation and political equality, effectively turning citizens into colonial subjects of the Nazi regime.[32]

Though the mass denationalization of Jewish citizens in Nazi Germany struck observers as extreme, it remained within the arena of justifiable behavior. Durward Sandifer, a member of the US State Department legal office specializing in nationality and immigration, argued that the comparative study of nationality law was the "chief hope of progress in the direction of securing any degree of harmonious interlocking of the laws on this important subject." He described the law adopted in Germany in July 1933 providing for the cancellation of any naturalization between 1918 and 1933 of undesirables as "especially noteworthy" but within the acceptable bounds of state practice.[33]

When British officials sought precedents to justify the evolving conception of nationality in the empire, they drew on the Nazi denationalization acts to reason through their own presumptions about sovereignty and citizenship. British civil servants and legal advisors involved in negotiating an acceptable constitutional arrangement between Britain and its dominions, particularly the legal position of nationality in the event of Irish secession, referenced the treatment of the Jews in Germany to suggest that elimination of a common, empire-wide, citizenship might generate public comparison between imperial constitutional reform and Nazi legislation. Home Office officials discussed whether the recognition of an independent sovereign state implied that former British subjects had ceased to be legally connected to the state. "Could the king," one Home Office correspondent inquired, "declare that Irish subjects were no longer 'British subjects?' Could he, for example, relieve all the Jews who are British subjects of their allegiance and turn them into aliens? And if not, by what greater right can he bring this about in the case of Irishmen?"[34] The response to the letter assured the official that no one was suggesting that the king would be able to deprive any particular British subjects or class of British subjects of their allegiance. According to the common law, the king could recognize by treaty that part of his dominion was independent and that those inhabitants were thus discharged of their allegiance by their own volition.[35]

Lawyers in Britain and the United States confirmed the claim that it was within the right of any state to exert full control over nationality. Claus von

Stauffenberg, a lawyer in the Nazi regime (and later part of a failed plot to assassinate Hitler), argued for the legitimacy of Nazi denationalization policy by comparing the law with the racist character of US immigration policy.[36] In response to the international legal scholar Georges Scelle's reproach—that Nazi legislation was incompatible with the essential principles of the international community—Stauffenberg responded that it was the state's prerogative to denationalize. Since France also had legislation imposing loss of nationality as a penalty, Scelle was "in the position of a man who sits in a glass house throwing stones."[37] According to James Garner, an American political scientist, "it probably cannot be successfully argued that the law violates any positive prescription of the law of nations."[38] In a seminal article on the subject of denationalization, Lawrence Preuss, a professor of international law at the University of Michigan, provided ample precedent for the German law of July 4, 1933.[39] Before World War I, France decreed that those found guilty of trafficking slaves would automatically lose their nationality. And in 1913, a German law provided for the denationalization of deserters and German residents abroad who refused to return to Germany. Preuss also cited the mass denationalization of Romanian Jews, who until 1918 were treated as foreigners subject to expulsion whenever their presence was deemed a threat to state security, as the last major instance before the mass denationalization of Russian émigrés by the Bolsheviks.[40]

In 1938, the Polish parliament passed a law establishing a number of conditions under which Polish citizenship could be taken away from any citizen living abroad. After the Nazi annexation of Austria in March of that year, thousands of Jews who possessed Polish citizenship tried to return to Poland from Austria and Germany. The Polish state had hoped to encourage mass Jewish flight, not mass return; the foreign ministry hastily excluded Polish Jews abroad from the protection of the Polish government. They demanded that citizens living abroad register with embassies, instructing the Polish ambassador in Berlin not to stamp the passports of Jewish migrants. A Vichy law from October 1940 overturned the Crémieux Decree of October 1870 that had naturalized Algerian Jews to reestablish "equality of status" between Jews and Muslims.[41] Vichy France in turn borrowed from the Nazi example, establishing that officials could withdraw French nationality without cause from anyone who had acquired it after August 10, 1927.[42]

Publicists and legal scholars scrambled to redefine statelessness after the expansion of the refugee crisis and the perceived failure of international efforts to minimize statelessness through the codification of nationality law. They shifted away from addressing statelessness in relation to international legal order, emphasizing the fact that The Hague conference had failed to produce a definitive statement on the legitimacy of denationalization. The collapse of faith in League mechanisms for policing nationality, and the widely acknowledged failure of The Hague conference to produce consensus on the international regulation of nationality, motivated the turn toward the internationalization of the refugee question by identifying the inherently international nature of foisting an unwanted population on another state.

What was the basis for protesting against stripping the Jewish population of the rights of citizenship? The arguments invoked against discrimination and persecution marked a retreat from claims about the supremacy of international legal order and the capacity of supranational rules to dictate the legitimacy of state practice discussed earlier. Publicists had placed their support behind a final effort in 1933 to legitimate the minority protection regime by supporting a petition by Franz Bernheim, a German Jew, to submit a complaint about Nazi racial discrimination in Upper Silesia, where individuals were allowed to bring petitions on behalf of their group. It ultimately served to highlight the limitations of the regime.[43] When James G. McDonald resigned as high commissioner as a public act of protest in December 1935, the *Petition in Support of McDonald's Letter of Resignation* argued in terms of the imperial right to intervene for humanitarian reasons: "Many eminent authorities from Grotius to those of our own day have recognized the right of intercession to protect the victims of persecution and oppression." This right, the letter maintained, was also based on the precedent of aiding coreligionists in foreign lands to maintain "human rights."[44] Human rights were thus invoked to recall imperial interventions in the Ottoman and Russian Empires during the nineteenth century to defend religious minorities.[45]

The results of The Hague Codification Conference convinced advocates of the implausibility of publicizing the issue of denationalization as a violation of international law. In 1935, Neville Laski, the president of the Board of Deputies of British Jews, asked Hersch Lauterpacht to write a letter to the British and French governments encouraging them to protest the recent acts of denationalization. Laski and Norman Bentwich actively monitored the German situation and worked with McDonald, the High Commissioner for Refugees at the League of Nations, to publicize it as an international, rather than a domestic, issue.[46] Lauterpacht, however, doubted the efficacy of the proposal. The deprivation of nationality, he explained, was not a new issue. It was just a larger-scale version of what the Italian government had already done by denationalizing several thousand of its subjects, an act that had met with international silence. Moreover, the Hague Codification Conference in 1930 had, Lauterpacht stated, been a disappointment: it provisionally addressed denationalization but did not assert that it was contrary to international law.[47]

Laski persisted, however, and sent his request to Morris Waldman at the American Jewish Committee, who in turn sent the question over to Arthur K. Kuhn and Alexander Sacks, both American professors of international law. Kuhn advised the American Jewish Committee that a public protest to the British and French governments, would, as Lauterpacht had already said, only cause aggravation. In addition, the "acquisition and loss of nationality is a question within the jurisdiction of each nation." Nevertheless, since the League had addressed statelessness at the 1930 Hague Codification Conference, he thought they could at least submit their protests there. Cyrus Adler, an American Jewish lobbyist, perfectly articulated the prevailing sentiment of the moment. He argued that there was simply no evidence to suggest any restrictions limiting a government's ability to deprive citizens of their citizenship.[48] Adler added that at the end of the American Civil War, rebels were denationalized. This, he explained, was sufficient evidence to suggest that there is no act by which a state could "be obliged by international control to prevent it from withdrawing citizenship or nationality." The only point at which it did become an "international" issue was when such persons entered another country.[49]

If the act of stripping someone of citizenship was domestic rather than international, then perhaps a different formulation of the problem could be contrived. Properly international issues were those that involved shared experiences of global disruption. The threat of uncontrolled population movements fit in well with the link drawn by peace activists after World War I between global population dynamics and geopolitics.[50] Donnedieu de

Vabres, who would become the French judge at the Nuremberg trials and one of the authors of the Genocide Convention after World War II, argued that expulsion was an inherently international problem since the stateless had nowhere to go.[51] Once it became clear, however, that nationality was no longer a viable target for international regulation, publicists placed more emphasis on the distinction between refugees and the stateless, and in particular the fact that persecution was the driving force behind migration. The lawyers began to disentangle the problem of those without any legal connection to the state from those that were vulnerable due to an effective absence of state protection. By the mid-1930s, legal academics worked to refine a definition for refugees that did not coincide with statelessness. In an article titled "International Measure for the Relief of Stateless Persons" in 1936, Arthur Kuhn distinguished between the large numbers of political refugees "enjoying temporary or permanent asylum in other countries" and stateless persons who had lost the diplomatic protection of their national state. He nevertheless recommended the expansion of the 1933 convention in order to ensure all stateless people a normal juridical status.[52] At a conference in Brussels organized by the Institute of International Law in April 1936, Arnold Raested of Normandy presented a comprehensive report on the legal status of stateless persons and refugees. He stated: "the conference recognized the principle that stateless persons ought to enjoy all the rights accorded under parallel circumstances to other foreigners."[53] At a meeting of the Institut de Droit International in 1936, de Vabres maintained that the status of the stateless person was characterized by no nationality, whereas that of the refugee was determined by his having lost diplomatic protection.[54] He was clearly splitting hairs. Yet the attempts to define the difference between refugees and the stateless represented a new phase of the crisis.

French officials established a hierarchy of need in justifying how they distributed visas granting entry into the country. They recognized only two groups of refugees—those who possessed German nationality and those who carried the Nansen passport. The French foreign minister Joseph Paul Nicour instructed the French consulate in Germany to liberally grant visas to Nansen refugees, including Russians, Greeks, and Armenians. According to Nicour, the situation of the stateless refugees "is even more precarious than that of the German Jews themselves."[55] Stateless people who did not have the Nansen passport were frequently expelled because they were not recognized as stateless. There were a number of officials who protested this policy, arguing that the "uprooted unfortunates" who had lost their nationality of origin—including Polish, Russian, or Romanian—as a result of war, migration, or political upheaval should also be exempt from expulsion.[56]

What did the refugee crisis mean for international politics? In an article in *International Affairs* from 1936, J. L. Rubenstein called for "the continuous existence of an international organization to deal with refugees." The previous few years had demonstrated the need for an international center concerned with the registration of refugees that could function as an employment bureau and stay in touch with governments, trade unions, and transport companies.[57] However, the leadership of the international refugee agencies argued that the crisis did not imply the need for a permanent organization that could provide international protection for anyone without the protection of a government. Sir Hubert Emerson, a former British imperial governor in India, took over leadership of the High Commission for Refugees as the organization expanded to incorporate the High Commission for German Refugees and the Nansen Office. In a 1939 address to the Intergovernmental Committee Dealing with Refugee Problems in Washington, DC, Emerson discussed expanding the work of the commission to include all refugees, not only those from the former Russian Empire. Emerson warned against the impulse to naturalize the existence of refugees as an inevitable feature of modern life. According to Emerson, the real goal of the organization had to be finding a permanent national home for stateless people and to "convert refugees into citizens." Only a more defined group of people who could not be resettled on a large scale would continue to require international assistance, which represented a responsibility that could be delegated to an international refugee authority.[58]

The urgency of establishing an organization to provide assistance and protection to refugees on a more permanent basis, and of clarifying the distinction between refugees and stateless persons, appeared vividly in John Hope Simpson's influential 1939 study *The Refugee Problem: Report of a Survey*. Simpson, a British liberal politician who had served as the vice president of the British Refugee Settlement Committee in Greece during the 1920s, distinguished stateless persons, as an "important and unfortunate class," from the class of "refugees."[59] Simpson had been commissioned by the Royal Institute of International Affairs in London in 1937 to prepare a survey of refugee populations and of the countries of asylum. He cited Red Cross rolls and the records of refugee organizations, as well as official statistics provided by the countries of asylum and the League of Nations.[60] Drawing on these materials, Simpson argued that both groups deserved the protection of the League of Nations but that remedies should be pursued separately. According to Simpson, refugees were characterized by the fact that they "did not enjoy the protection of their government or country of origin." In many cases, refugees may have become stateless, but this was neither a necessary nor sufficient condition to be defined as a refugee.[61]

IV

The Hague Codification Conference and its aftermath was only part of the picture. As we saw in Chapter 3, legal theorists who confronted mass statelessness in the 1920s saw it as fundamentally linked to wider debates about the foundations of political and legal order. In order to grasp how the crises of the 1930s informed reflections on the concept of statelessness, it is necessary to contend with the transatlantic realist challenge to the abstract and philosophical approach to law embodied by Hans Kelsen and his students.

Debates about legal theory and international law among Kelsen and his students continued in exile. The migration of European legal scholars to escape fascism initiated a new phase in the conceptualization of statelessness. In the 1930s, realist challenges to formalism began to more directly target legalist approaches to international law and political order. Kelsen came under particular attack in these years for failing to account for the fact that what we encounter as morality or law are both rooted in custom and practice rather than in a prior logical norm.[62] Kelsen's doctrine had, according to a reviewer in the *Archives de philosophie du droit et de sociologie juridique*, suffered vigorous attack in the last years, and had "ceded ground" to the new principle of "reality."[63] Legal realism's challenge to formalism preceded the First World War, when a generation of legal theorists across the Atlantic revolted in varying ways against the idea that judicial decisions represented the deductive application of rules and began to pay more attention to the foundation of law in power, history, and custom. They argued that legal outcomes ought to depend on sociological and political considerations and on the social impact of judicial decisions. In the United States, legal realists challenged the classical liberal insistence that judicial application of common rules created genuine equality under the law. They rejected the "formal style" based on the premise that judicial decision followed a deductive form of analysis, since adjudication and the application of rules cannot take place without recourse to policy arguments or the assessment of principle. Debates over formal law crystalized in the United States amid controversies over the expansion of the administrative apparatus of the welfare state; however, the challenge to formalism occupied legal theorists and shaped debates about the nature of law across the Atlantic.[64] By attacking legal abstractions and metaphysical claims about personhood, legal realists sought to uncover the relations of power that such theory concealed, and they articulated this attack in world historical terms. For Felix Cohen, an American legal realist, arguments about corporate personhood symbolized an age "in which thought without roots in reality was an object of high esteem." When the US Supreme Court, for example, argued that a labor union is a legal person and can therefore be sued, the court veiled its own role in recognizing the union as a legal entity. It obscured the creative power of the court by indicating that the court simply recognized an entity that already existed.[65]

The concept of substance as opposed to form became important to a number of academic fields after the turn of the century and took on a distinctly political meaning. Understanding politics required confronting the fact that it represented the clash of wills. As theorists began to emphasize this feature of domestic and international relations, they portrayed the domain of law as problematic in one of two ways: either as saturated with political will—though a will that was often hidden behind the abstraction of legal argument—or as ineffectual in the face of willful decision and action. In his doctoral dissertation from 1936, the German legal scholar Wilhelm Grewe observed that formalist jurisprudence had begun to collapse in the face of a science of law attuned to the reality of social existence. Instead of building a "normative illusory world of law," legal theorists had begun turning to "the concrete forms of community" and the "law creating forces of a nation in general."[66] Carl Schmitt's search for the "substance" of the nation, for example, represented a direct attack on legal formalism.[67] In his 1933 essay, "Forms of Modern Imperialism in International Law," Schmitt argued that the League of Nations served as the burial ground for the repertoires and languages of rule underpinning European imperialism. The new age characterized by the dominance of American power, he predicted, would be governed by the principle of the sovereign equality of states under international law rather than civilizational difference. Since the early 1920s, Schmitt had emphasized the way the formal and technical features of law concealed the fact that its creation and enforcement depended on power.

By the mid-1930s, students of international law who had studied with Kelsen began to align themselves with Schmitt's views, against those of their mentor. Criticism of Kelsen by his intimate associates established the foundation of the realist theory of international relations. Hans Herz grappled with Kelsen's legal theory through the 1930s. In his writing from this period, Herz argued that the question of how to comprehend the legal continuity of a state after regime change or revolution was central to comprehending the primacy of international law.[68] Kelsen and his students insisted on the capacity of legal analysis to redefine the threshold of the state. Only international law, Kelsen had argued in his writings on the legal concept of the state, could determine its borders. But by the mid-1930s, Herz had become thoroughly skeptical of Kelsen's legal theory. Herz, who had been Kelsen's research assistant and student in Cologne, began distancing himself from Kelsen's legal philosophy after joining him in exile in Geneva. Along with Hans Morgenthau, Herz became one of the founders of the discipline of international relations in the United States. He began to develop a theory of international relations that claimed to be more firmly oriented toward the reality of power politics.[69] By the time he emigrated to the United States, Herz began to argue that the previous decade had proved decisively "how far international law is but a barely veiled legal and ideological superstructure raised upon the political relationships of power."[70]

Morgenthau, a German Jewish legal and political theorist, similarly attacked Kelsen's legal theory in 1934 during his exile in Geneva.[71] In Weimar Germany, Morgenthau worked with Hugo Sinzheimer and other socialist lawyers developing social and labor regulation in an effort to move Germany toward social democracy.[72] This group distinguished between formal legal equality and the social reality of dependence and inequality but relied on formal law and legal interpretation to transform the state. In 1929, Morgenthau argued that the static nature of international law did not take into account political and social change, putting weaker states in the position of having to "abide for all eternity to norms privileging the great powers." By the time he reached Geneva, however, Morgenthau targeted legal formalism in general and Kelsen in particular, faulting formalists for failing to pay attention to social phenomena. Determining the status of Czechoslovakia, for example, was never a matter of the interpretation of law but rather a political demand. Morgenthau rejected international law altogether as a relevant factor in the regulation of politics, turning toward psychological explanations for the dynamics of power and political conflict.

By 1938, Alfred Zimmern, a British theorist of international relations, described international lawyers as subsisting in a "permanent condition of malaise."[73] Their malaise can surely be attributed to a number of factors, including the growing evidence of the League's failure to successfully prevent further conflict. But the criticism of Kelsen's legal theory, especially its failure to incorporate social reality and the nature of power, resonated with a wider assault on legal fictions and juridical forms of identification across the Atlantic. One essay on legal personality from 1938 by an American legal academic compared the nonsensical and politically dubious use of the term "legal subjects of rights" with the abstractions of the Vienna School. "This 'subject' is so dreadfully apt to spin an 'object' out of its entrails and then the game is up. We are slipping with gathering momentum into the bottomless pit where the gorgons and chimeras of 'pure' law disport themselves."[74]

Against the gathering storm of criticism, Kelsen tried to clarify the antimetaphysical bent of his theory. He criticized the immoderate use of the concept of a "juristic person" as only a metaphor that supplied an aid for thinking. By misinterpreting the anthropomorphic metaphor, jurists "created sham problems whose solution jurisprudence vainly attempts"—the same argument proposed by Joseph Kohler to clarify the concept of the legal person in an earlier moment of debate.[75] The law, Kelsen pleaded, creates obligations and rights but does not create persons.[76] Kelsen did not back down in the face of the argument that what societies describe as "law" is only an expression of more profound social or power dynamics, and he sought to defend his theory against the claim that it exemplified the tendency of formalist legal thought to lapse into pointless, or dangerous, abstraction.

By the end of the 1930s, Kelsen faced insistent criticism from legal scholars who would become the influential founders of the realist theory of international relations, a tradition that took root in the United States as émigré international lawyers and political scientists took refuge from fascism

STATELESSNESS: A MODERN HISTORY

in American universities, government, and think tanks. The demise of the League of Nations and what it had stood for represented the fatal breakdown of the fragile legitimacy that had sustained the various experiments in international governance that it had initiated. The realists were the first to articulate the idea that internationalism up to the 1930s had rested on ideological faith in European civilization. In *The Twenty Years Crisis* (1939), the English historian and journalist E. H. Carr elaborated the relationship between law, morality, and politics. The idea that law represented a field morally superior to politics represented a "common illusion" of the age; law was politics by other means, and what made law unique was its capacity to confer stability on political society. It was the basis of organized political life but no more than that. As Carr argued persuasively, many acts of discrimination were undertaken legally: "It is not in itself any more moral to deprive Jews of their property by a law to that effect than simply to send storm troopers to evict them." Laws could be ethical but only if they sought to effect a good intention. Carr's interpretation of the crisis contributed to one influential view of the interwar era as a period that nourished dangerous idealism about international relations and the capacity of law to tame power politics.[77] Carr reduced the League's international experiment in governance to the heedless faith in progress and technocratic know-how, but he failed to account for the nature of the legal consciousness that the League helped sustain but did not create.

The League became associated with idealism in the sense that the organization, at least rhetorically, stood for the promise of international cooperation; it became identified with the expectation that politics should be oriented toward achieving the good rather than forestalling the terrible. And as the organization failed to prevent the Japanese invasion of Manchuria, German rearmament and the annexation of Czechoslovakia, and discrimination against minorities, the promise of the League as the means to achieving peaceful coexistence dissipated, giving way to pessimism about the capacity of international organizations to prevent the turn to war. The United Nations, by contrast, was founded on the more realist principle that a group of Great Powers would remain responsible for ensuring the preservation of peace and the status quo.

Yet the significance of the evolution of legal thought extends beyond this familiar narrative of international institutions in the twentieth century. Realist skepticism of legal formalism played a critical role in discrediting a form of reasoning that accounted for the dynamic nature of membership. The idea of nationality as a legal fiction that nonetheless conferred real security likewise seemed increasingly dubious in light of the particular situation of those in flight from fascism. Legal scholars in Europe and the United States involved in the international response to the European refugee crisis began to reexamine the tendency to emphasize the formal national link between individuals and states in the face of Nazi and Vichy nationality laws, which stripped Jews of their citizenship but preserved their status as legal subjects.[78] The emphasis placed on the formal category of legal nationality diminished as a more substantive connection between state and subject came to seem more vital. The Nazi regime applied nineteenth-century imperial legal practices to Europe, which undermined international legal thinking on the question of statelessness.[79] The majority of European refugees in the 1930s were Jews who retained their formal legal connection to Germany. The Nuremberg Laws defined a substantive conception of citizenship by distinguishing between nationality as legal membership and more robust forms of national belonging. After 1938, the question became whether Jews could even be defined as formal subjects since they had lost all semblance of political protection. From the perspective of the municipal laws of Germany, however, they never lost their ties of loyalty to the Reich and remained "Jewish subjects of the state."[80] In September 1939, anyone with significant assets that would be lost if they became a citizen of another state also became subject to denationalization. There was some concern that depriving Jews of citizenship would hinder their emigration, as countries were less likely to accept stateless immigrants.[81] In 1941, National Socialist jurists developed the legal framework for deportation and for stripping Jewish subjects of their German nationality, turning them into stateless subjects, once the deportation trains crossed the Reich frontier.[82]

Yet the question of how the boundaries of membership should be defined in international law remained in flux. Jurists turned from prioritizing formal membership to scrutinizing the nature of the connection between the state to an individual it claimed to represent. Depending on the context, nationality or a passport could be a meaningless "scrap of paper" or life-saving technology. In some cases, identification with a particular state is more of a burden then formal statelessness. The Harvard political philosopher Judith Shklar exemplified the predicament jurists sought to address when she and her family sought refuge in the United States in 1941. Born in Riga, the capital of the Latvian republic founded in 1918 after the dissolution of the Russian Empire, Shklar fled on the eve of the Second World War only to be detained as an alien without citizenship when she and her family arrived in Seattle before reaching safe harbor in Montreal.[83] In response to this dilemma, legal writers who continued to theorize the relationship between statelessness and international law transformed the terms of the problem by moving away from the idea of statelessness as a test case for the nature of the state and its sovereignty. Instead, they proposed that control over the definitions of nationality and national attachments could be explicitly placed in the hands of an international authority.[84]

The evolving significance of nationality in the era of fascism compelled Josef Kunz and his contemporaries to reconsider the role that international law might play in regulating nationality. However, they did so in the particular terms of the theoretical debates about legal realism that rose to prominence in the 1930s. Kunz had received funding from the Rockefeller Foundation to visit the United States in 1931 for a yearlong fellowship to research the "law of war of neutrality, with specific reference to American conceptions of social economic war, of alien enemy legislation, of maritime law and neutrality."[85] When he returned to Vienna, Kunz continued to advocate on behalf of the *heimatlosen*, alongside representatives from the International Union of League Societies, the Women's International League for Peace and Freedom, the International Council of Women, the League for the Rights of Man, and the International Alliance of Women for Suffrage and Equal Citizenship.[86] Kunz left Vienna in 1932, returning to the United States to visit American law schools as he searched for an academic appointment. While he looked for an academic post in the United States, Kunz spent time at Harvard, where he taught Manley Hudson's class on international law. He took up a position at Toledo Law School in Ohio in 1934, which he would hold until his death in 1970.

From his new position in the United States, Kunz introduced the concept of a substantive link in response to the imposition of German nationality on denaturalized Jewish subjects. In his revised view of the international nature of nationality, Kunz stated, "Within the limits of international norms

... no state is allowed to confer its nationality upon individuals who are not reasonably connected with the state in question."[87]

By the end of the 1930s, therefore, the scale of the European refugee crisis—as well as the particular predicament facing people compelled to flee from fascism who retained their prior national status—transformed the significance of statelessness for international thought. Legal theorists began to focus on the possibility of establishing an international authority with the power to adjudicate disputes over national status. Shortly after arriving in the United States from Vienna, the legal scholar Maximilian Koessler applied for funding from a New York–based independent research institute, the Social Science Research Council, to write a monograph on "nationality under international law." Koessler had worked as a lawyer in Vienna before leaving Austria for the United States in 1938. Before that, he graduated from the University of Czernowitz, which had been the capital of the Bukovina region on the outskirts of the Habsburg Empire before it became part of Romania after 1918.[88] The topic he proposed to the Social Science Research Council was close to the subjects taken up by the theorists of the Vienna School of Law and had become even more politically urgent since he left Vienna.

Koessler defined his topic as an examination of the limits that international law could impose on the scope of domestic control with regard to questions of nationality, especially in reference to the refugee problem and to the situation of persons without nationality.[89] He stated that the status of the "non-citizen national" would be the central object of his investigation because of the potential for international law to regulate nationality as opposed to citizenship, which could only come under the control of municipal law. Koessler sought proof for a substantive distinction between nationality and citizenship, which for him meant delineating a space in which international law had control over the boundaries of naturalization. In his proposal, he cited evidence to support the idea that in international law the concept of nationality was "materially distinguished from municipal law."[90] Koessler introduced the idea that international legal control over nationality implied that an international body possessed the authority to adjudicate whether nationality reflected a substantive connection between the individual and the state or was only a formal connection that unjustly bound an individual to a state that had effectively repudiated its responsibility to protect. He proposed to examine "whether international law is bound to recognize a nationality which by the provisions of the respective municipal law has become a hollow, if not farcical concept."[91] According to Koessler, "a person who is so alienated from this state and so fully disenfranchised by the latter, that international law cannot consider such an individual as still bound to retain his nationality of origin, may become stateless under international law."[92] By emphasizing the social connections that tied an individual to a state, Koessler indicated that this relationship had to rest on something more substantial than a state's willingness to acknowledge an individual as a national.

The urgent need to provide protection generated more support for a distinct legal category that defined the victims of persecution. Whether someone possessed the formal markers of nationality no longer sufficed; the refugee crisis in the 1930s compelled legal writers to contemplate the substantive ways a person could be counted as a member of a state and what happened when those ties were broken in all but name. At the same time, the realist criticism of the approach to law and politics embodied by Kelsen and his students resonated with the evolving terms of the crisis. As we will see in Chapter 5, the onset of the Second World War recast the meaning of statelessness, compelling theorists to reframe its significance for the future of world order.

In the years that followed, theorists of international law and nationality—including Koessler and Kunz—would be compelled to revisit Kelsen's challenge to the idea that social realities determine legal membership in a state. Kelsen's legal theory had been pivotal in establishing the significance of differentiating the sphere of the juridical from that of the sociological since his central objective had been to comprehend the distinctive normativity of law. As we will see, understanding the loss of nationality as a deprivation in moral terms, and as a problem of international order and collective security, depended on the preservation of the distinctiveness of these domains.

5

A Condition of World Order

IN THE AUTUMN OF 1940, bombs rained down on London relentlessly. The Luftwaffe began striking the city on September 7 and continued its attack for the next fifty-seven nights. Amid the bombing, a group of international lawyers calling themselves the Committee on Stateless Persons began meeting in central London. Formed under the auspices of the Grotius Society, a British professional association established in 1915 for the study of international law, the committee set out to assess how the outbreak of the war had changed what it meant to possess a nationality and whether they could conceptualize the legal issues afresh even as the future of international order remained profoundly uncertain.[1] London at that time teemed with political exiles forming interim governments, supporting resistance movements on the European continent, and envisioning possibilities for the future of statehood, empire, and international society. The exiles, from France as well as from Central European states under Nazi occupation, carried the remnants of states on their backs. Their governments functioned by the grace of British hospitality; recognition as a representative of a government in exile at a garden party at Buckingham Palace became one of the temporary symbols of statehood. In this context, the Committee on Stateless Persons sought to contribute their expertise not only to the immediately pressing questions about nationality that had emerged with the outbreak of the war but also to wider debates about the future of world order.[2]

The 1940s are usually associated with the moment when individuals became the subjects of international legal order and when international law began to make inroads into the sovereign domain of states.[3] However, without examining the place occupied by statelessness in these deliberations we cannot properly identify the transformation of international legal thought around the status of individuals in international law. This chapter and Chapter 6 trace the evolution of the significance of statelessness for theories of international law and global order from the outbreak of the Second World War through the creation of the postwar legal frameworks that define what it means to be a refugee or a stateless person. In this chapter I focus on the period from 1940 through the creation of the Universal Declaration of Human Rights in 1948. During and immediately after World War II statelessness once again became central to debates about rights and the postwar order, but the problem was more readily mobilized in this period to advocate for the validity of the sovereign state as the primary source of rights and law, rather than as evidence for the future of non-state political order. The jurists who had considered the legal status of the stateless as the key to unlocking the nature of international legal order in the interwar period now made the sovereign state the premise of their analysis of rights and legal order. The legal category of statelessness thus became bound up in a new way with the idea of rights and the boundaries of political order in this period as the lawyers who contributed to the institutional development of international law and human rights after the war understood their work as part of the development of a new world order premised on sovereign equality. This chapter investigates how legal debate evolved during the Second World War and situates the wider turn among international legal scholars toward ensuring a basic right to possess a nationality, a right ultimately enshrined in the Universal Declaration of Human Rights in 1948. Though legal scholars continued to emphasize the role of international law in the protection of the individual, even in ensuring that individuals possess some nationality, these discussions indicate how broader criticism of interwar legalism and the revaluation of state sovereignty informed their perspective on the meaning of statelessness and the arguments they put forward about its significance for international politics. As we will see, international legal writers began to move away from tying the supremacy of international law to the problem of statelessness, linking it in other ways to the political organization of humanity. The first part of the chapter shows how debate evolved from 1941 to 1945, while the second section turns to a discussion of how the postwar problem of statelessness became bound up with debate about the future of world order. The third section discusses the inclusion of a right to a nationality in the Universal Declaration of Human Rights, which was articulated in the context of the entrenchment of the doctrine of sovereign equality as the central principle underlying interstate order. The final section turns to the political

156

theorist Hannah Arendt's postwar reflections on the stateless, contextualizing her analysis of rights and citizenship within wider critical reflection from the period. Though Arendt rejected the interwar legalist approach to political order associated with international thought after World War I, she portrayed statelessness as a fundamental problem of global politics, a position that would become increasingly marginalized in the succeeding postwar decades.

I

Many of the central theorists of statelessness discussed in the preceding chapters fled from fascist regimes or chose to escape Europe once the war began. War constrained the networks of international legal debate but lawyers nevertheless continued to carefully tend their established transatlantic partnerships. Between 1940 and 1943, Hersch Lauterpacht served as the linchpin linking the British and the American international legal communities, traveling to the United States in 1940–1941 to drum up support for international law before returning to Britain to take part in discussions as a member of the Committee on Stateless Persons. The Carnegie Endowment for International Peace had invited Lauterpacht to undertake a lecture tour in autumn 1940 to promote the teaching of international law in law schools, which at the time was not part of the regular curriculum in Britain or the United States. Josef Kunz had undertaken a similar grand tour of American law schools between 1932 and 1934 funded by a Rockefeller Foundation grant.[4] In the course of his visit to nine law schools across the country, Lauterpacht attempted to drive home the point that American and British courts were often called on to decide issues involving the application of international law and to highlight the importance of its progressive development.[5]

Lauterpacht's American colleagues hoped that his visit would inspire support for the study of international law in the United States but they were also concerned that his trip threatened US neutrality, and that Lauterpacht would press the case for intervention in World War II during his travels. Philip Jessup, at that time the director of the Carnegie Endowment's International Law Division, met with Lauterpacht when he arrived in New York and asked him not to speak of the war during his public meetings in such a way as to "suggest a role for the United States." Behind the scenes, Jessup assured Manley Hudson of Lauterpacht's pledge not to do so, indicating the collective worry among the American branch of the international legal profession that their European counterparts would compromise American neutrality.[6] This concern was not unfounded since Lauterpacht received financial support from the British Foreign Office, who wanted his trip to motivate American support for the British war effort. He had even more personal reasons to advocate for American intervention due to his worry about the fate of his remaining family in Poland, and the danger facing his wife and son in Cambridge during the Blitz.[7] Lauterpacht's objective for the trip clearly went beyond the official goal of promoting the study of international law, though he remained committed to the broader project to further develop the field and the profession. As we will see, in the years that followed his visit he became increasingly impatient with the idea that the stateless embodied the possibility of rights beyond those granted by the state through citizenship and the capacity of international law to confer rights directly to individuals without nationality.

Even among the community who remained committed to the importance of international law and its development, the subject of statelessness no longer occupied the central theoretical position it had served in international thought in the interwar years. After his emigration to the United States, Mark Vishniak provided a clear assessment of how the study of statelessness had transformed in the years since his systematic analysis of the subject in his 1933 lecture at The Hague on the legal condition of the *apatride*. Vishniak had fled from France in 1940 one week before the German Army entered Paris. When he arrived in the United States, he resumed his writing on statelessness, revising and updating his 1933 study.[8] Vishniak's draft manuscript, eventually published in 1945 under the auspices of the American Jewish Committee, elucidates the shift in his own thinking, as well as a broader change in the significance of statelessness for theorists of international law.[9] In his writing and public speaking engagements before his emigration to the United States, Vishniak had portrayed the League of Nations as a platform or parliament in which minorities could defend their interests. He had put forward a similar claim about how the stateless had become a distinct legal group within international public law. In Chapter 3, we saw how Vishniak's 1933 lecture presented the phenomenon of statelessness as a "pathogen" that illuminated the anatomy of the state. The stateless, and the legal and political rights they were able to exercise even without national status, provided critical evidence for debates about sovereignty and the nature of the state and international society. However, in the draft of his new work on statelessness from 1941, Vishniak lamented that the problem of statelessness had lost its powerful heuristic significance as much for international legal scholars as for statesmen and policy makers, bitterly noting that "the stateless of recent times is the step-child, not of the scientific literature and domestic legislation alone, but of international law too."[10]

In his writings from the period after his emigration to the United States, Vishniak began to move away from the analysis of the legal significance of statelessness that characterized his earlier approach. Reflecting on the decades in which mass statelessness emerged as a feature of international politics, Vishniak wrote, "When the ranks of stateless people were swelled in Europe, the consequences were world wide. No country could fully isolate itself from this phenomenon, and none could render statelessness harmless or prevent it by independent action."[11] Like many of those who had advocated for the establishment of a permanent international agency for refugee relief in the 1930s, he framed his argument in terms of the wider issue of international order and security. The centrality of statelessness for international politics, according to Vishniak, rested on its constitutive internationalism, on the fact that it represented a collective problem that demanded a collective response.

Vishniak was not entirely correct in his assertion that statelessness had become the "step-child" of international law or legal theory. However, he identified an important shift in the significance of statelessness for international thought, particularly after the United States entered the war in December 1941. As we already saw in Chapter 4, legal writers began to portray statelessness in terms of the sovereignty of international law over nationality in a way that represented a departure from the international legal thought of the 1920s, when jurists had argued that the status of individuals without a nationality hinged on what kinds of agents counted as subjects of international law. By the later 1930s, with the acceleration of the European refugee crisis, they envisioned an international legal authority with the power to adjudicate nationality claims rather than defining the nature of sovereignty in terms of the logical limits of the concept. In light of the real plight of those who retained their formal connection to the Nazi state but lost the protection of nationality, the mere marks of national membership began to appear dangerously fictional, divorced from reality in any meaningful sense.

However, the novel status of sovereignty in international thought took shape in the context of the ideological vision of international order promoted by the Allied powers. Even before the United States formally declared war the planning for the postwar order had already commenced. The joint Anglo-American effort to create a blueprint for the postwar order began with the Atlantic Charter in 1941, a watershed document that helped establish the ideological terms with which the Allies would wage the war of ideas against the Nazis.[12] The Atlantic Charter proclaimed a conception of world order premised on the centrality of sovereignty and the state. Directed toward Nazi-occupied Europe, the Charter asserts, "the states of the world form a community of states and the protection and advancements of their common interests requires continuous development of the organization of the community."[13] The vision of the Atlantic community evoked by Roosevelt and Churchill initiated new plans for reimagining the order that defines interstate relations. In this ideological setting, Hans Kelsen and Léon Duguit—the French jurist whose sociological jurisprudence and state theory was equally influential in the interwar period—came under particular attack in transatlantic political thought for undermining the concept of state sovereignty.

Kelsen arrived in New York in June 1940. In exile, he returned to the questions about the foundations of statehood and its relationship to international law. Only after the collapse of the French Front did he ask his US contacts to help him obtain a position in the United States. The Supreme Court justice Felix Frankfurter, himself a Viennese immigrant, had introduced the Harvard jurist Roscoe Pound to Kelsen's work in the 1920s, and it was Pound that Kelsen asked to find a position for him in the United States after his expulsion from the German University of Prague. Pound was able to furnish Kelsen with a temporary position as the Oliver Wendell Holmes lecturer at Harvard Law School, supported in part by the Rockefeller Foundation. Despite his transatlantic prominence, Kelsen remained in a precarious position professionally because of the damage sustained by his intellectual reputation in the 1930s. It is striking that the file on Kelsen created by the Rockefeller Foundation, which kept records of all the refugee scholars who applied to the organization for assistance moving to the United States,

states that the "irrelevance of his philosophical approach when war conditions have weakened American law schools make him a difficult problem."[14] As the Foundation predicted, finding Kelsen a new academic home in the United States would prove difficult.

Kelsen was, however, given an opportunity to try out for a more permanent position at Harvard when he delivered the Oliver Wendell Holmes lectures at the law school in 1940–1941, though the substance of his lectures did little to endear him to the faculty. Kelsen's lecture, titled "Peace Through Law," returned to the theme that had defined his signature intellectual approach to the study of law and the state, and shaped his response to the problem of statelessness in post–World War I central Europe. As the audience contemplated American involvement in yet another global conflict Kelsen presented the problems of peace and war, and the potential of international law to regulate international society, in terms of his prior theoretical presuppositions about the nature of political and social order. Against the argument that the breakdown of the League and the outbreak of war had shown that only an international community based on fellow feeling would preserve peace, Kelsen returned to his earlier claims about the foundations of social order resting on the fact that it is "the order itself that regulates the conduct of these individuals." Individuals, he went on, "comprise a group, a community, only to the extent that their mutual conduct is regulated by an order. Without this order they are a chaotic, structureless mass."[15] In any case, establishing any facts about international phenomena, Kelsen insisted, still depended on prior legal recognition. As he wrote, "it is cognition rather than re-cognition. It has the same character as the establishment of a legally relevant fact by a court."[16] The practical focus of American law schools meant that Kelsen's European-style expertise—combining jurisprudence, philosophy, and political theory—would never have been an easy fit in US law faculties. However, the hostility that his lecture provoked suggests that his vision of the regulative properties of legal order appeared particularly out of step with the times.[17]

By 1941 European émigré political scientists theorizing the future of democracy presented the war as a referendum on the pluralist theory of the state. Though Kelsen's theory was not pluralist, his theory of law and the state became fatefully associated with the critique of sovereignty. Policy intellectuals and refugee academics sought to rescue a conception of political community that broke with prewar concerns about legal personality and the political autonomy of groups within the state. Notably, when they initially faced the challenge of describing and analyzing the Nazi state as a type of political regime, theorists initially presented it within the paradigmatic interwar criticism of the orthodox theory of sovereignty. The Nazi state, like other states, represented a product of human imagination and law that assumed monstrous proportions when attributed with real powers. Carl J. Friedrich, a German political theorist from Harvard, for example, used terminology familiar from the post–World War I era to analyze the Nazi state. For Friedrich, Nazi Germany was just one example of the dangers of metaphysical abstractions and idolatrous worship. "The contemporary mind," he wrote, "has made the 'state' into a golden calf of misplaced concreteness." Friedrich placed Stalin and Hitler in the same tradition as Hobbes, Rousseau, and Bentham and attributed the adulation of the state to the decline of Christian faith.[18] He insisted along the lines of the interwar critique of sovereignty that proper methods of analysis would reveal the state for what it was; once stripped bare of its adornments and inflated proportions, the state would be less of a bogeyman. In other words, in the initial evaluation of Nazism for the theory of the state, theorists deployed the more familiar idea from the interwar era that the excesses of state power derived from the human impulse to project fantasies of divine authority and power to the state.

But soon after, theorists began to insist on the value of the sovereign state, and European exiles played a critical role in preserving the centrality of the state for political science. Political scientists, especially émigrés from Germany and Austria, provided a significant challenge to the critique of sovereignty that Kelsen had begun to represent. Any constraints on sovereign power would now have to be institutionalized, made real through practice and agreements that transformed state interaction. In 1942, Heinz Eulau, a German émigré political theorist trained in Berkeley, intervened in what he called the "contemporary crisis in the theory of sovereignty" in which he repudiated the distinction propagated in the 1920s between legal and political sovereignty by directly attacking Kelsen and Duguit. Despite the important doctrinal distinctions between the two jurists, Eulau placed them both within the same interwar tradition that had "depersonalized" the concept of sovereignty in order to expose the state as the product of "mythological thinking." Both theorists, Eulau argued, had missed the opportunity to develop a conception of political community that did not fall prey either to a depersonalized conception of sovereignty or to the dangerous idea of an organic collective will. In their haste to prove either that an organic unity knit together an international social order (in Duguit's case) or that the force of law within independent states depended on a prior international legal norm (in Kelsen's), both had missed what Eulau called the "democratic constitutional state," an entity "based on the consent of the people to be governed by its elected or appointed representatives." It was this kind of political community, Eulau insisted, that required a new robust theory—a resacralization of the practice of politics. In order to counter Carl Schmitt's powerful assertions about the nature of sovereign authority, the theory would need to prove theoretically persuasive as well as serve as what Eulau called "a fighting weapon in the struggle of ideologies." In this vein, Eulau argued that the theory of totalitarianism would "shield a conception of a state political community untainted by the crimes of fascism."[19] In Eulau's presentation, the introduction of the concept of totalitarianism facilitated the revaluation of state sovereignty by asserting a radical break between the normal functioning of sovereignty and the distortion of the state at the hands of totalitarian regimes. The Nazi Empire had highlighted the virtues of sovereignty and the danger of undermining the ultimate control of political communities over their own fate. By describing the Nazi state as totalitarian, a liberal democratic vision of sovereign authority over individuals and civil society would be safeguarded.[20]

Other émigré political scientists in the United States noted the transformation in the tone and substance of discussions of sovereignty, which stood in striking contrast to the popularity of the attack on the sovereign state in the period after World War I. In an article from 1942, Erich Hula, a Viennese émigré who had also been Kelsen's student and research assistant, argued that the question for postwar planners was how to define the legitimate boundaries of the state's legal independence in relation to other states. Hula had followed Kelsen to Cologne in 1931 and emigrated in 1938 to Prague and then Geneva before reaching the United States, where he took up a position at the New School for Social Research.[21] According to Hula, the war had not proved the dangers of the sovereign state. He cautioned that much of the literature on postwar reconstruction mistakenly applied the term *sovereignty* when the objects of their criticism should have been Hitler and Germany. "The sovereign state," Hula stated, "is not only under the attack of the internationalists, but also of the racists in Europe and as well as in other continents."[22] In a later analysis, Hula emphasized the distinction between "national self-determination" in the Atlantic Charter and the principle of national self-determination proclaimed after the First World War. These constituted, Hula insisted, "fundamentally different conceptions," and it was necessary to separate the principle that governments should be based on consent from the "principle of nationalities" that had inspired the interwar population transfers carried out under the Treaty of Lausanne.[23] By 1944, Otto Kirchheimer, a political theorist associated with the Frankfurt School, declared that "fashion in political theory seems to change quickly in our days. Hardly more than ten to fifteen years have elapsed since the state was declared moribund in pluralistic theories."[24]

The revaluation of the sovereign state—against the dominant perspective of the post–World War I years—took place in more academic, disciplinary contexts as well as in policy circles in the United States. James Ludlow, an American Foreign Service officer and later UN advisor, wrote a confidential report in 1943 that advocated the use of the term *state* rather than *nation* to describe a political community that was not subordinate to any other community. The term *state*, the report noted, was more accurate than *nation*, which implied ties of race or culture. One American vision for the postwar order included both the promotion of international law as a limitation on state action and the principle of nonintervention. Revitalizing and strengthening international law meant asserting that the sovereignty of a state would be subject to the limitations imposed by international legal order and that each state should have a legal duty to refrain from intervention in the internal affairs of other sovereigns.[25]

The analysis of sovereignty and international law among émigré political scientists and American policy experts illuminates the trajectory of the discussions about the legal significance of statelessness among the members of the Committee on Stateless Persons, the group mentioned at the beginning of this chapter. Their discussions about international law and nationality indicate the continued importance of statelessness for theoretical debates about the status and future of international law. The goal of the committee was to "prepare a study on the problem of stateless persons, their status and protection in circumstances which have increased their number and varied the causes of their condition."[26] However, these debates reveal how legal writers who had previously tried to undermine the statist premise of

164

international legal order now connected the question of statelessness with the state as the basis and foundation for rights. Those who had been most vocal in critiquing the doctrine of sovereignty before the war began to revalue the particular normative validity of the state.

Paul Weis joined the committee shortly after his release from a British internment camp. Born to a Jewish family in Vienna in 1907, Weis studied law at the University of Vienna, absorbing the legal philosophy of the Vienna School of Law from close range as Kelsen's research assistant. After leaving university, he spent a few years managing the family business before joining Vienna's social welfare administration as an arbitrator for the Austrian national health insurance board in 1934. As a member of the Austrian national bureaucracy responsible for delivering and managing the state's health insurance system, Weis confronted the predicament facing people without a claim to public welfare. These early encounters would have been at some remove from his own position as a member of Vienna's Jewish bourgeois elite. However, in 1938 Weis was sent to the Dachau concentration camp, and on obtaining release in 1939 he fled to Britain, where he was promptly interned in the Richborough Camp for enemy aliens in Kent before Britain decided to mobilize the prisoners as soldiers on the eve of the German invasion. Weis did not regain citizenship until 1947, when he naturalized as a British subject. It is worth noting here, though it will be discussed in greater detail in Chapter 6, that Weis wrote his doctoral dissertation under the supervision of Lauterpacht at the London School of Economics on nationality in international law. His book based on the dissertation, *Nationality and Statelessness in International Law*, published in 1956, is still considered the most authoritative study of the subject. Later in his career, Weis merged theory and practice when he agreed to serve as a legal advisor to the International Refugee Organization before becoming the head of the legal department at the United Nations High Commission for Refugees.[27]

In one of his first interventions in the Grotius Society debates on statelessness after joining the group in 1940, Weis pointed out that the discussions among committee members could only amount to speculation as long as the outlines of future international organization remained uncertain. The future of citizenship and noncitizenship depended on what the world would look like after the war. The work of the Committee on Stateless Persons was thus "inseparably bound up" with postwar political planning.[28] Rather than

165

the legal status of the stateless marking out a potential future for international legal order, which had been a central feature of the interwar discourse, its significance rested on other factors that would determine the ultimate shape of world politics.

The concept of human rights in turn appeared as a critical touchstone in the committee's speculations about the future of world order. However, these discussions indicate how international legal scholars understood the turn to human rights as a revision of the earlier emphasis among legal theorists on the nature of sovereignty and on the legal status of individuals as subjects of international law. Members of the committee disagreed over whether to support the idea of enforcing the principle that every individual should have a nationality or to de-emphasize nationality in favor of universal rights. Erwin Loewenfeld, a German émigré lawyer who had recently turned his legal practice to international questions, began his statement with the positivist orthodoxy that for individuals "who do not own a nationality, the principle link by which they could derive benefits from international law is missing and thus they lack protection, as far as international law is concerned. Their position is comparable to vessels on the open sea not sailing under the flag of a State." He suggested that they collect a survey of municipal and international legislation on nationality and attempt to write a charter of legal protection granting stateless persons a minimum of rights.[29] In the Grotius Society's revised draft on the proposed rules regarding nationality and the prevention of statelessness, the authors stated, "Every individual has a basic right to be born a national or subject of a state and thereby to obtain nationality which is recognized by the law of nations and forge the necessary link for his obtaining the benefits of that law."[30] A different member of the group, by contrast, objected privately to the committee's presentation of nationality as an all-important, universal, and inescapable condition of every individual since it signified submission to the statist foundations of individual rights.[31]

Discussants noted the self-conscious turn away from the antistatist, pluralist perspective that marked the analysis of statelessness in the interwar period. In his remarks before the Grotius Society, H. R. Pyke emphasized the idea that international lawyers should promote individual human rights rather than the rights of the "corporate body called the state." However, rather than focusing on the nature of state personality in order to determine the status of individuals, Pyke asked, "Is there anything inherently impossible, illogical, or impracticable in the conception of a system of international law which clothes an individual with legally enforceable rights against his own if not also other states?" He argued that it was the job of governments and politicians rather than lawyers to "establish the machinery of international government."[32] This was a striking turn from the idea that the science of international law was primarily a discipline for discerning the invisible mechanics of the system. Instead, Pyke identified the agents responsible for setting the rules of the game.

Discussions among the members of the American Society of International Law reflect some of the same dilemmas as well as the shared professional concern that international law had lost its hold as an important way of theorizing the state and international society. At a meeting of the society held in April 1941, Frederick Dunn, a professor of international law at Yale, proposed that the lack of protection for individuals was the principal reason that people held such a poor opinion of international law. Alwyn V. Freeman, an American legal scholar, disputed Dunn's reasoning and insisted that one had rights only as the national of some country. Lawyers should recognize the current limitations of international law and take steps to correct them rather than pretend that what was then aspirational was actually true.[33]

Lauterpacht, the figure perhaps most associated with the turn to human rights after the Second World War, likewise advocated a revision of the international legal community's prewar preoccupation with determining the subjects of international law. Though Lauterpacht was certainly one of the preeminent advocates in the postwar era for the doctrine of human rights and for international law as an instrument of individual rights claims, his understanding of these developments was wrapped up in his own concern about the problem of statelessness. From the late 1930s through the drafting of the Universal Declaration of Human Rights, Lauterpacht appealed to the problem of statelessness to argue for a more pragmatic approach to the question of who, or what, were the proper subjects of international legal order. By 1937, Lauterpacht began to look back on the cosmopolitan theories of the 1920s as part of a time that already lay deep in the past. An essay from that year gently put the full range of interwar intellectual legal innovation in its historical place. The impulse to assert the rights of groups against the state, he argued, only served to reinforce the idea of the real personality of the state itself. The trend after the war was to question the premise that sovereignty remained the foundation for international law. "The resulting development," he stated, "was described as the emancipation of the individual in the international sphere." And yet, the regular assertion that rights inhere in individuals rather than states amounted to little more than wishful thinking since "there was no attempt to answer these questions critically." Just because there was no agency, either national or international, to enforce the protection of the rights that international law grants to individuals as such did not mean that the individual did not have fundamental rights in the international sphere irrespective of nationality. Yet, if nationality remained the only link between the individual and the benefits of international law, then international law must "charge itself with securing the individual some nationality."[34]

The role of international organizations or agencies in the resolution of conflicts over national status would not impinge on the ultimate question of where sovereignty resides or what sovereignty means. Instead, such agencies would play a critical role in the resolution of a major humanitarian problem, as well as a problem of public and international order. In the draft produced by the Grotius Society members in 1942, Lauterpacht defined nationality as both the quality of being the subject of a certain state and the embodiment of the link between the state and the law of nations. Lauterpacht took it as given that there could be states that were not "soulless superstructures over and above the human group which forms its body." Since the state was not to be considered as such, the individual member of a state had an indirect and direct interest in international organization, and "through the medium of his nationality, that is to say his citizenship or membership . . . he can normally enjoy benefits from the existence of the law of nations." If nationality was indeed the link between the individual and enjoyment of the benefits of the law of nations, the individual was entitled to invoke the protection of the law of nations against the state that severed such a link. It was therefore essential, he asserted, that the protection of the individual against his own state be recognized as an international right.[35] According to Lauterpacht's formulation, international agreements would complete the protection gap experienced by the stateless. Conventions between states would limit the possibility of becoming stateless or mitigate the condition by providing international protection.

The French jurist René Cassin, who would become one of the legal architects of the postwar French state and of the Universal Declaration of

Human Rights, provided one of the clearest articulations of the view that international society should ensure a right to membership in a state. The evolution of his arguments about sovereignty and nationality further illustrates the broader transformation we have been tracing. In his lecture in The Hague in 1930 on the subject of domicile, Cassin cited the plight of Russian and Armenian refugees whose personal status had been thrown into doubt by war and revolution. Cassin argued that privileging domicile over nationality would mitigate the personal tragedies arising from the absence of citizenship.[36] Unlike some of the other proponents of a supreme unified international legal order, he did not rhetorically draw on statelessness to demonstrate the plausibility of legal personality outside the confines of the state.[37] Like Kelsen, he used statelessness to examine the legal boundaries of sovereignty and to prioritize territorial claims over other forms of collective membership.[38]

Cassin, however, understood the turn to the state as the condition for accessing international law among international legal publicists during World War II as a revision of the prewar approach. As president of the legal committee of the French government in exile, Cassin addressed questions of nationality for the resistance.[39] On November 5, 1942, the Vichy government published a decree stripping Charles de Gaulle, Pierre Mendès France, and other members of the Free French government of their nationality. The commissioner of justice of the Free French later wrote confidentially to Cassin in 1943 that the Vichy regime's denaturalization law of July 1940 should remain in effect after liberation.[40] At a meeting of the Society for French Combatants studying the intellectual and legal problems of the postwar order, the group proclaimed the "right of the individual to the state" and that "the state is the right of man. All men have the right to obtain integration in a particular state. No one can be deprived of their nationality unless they possess another one."[41] Cassin's position is not surprising given his loyalties to the French Empire and his later support for the establishment of a Jewish state. He endorsed plans to introduce more robust state programs for citizens after the war, and met with William Beveridge in March 1941 to discuss his vision for a new welfare system in Britain.[42] Yet the insistence on a specific right to the state represented a significant shift away from the argument he had offered about domicile as a solution to the problem of statelessness in 1930. Rather than advocating a different legal basis from which to conceptualize the boundaries of statehood, Cassin now made belonging to a state the foundation for rights.

Most of the lawyers who participated in these wartime meetings agreed that their emphasis should no longer be on the legal personality of the individual but rather on limiting the state's ability to deprive individuals of their only connection to international law. For some participants this move represented a dangerous retreat from the individualist cause. One participant in the Grotius Society meeting in 1944 on "The Law of Nations and the Individual" insisted that anyone promoting international protection for individual rights had injured this goal by "harping on the fact that you need to have a nationality before you acquire rights under international law."[43] Lauterpacht remarked that the time had come for more practical measures rather than theoretical reflection on the nature of international law itself. He stated that though he wished that the individual might be the subject of international law to a larger extent than at present, international law still permitted statelessness. Moreover, Lauterpacht mused, "it is possible that we are apt to attach too much importance to the question whether international law confers rights directly upon the individual and renders them enforceable at this instance (in which case he is a subject of international law) or whether benefits are conferred upon him through the instrumentality of his state and are made enforceable by it (in which case he is said to be an object of international law.)"[44] This question, which had been described by Lipovano in 1935 as the "question of questions," now seemed pedantic and insufficiently pragmatic.

II

Though the Second World War strengthened the concept of the sovereign state as a normative ideal, the prospects of global political organization remained far from determined from the perspective of those forecasting the future of international order. The future of citizenship and statelessness depended on how the map of the world would be reordered in the war's aftermath. The idea of federation represented one such option for the remaking of regional and international order. Multilayered government, with a palimpsest of legal jurisdictions, softened the problem of exclusion since a baggier form of citizenship within a federal system held out the promise of preserving associational life and the autonomy of communities. It represented an alternative mode of political organization that allowed people who did not feel they shared the same history to share a common territory.[45] Visions of federalism encompassed both liberal dreams of a free trading area as well as ambitions for establishing planned economies that combined dreams of a borderless Europe with social equality.[46] Clarence Streit's 1938 proposal for a federal union of democracies in the North Atlantic, envisioning a common citizenship and common currency, went through seventeen editions by 1940. Governments in exile, including those for Poland, Czechoslovakia, Yugoslavia, and Greece, likewise discussed European federation or regional confederation.[47] During the war, groups such as Federal Union and Student Federalists organized supporters around programs for universal world federation.[48] In 1943, the French government in exile under de Gaulle reached an agreement on the project for a regional federation in the West, and de Gaulle instructed his liberation committee to study "the project for a federation of western Europe."[49]

Evaluating the meaning of statelessness in this context therefore depended on whether Europe would become a union or federation at the end of the war. As Vishniak observed, if the plans for "union now" or "world federation" were achieved after the war, it would be easier to solve the problem of statelessness because a stateless person could claim European citizenship.[50] Jacob Robinson, a Jewish legal scholar from Lithuania who wrote prolifically on international questions and was part of a Zionist group in the United States, emphasized the challenge of outlining the future of international minority protection when the future of international order remained so uncertain.[51] Should they assume that postwar Europe would be territorially organized on the basis of nation-states? Would it be territorially organized into nation-states but governed by a universal organization like the League of Nations? Would it be a federation, as so many dreamed it would become, or would the postwar world be characterized by a "Pax Britannica," in which part of Europe would be supervised by a modified mandate system after proving unfit for democratic organization and institutions?[52] It was not clear whether the system of minority rights protection would be revived in Eastern Europe, expanded to other regions, or dissolved altogether.[53]

Such plans did not meet with agreement by the United States and the Soviet Union, who had already begun to envision a different basis for postwar international organization. Roosevelt and Stalin resisted the plans envisioned by the governments in exile and by members of the European resistance for a postwar federation. Instead, they promoted an alternative vision based on the idea that the security of the international states system was to be ensured by preserving the sanctity of state boundaries. In late 1944, representatives of Britain, China, the United States, and the Soviet Union met at Dumbarton Oaks to prepare the UN Charter. At Bretton Woods in July 1944, the Allies had established the main institutions of the postwar economic order, the International Monetary Fund and the International Bank for Reconstruction and Development.

Though some nationalist movements turned decidedly toward statebuilding in the early years of the Second World War and away from other postimperial alternatives, the nation-state—based on the idea of equality for all citizens and tightly bounded borders—hardly seemed a foregone conclusion after 1945. The democratic left, including socialists and left-wing Catholics, in Europe continued to promote the dream of a united Europe. Countries decimated by the war sought an influx of population and labor in these years—even as some of them, like Czechoslovakia and Poland, sought a more homogeneous population—and with the blessing of Britain and the United States they imported thousands of Italian workers.[54] Colonial subjects seeking autonomy and independence also put forward plans for postimperial federations.[55] Both the British and French empires reconceptualized the relationship between metropole and periphery by reforming the political structure of rule over nonwhite subjects. In 1946, the French Empire was renamed the French Union, and its colonies became part of a complex state in which political status was unevenly distributed. The federal structure of the Union was made possible by these new negotiated forms of belonging and the redefinition of legal statuses, rather than fully equal French citizenship.[56] In 1945, the Pan-African Congress brought together an imagined African diaspora against colonialism but did not advocate a specific future political order to replace it. By 1946, Algerian Muslims were advocating for equal citizenship in a federal republic. In the context of the constitutional reform of the French Empire, left-wing movements drew on the egalitarian rhetoric of imperial republicanism present in the 1946 law on imperial citizenship to ground rights of political participation, wages, and social services. They sought more substantial institutional integration in an empire transforming into a unified multinational state. The broader issue of citizenship in the postwar world thus hinged on the future of empire and on the kinds of political communities that would emerge after the war.[57]

Apart from uncertainty about the nature of imperial reform and citizenship, the political and legal implications of being a stateless person in the postwar world likewise depended on the future status of international political authority in the context of global political order. It is necessary, therefore, to return to the establishment of international refugee agencies called upon to conceptualize the nature of displacement and their own authority over people without states of their own. During the war, the Allied powers created more expansive institutions to handle the problem of mass displacement in Europe. The founding of UNRRA (United Nations Relief and Rehabilitation Administration) in 1943 transformed the international response to refugees, granting more resources and authority to the organization than the interwar High Commission for Refugees.[58] When the war ended, it was clear that the problem of mass displacement had reached unprecedented proportions and would have to be a factor in shaping the postwar world. As the Allies entered Germany in 1945, they estimated that nearly 350,000 people had been displaced in Western Europe. After the Nazis surrendered, the total increased to seven million. The Soviets also reported catastrophic numbers: a total close to fourteen million by the autumn of 1945.[59]

Postwar displaced persons camps marked a significant break in diplomatic practice as institutional responsibility was divided between the Intergovernmental Committee on Refugees and UNRRA. UNRRA would fulfill "physical needs" for what they called "short-term" refugees, while the Committee would handle less tangible matters such as nationality status, identity papers, travel documents, and the rights and obligations of particular groups and individuals considered "long-term refugees" in the countries they were living in temporarily.[60] Together, the Intergovernmental Committee on Refugees and UNRRA aimed to "re-territorialize" the displaced.[61] The rise of large-scale international institutions to manage the refugee crisis created a class of professional experts, often social workers or psychologists, to manage and care for refugees. While experts and international administrators pursued the strategic development of permanent institutions to manage refugees, postwar humanitarian workers and child welfare experts sought to reestablish the sovereignty of families as well as the sovereignty of nations.[62] The Soviets insisted that displaced persons were not stateless but were nationals that had to be repatriated. French, Belgian, Dutch, and Italian displaced persons returned quickly while Eastern European displaced persons often resisted repatriation until the policy was abandoned in mid-1947 in favor of resettlement. After the Yalta agreements, American, French, and British authorities helped repatriate Soviet nationals despite great resistance.[63]

Though the Allied powers sought to resolve the refugee problem through repatriation, statelessness represented a concept intrinsically bound up with the fundamental issues of international politics. Without formal legal definitions to organize the masses of victims and displaced people under the supervision of Allied forces, the military and international organizations invoked the term *stateless* as a catchall phrase. In displaced persons camps, officers and social workers examined residents to discern their nationality for the purposes of repatriation.[64] Officers used the rough definition "a stateless person is one who has no protection from any government," which served as a blanket definition for anyone who was de facto stateless. One colonel wrote to the Foreign Office to confirm a statement he made when visiting Bergen Belsen that "a person who considers he/she is stateless need not retain that status if at a later date he/she desires and is accepted as belonging to a 'state.'"[65] An article in the *Social Science Review* from 1946 defined the stateless as "those who cannot or are unwilling to return to their country of origin."[66] The conceptualization of the stateless as generally unprotected in turn encouraged comparison with other extraterritorial groups. Social scientists and commentators discussed two alternative plans. The first was to create a new state in some sparsely populated area of the world and import all the stateless there. The second solution was more in line with the League of Nations passport system and would create an extranational citizenship sponsored by the United Nations such that the stateless would become the first world citizens.[67]

A memo from the French state archives from July 1946 on the solution to the statelessness problem indicates the imaginative possibilities of the moment. The *apatrides*, as the memo argued, could be seen as one small part, a symptom even, of the enormous category of wartime victims. On the other hand, together they constituted a distinct political community in their own right.[68] The author used the terms *refugee* and *stateless* interchangeably and purposefully: "Can one then artificially enclose the definition of *apatridie* in a legal formula? Or is it just the category of men in revolt against the diverse inhumanity of terrestrial countries?" The author connected the concept to the deep history of those placed outside the political order and to revolutionary group action, citing the proletariat in Rome as the "sans-patrie," Marx's "men without a country," and the French Syndicalists who took the title "sans-patrie" at an International Congress in Stuttgart in 1907. As much as this dejected group elicited compassion, they constituted a cause of disruption, a source of possible epidemics, a danger to public finance and public order. The memo also compared the stateless to the millions of slaves at the end of the Roman republic, who contain "in germ an army of anarchists even as they regard themselves as provisory citizens." "These deracinated masses," he claimed, "portend the virus of civil war."[69] The United Nations, the memo argued, in turn faced a choice between two contradictory systems. The organization could choose to spread the mass of the stateless across various states, or it could organize a separate community, which would fulfill the ambition of a "state without territory." This second option, the memoirist stated, would be a logical extension of the Nansen passport. The community of the stateless constituted nothing more than the "embryo of a quasi-state." To be a "true" or even a "quasi" state it would be enough for representatives of the *apatrides* to have representation in every country. This "state for the stateless" would not have to be territorial but could constitute a political form separate from the territorial state that showed that nationality was "neither the only nor the most ancient form of affiliation and of public power."[70]

The central issue in contention was over which body—domestic, international, or intergovernmental—had the final word over nationality disputes. Internationalist publicists were engaged in a very particular debate about what kind of authority should adjudicate conflicts over nationality. In this context, Maximilian Koessler contributed a pivotal essay in which he proposed that the significance of nationality rested on the future of world order. A recent émigré to the United States, Koessler at this point worked as an attorney in the War Crimes Branch of the United States army charged with preparing for the prosecution of war criminals. By 1946, he concluded that any "realistically anticipated future world order will not be able to do away with the legal concept of nationality." Returning to his earlier thesis, discussed in Chapter 4, he argued that such a future would necessarily entail the elaboration of specific rules of international law determining the acquisition and loss of nationality as well as the basis for national membership in domicile rather than birthplace or filiation.[71] It is worth noting that in his elaboration of the international legal significance of nationality, Koessler distinguished between the idea that belonging to a state is primarily a "legal concept," and the premise that belonging is a "sociological conception" with political implications. As a legal concept, nationality, Koessler insisted, "is not more than a formal frame, surrounding a picture of changeable character." When it denoted a conception of international law, nationality remained a "purely formal proposition."[72] As we will see later on, conceptually differentiating between nationality as a "legal" as opposed to a "sociological" category became one of the central ways that legal theorists argued for the importance of statelessness for comprehending the conditions for world order.

Koessler's essay provided a more direct intervention into a specific debate that took place in the immediate postwar moment over the nature of international authority in determining national status. Sources from this period that seem, at first glance, to be proposing that individuals had for the first time become the subjects of international law, in fact were contributing to this other controversy about sovereignty over nationality disputes. Georges Kaeckenbeeck's study of the interwar "experiment" in Upper Silesia, in which a mixed international court settled controversies over nationality, has been cited as an example of postwar efforts to establish individuals as directly subject to international law. Yet on closer inspection he was far more concerned with demonstrating the success of the interwar international tribunal in adjudicating nationality questions. In an article from 1946 on the international court in Upper Silesia, he asserted that there must be a "right to a nationality" and that international bodies should have wide remit to adjudicate these claims.[73] Rather than revisiting an interwar institution in order to revise doctrine on the subjects of international law, Kaeckenbeeck intervened in a more contemporary debate about jurisdictional authority over nationality-related disputes.[74]

Lauterpacht also addressed the question of which body should have ultimate control over nationality issues. In early 1946, the Intergovernmental Committee on Refugees asked him to write a legal opinion on the effect of the laws issued by the Allied military government and by the Allied Control Council in Germany. By arguing that international organizations should have oversight over questions of nationality, Lauterpacht presented the claim that the decision of states to denationalize should be respected but that international organizations should have ultimate oversight over such determinations. He cited relevant cases, including *Stoeck v. Public Trustee*, insisting that statelessness could be beneficial if it was the result of losing the nationality of a state where national status did not confer security. He argued that *Stoeck* had given expression to a general principle of international law: that the legislation of a state divesting its subjects of their nationality was decisive for determining their status abroad.[75]

The broader question Lauterpacht set out to address, however, was whether it was within the limits of the International Refugee Organization to appeal to an international body, like the United Nations or the International Court of Justice, to provide a judgment on the legitimacy of the repeal of denationalization. He determined that "the problem raised by the Germanization of stateless persons previously deprived of German nationality involved the issues of nationality and respect for human personality in a manner so compelling that the IRO would be justified in an attempt to use the machinery of the UN and of the ICJ." Lauterpacht was careful in his opinion not to extend international jurisdiction too far, and he emphasized that the ability to turn to an international court should only be a last resort; ideally municipal courts and authorities would apply the law of nationality in a manner "consistent with justice and with the dignity of man so as not to re-impose upon victims of persecution a nationality of which they were divested in circumstances which outraged the conscience of mankind."[76] Joseph Chamberlain, a professor of law at Columbia University who worked with many refugee aid organizations during the 1930s and 1940s and was chairman in 1946 of the National Refugee Service, questioned Lauterpacht's brief on the grounds that even with its careful efforts not to grant international organizations ultimate authority over nationality issues, his proposal still accorded international organizations too much power. In a letter to the American representative of the Intergovernmental Committee on Refugees in May 1946, Chamberlain wrote that he agreed with Lauterpacht's claim that it would be repugnant to compel a former German national who had been rendered stateless to resume his old nationality. It would be a bridge too far, however, to say that an international court could provide a ruling on national law: "I think that the international court would have to accept the national law as interpreted by the national authority, and then decide whether it was a breach of international law."[77]

In other words, an international court could only assert jurisdiction over whether or not national law or government policy violated a norm or convention of international law. If such a court claimed the authority to adjudicate the laws governing how nationality was gained or lost, it would be in violation of the principle of sovereignty itself. In comparison with Chamberlain's dualistic perspective on the relationship between state sovereignty and international law, Lauterpacht may have appeared to be proposing an international court as a trump on the authority of states on an issue that went to the heart of what it meant to claim sovereignty. Yet Lauterpacht's intellectual trajectory from the 1920s through the 1940s revealed the critical shifts in his own perspective on the limits of international law and the normative validity of national sovereignty. In his later thought, Lauterpacht portrayed the question of international adjudication over nationality as a practical issue over where to agree to draw the line between international and national legal authority rather than in terms of the ultimate foundations of law and statehood.

Federalist and internationalist options for postwar order, with implications for the future of nationality and statelessness, narrowed considerably toward the end of the decade. By rejecting proposals to revive international minority protection after the war, the Great Powers tacitly endorsed a vision of statehood undivided by claims to international jurisdictional authority or the autonomous legal life of national groups within the formal borders of the state. In August 1946, one year before the creation of the independent states of India and Pakistan, Mohammed Ali Jinnah and Jawaharlal Nehru debated the proper distribution and organization of power once the British departed. At that moment, a federal structure remained part of negotiations. Would power be concentrated in a centralized state, legitimized by democratic voting, or would power be divided in ways that recognized Indian Muslims as a distinctive nation?[78] In the 1940s Jinnah pursued a form of federation that would ensure provincial autonomy and in which Muslims would be represented as a group. However, by Indian independence in 1947, Nehru overrode Gandhi's vision for village-based, bottom-up sovereignty and embraced the modern state and monopoly sovereignty, which he argued could best facilitate planned economic development.[79]

The transformation of legal internationalism in this period, as well as the broader surge of interest in the subject of human rights, also provides new insight into the normative grounding of the state in the postwar era. The origins of human rights after the Second World War were diverse and reflected varying political objectives. Many people across the political spectrum and around the world articulated the need to return to moral fundamentals after the war. In postwar Europe, conservatives turned to human rights and toward the creation of supranational legal institutions in response to the electoral success of labor and socialist governments in the immediate postwar years.[80] The elaboration of a universal declaration of human rights at the United Nations embodied a different politics and was envisioned as a common moral basis for postwar welfare states. The purpose, however, of the declaration was not to establish the postwar order on a set of common moral principles to define the international community of states. Rather, contemporaries understood the declaration as part of the project to rebuild the postwar world. The Thomist French philosopher Jacques Maritain offered one of the most striking responses to the 1947 survey undertaken by UNESCO of prominent intellectual and cultural figures on the philosophical foundations of human rights. Maritain concluded that it was possible to agree on a list of universal rights, "on condition that no one asks us why."[81]

The introduction of the concept of human rights as part of the Allied vision for the postwar world before the end of the war appeared to some as an affirmation of the idea that individuals are the primary subjects of international law. In a 1946 address before the American Society of International Law, Clyde Eagleton stated that the Institut de Droit International at its Briarcliff meeting in 1929 had already adopted the principle that individuals had international rights even against their own states. By reaching back to this earlier articulation of the idea of rights beyond the state, Eagleton suggested that the long-promised doctrine was approaching realization. After Eagleton spoke, another member of the American Society, George Finch, responded, "I would rather feel I had my own government behind me to give me protection."[82] The idea that individuals rather than states were the subjects of international legal order meant something different from what had come before, at least for the legal scholars who had held out hope for this possibility at an earlier date. In his 1946 article "The Grotian Tradition in International Law," Lauterpacht proclaimed that "the individual is the ultimate unit of all law ... in the double sense that the obligations of international law are ultimately addressed to him and that the development, the well being and the dignity of the individual human being are a matter of direct concern to international law."[83] Yet as we have seen, the turn to human rights among European and American international lawyers who had pursued a vision of the autonomy of international legal order in the interwar era signified the revision of their understanding of the relationship between international law and state sovereignty.

The idea of a right to a nationality introduced in this period implied that human rights should be grounded in a more basic right to national membership. An early draft of the Universal Declaration of Human Rights included an article detailing that anyone who was not protected by a government would be placed under the protection of the United Nations. René Cassin advocated a more robust and descriptive version of the article. If he had his way, the declaration would have included the following elaborated statement: "Everyone has the right to a nationality. It is the duty of the United Nations and Member States to prevent statelessness as being inconsistent with human rights and the interests of the human community."[84] Not everyone agreed. Eleanor Roosevelt—the Chairperson of the Commission on Human Rights at the UN—argued that the issue of statelessness and nationality should be avoided altogether in the declaration.[85] The Commission ultimately rejected the French plan to make "the fate of all the stateless the direct concern of the international organization."[86] By the commision's third session, Cassin's version of the clause had disappeared and was replaced by the final form that excluded the UN as a separate site for protection and legal identification.[87] The final version of article 15 of the declaration stated, "Everyone has the right to a nationality, no one shall be arbitrarily deprived of their nationality."[88]

In light of Cassin's intellectual development from the interwar period through the postwar era, a speech that he delivered in 1948 in defense of the declaration should be read as an attempt to console legal internationalists, who had placed their hopes in the creation of a more elaborated sphere of international authority. The declaration, Cassin told his colleagues, was "a way to move ahead." It was the first move toward bringing the legislation of member states "into conformity with the principles formulated in it and set up within the sphere of their jurisdictions . . . in order to prevent or correct violations of human rights which may have been committed within their territory."[89] Rather than searching for signs that international legal order already recognized individuals as subjects of international law, or that legal sovereignty was already defined by principles like domicile, he suggested that principles would eventually be constitutionalized and legalized by independent states. This should not suggest that the aspiration that individuals should be the subjects of international legal order continued to inform the analysis of the system of refugee relief. One legal scholar commenting on the evolution of international refugee policy argued that the decision to have the International Refugee Organization board hear appellants directly to determine their status was "from a juridical standpoint, the most interesting institution created for the displaced persons." Such assertions might lead one to suggest that the postwar era, and perhaps even postwar refugee relief, marked the moment when individuals became directly connected to an international legal order that could provide at least conceptual protection against the state. But the sentiment expressed here is the same one that informed international legal analysis of interwar institutions like the mixed court in Upper Silesia that determined nationality on the basis of individual testimony. The speaker found this development interesting because of its long-standing import in international legal debate.[90] Cassin's speech also highlighted the limits of universal human rights in the absence of state protection. The Universal Declaration of Human Rights did not conform to a legal positivist conception of law because it reflected moral aspiration rather than law backed by force.

Though Lauterpacht had never been a strict positivist, he expressed disappointment that negotiations had led to a declaration of rights rather than to covenants agreed to by member states. The legal scholars who had addressed statelessness since the 1920s revised their perspective on the role of international law; however, they also insisted on the centrality of the problem of statelessness for global political order. Postwar international conventions and treaties promised to limit the domain of sovereign right, but the lawyers who sought to develop human rights into a body of law ceased to deny the primacy of this sphere of authority altogether. Instead of searching for indications that international law already recognized individuals as subjects of law, or for the fundamental supremacy of international legal order, they pivoted toward the proposition that the rights listed in the Universal Declaration of Human Rights would eventually be codified into law by sovereign governments. The adoption of the Universal Declaration of Human Rights by the UN General Assembly on December 10, 1948, did not mark a moment of triumph from the perspective of those who sought to legalize human rights. Nor was it received as an expression of the cosmopolitan spirit that motivated Garry Davis, an American former pilot and Broadway actor, to renounce his citizenship in Paris in May 1948 and declare his intention to start a movement for world citizenship.[91] As the political philosopher Giorgio Agamben would later observe, "the post 1945 declarations of rights are not values that bind the legislator to respect eternal principles. Instead, they serve as the earthly foundation of the state's legitimacy and sovereignty."[92] At issue, however, is how the entrenchment of rights in the state evolved over the period of the two world wars in international thought.

It is worth pausing on an illustrative debate between Lauterpacht and Jessup on the significance of nationality in the postwar world. Two different forms of statelessness were at stake in their disagreement over an international right to a nationality—the fundamental freedom of the private economic actor in relation to the state, and the obligations of the international community toward those without the protection of nationality. Lauterpacht and others who insisted on the primary international guarantee to a nationality in the postwar period arrived at this position through a pragmatic assessment of international law's failure to achieve the universality to which it had aspired after World War I. By urging his colleagues to loosen their commitment to the doctrinal position that international law could become a potent force in international affairs only if it had direct access to nonstate entities, Lauterpacht suggested that nationality, rather than its absence, could become subject to the gentle hand of international law.[93] Lauterpacht's postwar writing on human rights described nationality as an "essential attribute of human personality."[94] However, faced with the predicament of Jewish displaced persons who sought to free themselves of their German national affiliation, he argued in a separate essay on denationalization that the experience of not having a nationality was context dependent and could not be described as an unequivocal deprivation.[95] Lauterpacht's sensitivity to the difference between theory and practice accounted for the ambivalence in his writings in the 1930s and 1940s on who counted as a subject of international law. In theory, individuals have rights by virtue of their humanity. In practice, however, Lauterpacht insisted on the necessity of an internationally guaranteed right to a nationality. His *An International Bill of the Rights of Man* from 1945 fit harmoniously with the San Francisco Charter, the founding document of the United Nations. There, he cited Immanuel Kant on the idea that good government through the instrumentality of the state was a paramount condition for the enjoyment of the "natural rights of man."[96]

A comparison with Jessup's approach to the relation between statelessness and human rights in the 1940s underscores the particular balance between the normative values of state sovereignty and human rights that Lauterpacht tried to strike. Jessup, as we have seen, had been searching for evidence of the supremacy of international legal order since the 1920s and he now argued that the UN's mechanisms of enforcement could be directly applied to individuals. Jessup's arguments in favor of the idea that individuals were now the subjects of international legal order were qualitatively similar to those offered as proof in the 1920s that nonstate entities had international legal personality. The United Nations, as he argued, represented the culmination of the history of internationalism and the realization of the supremacy of international legal order, and he cited interwar authors who had argued that international law should be concerned with individuals rather than states and suggested that the UN represented the fruition of their ambitions.[97] In the period before decolonization took hold of the General Assembly, Jessup continued to draw on examples of political dependencies and limited sovereignty to prove his case about individuals in the law of nations. In a 1948 essay on "The Subjects of a Modern Law of Nations," Jessup pointed to a variety of nonstate subjects, including the Holy See, the chartered companies of the early modern era like the Dutch East India Company, the princely states of India, and the status of the Philippine Commonwealth in US courts. Strikingly, Jessup used statelessness to demonstrate his point. He argued that a contract between a corporation and a state, or between a corporation and a stateless person, constituted an international law agreement that could in turn be adjudicated by special international tribunals.[98]

Jessup was not entirely insensitive to the injuries sustained by international law's reputation in the preceding decade, and he remained in close contact with its most eloquent critics.[99] Conscious of such criticism, Jessup crafted a formula that carefully balanced the legal principle of the equality of states and the principle of equality of subjects of law, whether states or individuals. He insisted that the conviction that individuals are subjects of international legal order no longer required the theoretical destruction of the personality of the state. By carefully delineating between legal equality and political equality, Jessup argued that all entities—individuals, corporations, and states—could appear as equal subjects before the General Assembly.[100] *A Modern Law of Nations*, Jessup's book on the transformation of international law since the Second World War, from 1948, directly addressed Lauterpacht's formulation of the relationship between human rights and the right to a nationality. Jessup acknowledged Lauterpacht's reasoning—ending statelessness required that states accord nationality to all persons born on their territory—but argued that this thesis lay in direct contradiction to the notion of basic rights against the states. The remedy for statelessness, he wrote, "is not inconsistent with the hypothesis on which this book is based: that is, the acceptance of the position that the individual is a subject of international law." If the individual has rights, he does not have them derivatively through the state of which he is a national. "His possession of international rights thus ceases to be dependent on his possession of a nationality."[101]

For Jessup, then, statelessness held out the same promise that it had represented after World War I to make individuals the subjects of international law, though this prospect no longer depended on denying the personality of the state. By contrast, Lauterpacht had by this point turned decisively away from interwar expectations linking the future of an expansive international legal order to the phenomenon of statelessness. Lauterpacht's insistence on the "right to a nationality" could certainly be read as part of his larger commitment to Jewish national self-determination and the rights that follow from collective political emancipation in this period.[102] Recent studies of Lauterpacht's life and thought demonstrate how difficult it is to disentangle his personal politics from his broader international legal interventions, and the general value of uncovering the particular commitments and interests that lie behind the abstract and seemingly universal claims about the nature of law, rights, and international order articulated by international legal scholars. However, without denying the importance of Lauterpacht's political convictions or his lawyerly capacity to present different arguments depending on the particular setting, his conflict with Jessup highlights the existence of two distinct perspectives on the significance of statelessness for the future of world order.

III

The most celebrated reflections on the significance of statelessness for global political order from the 1940s do not spring from the tradition of international law or the discipline of political science but from the political thought of the German Jewish émigré intellectual Hannah Arendt. Unlike most of the figures discussed in this book, Arendt was not an international lawyer or a jurist, and she developed her analysis outside the internal institutional confines of the United Nations. A selective reader of international legal literature, Arendt's political writings from this period tended to mischaracterize the significance of statelessness in international legal thought. Her celebrated and influential analysis of modern statelessness, presented comprehensively in *The Origins of Totalitarianism*, contributed to the representation of the interwar legalist generation as relics from a lost liberal age. Moreover, her account did not capture the extent to which the problem of mass statelessness had been a critical resource for theorizing the boundary between national and international domains of authority since the First World War. Yet, as we will see, by linking the problem of statelessness to the future of global political organization, Arendt joined theorists like Lauterpacht in her insistence on political inclusion as a basic postulate for collective security and world order. Read in isolation, her reflections appear as a response to the inevitability of a world divided into states jealously guarding their sovereign authority. However, situated in the context of wider debate and uncertainty about international political order, Arendt's intellectual evolution over the course of the 1940s demonstrates the significance of her interventions in light of the broader movement to legitimate the state as the fundamental unit of governance against nonstatist alternatives for the political organization of humanity, and the centrality of the problem of statelessness for this proposition.

Arendt's initial turn to politics began once she was forced to contemplate exile from Germany after the rise of Nazism. She had studied philosophy with Martin Heidegger in the atmosphere of intellectual crisis of Weimar Germany, and her first major work took up the themes of intersubjectivity and humanity's relationship to the divine through a study of St. Augustine's conception of love. The collapse of the Weimar Republic and the growing discrimination against Jewish citizens in Germany spurred Arendt to turn her attentions to modern European history, particularly the history of Jewish emancipation and assimilation in European modernity. After fleeing Germany in 1933, Arendt observed interwar European internationalism up close when she worked briefly at the International Labor Organization

(Bureau International du Travail) in Geneva, before leaving for what she hoped would be more permanent settlement in France, where she became involved in Jewish politics.[103]

Arendt began writing more systematically about statelessness after arriving in the United States in 1941—a move that followed a period in a French concentration camp and was only made possible through the securing of a Nansen passport and a US emergency visa. Her initial writings on the subject emphasize the breakdown of the ideal of civic emancipation and assimilation—the promise of equal citizenship represented by the idea of the "rights of man" in the nineteenth century. These essays stress the inescapability of group identification. The distinctiveness of modern statelessness, compared to the minor phenomenon of the nineteenth century, is that it attaches to whole peoples rather than to individuals. In "We Refugees," an essay published in 1943, Arendt reflects on the futility of Jewish refugees assuming new national identities. Instead, she concludes that the refugees could embrace their pariah status rather than desperately cling to the ersatz security provided by a new national status. Her essay "The Stateless People" from 1945 similarly emphasizes the novel impossibility of assimilation in modern history, linking it to the collapse of the medieval principle of territorial jurisdiction and the rise of modern international treaties ensuring that states protect their nationals even beyond their own borders.[104]

Arendt based her analysis primarily on the German, French, and English-language legal and political literature on the interwar minority protection treaties, as well as work by the international legal scholar Lawrence Preuss on the deprivation of nationality in international law, which took for granted that "the national state's sovereign power in the sphere of international law is nowhere greater than in matters of emigration, naturalization, nationality, and expulsion."[105] For Arendt, the stateless represented an extension of the wider minority problem facing interwar Central Europe. People who did not acquire citizenship after World War I were generally members of minority groups who faced discrimination in the new national states of central Europe, which viewed the members of national minorities living within their borders as a threat to their territorial sovereignty. At the same time, members of the majority national group living as protected minorities in other states provided the basis for revisionist claims to extend the territory of the state.

These early essays reflect Arendt's commitment to the ethical and political value of national identification and community. Her writing also testifies to the perceived openness in the early 1940s to a variety of postwar schemes for global political organization. Essays published in 1945–1946 appealed to the ideal of European federation put forward by underground movements fighting for a federation of European peoples who sought to "amputate" nationality from territoriality. According to this proposal, national groups could retain their political autonomy within a broader constitutional structure. Arendt drew on the proposal created by Austro-Marxist theorists Otto Bauer and Karl Renner, who elaborated a way to reconcile imperial governance with national autonomy. Since people naturally belonged to a national group, a federation of peoples that separated territory from political community meant that each person would find a political home in the world. In a 1937 essay, Renner had argued that global peace was attainable through a free federation of nations. The surface of the globe would be covered by a "precious patchwork, characterized by an infinitely heterogeneous spirit and mankind."[106] Diversity itself constituted the conditions for peace, as people found community through an affinity or natural connection to particular groups. A constitutional and legal order, Renner imagined, would regulate relations among these communities. Federalism combined the collective spiritual life of national groups with international stability.[107] Building on this idea, Arendt argued that a wider imperial territory would constitute the real "national homestead," in which the diverse nationalities could still administer their collective lives through national councils.[108] National states created masses of stateless people, Arendt argued, while a European federation of peoples would not pose the same exclusionary dilemmas. Federation represented a solution because it would "amputate nationality from state and territory and make nationality portable."[109] Arendt concluded that federalism would restore the "inalienable rights of man" to the stateless by preventing millions of people from living outside the boundaries of political order. She portrayed this option as a direct answer to Allied proposals to transfer populations in order to create more homogenous national states.[110]

In response, however, to the on-the ground realities of international politics, by 1946 Arendt began to insist that the dream of politically autonomous groups interconnected in a federal system was no longer sustainable. Surveying the political reorganization of Europe after 1945, she concluded that the

Great Powers had foreclosed the possibility of European federation. Arendt noted in her review of a 1945 study of the revival of minority protection in Central Europe that the proposal to reintroduce protection was premised on the faulty assumption that the region could be organized along federalist lines.[111] Arendt bitterly stated, "The time for which this excellent proposal was written, the time when the UN would be in a position to assess the 'true relationship between the various nationalities and east central Europeans, and the national requirements of majorities and minorities alike' has passed into history. This time, the United Nations may even claim that they did not fail, for the simple reason that they did not try."[112] The time, in other words, for innovative internationalist solutions to national conflict, had passed, and given way to a Great Power system less amenable to the experimentation of the interwar era.

From this point on, Arendt's writings portray citizenship as the basis for human security and moral and legal personhood. Read against her earlier essays, it becomes clear how Arendt provided a normative vision of the state—albeit a highly idealized republican version of it—that was part of its broader relegitimation in the postwar era. Arendt was part of the broader movement to reevaluate the normative value of the sovereign state. In her review of a 1946 book, *La Nation*, by the Catholic social and international theorist J. T. Delos, Arendt responded to those like Carl Friedrich who argued on the eve of World War II that misplaced worship of the state lay at the root of fascism and the collapse of the peace. Instead, Arendt shifted responsibility to the excesses of national identification and stated, "It is therefore quite erroneous to see the evil of our times in a deification of the state. It is the nation which has usurped the traditional place of God and religion."[113]

Arendt was prompted to write about human rights at the UN by an essay written by Hermann Broch, "Considerations on the Utopia of an International Bill of Rights and Responsibilities in 1946." In this essay, Broch criticized the lack of realism among the jurists, proposing the standard of "human dignity" as a source of common morality. By contrast, Arendt focused on the foundations of political order.[114] The "lack of reality" evident in the developments at the UN stemmed from the fact that the declaration asserts what human rights are without acknowledging their true source. Her discussion had clear implications for the ongoing debates at the United Nations about human rights. When Arendt submitted her essay titled "The

Rights of Man: What Are They?" in April 1949 to *Foreign Affairs* magazine, the editor noted that the piece would be "interesting in conversation with the UN declaration of rights of man."[115] In the essay, Arendt underlined the contradiction embedded in the declaration, which proclaimed that rights are universal but provided no institutional measures for the enjoyment of rights beyond those assured through membership in a particular state. "Recent attempts to frame a new bill of human rights have demonstrated that no one seems able to define with any assurance what these general human rights, as distinguished from the rights of citizens, really are."[116] Arendt concluded that the Universal Declaration of Human Rights offers a "welter of rights of the most heterogeneous nature and origin" but did not account for the "one right without which no other can materialize—the right to belong to a political community. This human right, like all other rights, can exist only through mutual agreement and guarantee. Transcending the rights of the citizen—being the right of men to citizenship—this right is the only one that can only be guaranteed by the comity of nations."[117] Arendt's 1949 essay proceeded to polemically challenge the declaration by offering a singular "right to have rights" as a prepolitical guarantee. The essay portrays well-meaning jurists as failing to confront the fundamental challenge of statelessness or to acknowledge the true source of rights; she reveals her own sensitivity to the limits of idealism and the dangers of exceptional status and of subjection to philanthropic sympathies. She thus positioned herself against the jurists who failed to grasp the essential truth revealed by the plight of the stateless.

Arendt's discussion of statelessness in *The Origins of Totalitarianism* wove together her criticism of interwar legal idealism with a genealogy of the rise and fall of what the historian Faisal Devji has called "the enlightenment state."[118] At the conclusion of a longer discussion of the history of European imperialism, Arendt turned to the collapse of the national state governed by the principle of equality among all citizens. She presented an ideal type of the nation-state corrupted by the rise of pan-national movements and limitless imperial ambitions, arguing that "the inner contradiction between the nation's body politic and conquest as a political device has been obvious since the failure of the Napoleonic dream."[119] Since the French Revolution, the European nation-state had based its authority on the sovereignty of the people and on equality under the law. The French Revolution promised political equality in the name of all human beings but turned almost instantaneously into a revolution for the nation. Jewish emancipationist and assimilationist liberals in the nineteenth century placed their faith in culture and the bourgeoisie, evading the authentic promise of political freedom. Nationalism, in conjunction with imperialist liberalism, produced movements that sought to extend beyond all boundaries. Once the expansive imperialist practices reached Europe, the fragile nation-state system broke down. The breakdown of the ideal of legal and political equality, Arendt argued, found its most articulate expression in the "supranationalism" of nineteenth-century anti-Semitism, which sought to "destroy all home grown national structures alike."[120] The meaninglessness of rights without national guarantee meanwhile demonstrated that the structure of declarations of rights since 1789 (and really since the American Revolution) were not about the assertion of natural rights but about the necessary connection between rights and membership in a political community.

Arendt further offered a bitter assessment of recent attempts by well-meaning internationalists to protect the rights of humanity: "Even worse was that all societies formed for the protection of the rights of man, all attempts to arrive at a new bill of human rights were sponsored by marginal figures—by a few international jurists without political experience or professional philanthropists supported by the uncertain sentiments of professional idealists."[121] True equality demanded complete equality under the law for all the subjects of a particular sovereign. Her interventions, like other writings from the postwar era evaluating interwar political aspirations, reflected on the failure of internationalism over the previous thirty years. "The moment human beings lacked their own government and had to fall back upon their minimum rights, no authority was left to protect them and no institution was willing to guarantee them." Only when individuals had a place in the world, a right to belong to some kind of organized community, could human rights be guaranteed.[122]

Yet, as we have seen, it is important not to relegate the history of statelessness and its impact on international political and legal thought to Arendt's claim that the relevant historical fact was the absence of the "ordinary functioning of the nation-state."[123] In the period after World War I, legal scholars did not suppose that the nation-state had an "ordinary function." Instead, statelessness appeared as a way to test their theories about the legal boundaries of the state and to examine the question of whether individuals could be said to possess legal personality outside of state guarantee. Arendt's polemical engagement with the proposals for universal rights fatefully misrepresented the significance of statelessness for international thought.

Arendt contributed to the argument affirming the normative value of states and the importance of statelessness as a principle or condition of world order. She concluded that the problems of humanity are inescapable because we live in one world. The only answer is mutual agreement, a covenant that arises from conditions that led to catastrophe. In the preface to *The Origins of Totalitarianism* from 1951, Arendt proposed an international law that could guarantee a "new law on earth, whose validity this time must comprehend the whole of humanity while its power must remain strictly limited, rooted in and controlled by newly defined national territories."[124] Global political organization, Arendt argued, arose from the historical effect of imperialism and conquest in unifying space. The covenant that followed from this fact in turn seemed to bear a Biblical imprint. Just as God promised Noah after the flood to never destroy the earth again, humanity must limit itself in this one key respect. The problem of statelessness for Arendt meant grappling with political minimalism—with the threshold conditions for an inescapably limited and unified world system. Through violence and coercion, imperialism ensured that all humanity lived the same history but a common political order that took account of this fact would have to be instituted and created.

Arendt's minimalist cosmopolitan argument bore a striking similarity to Kant's argument for the right to hospitality in *Perpetual Peace*.[125] A similar vision of global historical development underlies Kant and Arendt's justification for their cosmopolitan principles. In *Perpetual Peace*, Kant defined cosmopolitan right in the limited terms of the universal right to hospitality. For Kant, the settlement of the whole earth, and the limited nature of territorial space, was the essential foundation for practical ethics on a global scale. All humans, Kant argued, had a claim to present themselves to society "by virtue of the right of common possession of the surface of the earth." The very shape of the globe, in turn, dictated this principle: "Since it is the surface of a sphere, they cannot scatter themselves on it without limit, but they must rather ultimately tolerate one another as neighbors, and originally no one has more of a right to be at a given place on earth than anyone else."[126] Kant's claim about cosmopolitan right depended on an empirical argument about territorial limitation. Similarly, Arendt's proposal for a "new law on earth" ensuring that all human beings could claim membership somewhere followed because imperialism had unified the globe.[127] As opposed to the idea that sovereignty should be contingent on states abiding by certain su-preme moral principles, Arendt portrayed the basic entitlement to political inclusion as a precondition of international order. She presented a world of states defined by their exclusive control over their borders and boundaries, each of whom might be willing to acknowledge their mutual interest in very specific domains. The "right to have rights" represented a cosmopolitan prop-osition in the sense that it is a principle of international order providing the foundation for a minimalist threshold for inclusion that must be accepted and applied universally. Statelessness therefore represented a common ex-istential predicament, and the principle of a "right to have rights" affirmed the centrality of states to solving a common dilemma in an age of inevitable interconnection and interdependence.

In his classic 1946 essay, Maximilian Koessler described nationality as a "purely formal proposition," and as a "formal frame surrounding a picture of changeable character." Arendt's critical reflections on the meaning of mass statelessness in modern history supplied a far more textured, explanatory picture of modern rightlessness and vulnerability. Her account in *The Ori-gins of Totalitarianism* targeted the legalists who focused on the formalities of legal status rather than on the agents responsible for mass death and home-lessness. However, read together, we see how Arendt joined the international legal theorists in the postwar presentation of statelessness as intrinsically bound up with the prospects for global order. As opposed to conceptualiz-ing legality and the rule of law in terms of its predictability and generality, she described being part of the organized political world as the capacity to exercise agency, which she portrayed as a kind of theatrical performance—a characterization that echoed Otto von Gierke's theory of legal personality. The state, in addition to being the primary agent that assumes responsibility for the stateless, serves as the stage upon which actors can perform. It is a formal condition for the exercise of personality that depends on maintain-ing the distinction between the juridical and the sociological foundations for political membership, and on an appreciation of the artificial nature of political order.

6

Nationalizing International Society

In a letter dated October 21, 1960, Hélène Batresco petitioned Dag Hammarskjöld, then the secretary-general of the United Nations, to grant her French citizenship, an intervention that would bring decades of living as a stateless person to an end. In her letter Batresco highlighted the dramatic collision between her own personal struggles and the drama of high politics in the twentieth century, reporting to the secretary-general that her story was to be the basis for a book she was writing on the experience of being *apatride*. Born in Brussels in 1905 but raised in France, she had never managed, despite great persistence and effort, to acquire French citizenship. Married at nineteen to a man with a Polish passport, she thought she had become a Polish national through her marriage. Then—just as she and her husband applied for French citizenship in 1932—the French president Paul Doumer was assassinated, and in the agitation of the moment their naturalization file was lost. As Batresco explained, all of her subsequent efforts to establish legal residence in France failed, too, during the period of Nazi occupation. When her husband was deported during the war, she and her son lived without French nationality while she worked as a guide for the blind, a position that left her unable to enjoy social security and other social benefits that French citizens could claim once the war ended.[1] It is not clear from the letter why her husband was deported or how she became stateless, though Batresco's fate mirrored that of many women married to men without national citizenship. She stated plainly that she did not seek to obtain material assistance from the United Nations. Rather, she wrote to the secretary-general to demand that he put an end to her condition as a stateless person, writing in bold capital letters, "I do not want to die apatride," and adding, "What is it to be human if not to have the right to a nationality?"[2]

The letter features a number of noteworthy elements, including Batresco's expectation that the UN secretary-general would be able to intercede with the French government, the way she framed her personal narrative in terms of the wider history of the twentieth century, her plans to write a memoir about the experience of being a stateless person, and the connection between possessing a national status and access to national welfare provisions. Most striking, however, is her strategic use of the central terms of debate around the concept of a right to a nationality. Her statement invoked the tension between the claim that human beings possess rights by virtue of their humanity and the view articulated by many at the time of the creation of the Universal Declaration of Human Rights that rights flow only from national membership.

Nearly a year after the Human Rights Division at the United Nations received Batresco's letter, the Convention on the Reduction of Statelessness was adopted on August 30, 1961, setting down rules for the conferral and nonwithdrawal of citizenship to prevent new cases of statelessness from arising. Yet what is most noteworthy about the adoption of the 1961 Convention is that it coincided with the broader marginalization of the loss of nationality as an object of international concern, and the entrenchment of the idea that not being in possession of a nationality was indeterminate from a moral perspective.

As we saw in Chapter 5, during the Second World War the problem of mass numbers of individuals without the protections of citizenship once again become central to debates about rights and the postwar order. Unlike in the 1920s, statelessness was more readily mobilized in the 1940s to advocate for the value of the sovereign state as the primary source of rights and law. Statelessness transformed from a central theoretical resource for those arguing for political and legal order beyond the state to a touchstone for those trying to establish the normative legitimacy of sovereign statehood, and the primacy of states for international politics. Rather than contributing to a body of legal norms that could be used against the power of the state, the legal scholars who contributed to the institutional development of international law and human rights after the war understood their work as part of the development of a new world order premised on the sovereign equality of states. Theorists who had considered the problem of statelessness as the key to unlocking the nature of international legal order in the interwar period now made the sovereign state the premise of their analysis of rights. Batresco's appeal to the right to a nationality, and her invocation of the idea that the possession of formal political membership was intrinsically bound up with human rights, recalled an earlier moment after the Second World War when theorists like Hersch Lauterpacht and Hannah Arendt insisted that the future of global order depended on a cooperative international approach to ensure that everyone possessed a nationality.

This chapter seeks to establish how the idea of nationality as a formal legal status designating membership and a basic threshold condition of rights became so discredited in the postwar era. As we will see, high politics contributed to the legal frameworks that define what it means to belong to a state. But the distinctions developed after the Second World War to define the displaced were conditioned by the emphasis placed on the substance of citizenship—and on social and psychological experience in particular. Nationality as a form of legal identification represented the formal basis for an individual's inclusion within international legal order. The abstract right to nationality ran up against the widespread turn in the postwar era toward more substantive definitions of citizenship that emphasized the social, as opposed to formal-legal, nature of political membership.

The socialization of citizenship in the postwar period, and the transformation of legal thought that underwrote the shift, shaped approaches to the problem of political exclusion. To say that the presence of the stateless reveals a condition of lawlessness and affects us all is a formal or categorical statement. It is not an inquiry into the particular experience of the stateless person or the refugee. The emphasis on social experience rather than formal membership to describe the significance of nationality—and to define the relation between citizens and states—made the loss of nationality more obscure from a political and moral standpoint. The establishment of statelessness as an international legal category indicates how the creation of discrete categories of noncitizenship shaped the formation of the postimperial world of states. Postwar international legal institutions redefined nationality as a thick social bond, with the international community and its legal institutions in a privileged position to determine the nature of those attachments. We cannot begin to account for how nationality and its absence became so illegible without comprehending the intellectual conflicts that shaped postwar international organization and the legal frameworks established to define those who did not fit within a bounded polity.

I

Legal statelessness was not initially thought of as a separate problem from the broader refugee crisis. Individuals without the protection of any state represented a broad general group who posed a fundamental challenge to the reestablishment of international order after the war. After the adoption of the Universal Declaration of Human Rights in 1948, work began on an international agreement to provide legal protections for both refugees and the stateless, who were considered to be twin challenges for postwar order. In "The Refugee, a Problem for International Organization," Patrick Murphy Malin argued that of the two million refugees and displaced persons relatively few were legally "stateless," but all effectively lacked legal and political protection, especially consular and diplomatic protection.[3] Similarly, according to the author of a 1948 resolution at the UN to alleviate the plight of stateless persons, "stateless persons" should be defined as "persons legally deprived of their citizenship and non-repatriatable refugees."[4]

For a brief moment following the inclusion of article 15 in the Universal Declaration of Human Rights, the Economic and Social Council of the United Nations directed its attentions toward the general problem of political homelessness and entertained the possibility of instituting broad protections for individuals without the security of citizenship. The Economic and Social Council called for member states in cooperation with the United Nations "to ensure that everyone shall have an effective nationality." The council requested that the secretary-general undertake a study of the protection of stateless persons and recommend whether a separate convention defining the obligation of states toward stateless persons was desirable.[5] The International Law Commission decided at its first session in 1949 to include "nationality including statelessness" in the list of topics selected for codification. Manley Hudson, Vladimir Koretsky, Shuhsi Hsu, Robert Cordova, and Hersch Lauterpacht were commissioned to take up the codification of nationality.[6] As a result of these efforts, the commission produced a draft of recommendations for governments, as well as a pamphlet surveying the history and legal issues called *A Study of Statelessness*.

Preserving a broad definition of statelessness fulfilled strategic requirements, at least for a time. The US State Department insisted on keeping refugees and the stateless conceptually together in order to avoid incurring any
concrete obligations toward the European refugees. In private discussions
among the US delegation to the Economic and Social Council in June 1949,
advisors concluded, "Care should be taken at this stage not to project any
particular organizational pattern or to segregate the problem of displaced
persons from the overall problem of statelessness."[7] By 1949, mass displacement had become a global phenomenon, and the center of refugee movement
shifted from Europe to the Middle East and Asia. Demands for assistance
from refugee relief agencies followed the partition of India and the creation
of a Jewish state in Palestine. The United Nations Relief and Works Agency
(UNRWA) was formed in December 1949 to assist dispossessed Palestinians. Hundreds of thousands of mainland Chinese fled to Hong Kong and
Taiwan. After the outbreak of the Korean War in 1950, the director of the
International Refugee Organization established the United Nations Korean
Reconstruction Agency (UNKRA) to help civilians in South Korea. At this
time, by emphasizing statelessness as an all-encompassing category, officials
could minimize their exposure to refugee asylum claims.[8]

General attention within the UN to the broadly defined problem of statelessness, including to the rising numbers of people who could no longer claim
imperial protected status as former imperial colonies gained independence,
led British officials to carefully weigh the potential pitfalls of internationaliz-
ing postimperial nationality questions. In that same year, the president of the
Greek Fraternity of Cypriots in Egypt petitioned the British government for
the protection of "stateless Cypriots." Cyprus had been a British protectorate
since 1878 and was formally annexed in 1914. Natives of Cyprus had been
entitled to British protection but were not British subjects. Many of those
residing in Egypt had fought for the British in World War II and expected
to remain under British protection. Only a few years earlier, in 1943, the Foreign Office had strongly considered granting British nationality to Cypriots
in Egypt who were willing to serve in the British forces. By 1949 the chances
of former British subjects holding on to this status had diminished. Cypriots would be left without the status of British protected subject and could
not obtain Egyptian nationality; they would therefore become stateless. The
British Foreign Office in Cairo proposed in a confidential memo that they

could avoid embarrassment and assist the Cypriot community by referring the problem to the United Nations, and conferred with Ernest Bevin, then the foreign secretary in the Labour government, about whether to refer the case to the Economic and Social Council committee charged with studying statelessness.[9]

Notably, when confronted with the possibility of being taken to task before the UN's Economic and Social Council for relinquishing responsibility for the Cypriot community in Egypt, British administrators sought to evade public censure, a move that demonstrates the status of the problem within the confines of the UN, at least briefly. Rather than risk facing criticism in the Economic and Social Council, British officials quietly ignored the Cypriot petitions and declined the proposal to assist in the internationalization of the statelessness problem in Egypt. The Foreign Office instructed the chargé d'affaires in Alexandria not to proceed with the plan to quietly send the petitions to the UN. As the author stated, "I think we should not run the risk of having to defend our attitude at the Economic and Social Council."[10] If the question of how to nationalize or protect the stateless Cypriots in Egypt were raised in the Economic and Social Council, the author concluded, the decision of the British government not to grant British nationality to the Cypriots could subject it to public scrutiny.[11]

In 1949, a comprehensive definition of international homelessness received institutional backing in the UN's *Study of Statelessness*. The study elaborated how countries would grant the legal status of "protected persons" to any stateless individual in their country of residence, providing the same rights enjoyed by nationals. It unequivocally endorsed the perspective voiced by René Cassin and others during the deliberations over the Universal Declaration of Human Rights: statelessness in all forms was contrary to the rights of humanity and counter to the interests of the human community.[12] Yet the UN's *Study of Statelessness* demonstrated the new importance of psychology and a growing understanding of trauma in comprehending postwar refugees. The 1949 report emphasized the traumatic consequences of losing or living without a nationality. Statelessness was a problem for the individual because, as the authors stated, "the fact that the stateless person has no nationality places him in an abnormal and inferior position which reduced his social value and destroys his own self-confidence."[13] The description of the consequences of statelessness in terms of its psychological impact on the individual represented a decisive turn away from the emphasis on its legal implications in the decade after the First World War. This is not to say that the material deprivations that resulted from becoming stateless had not been an important factor for legal advocates and international agencies in the early confrontation with statelessness as a mass phenomenon. However, the study's stress on the psychological consequences of statelessness placed a different emphasis on the nature of the problem, honing in on the experience rather than on the anomalousness of not possessing membership in a state in a world where membership is a basic condition for security.

The presentation of the problem in the *Study of Statelessness* previewed the dominant terms of debate over the relationship between individuals without a national status and the concept of the refugee in the years preceding the creation of the 1951 Refugee Convention. Was the mere fact of statelessness—the condition that Batresco described in her letter to Hammarskjöld—a deprivation comparable to the suffering experienced by the victims of persecution and mass atrocity? Or did the absence of national status constitute a deeper deprivation of rights, not only because it limited the ability of the stateless person to access goods and services but also because of the link between legality and moral personality?[14] Did it make sense to evaluate the phenomenon from the perspective of individual experience at all? As we will see in a moment, the emphasis on social experience rather than formal membership to describe the significance of nationality—and to define the relation between citizens and states—made the loss of nationality appear more obscure from a political and moral standpoint. In December 1950, the General Assembly voted to convene a diplomatic conference to consider the draft agreements on the status of refugees and of stateless persons. The question of whether to create a more inclusive document was strongly contested during the drafting sessions for the convention. Paul Weis reported that during deliberations there was a clear tendency to define "refugees" against "the stateless" and to argue for a separate convention for individuals without a nationality.[15]

By this time Weis had become sought after as an expert on legal matters relating to refugees and the stateless, eventually gaining a position as legal advisor to the International Refugee Organization in Geneva. He had recommended a broader regime that would ensure international protection for anyone living without the protection of a state by expanding the authority of the International Refugee Organization.[16] During negotiations over the convention, only the United Kingdom supported his proposal by arguing that both refugees and the stateless should stand under the same category of "protected persons," well aware that broader international institutional measures for noncitizens in postcolonial states could help minimize their responsibilities toward former protected imperial subjects.[17]

However, the proposal to draw together those without a nationality with those forced to flee who may not have formally relinquished a former national tie, struck some representatives as a bridge too far. "What legal revolution was afoot," the French delegate to the UN wrote privately to the Ministry of Foreign Affairs, "by the proposed assimilation of the concept of the refugee with that of the *apatride?*" Before the war, the author stated, there were two sorts of conventions, one addressing the legal conflicts—primarily contradictions that arose between states that naturalized on the basis of *jus sanguinis* and states that applied *jus soli*—and the other on international protection for refugees. By assimilating the terms, they risked transforming statelessness from a "state of exception" to a regulated legal condition. The stateless did not belong, the author argued, from either a legal or psychological perspective in the same international category as refugees.[18] As the UN secretary-general admitted in a memo from January 1950, a separate treaty on statelessness would be necessary because no government would agree to such broad provisions that obligated them to accord citizenship to any stateless person and would inevitably impinge on domestic legislation.[19] The framing of statelessness as a fundamentally moral problem, though a highly ambiguous one, allowed representatives to evade the more fundamental questions of political order introduced by the possibility of regulating the problem of statelessness internationally. Some representatives, such as the representative from Belgium, argued that whereas refugees represented an acute humanitarian crisis, deserving of the coordinated efforts of member states, stateless individuals who did not possess any nationality represented administrative anomalies and were a long-term concern of the world community rather than an acute humanitarian emergency.[20]

The second option for state officials was to present statelessness as a humanitarian disaster but of a fundamentally different kind from the one presented by refugees. Louis Henkin, an American international lawyer, brought the US State Department's shifting agenda to the Refugee Convention preparatory meetings.[21] Turning about-face from the position that the United States had taken in 1949, when the US delegation had insisted on not separating refugees from the general problem of statelessness, the US State Department directed Henkin to argue that refugees and stateless people both represented a fundamental deprivation of rights but that the Refugee Convention should apply strictly to refugees.[22] The State Department instead supported the recommendation to send the statelessness problem to the International Law Commission, with instructions to draft a separate international convention designed to eliminate or reduce statelessness by working on resolving contradictory naturalization regimes. The convention, as the United States set out, would maintain the special interest of the UN in the field of refugees and "protect the position of the United States in insisting on a defined definition of refugees by not throwing it open to stateless people generally." Stateless people who were not refugees would be covered by a separate agreement that remained untethered to the UN's refugee machinery.[23]

When the United Nations Convention Relating to the Status of Refugees was adopted at a conference held in Geneva in July 1951, the final text reflected the fundamental assumption that refugees already possessed birthright citizenship. Article 1 of the convention defined *refugee* as anyone who "owing to well-founded fear of being persecuted for reasons of race, religion, nationality, membership of a particular social group or political opinion, is outside the country of his nationality and is unable, or owing to such fear, is unwilling, to avail himself of the protection of that country; or who, not having a nationality and being outside the country of his former habitual residence as a result of such events, is unable or, owing to such fear, is unwilling to return to it."[24] The convention thus had little to say about the predicament of people like Batresco who did not face the challenge of repatriation due to fear of persecution or violence but simply lacked a formal legal connection to the territory she had never left. At the conference, delegates adopted a resolution to consider the status of stateless persons in a more detailed study and deferred determining the role of international law and international agencies in the regulation of statelessness, now defined in much narrower terms.

By separating refugees from the stateless, international legal experts and representatives at the United Nations placed priority on persecution rather than the security that derived from possessing a formal political status in one of the world's states. The convention universalized the category of the refugee far more than earlier agreements but remained directed at a particular group by stipulating that anyone defined as a refugee must have fled owing to events occurring in Europe before 1951. There is no question that the postwar conventions established more extensive rights for noncitizens than previous international agreements. The 1951 Refugee Convention introduced the principle of non-refoulement, or the prohibition against expulsion or return of anyone who might be endangered if sent back to their place of origin. Moreover, despite the importance placed on the separation of the legal category of statelessness from that of refugee, the convention furnished protection for persons without any nationality.[25] However, the codification of the category of the refugee, as well as the concept of asylum elaborated in the convention, affirmed the basis of global organization in national communities with certain ethical or political obligations. It is, therefore, critical to appreciate how the new regime of refugee protection strengthened international cooperation among agencies and relief workers and provided an argument for rebuilding strong states that could care for those placed under their protection.[26]

Once the argument that statelessness and refugees should be treated separately won the day, the task of preparing research material for the future conference on statelessness fell to a subcommittee of the International Law Commission. Manley Hudson, the Harvard Law professor who had led the effort to research and codify nationality law in the interwar period, once again took the lead in drafting the Convention on Statelessness. Hudson was joined by Weis, now serving as legal adviser to the UN High Commissioner on Refugees. Ivan Kerno, a former member of the League secretariat and Czech diplomat, undertook most of the logistical arrangements and original research for the convention.

Rather than a more generalized agreement that placed obligations on states to accord rights to individuals without the reciprocal protection of another state, or expanding the authority of an international agency such as the International Refugee Organization, the 1951 Convention defined the problem of the refugee in terms of the moral problem of persecution. When it came time to create a separate agreement on the problem of statelessness, now formally separated from the concept of the refugee, drafters likewise sought to frame the problem in terms of a particular kind of deprivation experienced by stateless persons. In anticipation of a separate conference to agree on a convention relating to the status of stateless persons, Kerno produced a remarkable report entitled "Is Statelessness an Evil?" Kerno's report documented the contradictory ways that legal scholars and politicians had characterized statelessness since the late nineteenth century in an attempt to discern whether there was an emerging normative consensus over its moral status. He drew on the history of debates over the meaning and consequences of statelessness since the period after World War I to consider how the International Law Commission should evaluate the phenomenon. Kerno's research reaffirmed the ambiguity that had first authorized the separation of the statelessness question from that of refugees. His report captures the range of debate over what it meant to be a stateless person and the nature of the deprivation that it represented. Not being in possession of a nationality, he reported, had proved to be at times a source of evil and at times a useful transitional category on the road to citizenship, or a source of freedom for individuals liberated from the state. It remained an open question whether statelessness should be conceived of as "an evil" or a strange anomaly that retained its Janus-faced character—at times a curse, at other times a source of individual freedom. Kerno had personally experienced the dual quality of statelessness. In his numerous travels on behalf of the United Nations, he listed his nationality as "stateless," traveling with an affidavit of identity and nationality in place of a passport. Kerno thus portrayed statelessness— whether it should be viewed as a clear "evil"—as fundamentally ambiguous once analysis of the phenomenon shifted onto the terrain of moral judgment.[27]

As opposed to evaluating the meaning of statelessness from the perspective of experience or victimization, Weis argued that statelessness represented an intrinsic problem of international legal order. Unlike Kerno, Weis insisted that not being in possession of a nationality represented a fundamental deprivation since the absence of a formal legal status left stateless persons excluded from international legal order. Weis hoped that states would agree on an "international nationality" for the stateless and argued that the Statelessness Convention should accord more authority to the International Refugee Organization to provide consular services to refugees and stateless persons.[28] Similarly, reflecting on the problem of statelessness under consideration by the International Law Commission at the UN, the international legal scholar Georges Scelle argued that the situation of stateless nonrefugees was the "most cruel of all" since it meant that an individual did not possess a direct connection to international legal order, which in turn "refused to him all the blessings of sociability." The solution, he argued, would be to ensure that subjects are directly tied to international law, which confers the equivalent of a nationality, or an international citizenship.[29]

Correspondence between the main legal experts charged with the drafting of the statelessness convention illuminates the decline of the symbolic stakes of statelessness for cosmopolitan lawyers. Lauterpacht cautioned Weis, who had been his student in Cambridge, "not to get bogged down" in turf wars with states over the International Refugee Organization's jurisdiction over consular services for refugees. "Do be willing," he advised Weis, "to admit that many of the quasi-consular functions can be carried out just as well by national offices as international."[30] As the premier international legal scholar of his generation, Lauterpacht was called on to advise more generally on the statelessness convention. In this context he argued that it would not be advisable to put forward a more radical version of the convention, which some of the lawyers had called for, since it would "saddle" states with a large number of stateless people whom they would be obligated to nationalize and would forestall the more practical measure of preventing future cases of statelessness. Instead, he suggested that the convention require signatories to confer nationality on stateless persons that had been habitually resident in a territory for a period of ten years, provided that they first applied for nationality.[31] Lauterpacht argued in the fifth session of the International Law Commission meetings on nationality and statelessness that the subject of existing statelessness was of a political nature and was probably outside the competence of the Commission. The function of the commission, he contended, was the progressive development and codification of international law. Weis, meanwhile, resigned himself to the convention as a pragmatic resolution. He nevertheless continued to hold out hope that states could one day agree on an "international nationality" for the stateless and expressed his view that formalized protection for stateless persons through an agency like the International Refugee Organization would provide more practical benefits.[32]

The separation of refugees from stateless persons in two separate international conventions, and the debates over the content of the separate convention on stateless persons, revealed a fundamental disagreement over how to conceptualize what it meant to not possess formal membership in a state. Ultimately, the text of the Convention Relating to the Status of Stateless Persons, adopted on September 28, 1954, defined statelessness in formal legal terms. A stateless person, according to the first article of the convention, is "a person who is not considered as a national by any State under the operation of its law." In theory, states that agreed to the convention would ensure that everyone possessed a legal status and thus basic rights under the law.[33]

The conventions introduced two kinds of persons to be regulated by international law: the refugee and the stateless person. Yet as we will see, the more narrowly defined problem of statelessness would become increasingly marginal in the years following the creation of the 1954 Convention. The marginalization of the problem should certainly be attributed in part to exogenous political developments, including the fact that the US representatives remained largely detached from negotiations over the convention.[34] However, it is necessary to reckon with how the turn away from a prior preoccupation with the special status of law in legal and social thought reverberated in subsequent debates.[35] Attention to questions of juridical status began to seem too formalistic, despite the fact that the 1954 Convention defined statelessness in terms of the absence of a formal status.[36] The fact that the absence of nationality as a formal legal status began to seem increasingly illegible from a moral standpoint, a view intrinsic to the formation of the two major conventions, proved to be critical as a world of states after empire began to take shape.

II

It is necessary to turn once again to Arendt's writings on statelessness in the years following her initial major intervention in *The Origins of Totalitarianism*. Arendt's reactions to the legal framing of statelessness further clarify the argumentative terms that defined legal and political approaches in this period. Her reflections on the subject of statelessness provide crucial insight into the shift over the period of the two world wars from emphasizing the nature of the problem in terms of its formal, structural, implications for international legal order, and the later focus on its experiential and moral consequences.

Arendt did not participate in the international negotiations over how to provide protection for refugees and the stateless. She did, however, pay careful attention to the proceedings. As lawyers and diplomats negotiated the terms of the convention on statelessness, Arendt defended her original thesis that the absence of formal state protection represented one of the great dangers of the contemporary world. While preparing to deliver a series of lectures at Princeton University in 1953 on the Western tradition of political thought, Arendt considered the problem of carving out separate legal-bureaucratic categories to define refugees and stateless people. She cautioned against the impulse to separate the refugee from the stateless and to define legal-bureaucratic distinctions that elided the basic fact that both were fundamentally vulnerable in a totally organized global order. The distinction between someone who technically retained a legal connection and someone who was legally without a nationality mattered less than the meaning and consequences of exclusion. In her 1953 lecture, Arendt described statelessness as the condition of the modern world—the condition of not being part of politics.[37] Though she portrayed the meaning of modern statelessness in light of the particular conditions of global order in her time, her analysis rested on a more profound philosophical claim about the intrinsic value of citizenship and public freedom. Statelessness described a condition of alienation and homelessness more fundamental than any legal category. To lose one's nationality automatically cast one out of the sphere of politics. In an entry from her intellectual diary from August 1953, Arendt linked the Greek idea of *apolitia* with the newer term *staatenlosigkeit*.[38] An account of how one suffered by not having a nationality missed the point: the post–World War II organization of the world into defined, bordered communities rendered nationality a baseline requirement, regardless of whether one could establish its social or experiential consequences in any given case.

As Arendt conceptualized the meaning of citizenship in these terms, her attention was focused on how citizenship in the United States conferred more social rights and protections than ever before, but that federal power to deprive someone of their nationality had expanded. By the early 1950s, American prosecutors increasingly applied wartime legislation depriving anyone accused of treason or desertion of citizenship, while anticommunism motivated a growing willingness to strip suspected communists of their citizenship.[39] Arendt portrayed this development as a fundamental threat to the American republic, and kept a clipping from the *New York Times*'s report on the UN's planning sessions on the statelessness convention from October

1954 detailing how "punitive deprivation of citizenship" had become increasingly widespread.[40]

In the course of her nomadic academic life, Arendt continued to reflect on the significance of the deprivation of nationality and to anxiously observe developments both in the United States and at the United Nations relating to such questions. In 1955, when she was appointed visiting professor of political science at the University of California, Berkeley, Arendt prepared notes for a lecture to be delivered at the university on the topic of statelessness and revisited the idea of a "right to have rights" in the context of the American denaturalization cases. Here she claimed, "No state, no matter how draconian its law, should have the right to deprive citizenship."[41] Once again, she sought to ground this limiting principle in international reality. It was the only conclusion to draw from the fact that "no international body can supplant sovereignty" and therefore "even the most elementary human rights function as citizen rights." According to Arendt, the deprivation of citizenship "could be counted among the crimes against humanity." At this time legal scholars at the United Nations, disappointed with the nonbinding character of the Universal Declaration of Human Rights, worked toward the completion of an international bill of human rights with legal force. Arendt, though, responded by insisting that there remained only one relevant right. She proposed "one internationally guaranteed right to citizenship—whatever this citizenship happens to be" rather than "a bill with innumerable human rights which only the highest civilizations enjoy."[42]

Arendt's 1955 lecture concisely and forcefully articulated the destructive consequences of statelessness for individuals and for international order. Such an argument had not received a hearing in the drafting of the Convention on Statelessness, where the lawyers and civil servants concluded that the psychological and social consequences of not having a nationality were indeterminate. By contrast, Arendt insisted in her lecture that those who became stateless lost contact with humankind along with the loss of their citizenship. Her lecture provided an abstract formula—one internationally guaranteed right to citizenship—that would serve as the basic condition of international society. The argument, moreover, did not depend on the particular consequences of statelessness for individuals. Along classical republican lines, Arendt argued that the presence of those who lived outside the law infected the lawfulness of the surrounding political order, just as imperial expansion threatened the virtue of republics.[43] The lecture therefore provided an argument for why individuals without political or legal status threatened the integrity of democratic states. Though she is partly responsible for reviving a classical republican ideal of citizenship in the twentieth century, in her reflections on the subject of statelessness she reverted to the more minimalist legal ideal of protection. Arendt protested that a threshold condition for political membership remained vital even as the substance of citizenship became increasingly robust in the era of welfarist reform that promised true social equality among citizens.

Arendt's insistence on an abstract right to citizenship ran up against the widespread turn in the postwar era toward more substantive definitions of citizenship that emphasized the social, as opposed to formal-legal, nature of political membership, and the way such arguments were mobilized to justify the marginalization of statelessness. The idea of a basic promise of inclusion placed Arendt at odds with the turn to social and psychological explanation to assess the significance of nationality in the decades following the Second World War.[44] Unlike in earlier periods when, as we have seen, theorists of the state posited a clear separation between the regulatory apparatus of the state and the society within it, the difficulty of conceiving the state apart from particular groups and interests arose as a distinctive feature of postwar society. This is not to say that state and society had actually functioned as separate entities in earlier periods but that state theory and international legal institutions began to insist on their fundamental unity.[45] Societies that could sustain redistribution and control the market in ways that would promote social equality demanded a heightened sense of obligation and solidarity rather than mere membership held together by the fiction of legal entitlement.[46]

Arendt joined the chorus of criticism from legal experts concerned that the socialization of citizenship—or the attempt to imbue the concept of citizenship with particular social entailments—undermined the particular legal situation of persons who could not claim citizenship anywhere. Yet her insistence on the priority of legal status positioned her against the substantive moral and psychological analysis prominent in the postwar era. In her interventions on the subject, Arendt repeatedly insisted that an account of how one suffered by not having a nationality missed the point that the formal structure of international order rendered nationality a baseline requirement regardless of whether one could establish its social or experiential consequences in any given case.[47]

It must be said that Arendt's perspective on legal order was not formalist in the way that, for example, Max Weber or Hans Kelsen understood the basis of modern legal rationality in its separation from norms such as morality or politics. She nonetheless rejected the broader turn to social or sociological explanation that characterized much of the policy and legal debates around statelessness. In *The Human Condition*, published in 1958, Arendt updated the Aristotelian distinction between the sphere of political activity and that of the household for the administrative state, where, as Arendt claimed, social, economic, and scientific imperatives marginalized the shared plural political world.[48] The idea that nationality depended on an individual's broader social ties and commitments exemplified the historical process Arendt set out to diagnose. Her contemporaries at the University of Chicago had been railing against the expansion of the state in the name of social welfare for far longer.[49] However, she published the book at the moment when the colonization of the political by the social, in Arendt's terms, took a particular form relevant to her long-standing concern with stateless people. The entanglement of state and society, and the impossibility of conceiving the state apart from particular groups and interests, emerged as a distinctive feature of postwar society. The internationally guaranteed right to citizenship that Arendt proposed would not be grounded in the logical necessity of a supreme international legal order. But her account of what it meant to be stateless in the modern world did not depend on an analysis of how the experience might impact individuals in particular. It was, rather, a general rule based on the structure of global order.[50] Arendt placed the imperative to ensure the distribution of people into the secure boundaries of some political community at the heart of her vision of global security.

III

Arendt's worry that the socialization of citizenship would obscure the significance of not possessing a formal legal status materialized in *Nottebohm* (*Liechtenstein v. Guatemala*), a case brought before the International Court of Justice (ICJ) in 1955 by the governments of Liechtenstein and Guatemala. Originally a citizen of the German Reich, Friedrich Nottebohm had established a prosperous business in Guatemala before the First World War.

As a businessman who worked around national borders, Nottebohm represented the class of cosmopolitan entrepreneurs prominent in Latin America in the first half of the twentieth century. In 1939, right before the outbreak of World War II, Nottebohm acquired citizenship in Liechtenstein at the cost of 37,500 Swiss francs, concerned that as a former German national he would lose his business and property in Guatemala if he were designated an enemy alien during the war. As a national of Liechtenstein, Nottebohm would have to be considered a neutral subject and thus protected from the seizure of enemy alien property and detainment in a wartime camp for enemy nationals.[51] When he returned to Guatemala, Nottebohm resumed his life, only on a Liechtenstein passport, until November 1943 when Guatemala officially declared war on Nazi Germany. At that point, officials in Guatemala deported Nottebohm to the United States, where he was interned as an enemy alien until his release in 1946.[52]

Acting on behalf of Nottebohm, Liechstenstein sought a ruling from the court to force Guatemala to recognize him as a national of Liechtenstein. Established in 1945 by the Charter of the United Nations to settle legal disputes submitted to it by states in accordance with international law, the court consisted of fifteen judges elected by the UN General Assembly and Security Council, and seated at the Peace Palace in The Hague. Though he had technically obtained citizenship from Liechtenstein, Guatemala argued that Nottebohm's formal connection should not allow him to remain exempt from an Agrarian Law that would nationalize and distribute his holdings. The question entertained by the court of whether Guatemala must respect Liechtenstein's right to extend diplomatic protection on his behalf tested Arendt's vision of an internationally guaranteed right to a nationality—whatever that nationality happened to be. It also provided a prominent public international setting for debate over the basis for individual membership a state. The majority judgment determined that at the time of his naturalization in Liechtenstein, Nottebohm had not possessed a "genuine" link with the country, thus upholding Guatemala's claim. In *Nottebohm*, the court determined that nationality was not a rubber stamp that could be picked up and relinquished at a moment of emergency but a social category that reflected an authentic bond between the individual and the state. Nationality, according to the court, was a "legal bond having as its basis a social fact of attachment, a genuine connection of existence, interests and sentiments, together with the existence of reciprocal rights and duties."[53] As John Mervyn Jones—a British legal expert on nationality and international law—argued in his own reflections on the judgment, the court did not deny that Liechtenstein had, in accordance with its naturalization law, conferred citizenship to Nottebohm. Instead, the tribunal affirmed that Liechtenstein could not exercise the protection that came with national status because of the *quality* of the nationality acquired.[54]

The decision thus deferred to the "factual," or real, bonds that connect an individual to a particular state; though an international court claims the jurisdictional power to adjudicate the reality of such a relationship, the principle that governs such a determination is the idea that nationality marks a deep social fact rather than a merely formal legal connection. It implied that states were only bound to recognize another state's rights to extend protection if their national status represented that individual's strongest "organic link" to a territory.[55] The ruling notably emphasized the concrete ways individuals build lives and communities, stating, "habitual residence of the individual concerned is an important factor, but there are other factors such as the centre of his interests, his family ties, his participation in public life, the attachment shown by him for a given country and inculcated in his children etc." The court therefore prioritized the substantive nature of nationality rather than its basis in bureaucratic procedure.[56]

The Nottebohm case also challenged the presumption that states should have little leeway in assessing the naturalization—and denaturalization—practices of other states. In the 1921 *Stoeck* decision, the judge decided that the determination made by another sovereign nation about the national status of one of their subjects must be respected—whatever the basis for how that country determined who counted as a national. In this sense, the ruling placed some limit on the state's sovereign ability to naturalize or denaturalize while tacitly accepting the occurrence of stateless individuals if it meant that states no longer had the epistemic privilege of determining the legitimacy of nationality rulings.[57] By asserting the principle of the "genuine" or "effective" link, the court raised the bar to citizenship while at the same time providing a rough transnational criterion for evaluating the domestic affairs of states. The genuine link principle indicated that nationality only entitles states to exercise protection against another state if a person's national status reflects their real connections with the state in question. Unlike in *Stoeck*, therefore, the court asserted the supremacy of international law in the evaluation of national status. Muhammed Zafrulla Khan, a judge on the court representing Pakistan, recollected that the *Nottebohm* judgment was one of the most important cases during his tenure on the court because it set a new precedent for the jurisdiction of international law over nationality.[58]

Leaving aside the internal logic of the arguments put forward in the course of the proceedings for a moment, it is important to consider how the background politics of decolonization informed how contemporaries understood the significance of the case. Behind the scenes of the legal proceedings before the ICJ, the older powers at the UN debated how the judgment would impact the emerging struggles within the UN over decolonization and the end of empire. British officials were particularly eager for the ICJ to find in favor of Guatemala as the global balance of power, at least in the formal confines of the UN, began to tilt away from Anglo-American hegemony. As one memo stated, "A decision against Guatemala would embarrass new governments from the standpoint of international politics."[59] Originally envisioned as a way to preserve the basic hierarchical structure of imperial international order, the UN had rapidly become the setting for adjudicating the injustice of imperial rule. In the same year as the *Nottebohm* judgment, debate over the inclusion of the right to self-determination in the draft covenants on human rights rocked the General Assembly. In North Africa, Moroccans, Algerians, Tunisians, Egyptians, and Libyans demanded independence from the French and British Empires. A proposal to implement international oversight to survey the status of the permanent sovereignty of peoples and nations over their national resources threatened to further complicate relations between the countries of the global south and the richer nations of the global north. Developing countries and recently independent nations pushed back through their agitation for the right to self-determination and against the implementation of international oversight to determine their sovereign control over natural resources.[60]

Yet in its re-imagining of the relationship between nationals and states, the judgment clarifies how the deformalization of law and legal thought contributed to the marginalization of statelessness in the postwar decades as a world of states emerged from a world composed largely of empires. The idea that nationality—as opposed to citizenship—represented a thicker tie between states and subjects rather than a contractual relation of protection challenged the previous doctrinal treatment of the subject. Until this point international legal opinion had preserved the understanding of nationality as the formal link tying an individual to a state. In affirming the social foundations of national status, the court privileged a more robust conception of nationality that appeared to marginalize the problem of statelessness. In a dissenting opinion, Paul Guggenheim, a Swiss judge seated on the ICJ, objected to the court's introduction of the genuine link principle because by rejecting Liechtenstein's claim to exercise diplomatic protection for Nottebohm, the court had tacitly accepted the creation of stateless persons. This result, he argued, further weakened the protection of the individual under international law and was "contrary to the basic principles embodied in the UDHR according to which everyone has the right to a nationality."[61] No one was more surprised about the court's decision to invoke "effective nationality" than Hersch Lauterpacht. At this time, Lauterpacht had been elected as a judge on the ICJ but had been precluded from taking part in the case because before his election he had advised the government of Liechtenstein about Nottebohm's case. He did not anticipate the use of this legal argument since the genuine link had never been invoked except in cases of dual nationality, where an individual would have to choose between two possible allegiances.[62]

Nottebohm continued to be a source of controversy among international lawyers who divided over their interpretation of the case and its implications. At the Annual Meeting of the American Society of International Law in 1956, members of the society, many of whom had been involved in debates about the nature of the legal link tying individuals to particular states, discussed *Nottebohm* and its implications for establishing an international consensus on the problem of statelessness. Dr. Ivan Soubbotitch, an émigré from Serbia who had served as chief of the political department in the Yugoslav foreign ministry in the 1920s, and who after 1935 was Yugoslavia's permanent delegate to the League, reminisced in his comments about longstanding debates with other legal experts on the legal nature of the link between the state and the individual since the 1930 Hague Conference.[63] The discussion in turn pivoted around the question that Kerno had taken up in his memo before negotiations over the 1954 Convention on the Status of Statelessness—whether it was a clear "evil" that the international community should strive to eliminate, or whether the consequences of statelessness could not be determined in advance.[64]

The answer depended on the type of reasoning applied, and in his landmark 1956 treatise *Nationality and Statelessness in International Law* Paul Weis attempted to clarify the particular juridical, in contrast to the "factual" or "social," significance of nationality. Weis completed the study before the judgment, although he managed to include some references to the case before the book's final publication. As he defined the concept:

> The term "nationality" in the sense in which it is used in this book is a politico-legal term denoting membership of a State. It must be distinguished from nationality as a historico-biological term denoting membership of a nation. In the latter sense it means the subjective corporate sentiment of unity of members of a specific group forming a "race" or "nation" which may, though not necessarily, be possessed of a territory, and which, by seeking political unity on that territory, may lead to the formation of a state. . . . Nationality in that sense, which is essentially a conception of a non-legal nature belonging to the field of sociology and ethnography, is not the subject of this work.[65]

Weis cited Vishniak's 1933 Hague Lecture, "Le Statut International des Apatrides," to define the term "nationality" as a "politico-legal" concept in contrast to a definition that derived from sociological or ethnological investigation. As Weis argued, an international legal conception of nationality depended on keeping the concept carefully segregated from the domains of sociology or ethnography. Shortly before publishing *Nationality and Statelessness*, Weis had asserted that refugees and stateless persons were "anomalous" in international law, comparable to vessels sailing on the open seas without a flag, in response to the deliberations on the separation of refugees and stateless persons in international law, and argued that the general problem should be conceptualized in positivist terms.[66] Though Muhammed Zafrulla Khan portrayed *Nottebohm* as introducing the supremacy of international law in matters relating to national status, Weis asserted that international law could only remain in a position to make claims about the boundaries of membership if the international legal sense of the word remained relevant. *Nottebohm* implied that this might not be the case by insisting that international law could evaluate the social ties that bound individuals to states. The court could, in other words, ratify a country's nationality legislation if it reflected a more profound social reality.[67]

In the 1950s and 1960s national governments seized on the genuine-link principle articulated in *Nottebohm* to formulate the foundations of citizenship in new state constitutions. Constitutions written after 1955 gave expression to the idea that nationality rests on relations more profound than the formal connection conferred by naturalization.[68] Echoing the logic articulated in *Nottebohm*, governments argued that legislation on the basis for membership in a state should reflect given "sociological" factors, as opposed to the idea that the constructions, or fictions, of law contribute to the making of social reality. In preparation for the Conference on Elimination or Reduction of Future Statelessness, Denmark submitted a memorandum in March 1955 stating the following: "In the opinion of the Danish Government it would be unrealistic to ignore the sociological and other factors underlying the choice by States between *jus soli* and *jus sanguinis* as a fundamental principle of their nationality laws. Just as unrealistic would it be to ignore the changes in attachment between the individual and the state which may occur, particularly during the period from birth and until the individual reaches the age of maturity."[69] One critical implication of the Danish government's comments was that the nature of the attachment between nationals and states should assume greater importance than shaping legislation responsive to the entry of new citizens, or to the international problem of statelessness. What is so striking about the comments from the Danish government is how they address the explicit terms of the controversy, weighing the distinct values at the heart of the debates over the convention.

The genuine link principle likewise contributed to the nationalization of international order by establishing what it meant for ships flying a national flag to earn broader recognition as an extension of a particular sovereign territory in the socialized terms set by the judgment. Following *Nottebohm*, the 1958 Convention on the High Seas dictated that "each state shall fix the conditions for the grant of its nationality to ships, for the registration of ships in its territory, and for the right to fly its flag. Ships have the nationality of the state whose flag they are entitled to fly. There must exist a genuine link between the state and the ship; in particular, the state must effectively exercise its jurisdiction and control in administrative, technical and social matters over ships flying its flag."[70]

In his response to the judgment published a few years later in the *American Journal of International Law*, Josef Kunz argued unequivocally that the ICJ judgment had perpetrated an injustice because it left Nottebohm a stateless person, depriving him of all legal remedy. Kunz placed part of the blame on the group he called the "defenders of human rights," who had misleadingly presented the idea of individuals as subjects of international legal order as a real possibility, which in turn helped neutralize the act of rendering Nottebohm stateless. Kunz argued that the ruling did not further the doctrine of human rights because it did not confirm the principle that individuals held standing under international law. To make matters worse, it also severed the obligation of the state to protect its nationals, which had only become more necessary with increasing migration and the rise of insecure new states. Kunz therefore proposed a different kind of instrumental reasoning that took the formal dimensions of international legal order into account.[71]

The idea that national status should rest, even at the cost of some people becoming stateless, on more substantive criteria appeared justifiable during a legal realist, policy-oriented moment in international legal thought when demonstrating the importance and validity of international law meant embracing its intrinsic politicization.[72] Among professional international lawyers, defenders of the *Nottebohm* decision insisted that there should be a "genuine relation" between the individual and the nation. Ian Brownlie, a British international legal scholar, criticized Kunz's claim that statelessness represented a failing of international order. Brownlie argued that the presumption against statelessness would "work mischief" by creating cases in which individuals retained formal membership but were in practice excluded from the benefits of statehood. Instead, it would be better to prove the "solidity" of the individual's links with the state as not a matter of "mere formality."[73] Along similar lines, Brownlie commented in a separate piece on the international legal status of individuals, "to say the individual is, or is not, a 'subject' of international law is, in either case, to say too much and to beg too many questions."[74]

In advocating a minimal international assurance of nationality without expecting that nationals demonstrate the more profound sources of their attachment to a country, Kunz—like Arendt—promoted a conception of legal nationality that had lost its salience as history had shown the drawbacks of formal national attachments and as more legal scholars became dismissive of legal form without socially concrete substance. Kunz shared Arendt's concern about the devaluation of the formal legal bond linking individuals to states. However, his later work bears the marks of a divided mind. He held on to the core elements of his teacher Kelsen's legal theory while conceding to the realist and sociological turn in the profession. What had appeared as a regulative order governed by law had in fact rested and depended on an underlying social cohesion. In an article titled "The Contributions of Law to Contemporary World Order" from 1961, Kunz argued that a legal order is prescriptive, normative, and coercive and regulates human conduct but that a shared system of values must underlie this order. Looking back on the development of international law, he concluded that a "regional law of Christian Europe" expanded in the period of the League of Nations. After 1945, the underlying beliefs and sentiments that buttressed this expansion fell apart. Kunz thus contributed to the discourse about the fragmentation of international law and to the idea that legal regulation can be effective only when it rests on deeper social ties.[75] His analysis echoed the premise of a prominent interpretation of the constitutional history of the Habsburg Empire put forward at this same moment. A system organized juridically might bring together disparate entities into a formal whole; but without a deeper experience of community this political arrangement would be unable to stand the test of time. In a 1957 study of the integration and disintegration of the multinational Habsburg Empire, the historian Robert Kann concluded that "organizations designed for the long run prevention of war (like the United Nations) can be effective only if they rest upon such a deep sense of community that the process of peaceful change has become assured over a long period of time."[76] As the number of member states at the United Nations expanded during decolonization, Kann and other commentators on international order, including Kunz, argued that any semblance of a real international community had already fallen apart.

In an important sense, however, the preference for separating the juridical sources of national membership from so-called sociological ones reproduced Kelsen's justification of the pure theory in the context of modern societies defined by value pluralism. Despite his growing skepticism about the formal legal foundations of political community, Kunz continued to insist on the urgent necessity of possessing a formal nationality in light of the fact that international law did not provide a separate blanket of norms and protections for individuals. He rejected the arguments proposed by legal commentators like Brownlie who argued that it was perfectly justified for the ICJ to claim the authority to assess the extent that a national status reflected the "real" relations binding an individual to a particular political community, even if it meant overriding the decision of a sovereign government such as Liechtenstein to naturalize a particular person. A stateless person could claim no legal connection to international legal order, and on those grounds Kunz argued that international law should err on the side of ensuring a formal status, rather than validating the idea that national membership rested on more substantial attachments.

Jurists had another opportunity to consider whether the nature or quality of the connection between an individual and a country should inform whether other governments were obliged to respect the national link during the widely publicized trial of Adolf Eichmann in Jerusalem in 1961. In their reflections of the capture of Adolf Eichmann by Israeli agents in Argentina, where the Nazi SS leader had been living under a false name and passport, jurists tended to affirm the virtues of the genuine link as the basic principle governing nationality law around the world. One commentator argued that formal nationality was not sufficient for the exercise of international protection, citing the *Nottebohm* case to support the idea that Germany could not protect Adolf Eichmann from trial in Israel. Since nationality had to be "real and effective" and express "a social fact," Germany could not exercise diplomatic protection for Eichmann because although technically Eichmann remained a national of the German state, his substantial ties to the state had been severed with the defeat of the Nazi regime.[77]

From Arendt's standpoint, the case of Eichmann revealed broad public denial about the predicament of statelessness, a denial that manifested in the silence surrounding this aspect of the case. When Arendt began reporting on Eichmann's capture and the subsequent televised trial in Israel, she found confirmation of her original observation that the problem of legal statelessness had not achieved any public traction. Once Arendt decided to report on the Eichmann trial for the *New Yorker*, her main source for the international legal dimensions of the trial was a pamphlet by Yosal Rogat, a colleague at the University of Chicago, on the legal issues surrounding the case. Rogat never mentions the fact of Eichmann's statelessness in his analysis of the legal issues surrounding the kidnapping, and in her handwritten annotations on the pamphlet, Arendt added, "The case of E: stateless."[78] She revisited this point in *Eichmann in Jerusalem*, published in 1963, where she noted that Eichmann was available for kidnapping only because he did not possess a nationality.[79] Her arguments for the ultimate justifiability of his capture and trial did not rest on positivist legal principles. As she argued in her reporting on the trial, Eichmann was guilty of violating the plural and diverse nature of the world inhabited by many different peoples. Eichmann's capture and trial, Arendt argued, was justified because the Israeli court could claim to act on behalf of the universal principle of plurality. However, the irony that Arendt noted in her annotations on Rogat's pamphlet is that Eichmann became the universal subject who could face this charge only because he had no nationality to protect him.

In addition to the fact that few jurists or public commenters seemed troubled by what Eichmann's statelessness implied about the broader status of the problem, Arendt also registered concern about the loss of appreciation for the virtues of law's formality that the case illuminated. Her resistance to the idea that any political body—either national or international—should possess the power to evaluate the "genuine link" between an individual and the national state echoed her arguments about the dangers of removing the mask afforded by legal personality in pursuit of the authentic moral character within, a point she made in *On Revolution*, published in 1963. In this study, Arendt reached back to interwar sources on legal personality to compare the divergent trajectories of the French and American revolutions and cited the British pluralist theorist Ernest Barker's introduction to Otto von Gierke's *Natural Law and the Theory of Society* approvingly in her biting analysis of the French revolutionary impulse to liberate natural humankind from the fiction of legal form. The term *persona*, Arendt points out, originally served as a metaphor derived from classical theater. Law for the Roman citizen was like an actor wearing a mask because it separated the citizen from the private person and enabled participation on a public stage. According to her argument, the French Revolution fatefully conflated the realm of the social and that of the political by insisting on ripping off the fictional mask of legal personality to identify authentic virtue.[80]

The critics of the turn to the social thus prioritized assuring that no one face statelessness in a world of states, and emphasized the necessity of comprehending nationality in more formal terms to achieve this goal. However,

in their focus on the formal nature of nationality, these critics risked undermining the robust vision of social citizenship that began to achieve legislative
victory in the postwar era. Indeed, their arguments brought them into close
proximity with liberal critics of the national welfare state, who prioritized
the rights of the stranger to the security of the rule of law and above all
the protection of property rights during the era of the establishment and
growth of national states. Friedrich Nottebohm, like Max Stoeck, exemplified the merchant freedom that Friedrich Hayek, the Austrian-born theorist
of economic liberalism, had in mind when he asserted the economic rights
of individual investors over the sovereign rights of states. According to this
understanding, one's national status provided an entry ticket for enjoyment
of the rule of law. In other words, put in terms native to Hayek and the Austrian School of Economics, those who argued for the centrality of statelessness emphasized the constitutional structure of international society. They
positioned the formal features of the rule of law over substantive equality
among citizens. Yet Hayek, and other conservative critics of the administrative welfare states, did not imagine the human rights of capital extending to
protect vulnerable individuals without the protection of a state. Neoliberal
theorists worked to encase the world in the rules of the borderless market
while preserving and depending on the political sovereignty of states to enforce them. Despite the resonances of their arguments about the rule of law,
and the shared origins of many of the legal scholars discussed in this book in
the Habsburg Empire (though not Arendt), these visions of global order in
the postwar years ultimately conflicted more than converged.[81]

IV

In debates over the significance of statelessness, the dominant question became whether there is a principle that can not only establish what statelessness is but also explain why it represents a particular kind of deprivation that
requires a solution in the first place. Since World War I, the US Supreme
Court had upheld Congress's constitutional authority to enact legislation
authorizing the denaturalization of American citizens for desertion or other
crimes committed during war. In a series of cases brought before the Supreme Court in the 1950s, the justices considered the constitutional status
of the Expatriation Act and the consequent imposition of statelessness as a
punishment. The conceptual uncertainty appeared vividly in two landmark

US Supreme Court decisions on the constitutional status of involuntary expatriation. The arguments put forward by the American justices further illuminate the terms of debate and justification in the postwar decades about the status of nationality in a world of states and the wider international and intellectual contexts that informed seemingly internal, domestic legal disputes.[82]

Trop v. Dulles, a case that came before the Supreme Court in 1958, marked the culmination of the court's deliberations on this constitutional question. The reasoning articulated by the justices turned on the question of the material consequences of the loss of nationality, and on whether its effects could be determined *a priori*. In his opinion, Justice Earl Warren explained why revoking nationality as a form of punishment qualified as "cruel and unusual" in constitutional terms. The loss of nationality, Warren argued, led to the "total destruction of the individual's status in organized society." His opinion invoked the idea that statelessness represented an injustice to the individual forced to live in a state of "international outlawry," and that it was in the "interest of organized society to admit of no person being without a political status." Stripping a naturalized person of their citizenship therefore constituted a "punishment more primitive than torture" that certainly violated the US Constitution's injunction against such a sentence, but it also should be avoided because it undermined international order.[83]

Warren in turn drew on UN sources to support the view that the Expatriation Act violated the governing norms of international society: "The civilized nations of the world are in virtual unanimity that statelessness is not to be imposed as punishment for a crime." Citing the UN's survey of nationality laws, Warren argued that of the eighty-four countries polled, only the Philippines and Turkey imposed denationalization as a punishment. Significantly, Warren also cited the UN's *Study of Statelessness* from 1949, which was unequivocal in its condemnation of statelessness. The Eighth Amendment thus barred denationalization as a form of punishment because statelessness rendered the individual vulnerable both domestically and abroad and therefore met the criteria for "cruel and unusual punishment." According to Warren, "the American concept of man's dignity does not comport with making even those we would punish completely 'stateless'— fair game for the despoiler at home and the oppressor abroad, if indeed there is any place which would tolerate them at all."[84]

Negotiations over the Refugee and Statelessness Conventions in the public international setting of the United Nations had succeeded in establishing conceptual uncertainty around the problem of statelessness—what made it a problem in the first place. While Warren drew on an imaginary international consensus, stating that the norms of "civilized" nations had already dictated that denationalization was outside the bounds of state practice, in a dissenting opinion Justice Felix Frankfurter countered that the fact that the United States ensured the rights of noncitizens within its borders meant that a stateless person was not a legal "outlaw" forced to live outside the law's protection, a key factor that militated against Warren's conclusion about the necessarily cruel nature of this condition.[85] According to Frankfurter, the norms of "civilized states" did not dictate that it was in fact unusually cruel to render someone stateless because the progressive development of norms and institutions in international society had made the modern condition of statelessness neither cruel nor unusual. It was no longer the case, Frankfurter argued, that the stateless person was an "outlaw" in the international system. As Kunz had feared, the "defenders of human rights" had inadvertently lent support to the argument that the development of non-state forms of legal authority meant that being a stateless person no longer implied a clear deprivation.[86]

The process of delineating the category of statelessness from that of the refugee, and of creating two separate agreements to define the obligations of signatory states, had thus succeeded in shifting the terms of analysis toward the experiential. While Warren and Frankfurter reached opposing conclusions about the punitive consequences of losing national status, Justice William Brennan expressed skepticism about whether the results were really as clear as both justices claimed. Brennan argued that the damage caused by statelessness remained indeterminate, though he agreed with Warren that the uncertainty involved in being stateless, and the experience of becoming an outcast, represented a "psychological hurt" that would have to be an essential factor in reaching a decision. Yet, he added, the nature of such a punishment was fundamentally uncertain since "however insidious and demoralizing may be the actual experience of statelessness, its contemplation in advance seems unlikely to invoke serious misgivings, for none of us yet knows its ramifications."[87] Brennan's response suggested, therefore, that judged from the perspective of the experience of statelessness, the nature of the deprivation, whether it indeed met the criteria for cruel and unusual punishment, could not be determined *a priori.*

The conferences that ultimately established the legal framework for statelessness nevertheless proceeded on the assumption that statelessness represented an "evil" that states should collectively strive to overcome. Shortly after the Supreme Court reached its decision, representatives from UN member states met again to discuss the validity of denationalization, but the outcome of the international conference only confirmed the absence of international consensus about the nature of the problem of statelessness. In the lead-up to the meeting, the International Law Commission had drafted two separate conventions, one that aimed to reduce cases of future stateless- ness and another directed toward its elimination through more expansive provisions articulating the obligation of governments to naturalize anyone who would otherwise be stateless. Committee members likewise drafted provisions for the creation of a separate agency to adjudicate conflicts over nationality and to provide legal protection to stateless persons.

Thirty-five states were represented at the conference in Geneva from March 24 to April 17, 1959, but the conference fell apart soon after it be- gan due to serious disagreement about the inclusion of a clause forbidding the deprivation of nationality. The controversy over the inclusion of such a clause redrew the global battle lines over the notion of an international right to self-determination that had rocked the UN only a few years earlier. Older powers at the UN clashed with the emerging bloc of "non-aligned" and post- colonial states with much to lose by relinquishing their sovereign prerogative to grant—and take away—citizenship. There was little willingness on the part of states to entertain the proposal of the International Law Commission to submit disputes concerning the interpretation or application of the con- vention to adjudication by a specially established international tribunal, and still less to allow individuals access, even indirectly, to such a tribunal for the decision of their claims to nationality according to the convention.[88]

Despite the breakdown of the 1959 international conference, represent- atives reconvened at United Nations headquarters in New York in August 1961 to finalize the Convention on the Reduction of Statelessness. By de- lineating the positive obligations on states (at least those that agreed to the terms of the convention) to address the ways that individuals could fail to obtain a national status, the 1961 treaty marked a significant achievement in light of the longer history of international movements to regulate nationality. Nearly a year after Hélène Batresco's letter, the convention imposed positive obligations on states for the conferment of their nationality, delineating two main ways for states to share in the responsibility of guaranteeing that there are no stateless people. First, by ensuring that if a person is born without a nationality they are able to acquire the nationality of their place of birth, and second, by legislating that no individual should lose their nationality without acquiring another one. The multilateral treaty obligates signatory countries to extend citizenship to those born on their territory who would otherwise be stateless, providing a mechanism for avoiding statelessness either at birth or through inadvertent loss of a nationality, and prohibits the deprivation of nationality on racial, ethnic, religious, or political grounds.[89]

Although the extent of attention devoted to the refugee problem worldwide depended on a variety of historical factors, including the politics of refugee asylum during the Cold War, it is striking that, set in humanitarian terms, the problem of statelessness generally received far less attention in the succeeding decades. Beginning with the Hungarian refugee crisis of 1956, those defined as refugees came to be more widely conceived as a global problem. In 1959, the UN-sponsored World Refugee Year to raise funds to provide assistance to four nominated groups of displaced people—refugees in Europe, Palestinian refugees in the Middle East, Chinese refugees in Hong Kong, and Russian refugees in the People's Republic of China.[90] As many scholars have pointed out, the legal framework governing refugee status affirmed the state as the ultimate source of security, and the nationalization of international order depended on the selective devolution of responsibility to international agencies charged with administering to refugees. After all, the status of refugees and stateless persons in international law was established during a period when Keynsian principles of governance and the capacity of states to ensure the well-being of their citizens achieved widespread acceptance.[91]

However, in order to comprehend how the terms of the problem begin to shift we must first understand how the socialization of citizenship, and the transformation of legal thought, conditioned the nationalization of international order and the categories of political exception in the postwar era. Reconstructing the broader terms of argument clarifies how the idea of nationality as a formal legal status designating membership and a basic threshold condition of rights came to seem so discredited in the postwar era. Even as cosmopolitan legal writers turned toward the state as the ultimate source of protection and rights, they resisted the deference to social reality that justified the marginalization of nationality as an object of broad international concern as the universe of states expanded in the era of decolonization. Their interventions clarify how the emphasis on social experience, rather than formal membership, obscured the larger political significance of the loss of nationality. The arguments that justified the presumption that the boundaries of membership should be compatible with sociological and historical reality contributed to the naturalization of the boundaries of international legal order and international politics. While the League of Nations evaded the challenge to its own efforts to establish the limits of international authority by locating the problem of statelessness in the context of the conflict of laws, the United Nations framed it as a matter of harm and deprivation, in the process silencing the question of how states define their boundaries in the first place. Across the social sciences, meanwhile, the internal qualities of citizenship, of political representation, access, and equality, almost entirely overshadowed the fundamental question of political boundaries.

In the complex pathways out of a world organized around empires in the decades after World War II, a range of political and constitutional arrangements were proposed to minimize the consequences of exclusionary forms of national citizenship.[92] Just as in the post–World War I breakup of empire, international lawyers and bureaucrats once again needed to consider the implications of the breakup of states and the transfer of sovereignty for the subjects who lived within the boundaries of successor polities. They would again consider the status of a succession state from the perspective of international law, and whether it assumed the debts, promises, and obligations belonging to the previous government. The 1961 convention includes a provision directed toward the potential for the proliferation of statelessness during decolonization, stating that every treaty between contracting states concerning transfer of territory include provisions to ensure that no person shall become stateless as a result of such transfer. However, when they set out to address such thorny questions in the era of postwar decolonization, legal theorists generally avoided discussion of the nature of the "person" of the state, or the legal personality of individuals, unlike after World War I when these debates became critical to larger conceptions of the political.[93]

Upon achieving independence, new states that entered the international system pledged to respect existing frontiers lest the boundaries of new states face revision by secession or expansionism. Statehood held out the promise of collective emancipation, but the creation of new states threatened to destabilize a system based on respect for the principle of sovereignty. Theorists in turn debated whether decolonization implied the reemergence of sovereignty submerged during the decades of colonial rule or whether the boundaries of the colonial states had artificially fenced in a diverse array of people with distinct affiliations and allegiances. Without question, the principle of self-determination nurtured the proliferation of sovereignty, yet ideas about statelessness—what made it a problem from the perspective of international law—contributed to the postwar stabilization of the boundaries of international politics.[94]

As new states entered the international system, waves of migration and displacement followed. Statelessness proliferated as former colonial subjects navigated between novel regimes of protection and citizenship laws. Many who would become permanently stateless after decolonization were members of groups who sided with the wrong faction during the struggle for independence. Others were caught between the gradual disappearance of imperial status and the difficulties of obtaining citizenship in newly formed postcolonial states.[95] Some postcolonial governments justified exclusionary legislation by looking to extend imperial legal status. When Sierra Leone gained formal independence from Britain in 1961, the post-independence government proposed the creation of a "commonwealth citizenship" status to provide coverage for anyone who became stateless through the nationality laws of the new country.[96] The end of imperial governance involved the abolition of the varied forms of membership that characterized nationality in empire. However, officials continued to appeal on a case-by-case basis to extend the status of British protected subjects to individuals who did not regain a national status following the independence of former British colonies. The imperial dimensions of nationality as a formal status that conferred protection persisted for a time in the imagination of British officials. J. M. Ross, a lawyer who ran the nationality division within the Home Office, wrote that the concept of "citizenship of the commonwealth" now represented an unsustainable legal fiction since the commonwealth consisted of independent states and was not a federation. Ross concluded that commonwealth citizenship, without possessing the citizenship of an individual common-wealth country, represented an "empty concept" divorced from social or po-litical reality.[97]

Public focus shifted to the legal and political claims to independence and statehood as the international community of states expanded. In the UN General Assembly and in the anticolonial imagination more broadly, Pales-tinians began to exemplify the plight of people without citizenship, and the fact that overcoming statelessness remained bound together with the pros-pects for statehood.[98] By 1974, the UN High Commission for Refugees had become the main organization charged with receiving applications from any-one without a nationality. However, by this point the legally stateless had largely disappeared from public debate and from the attentions of interna-tional lawyers and civil servants at the United Nations. In his 1976 study of international law and statelessness, Peter Mutharika—a legal scholar and the future president of Malawi—began one of the few books devoted to the subject from this period with the statement that legal statelessness does not arouse the same kind of international interest as refugees within internation-al agencies or in international legal scholarship.[99]

The question often asked about human rights treaties is whether they make a difference, and whether they are only honored in the breach. As we have seen, when it comes to the codification of statelessness in international law, there is much more to consider since the provisions contained within the agreements do not fully capture the wider framing of the problem of statelessness in postwar international thought. In the postwar debates over the significance and meaning of statelessness, all parties appealed to values to articulate the nature of the deprivation represented by the loss of nation-al status. However, only the appeal to the idea that the loss of nationality was objectionable because of its effects on international order provided the strongest argument for the centrality of the problem for the world at large. Recasting the problem in terms of morally richer considerations shifted at-tention away from the legal status of individuals under international law and from the basic premises of global order.

Conclusion

W<small>HEN THE LEGALLY STATELESS</small> returned to international prominence at the end of the Cold War, the global visibility of the problem coincided with widespread conviction about the erosion of sovereignty and the death of the state. In the wake of the breakups of the USSR, Yugoslavia, and Czechoslovakia in the early 1990s, which generated new populations without national membership, a 1995 UN General Assembly resolution mandated that the UNHCR direct its attention to preventing statelessness. Toward this end, the agency established a designated post to work with states and other international agencies to promote compliance with existing conventions.[1] However, even as the state form spread across the globe, experts declared the era when states represented the central actors of international politics to be approaching its end. Reflecting on the dominance of a discourse about the erosion of sovereignty due to the forces of globalization, the historian of political thought John Pocock remarked in a 1997 lecture, "sovereignty and history are widely regarded as marked out for demolition."[2] Despite the fact that by the end of the twentieth century, the international system consisted of 191 states represented in the United Nations, with an estimated 575 potential states, in the 1990s policy elites and social scientists proposed that state sovereignty had begun to break down under the pressures of increasing economic interdependence and the growing prominence of nongovernmental organizations. Along similar argumentative lines, the establishment of the European Union in 1992 seemed to some a return to a time when identities and sovereignties, supranational, national, and local, vied for people's loyalties. Under the umbrella of American global political hegemony, policymakers proposed a return to earlier ideas about an international order composed of diverse political entities, including groups with national rights without sovereignty over a defined territory, or minority rights protection under the auspices of an international organization.[3] States would have to share authority with multinational corporations, nongovernmental organizations, and legally empowered minority groups and indigenous peoples who

228

had fought through the courts for local territorial rights and the recognition of treaty obligations.[4]

In the context of predictions about the end of states, or at least of conventional conceptions of sovereignty, the global stateless provoked revelations about the state's continuing importance—the need for its existence and protection at a moment when the denial of its power and necessity had achieved public prominence.[5] It was in this moment that Hannah Arendt's discussion of modern statelessness became the critical touchstone for comprehending the plight of anyone without the security of citizenship. Arendt's writings gained new adherents in the post–Cold War moment because of how they powerfully captured the melancholy of an international order that proclaimed the rights of individuals against the state but ensured that rights remained dependent on state power. Discourses of globalization and human rights in the 1990s bolstered the idea that the stateless represented a remnant of state power in an era of waning state capacity, a claim that often depended on tracing the history of exclusive sovereignty back to the 1648 Treaty of Westphalia. According to such narratives, a world of exclusive sovereign states had begun in the post–Cold War years to give way to a world that was more unified morally and politically. The idea of statelessness as a painful paradox in an age of rights therefore began to assume novel significance in liberal international thought, embodying the persistent tension between cosmopolitanism and nationalism, universalism and particularism, universal human rights and exclusivist rights to citizenship.[6]

One of the central aims of this study has been to clarify the conceptual and normative resources available for comprehending the significance of statelessness at the present moment. This book has sought to challenge the idea that the bounds of traditional sovereignty were only crossed after 1945, and that the stateless embody the contradiction between sovereignty and human rights. The history of critical reflection on the concept of statelessness, set in the novel international institutional settings established in the twentieth century, provides a more grounded, historical, perspective on the current relationship between state and nonstate legal orders.[7] As the journalist Atossa Abrahamian has detailed, for the wealthy, the world has become postnational and largely for sale; consumers can collect passports and claim citizenship in countries that house their wealth tax free. The decline of social citizenship as an ideal and a public policy in the later twentieth century coincided with the possibility of owning multiple nationalities. Citizenship by investment programs, along with offshore tax registries, have become prevalent among those who can afford it, while picking and choosing residencies and tax regimes helps those with means to live as if there are no borders at all. According to one libertarian version of this fantasy, states are no longer required to provide the basis for faith in the monetary system as a result of technological innovation. Identity is confirmed by a block chain app; money is made and spent through a stateless currency like Bitcoin that does not seem to depend on the guarantee of a government. Such new technology promises to overcome the clumsiness of the passport and to establish a world beyond government—though even if money flows digitally as though borders do not exist, the individuals who seek to move money around still need passports in order to visit their accounts.[8]

For the poor and disenfranchised, membership in a state is as important as ever. The ability to move across borders manifests global patterns of inequality—some people can collect dozens of passports while others languish without one. Today's legally stateless are often excluded from basic national provisions such as employment and education. Lacking passports and birth certificates, they are unable to make claims on the state and become vulnerable to a variety of predatory practices such as trafficking. The UN High Commissioner for Refugees has called on the agency to eradicate statelessness in a decade, initiating a campaign to end global statelessness by 2024. This advocacy has a complex relationship to older approaches to statelessness, and embodies both continuity and change. On the one hand, even as the problem of legal statelessness around the world assumed greater importance, the approach followed the segmented lines and institutional formations established in the postwar era. It is within the power of many of the countries where the majority of the legally stateless reside to register and confer citizenship, and lawyers, activists, and international organizations have developed techniques to persuade states to assume this responsibility. Their tactics have achieved some success based on the growing movement in the last few years to expand the number of countries that have signed on to the 1954 and 1961 UN conventions. On the other hand, though international and nongovernmental agencies rely on the script established by the conventions, existing frameworks are stretched to accommodate new causes of statelessness that have emerged in recent years due to forced migration.[9]

Indeed, from the perspective of present-day advocates, the notion of a baseline right to nationality—an assurance of a formal legal status—favored by Hannah Arendt and Josef Kunz, appears somewhat antiquated. Yet the argumentative context in which the legal frameworks were established in international law illuminates the terms of contemporary advocacy and legal argument. Arendt and Kunz feared that the emphasis on the substantive dimensions of citizenship would bear negatively upon the urgency of the matter of how people enter and gain membership within one of the world's states. For many years, their prediction proved accurate. However, as the legally stateless assumed greater importance within the UN and refugee agencies, legal scholars and activists have deemphasized the rigid divisions between legal categories in favor of practical examinations of the real conditions of actual human beings. The problem of functional statelessness has assumed priority in the activist imagination, leading to arguments emphasizing state obligation to recognize effective nationality. Activists discuss the problem with the distinction, for example, between *de jure* or *de facto* statelessness. *De facto* statelessness means that a person may have a nationality in a formal sense, but cannot turn to the state where they live for protection. As one UN report explains, a legally resident noncitizen may enjoy more protections in a particular state then a citizen of a state under a violent regime, while those who technically retain their legal connection to a state may effectively lack all substantive connection to it. Effective statelessness also means that a person is unable to prove their formal nationality or legal immigration status, a reality which affects the children of undocumented immigrants and those who belong to marginalized communities such as the Roma or the Rohingya who often lack the documents required to prove legal identity. The UNHCR estimates that at least 12 million people fall into this category.[10]

One dangerous consequence of the *Nottebohm* decision, from the standpoint of the international lawyers and commentators critical of the outcome of the case discussed in Chapter 6, was to deprioritize statelessness as an "evil." The principle of the effective link asserted in the judgment, however, is today thought to contain the resources to challenge governmental claims about whether an individual, or a minority group, possesses a national status.[11] Territory and communal ties are the two arguments often invoked in defense of the stateless and the undocumented. Territory is figured as a space of ethical obligation and as a way to show the true nature of attachment to place and polity even in the absence of formal recognition.[12] As opposed to the arguments presented by Kunz, Arendt, and others about visibility and personality in formal, legal terms, contemporary advocates tend to argue that it is better to emphasize the social linkages that bind someone to a particular community. They imply that there is a source of judgment about national status outside of any particular government, and that this judgment rests on the "real" connections that bind an individual to a place. The social bond and relationships that connect people to places circumvent or subvert the way states define the boundary of their citizenry and legal residency.[13] Focusing on the social basis of national membership removes the ultimate source of judgment about legal membership from the state to the domain of international law, and the guardians of that legal order. A person may be a national even if the state in question is unable or unwilling to confirm this fact, and migrants constitute a reality by building lives and communities in particular places. Presumptions about international law or the conventions of interstate order are less significant here than the facts on the ground produced by everyday practices and relationships.

Two of the major traditions of thought typically deployed to engage with migration from a normative standpoint are political philosophy and international law. The story told in this book places both traditions in historical perspective. It has explored the critical historical developments as well as the concepts that have framed debate and argument about the creation of borders and what it means to constitute and cross them. Political and moral philosophers have taken up the justice and legitimacy of membership and the boundaries of the state, particularly in the last decade, in a way that is markedly different from the legalist debates surveyed in this book. In contrast to reasoning that depends on existing legal frameworks, they apply principles and moral judgments to evaluate the justness of the categories and institutions that define citizenship and non-citizenship, at times building on the conventions, and at times questioning their validity from the perspective of justice.[14] It is not insignificant, in light of the particular genealogy elaborated in this book, that the foundations of modern political philosophy lie in the rejection of logical positivism and the formal separation of law from morality. Moral arguments about the principles governing the boundaries of membership, the rules of entry, exit, and asylum, have dominated political philosophy since the 1970s, and it has been the criticism of legalist approaches to distribution and membership that shifted analysis of boundary questions toward the arena of moral judgment.[15] The distance from the post–World War I era is also evident in the fact that the robustness of the discourse on human rights and human dignity in the second half of the twentieth century has made the debates about legal personhood, which characterized the first period of critical reflection, seem impoverished by comparison. Moral personality is envisioned as something more substantial than the capacity to sue or be sued in a court of law. Whereas the independent legal existence of corporate entities in the early twentieth century furnished a powerful example of legal standing independent of the state, the moral revolution in the second half of the twentieth century that figured the individual human being as the sacred object of rights and duties began to be exploited as a resource for according corporations greater standing within an emergent system of global law. The fact that "humanity" has become more than a legal category, that it carries certain moral assumptions not present in the concept of legal personhood, has made it seem less susceptible to appropriation by corporations seeking rights against the states of the world.[16]

Yet climate change as a cause of forced displacement has made contemplating the conceptual and legal foundations of global order inescapable. It also points to the problems that arise when the political implications of mass displacement are conceptualized only in terms of a static vision of international order. In the likely not so distant future, when whole nations— Micronesia, the Maldives or Tuvalu—become submerged, the dispossessed population would not under current regimes enjoy the protection of any government. They would therefore be *de facto* stateless. The boundaries of states are breaking down in new ways; forced migration is inextricable from this process. Territorial sovereignties face erosion by rising sea levels, raising the question of how to comprehend the continuing statehood of these nations as territory disappears. In a new era of climate change and mass migration, what will be the definition of statehood, and who will decide? Are disappearing states a new kind of subject under international law? Does territory remain one of the fundamental features of statehood?[17] If Maldivians, for example, were to retain some nominal "nationality" without the benefits of a territorial state, there would be no remedy for them under international law since they do not conform to the de jure definition of statelessness supplied by the convention. Political theorists have begun to emphasize the limits of

existing normative approaches to migration in light of the dynamic transformation of territory, but there is much work to be done. Paulina Ochoa
Espejo has recently argued that a country's given boundaries can be justified
democratically by assuming existing peoples and given territories but that
this strategy fails when immigration has challenged the existing boundaries of nations and states. Such approaches would, moreover, be insufficient
in the case of contested territorial claims or of territorial problems related
to massive migrations that will likely emerge from a global environmental
crisis.[18]

In the aftermath of the First World War, Kurt Schwitters's *Merz* collages
evoked the remaking of the map of the world. One of his collages from this
period is the cover image for this book. The image draws our attention to a
broader self-consciousness in Europe and the wider world about the breakdown and creation of political order in the years following the war. In those
years, a variety of theorists linked statelessness to debates about the conceptual foundations of political and legal order. By attending to the intersecting
histories of empire, sovereignty, internationalism, and legal thought, this book
has sought to explain the particular intellectual and ideological contexts in
which these debates about the meaning and significance of statelessness took
place. It has traced the origins and legacies of these doctrines and the institutions that enabled them, which continue to shape global politics. What the
story of the legal category of statelessness reveals about international history
is that ideas have played a more significant role in the creation of modern international order than is often assumed. It also suggests that the intellectual
history of law and legal thought is fundamental not only to making sense of
the history of ideas about nationality and statelessness, but to the history of
international order itself. Over the course of the twentieth century, the intellectual premises that sustained legal positivism and legal formalism were
eroded or challenged. These technical debates had important consequences
for how political and legal actors codified the problem of statelessness in
the postwar legal frameworks, which in turn contributed to the stabilization
of the conventional boundaries of international politics. These frameworks
thus had an important ideological function, which this study has tried to
make visible.

What resources are available for conceptualizing the ongoing and rapidly
accelerating crisis of statelessness today? The pandemic that has transformed

the world as I complete this book has shown the undeniable importance of national governments assuming responsibility for collective catastrophes. If states remain the most important actors or agents of global order, what frameworks and vocabularies can we use to comprehend that which does not fit within the boundaries of states? If we are to have answers to these questions today, we will have to connect them to the broader transformations of political and legal order that characterize our own time, just as the protagonists of this book did in the period of breakdown and creativity that characterized theirs.

ABBREVIATIONS

BT	Board of Trade
CO	Colonial Office Papers
DO	Dominions Office
FO	Foreign Office Papers
FRUS	Foreign Relations of the United States
HO	Home Office
LNA	League of Nations Archive
NUOI	Nation Unies et Organizations Internationales
TNA: PRO	The National Archives, Kew
UN	United Nations
UNHCR	United Nations High Commissioner for Refugees
UNRRA	United Nations Relief and Rehabilitation Administration

NOTES

INTRODUCTION

1 Kurt Schwitters, *Das Literarische Werk*, ed. Friedhelm Lach (Munich: Deutsche Taschenbuch Verlag, 2005), LW 5:335–336. Cited in Megan R. Luke, *Kurt Schwitters: Space, Image, Exile* (Chicago: University of Chicago Press, 2014), 4–5.

2 Jane McAdam, "Disappearing States, Statelessness, and the Boundaries of International Law," in *Climate Change and Displacement: Multidisciplinary Perspectives*, ed. Jane McAdam (Oxford: Hart, 2010), 105–131. Patrick Sykes, "Sinking States: Climate Change and the Next Refugee Crisis," *Foreign Affairs*, September 28, 2015.

3 Countries that have signed on to the 1954 Convention agree not to deport anyone who would otherwise have nowhere else to go. Together with the 1961 Convention, the postwar agreements establish the particular obligations of signatory states toward stateless people. See Chandran Kukathas, "Are Refugees Special?," in *Migration in Political Theory: The Ethics of Movement and Membership*, ed. Sarah Fine and Lea Ypi (Oxford: Oxford University Press, 2016), 249–269.

4 Convention Relating to the Status of Refugees, Geneva, July 28, 1951; Convention Relating to the Status of Stateless Persons (adopted September 28, 1954; entered into force June 6, 1960).

5 Kristy Belton, "The Neglected Non-Citizen: Statelessness and Liberal Political Theory," *Journal of Global Ethics* 7, no. 1 (2011): 59–71; Lindsay N. Kingston, "A Forgotten Human Rights Crisis: Statelessness and Issue (Non) Emergence," *Human Rights Review* 14 (2013): 73–87; Michelle Foster and Hélène Lambert, "Statelessness as a Human Rights Issue: A Concept Whose Time Has Come," *International Journal of Refugee Law* 28, no. 4 (2016): 564–584.

6 Judith Shklar, *American Citizenship: The Quest for Inclusion* (Cambridge, MA: Harvard University Press, 1991), 4.

7 Compare to an ontological approach to statelessness, or to the idea that the consequence of category formation is to create a certain kind of person. See, for example, Ian Hacking, *The Social Construction of What?* (Cambridge, MA: Harvard University Press, 2000). On the birth, life, or death of objects of research like "memory" or "the economy," see Lorraine Daston, "Historical Epistemology," in *Questions of Evidence: Proof, Practice, and Persuasion across the Disciplines*, ed. James Chandler, Arnold Davidson, and Harry Harootunian (Chicago: University of Chicago Press, 1994), 282–289.

8 See for example Michael Marrus, *The Unwanted: European Refugees from the First World War to the Cold War* (Philadelphia: Temple University Press, 2002); Claudena Skran, *Refugees in Inter-War Europe: The Emergence of a Regime* (Oxford: Oxford University Press, 1995); John Torpey, *The Invention of the Passport: Surveillance, Citizenship, and the State* (Cambridge: Cambridge University Press, 2000).

9 Jane Burbank and Frederick Cooper, *Empires in World History: Power and the Politics of Difference* (Princeton, NJ: Princeton University Press, 2010), 380–387; Pieter

Judson, *The Habsburg Empire: A New History* (Cambridge, MA: Harvard University Press, 2016); Manu Goswami, "Colonial Internationalisms and Imaginary Futures," *American Historical Review* 117, no. 5 (2012): 1461–1485; Susan Pedersen, *The Guardians: The League of Nations and the Crisis of Empire* (Oxford: Oxford University Press, 2015); Mark Mazower, *No Enchanted Palace: The End of Empire and the Ideological Origins of the United Nations* (Princeton, NJ: Princeton University Press, 2009); Sunil Amrith, *Crossing the Bay of Bengal: The Furies of Nature and the Fortunes of Migrants* (Cambridge, MA: Harvard University Press, 2015); Adom Getachew, *Worldmaking after Empire: The Rise and Fall of Self-Determination* (Princeton, NJ: Princeton University Press, 2019). On the historical emergence of an imagined world of states, see David Armitage, *Foundations of Modern International Thought* (Cambridge: Cambridge University Press, 2013); Jennifer Pitts, *Boundaries of the International: Law and Empire* (Cambridge, MA: Harvard University Press, 2018).

10 On the history of nationality and international law as fundamentally bottom-up, socio-legal or administrative, phenomena, compare Will Hanley, *Identifying with Nationality: Europeans, Ottomans, and Egyptians in Alexandria* (New York: Columbia University Press, 2017); Lauren Benton and Lisa Ford, *Rage for Order: The British Empire and the Origins of International Law, 1800–1850* (Cambridge, MA: Harvard University Press, 2016).

11 Patrick Weil, *The Sovereign Citizen: Denaturalization and the Origins of the American Republic* (Philadelphia: University of Pennsylvania Press, 2013), 6.

12 See Franz Neumann and Otto Kirchheimer, *The Rule of Law under Siege*, ed. William E. Scheuerman (Berkeley: University of California Press, 1996); Roberto Unger, *Law in Modern Society: Toward a Criticism of Social Theory* (New York: Free Press, 1976); Duncan Kennedy, "The Disenchantment of Logically Formal Legal Rationality: Or, Max Weber's Sociology in the Genealogy of the Contemporary Mode of Western Legal Thought," in *Max Weber's Economy and Society: A Critical Companion*, ed. Charles Camic, Philip S. Gorski, and David M. Rubek (Stanford, CA: Stanford University Press, 2005); Jürgen Habermas, "Law and Morality," in *The Tanner Lectures on Human Values*, ed. S. McMurrin, trans. K. Baynes, (Salt Lake City: Utah University Press, 1988), 8:217–279.

13 On the natural law foundations of Grotius's theory of the law of nations, see Benjamin Straumann, *Roman Law in the State of Nature: The Classical Foundations of Hugo Grotius' Natural Law* (Cambridge: Cambridge University Press, 2015).

14 In 1925 Sterling E. Edmunds offered a concise description of the problem: "The position, or lack of position, of stateless members of society in international law is significant. They are objects of the Law of Nations in so far as they fall under the territorial supremacy of the state on whose territory they live. But since they are without nationality, the tie by which they could derive the benefits from international law is missing and therefore they lack the protection as far as such law is concerned." *The Lawless Law of Nations: An Exposition of Prevailing Arbitrary International Legal System in Relation to Its Influence upon Civil Liberty* (Washington, DC: J. Byrne, 1925), 15.

15 Peter Sahlins, *Unnaturally French: Foreign Citizens in the Old Regime and After* (Ithaca, NY: Cornell University Press, 2004); Hanley, *Identifying with Nationality*; Saskia

Sassen, *Territory, Authority, Rights: From Medieval to Global Assemblages* (Princeton, NJ: Princeton University Press, 2006), 281. On the imperial, hierarchical dimensions of nationality, see, Lauren Benton, Adam Clulow, and Bain Attwood, eds., *Protection and Empire: A Global History* (Cambridge: Cambridge University Press, 2017); Emmanuelle Saada, *Empire's Children: Race, Filiation, and Citizenship in the French Colonies*, trans. Arthur Goldhammer (Chicago: University of Chicago Press, 2012); Karen Knop, *Diversity and Self-Determination in International Law* (Cambridge: Cambridge University Press, 2004), 8.

16 Compare Will Hanley, "Statelessness: An Invisible Theme in the History of International Law," *European Journal of International Law* 25, no. 1 (2014): 321–327.

17 Compare Astrid Kjedlgaard-Pedersen, *The International Legal Personality of the Individual* (Oxford: Oxford University Press, 2018). Anne Peters, *Beyond Human Rights: The Legal Status of the Individual in International Law* (Cambridge: Cambridge University Press, 2016).

18 The history of cosmopolitan law has generally been told from the perspectives of the individuals who had the most to lose as diverse empires gave way to national states in the decade after the First World War. By creating law that encompassed all humanity, they sought to circumvent or combat the consequences of national exclusion and mass violence. According to this interpretation, their efforts contributed to the heroic establishment of law that defines the rights and obligations of individuals and groups beyond the limits of recognized sovereign states. See, for example, Philippe Sands, *East West Street: On the Origins of "Genocide" and "Crimes against Humanity"* (New York: Knopf, 2016); Seyla Benhabib, *Exile, Statelessness, and Migration: Playing Chess with History from Hannah Arendt to Isaiah Berlin* (Princeton, NJ: Princeton University Press, 2018).

19 Marc Vishniac, "Le statut international des apatrides," *Recueil des cours de l'Académie de la Haye* 43 (1933): 217. (Generally cited as "Mark Vishniak" in this book).

20 On the virtues of thick description for grasping historical transformation, see William Sewell, *Logics of History: Social Theory and Social Transformation* (Chicago: University of Chicago Press, 2005), 184–185.

21 Hannah Arendt, *The Origins of Totalitarianism* (New York: Schocken Books, 1951), 278. Arendt promoted the idea that until after the Second World War, the stateless were considered "legal freaks" without law.

22 On the idea of bracketing the origins and foundations of fundamental conceptual and political boundaries, see Pierre Bourdieu, "Rethinking the State: Genesis and Structure of the Bureaucratic Field," trans. Loic J. D. Wacquant and Samar Farage, *Sociological Theory* 12, no. 1 (1994): 1–18.

1. FROM A SUBJECT OF FICTION TO A LEGAL REALITY

1 The files on *Stoeck v. Public Trustee* are located in the National Archives, CO/323/857 and HO 144/11489.

2 Chancery Division, *Stoeck v. Public Trustee*, Annotated Law Reports, http://www.uniset.ca/naty/maternity/19212Ch67.htm.

3 Compare Erez Manela and Robert Gerwarth, eds., *Empires at War, 1911–1923* (Oxford: Oxford University Press, 2014).

4 On an international order as a "matter of refined thought," see Herbert Butterfield, "The Balance of Power," in *Diplomatic Investigations: Essays on the Theory of International Politics*, ed. Herbert Butterfield and Martin Wight (London: George Allen and Unwin, 1966), 147.

5 "Denationalized Germans under the Treaty of Peace," *Times Law Reports*, April 29, 1921, HO 144/11489, TNA: PRO. On the unique significance of *Stoeck v. Public Trustee* in subsequent debates on statelessness, see Paul Weis, *Nationality and Statelessness in International Law* (London: Stevens, 1956); "Report by Mr. A Jaffe on 'Statelessness in English Law,'" Grotius Society Committee for the Status of Stateless Persons, September 27, 1940, Paul Weis Papers, PW/PR/GRSO 1, Social Sciences Library, University of Oxford.

6 Andreas Fahrmeir, "Passports and the Status of Aliens," in *The Mechanics of Internationalism: Culture, Society and Politics from the 1840s to the First World War*, ed. Michael Geyer and Johannes Paulmann (Oxford: Oxford University Press, 2001), 110; H. S. Q. Henriques, *The Law of Aliens and Naturalization, including the Text of the Aliens Act, 1905* (London: Butterworth, 1906). For the larger story of migration from the German lands to Britain, see John R. David, Stefan Maz, and Margrit Schulte Beerbühl, eds., *Transnational Networks: German Migrants in the British Empire, 1670–1914* (Leiden: Brill, 2012).

7 See generally Adam McKeown, *Melancholy Order: Asian Migration and the Globalization of Borders* (New York: Columbia University Press, 2008).

8 Friedrich Nietzsche to Georg Brandes, April 10, 1888, in *Selected Letters of Friedrich Nietzsche*, trans. Christopher Middleton (Indianapolis: Hackett, 1996), 293. Nietzsche traveled with a Swiss letter of protection from the Basel canton, though he was not a Swiss citizen and could not have become one since he had violated the Swiss residency requirements by joining up as a medical orderly in the Prussian military in 1870. David B. Allison, *Reading the New Nietzsche: The Birth of Tragedy, The Gay Science, Thus Spoke Zarathustra, On the Genealogy of Morals* (Lanham, MD: Rowman and Littlefield, 2001), 271.

9 On the ideology of "connectivity talk" in the late nineteenth century, see Vanessa Ogle, *The Global Transformation of Time, 1870–1950* (Cambridge, MA: Harvard University Press, 2015), 204.

10 David Feldman, "The Distinctiveness of Public Law," in *The Cambridge Companion to Public Law* (Cambridge: Cambridge University Press, 2015), 17–37; Morton Horwitz, *The Transformation of American Law, 1870–1960: The Crisis of Legal Orthodoxy* (Oxford: Oxford University Press, 1995); Karen Knop, "Citizenship, Public and Private," *Law and Contemporary Problems* 71, no. 3 (2008): 309–341. On the individual right to contract and property as the object of private international law jurisprudence in the nineteenth century, see Christopher Casey, *Nationals Abroad: Globalization, Individual Rights, and the Making of Modern International Law* (Cambridge: Cambridge University Press, 2020); Martti Koskeniemmi Koskenniemi, "Nationalism, Universalism,

Empire: International Law in 1871 and 1919" (paper presented at "Whose International Community? Universalism and the Legacies of Empire," Columbia University, New York, NY, April 29–30, 2005).

11 Stephen Kern, "Changing Concepts and Experiences of Time and Space," in *The Fin de Siècle World*, ed. Michael Saler (London: Routledge, 2015), 74–91. By 1907, the passport system was described in a French dissertation as "a dead part of legal history." Fahrmeir, "Passports and the Status of Aliens," 105.

12 "Two Electric Safety Lamps," *Coal Age Magazine*, September 21, 1921.

13 Metropolitan Police Criminal Investigation Department, "Stoeck v. Public Trustee," September 18, 1914, HO 144/11489, TNA: PRO.

14 On the creation of a new "crustacean type of nation" during the First World War, see Karl Polanyi, *The Great Transformation: The Political and Economic Origins of Our Time* (Boston: Beacon, 1944), 122.

15 Sara Abrevaya Stein, *Extraterritorial Dreams: European Citizenship, Sephardi Jews, and the Ottoman Twentieth Century* (Chicago: University of Chicago Press, 2016), 57–67; Salahi R. Sonyel, "The Protégé System in the Ottoman Empire," *Journal of Islamic Studies* 2, no. 1 (1991): 56–66.

16 Metropolitan Police Criminal Investigation Department, "Stoeck v. Public Trustee," September 18, 1914, HO144/11489, TNA: PRO. On the process of "deglobalization" in the interwar era involving protectionism, restrictions on international lending, and antimigration policies, see Harold James, *The End of Globalization: Lessons from the Great Depression* (Cambridge, MA: Harvard University Press, 2001).

17 J. C. Bird, *Control of Enemy Alien Civilians in Great Britain, 1914–1918* (New York: Garland, 1986), 17, 203.

18 London Metropolitan Police report on Stoeck's request for a certificate of naturalization on September 18, 1914, file: Alien Restrictions, Aliens Branch, HO 144/11489, TNA: PRO.

19 Bird, *Control of Enemy Alien Civilians*, 322.

20 Coleman Phillipson, *International Law and the Great War* (London: T. Fisher Unwin, 1915), 71; Michael Lobban, "Introduction: The Great War and Private Law," *Comparative Legal History* 2, no. 2 (2014) 163–183; Geoffrey Jones, *Multinationals and Global Capitalism* (Oxford: Oxford University Press, 2005), 286.

21 Imprisonment was not the original goal. Parliament initially prioritized a form of population exchange. Bird, *Control of Enemy Alien Civilians*, 173. For estimates of the numbers of civilian enemy aliens in France, Britain, Germany, the United States, and Australia, see Eric Lohr, *Nationalizing the Russian Empire: The Campaign against Enemy Aliens during World War I* (Cambridge, MA: Harvard University Press, 2003), 178. On the genealogy of the category of enemy aliens more generally, see Daniela Caglioti, "Waging War on Civilians: The Expulsion of Aliens in the Franco-Prussian War," *Past and Present* 221, no. 1 (2013): 161–195; Caglioti, "Property Rights in Times of War: Sequestration and Liquidation of Enemy Alien Assets in Western Europe during the First World War," *Journal of Modern European History* 12, no 4 (2014): 523–545. Also see J. M. Winter, "British National Identity and the First World War,"

in *The Boundaries of the State in Modern Britain*, ed. S. J. D. Green and R. C. Whiting (Cambridge: Cambridge University Press, 1996), 261–278. By an act of Parliament on April 7, 1915, France denaturalized many naturalized French citizens born in enemy countries except those living in Alsace-Lorraine who had been French citizens before the Prussian victory in 1871; the minister of justice could in accordance with his own judgment decide which naturalized Frenchmen were worthy of retaining their French nationality. On the discretion exercised by national bureaucracies in the determination of national status, see James Wilford Garner, "Treatment of Enemy Aliens: Measures in Respect to Personal Liberty," *American Journal of International Law* 12, no. 1 (1918): 27–55.

22 M. Stoeck to Richard Redmayne, August 1914, Aliens Branch, HO 144/11489, TNA: PRO.

23 M. Rouse to Prisoner of War Department, August 9, 1916, Aliens Branch, HO 144/11489, TNA: PRO.

24 Stoeck to Redmayne, August 1914.

25 Rouse to Prisoner of War Department, August 9, 1916.

26 "Denationalized Germans," *Times Law Reports*.

27 In a letter to Whitehall, Stoeck's solicitors noted that "a very large number of cases depend upon the decision of this action." Cruesemann and Rouse to Under Secretary of State, Whitehall, February 9, 1921, Aliens Branch, HO 144/11489, TNA: PRO. Also see the decision of the Belgian Court of Cassation of January 10, 1921, in *Procureur-General v. Schneider*. The court upheld the right of an "alien of indeterminate nationality" to oppose the order to seize the movable property of enemy aliens. Also see the Court of Appeals of Ghent of February 1, 1924, in *Belgian State v. Haupert and de Vuyst*. Cited in André Colanéri, *De la condition des "sans-patrie," étude critique de l'heimatlosat* (Paris: Librairie générale de droit et de jurisprudence, 1932), 176.

28 "Denationalized Germans," *Times Law Reports*.

29 Memorandum, May 27, 1921, HO 144/11489, TNA: PRO. A lawyer from Lincoln's Inn reviewed the issue of "stateless" German nationals based on the Treaty of Peace in 1919 and offered some general remarks on the varying evidence requirements between those born stateless and those claiming to have lost their nationality due to the details of the German law, but added, "I do not pretend to be familiar with German law . . . the questions I have drafted should be submitted to someone in the Foreign Office better qualified than I am to deal with this subject." BT 103/482.

30 Chancery Division, *Stoeck v. Public Trustee*.

31 In the later nineteenth century, British courts had begun moving toward the establishment of a rule that recognition would be denied if a foreign judgment contravened rules of natural justice. See Peter North, "Private International Law in Twentieth Century England," ed. *Jack Beatson and Reinhard Zimmermann Jurists Uprooted: Émigré Lawyers in Twentieth Century Britain* (Oxford: Oxford University Press, 2004), 483–517.

32 Jane Burbank and Frederick Cooper, "The Empire Effect," *Public Culture* 24, no. 2 (2012): 239–247; Edward Keene, *Beyond the Anarchical Society: Grotius, Colonialism*

and Order in World Politics (Cambridge: Cambridge University Press, 2002); Gerrit W. Gong, *The Standard of "Civilization" in International Society* (Oxford: Clarendon, 1984); Martti Koskenniemi, *The Gentle Civilizer of Nations: The Rise and Fall of International Law, 1870–1960* (Cambridge: Cambridge University Press, 2001), 174.

33 File: Alien Restrictions, Aliens Branch, HO 144/11489, TNA: PRO.

34 Chancery Division, *Stoeck v. Public Trustee.*

35 Cruesemann and Rouse to Under Secretary of State, Whitehall, February 9, 1921, HO 144/11489, TNA: PRO.

36 Cruesemann and Rouse to Under Secretary of State, February 9, 1921. It only helped Stoeck's claim that he had left before the passage of a law that allowed German subjects to retain their nationality even after settling elsewhere and to transmit German citizenship to their children. See Rogers Brubaker, *Citizenship and Nationhood in France and Germany* (Cambridge, MA: Harvard University Press, 1992), 115–119.

37 Chancery Division, *Stoeck v. Public Trustee.* See Brubaker, *Citizenship and Nationhood,* 21, 195.

38 He also cited the facts that the German military law of 1913 imposes the burden of military service on stateless persons and that the position of a stateless person is recognized in article 29 of the German Introductory Statute of 1896. Chancery Division, *Stoeck v. Public Trustee.*

39 "Denationalized Germans," *Times Law Reports.*

40 Chancery Division, *Stoeck v. Public Trustee.*

41 According to the British constitutional theorist A. V. Dicey, British judges should take into account the rules of a foreign government if the case demanded it, "distributing property for example as an Italian judge would." Russell, by contrast, did not attempt to discern German law. Instead, he deferred to the testimony of the legal experts from Germany that Cruesemann and Rouse had brought before the court. Dicey, *A Digest of the Law of England with Reference to the Conflict of Laws* (London: Stevens, 1908), 715.

42 "Denationalized Germans," *Times Law Reports.*

43 Edmund Burke, "Inquiry into the Seizure of Private Property in St. Eustatius," in *The Speeches of the Right Honourable Edmund Burke in The House of Commons and in Westminster Hall* (Piccadilly: Longman, 1816), 11:251. On Burke's invocation of the law of nations in the case of the property seizure and banishment of the Jews of St. Eustatius, see Jennifer Pitts, *Boundaries of the International: Law and Empire* (Cambridge MA: Harvard University Press, 2018), 98. On the context of imperial reform, see Richard Bourke, *Empire and Revolution: The Political Life of Edmund Burke* (Princeton, NJ: Princeton University Press, 2015), 434–438. On the concept of the outlaw in international thought generally, see Renée Jeffery, "The Wolf at the Door: Hospitality and the Outlaw in International Relations," in *Hospitality and World Politics,* ed. Gideon Baker (London: Palgrave, 2013), 124–145.

44 According to the *corpus iuris civilis,* the medieval codification of Roman law, Roman citizens deported as a punishment lost the rights and privileges that derived from a connection to civil law, but retained the rights that derived from the law of nations.

See Cornelius M. Riethdorf, *Citizenship, Exile, and Natural Rights in Medieval Roman Law, 1200–1400* (PhD dissertation, Cambridge University, 2016).

45 *Talbot v. Janson*, 3 U.S. 133 (1795); James H. Keitner, *The Development of American Citizenship, 1608–1870* (Chapel Hill: University of North Carolina Press, 1978), 278–280. On nationality and its accompanying paperwork in the age of revolution, see Nathan Perl-Rosenthal, *Citizen Sailors: Becoming American in the Age of Revolution* (Cambridge, MA: Belknap Press of Harvard University Press, 2015).

46 Jean-Pierre Tabin, Arnaud Frauenfelder, and Carola Togni, "The Recipients of Public Welfare: The Example of Two Swiss Cantons around 1890," *Social History* 34, no. 3 (2009): 321–338.

47 Jean Holloway, *Edward Everett Hale: A Biography* (Austin: University of Texas Press, 1956), 238.

48 "A Man without a Country—a Curious Article," *The Atlantic Monthly*, December 28, 1863. On statelessness in American history, see Linda Kerber, "The Stateless as the Citizen's Other: A View from the United States," *American Historical Review* 112, no. 1 (2007): 1–34.

49 In 1865, Denmark ceded the provinces of Schleswig-Holstein to Prussia. After the cession, the inhabitants of these provinces were granted the right to opt for either Danish or Prussian nationality. The children of those who had opted for Danish nationality but had not been expelled were regarded as stateless by the Prussian government and were required to be formally naturalized before being granted citizenship at the discretion of the Prussian government. Erik Goldstein, *War and Peace Treaties: 1816–1991* (London: Routledge, 1992), 9.

50 The development of nationality regulations allowed governments to expand their territorial control over populations that evaded incorporation such as the Roma in Central Europe and Native Americans in the United States. The Russian and Habsburg Empires encouraged "undesirable" populations to emigrate but developed new mechanisms for maintaining an increasingly tight grip on the subjects they wished to retain. David M. Crowe, "The International and Historical Dimensions of Romani Migration in Central and Eastern Europe," *Nationalities Papers* 31, no. 1 (2003): 81–94; Tara Zahra, "'Condemned to Rootlessness and Unable to Budge': Roma, Migration Panics, and Internment in the Habsburg Empire," *American Historical Review* 122, no. 3 (2017): 702–726. On the growth of state control over the territorial interior of states over the course of the nineteenth century, see Charles Maier, *Leviathan 2.0: Inventing Modern Statehood* (Cambridge, MA: Belknap Press, 2014).

51 The Ottoman nationality law of 1869 gave the Ottoman government the authority to adjudicate matters relating to nationality, often involving the legal status of the children and wives of foreigners, as well as of emigrants. David Gutman, "Travel Documents, Mobility Control, and the Ottoman State in an Age of Global Migration, 1880–1915," *Journal of the Ottoman and Turkish Studies Association* 3, no. 2 (2016): 347–368.

52 In the mid-nineteenth century, the convenience of establishing clear agreements between countries over the recognition of each sovereign's respective rules regarding naturalization led to the multiplication of treaties, such as the Bancroft Treaties, between

the United States and other countries, governing the nationality of children born in foreign territories. Patrick Weil, *The Sovereign Citizen: Denaturalization and the Origins of the American Republic* (Philadelphia: University of Pennsylvania Press, 2013), 83.

53 Brubaker, *Citizenship and Nationhood*, 27.

54 The role of this group in the creation of a hierarchical international order has been the focus of recent scholarship. See Pitts, *Boundaries of the International*. Rose Parfitt, *The Process of International Legal Reproduction: Inequality, Historiography, Resistance* (Cambridge: Cambridge University Press, 2019).

55 Ludwig von Bar, *The Theory and Practice of Private International Law*, trans. G. R. Gillespie (Edinburgh: William Green, 1892), 111. Compare the definition of *state* in a German encyclopedia from the 1860s: "the collectivity of sedentary peoples that is united into a moral organic personality under the superior force driven by their common interest." Cited in Holly Case, *Between States: The Transylvanian Question and the European Idea during World War II* (Stanford, CA: Stanford University Press, 2009), 14.

56 See Maier, *Leviathan 2.0*, 156; William Novak, Stephen Sawyers, and James Sparrow, "Toward a History of the Democratic State," *Tocqueville Review* 33, no. 2 (2012): 7–18. See also, for example, Johann Caspar Bluntschli, *Theory of the State* (Oxford: Clarendon Press, 1885). Theodore Woolsey's *Introduction to the Study of International Law* from 1860 does not mention the term *stateless*, though he has one passing reference to persons of "no nationality" in the context of a discussion of belligerents and neutrals in the laws of war: "the neutral ought to discharge the duties of humanity to both belligerents, for these are still due even to an enemy, and are due to persons of no nationality." (Boston: J. Munroe, 1860), 356.

57 See Lauren Benton and Lisa Ford, *Rage for Order: The British Empire and the Origins of International Law, 1800–1850* (Cambridge, MA: Harvard University Press, 2016); Stuart Banner, *Possessing the Pacific: Land, Settler, and Indigenous People from Australia to Alaska* (Cambridge, MA: Harvard University Press, 2007). On the partitioning of Africa among the colonial powers in 1884, see Koskenniemi, *Gentle Civilizer of Nations*, chap. 2.

58 David Dudley Field, *Outline of an International Code*, 2nd ed. (New York: Baker, Voorhis, 1876), 130.

59 See von Bar, *Private International Law*, 209; John William Burgess, *Political Science and Comparative Constitutional Law* (Boston: Ginn, 1891), 52; Anthony Anghie, *Imperialism, Sovereignty, and the Making of International Law* (Cambridge: Cambridge University Press, 2005). On the emergence of the historical distinction between "the domestic and the foreign" or the "municipal and the international" in international thought, see David Armitage, *Foundations of Modern International Thought* (Cambridge: Cambridge University Press, 2013), 10.

60 Chancery Division, *Stoeck v. Public Trustee*.

61 Abigail Green, "Intervening in the Jewish Question, 1840–1878," in *Humanitarian Intervention: A History*, ed. Brendan Simms and D. J. B. Trim (Cambridge: Cambridge University Press, 2011), 139–159; Abigail Green, "The British Empire and the Jews: An Imperialism of Human Rights?," *Past and Present* 199, no. 1 (2008): 175–205;

Constantin Iordachi, "The Unyielding Boundaries of Citizenship: The Emancipation of 'Non-Citizens' In Romania, 1866–1918," *European Review of History* 8, no. 2 (2001): 157–186. On the history of humanitarian intervention, see Davide Rodogno, *Against Massacre: Humanitarian Interventions in the Ottoman Empire, 1815–1914* (Princeton, NJ: Princeton University Press, 2012). Also see Max Kohler and Simon Wolf, *Jewish Disabilities in the Balkan States: American Contributions toward Their Removal, with Particular Reference to the Congress of Berlin* (New York: American Jewish Committee, 1916). Joshua Starr, "Jewish Citizenship in Rumania," *Jewish Social Studies* 3, no. 1 (1941): 57–80.

62 Duncan Kelly, "Popular Sovereignty as State Theory," in *Popular Sovereignty in Historical Perspective*, ed. Richard Bourke and Quentin Skinner (Cambridge: Cambridge University Press, 2016), 283. On international humanitarian law and the disciplining of democratic nationalism in the nineteenth century, see Eyal Benvenisti and Doreen Lustig, "Taming Democracy: Codifying the Laws of War to Restore the European Order, 1856–1874," (Legal Studies Research Paper Series, University of Cambridge Faculty of Law, June 2017).

63 J. C. Bluntschli, *Roumania and the Legal Status of the Jews in Roumania, an Exposition of Public Law* (London: Anglo-Jewish Association, 1879), 17. On Romania as a symbol in Anglophone literature for legal inequality within a "civilized" state, see H. S. Q. Henriques and Ernest J. Schuster, "Jus Soli or Jus Sanguinis?," *Problems of the War* 3 (1917): 119–131.

64 On the rise of statelessness as a common issue in private law cases in Egypt, see William Hanley, "International Lawyers without Public International Law: The Case of Late Ottoman Egypt," *Journal of the History of International Law* 18, no. 1 (2016), 98–119.

65 Legal publicists began to address the status of people with no national status after a series of international scandals involving migrants from the Russian and Habsburg Empires. In 1879, George Cogordan, a French diplomat and advisor to the foreign ministry, drew particular attention to the Russian emigrants to Argentina, who were denied reentry to Russia, in his treatise *La nationalité au point de vue des rapports internationaux*. The case of the Russian emigrants in Buenos Aires appeared in a number of other treatises on the nature of nationality and protection and the obligation of the Russian government. Ludwig von Bar's treatise on international private law from 1892 cited the examples of the Saratow colonists who emigrated to Brazil from Russia but eventually returned to Russia, despite Russia's original unwillingness to accept them. Von Bar, *Private International Law*, 160, note 7. Tara Zahra, *The Great Departure: Mass Migration from Eastern Europe and the Making of the Free World* (New York: W. W. Norton, 2016).

66 Chancery Division, *Stoeck v. Public Trustee*; William Edward Hall, *A Treatise on International Law*, 2nd ed. (Oxford, 1884); Franz Holtzendorff, *Handbuch des Völkerrechts: Auf Grundlage Europäischer* (Berlin, 1885).

67 See James Lorimer, *The Institutes of the Law of Nations: A Treatise of the Jural Relations of Separate Political Communities*, 2 vols. (London: W. Blackwood, 1883), 1:334–347; "Règles internationales sur l'admission et l'expulsion des etrangers, 9 September

1892 (1892–1894)," 12 Annuaire IDI, http://www.idi-iil.org/idiF/resolutionsF/1892_gen_01_fr.pdf.

68 Von Bar, *Private International Law*. In his widely used treatise on international private law, the French jurist André Weiss, who had served as the legal advisor to the French Ministry of Foreign Affairs, cited possible causes of loss of nationality including: emigration, evasion of military duties, acceptance of service with foreign governments, loss of nationality as a penalty, and marriage. Weiss, *Traité élémentaire de droit international privé* (Paris: L. Larose & Forcel, 1890).

69 See David Miller, *Strangers in Our Midst: The Political Philosophy of Immigration* (Cambridge, MA: Harvard University Press, 2016), 5. On refugee relief in British history, see Caroline Shaw, *Britannia's Embrace: Modern Humanitarianism and the Imperial Origins of Refugee Relief* (Oxford: Oxford University Press, 2015). On moral panics produced by immigration, see Saskia Sassen, *Guests and Aliens* (New York: New Press, 1999), chap. 6.

70 *U.S. v. Wong Kim Ark*, 169 U.S. 649 (1898); On the broader context of the case, see, Beth Lew Williams, *The Chinese Must Go: Violence, Exclusion, and the Making of the Alien in America* (Cambridge, MA: Harvard University Press, 2018).

71 Kai Raustiala, *Does the Constitution Follow the Flag? The Evolution of Territoriality in American Law* (New York: Oxford University Press, 2009); Christina Duffy Burnett and Burke Marshall, eds., *Foreign in a Domestic Sense: Puerto Rico, American Expansion, and the Constitution* (Durham, NC: Duke University Press, 2001); Gerald Neuman, *Strangers to the Constitution: Immigrants, Borders, and Fundamental Law* (Princeton, NJ: Princeton University Press, 1996); Robert C. McGreevey, *Borderline Citizens: The United States, Puerto Rico, and the Politics of Colonial Migration* (Ithaca, NY: Cornell University Press, 2018).

72 Frederick Coudert, "Our New Peoples: Citizens, Subjects, Nationals or Aliens," *Columbia Law Review* 3, no. 1 (1903): 13–32.

73 Coudert, "Our New Peoples," 13–32; Frederick Coudert, "The Evolution of the Doctrine of Territorial Incorporation," *Columbia Law Review* 26, no. 7 (1926): 823–850. Coudert's conceptual gymnastics struck the American jurist Oliver Wendell Holmes as problematically contradictory in light of the widespread condemnation of Romania's treatment of its Jewish subjects. In 1903, Holmes wrote to Frederick Pollock, a British legal theorist, about one of the US Insular Cases, in which the US Supreme Court ruled that the inhabitants of Puerto Rico owed allegiance to the United States but nonetheless remained alien. Holmes dryly commented, "The only parallel I can think of is the position assigned, in defiance of treaties, to the Jews in Roumania, against which the US has been protesting." Oliver Wendell Holmes to Frederick Pollock, January 17, 1903, in *Holmes-Pollock Letters: The Correspondence of Mr. Justice Holmes and Sir Frederick Pollock 1874–1932*, ed. Mark DeWolfe Howe (Cambridge, MA: Cambridge University Press, 1942), 111. The history of citizenship in the French metropole also revealed a core distinction between the active citizenship of male property owners and the more inclusive definition of French nationals in the first half of the nineteenth century. Peter Sahlins, *Unnaturally French: Foreign Citizens in the Old*

Regime and After (Ithaca, NY: Cornell University Press, 2004), 312. In the British Empire, non-European British subjects and British protected persons could not become fully naturalized members of the British Empire. Daniel Gorman, *Imperial Citizenship: Empire and the Question of Belonging* (Manchester: Manchester University Press, 2006), 164.

74 See Mathias Schmoeckel, "The Internationalist as a Scientist and Herald: Lassa Oppenheim," *European Journal of International Law* 11, no. 3 (2000): 699–712.

75 Treatises divide between jurists who believe that international law functioned as the "gentle civilizer" of nations and the strict legal positivists who seek to place international law on more secure theoretical foundations. See Benedict Kingsbury, "Legal Positivism as Normative Politics: International Society, Balance of Power and Lassa Oppenheim's Positive International Law," *European Journal of International Law* 13 (2002): 401–436.

76 Schmoeckel, "Internationalist as a Scientist and Herald."

77 Lassa Oppenheim, *International Law: A Treatise, Vol. 1* (London: Longmans, Green, 1905). Also see Sir Francis Taylor Piggott, *Nationality, including Naturalization and English Law on the High Seas and beyond the Realm* (London: W. Clowes, 1906), 1; Piggott, *Extraterritoriality: The Law Relating to Consular Jurisdiction and to Residence in Oriental Countries* (London: Butterworth, 1907). Piggott was a British jurist who served as chief justice of Hong Kong from 1905 to 1912.

78 Oppenheim, *International Law*, 1:366. Jurists debated the significance of the Romanian Jewish case for the meaning of the rights of humanity. See Fedor Martens, *Traité de Droit International* (Paris: Chevalier-Marescq, 1883); Johann Caspar Bluntschli, *Droit International Codifié* (Paris: Guillaumin, 1874).

79 On the metaphor of the lawless sea, see Hans Blumenberg, *Shipwreck with Spectator* (Cambridge, MA: MIT Press, 1997); "A Man without a Country: Neither Cuba nor United States Will Have Him and Ward Line Is in Quandary," *New York Tribune*, November 13, 1902.

80 Piggott, *Nationality*, 1.

81 J. Westlake and A. F. Topham, *A Treatise on Private International Law: With Principal Reference to Its Practice in England* (London: Sweet and Maxwell, 1905); von Bar, *Private International Law*. See also Will Hanley, "Statelessness, an Invisible Theme in the History of International Law," *European Journal of International Law* 25, no. 1 (2014): 326; Mary Lewis, *Divided Rule: Sovereignty and Empire in French Tunisia, 1881–1938* (Berkeley: University of California Press, 2014).

82 F. Meili, *International Civil and Commercial Law as Founded upon Theory*, trans. Arthur Kuhn (New York: Macmillan, 1905), 123.

83 Will Hanley, "What Ottoman Nationality Was and Was Not," *Journal of Ottoman and Turkish Studies* 3, no. 2 (2016): 277–298.

84 E. S. Zeballos, *La nationalité au point de vue de la législation comparée et du droit privé humain* (Paris: Université de Buenos-Aires, 1914), 1155. In his work on nationality and private law, Zeballos developed the doctrine of the extraterritoriality of domicile in private law, which favored foreign companies in Latin America. He noted, however,

that when it came to the status of a person without any national ties, "English law" was "silent on the subject."

85 Anonymous, "Notes," *Law Quarterly Review* 37 (1921): 407; Anonymous, "Recent Decisions," *Michigan Law Review* 50, no. 1 (1921): 139–170. On Stoeck and the legal foundations of "world citizenship," see Edward A. Harriman, "Virginia's Influence on International Law," *Virginia Law Review* 12, no. 2 (1925–1926): 135–145; Chester Rohrlich, "World Citizenship," *St. John's Law Review* 6, no. 2 (1931–1932): 246–257.

86 Edwin M. Borchard, *The Diplomatic Protection of Citizens Abroad* (New York: Banks Law, 1915). Borchard cited legal treatises by Felix Stoerck, an Austrian professor of public law who coined the term *volkerrechtsindigenat* to define a "citizen of the world" who enjoyed rights by virtue of his or her humanity, and by Oppenheim and von Bar. On the emergence of a transatlantic civil-liberties movement during World War I, see John Witt, "Crystal Eastman and the Internationalist Beginnings of American Civil Liberties," *Duke Law Journal* 54, no. 3 (2004): 705–763.

87 "An Interned German's Appeal," *The Times*, July 27, 1915; *Stoeck v. Public Trustee*, HO 144/11489, TNA: PRO.

88 "A Claim to Be of No Nationality, Ex Parte Antonius Charles Frederick Weber," *The Times*, February 18, 1916; *Stoeck v. Public Trustee*, HO 144/11489, TNA: PRO.

89 Similarly, in *Simon v. Phillips*, a case brought before the High Court of Justice in January 1916, Simon contended that he was not an enemy alien but a person of no nationality. Simon had received a discharge of nationality from Germany after emigrating to America in 1887. He was naturalized as an American citizen in 1894, but due to living and working in London until the outbreak of the war, he lost his status in the United States by failing to register with the American consulate until January 1915. When he claimed to be stateless, the magistrate agreed with the argument that the letter from the American consulate could not be admitted as legal evidence. See "A Claim to Be of No Nationality: *Simon v. Phillips*," *London Times*, Law Report, January 19, 1916.

90 "Protection of Egyptian Local Subjects by Foreign Powers," November 5, 1915, Intelligence Department War Office, FO 141/468, TNA: PRO. In *Simon v. Phillips*, the court cited a treatise by Westlake on private international law stating that in the absence of the applicability of foreign law a person's national status was to be determined in accordance with English law.

91 "International Law. Nationality. Statelessness," *Yale Law Journal* 27, no. 6 (April 1918): 840–841. See also *Kornfeld v. Attorney General*, Tribunal Civil de la Seine, June 20, 1915, reported in *Clunet* 44 (1917): 638.

92 On comparative law and the field of nationality law, see Helen Silving, "Nationality in Comparative Law," *American Journal of Comparative Law* 5, no. 3 (1956): 410–442.

93 Public Trustee Office to Colonial Office, October 2, 1922, CO/323/898/18.

94 Release of Property Hugo Hoffman, September 22, 1922, Miscellaneous Correspondence Colonial Office 1922, CO/323/898, TNA: PRO.

95 Memo from the British Board of Trade on the case of P. G. Ernst, 1922, BT 58/2599, TNA: PRO. Pitt Cobbett's *Leading Cases on International Law* cited *Weber* (1916),

Liebmann (1916), and *Stoeck v. Public Trustee* (1921) on the question of discharge of nationality. Stoeck was acknowledged as a leading case in a 1925 dispute between a claimant, Otto Johann Ettinger, arguing that he was a stateless person—and British officials in Cairo—who maintained that the claimant remained a German subject and was therefore subject to property seizure according to the terms of the Versailles Peace Treaty. Office of the Public Custodian to the Foreign Office, January 23, 1925, Nationality: Protection of Egyptian Local Subjects by Foreign Powers, FO 141/468, TNA: PRO.

96 "The Advantage of No Nationality," *Times*, July 11, 1922; *Stoeck v. Public Trustee*, HO 144/11489, TNA: PRO. In his essay *Roman Catholicism and Political Form* from 1923, the German jurist Carl Schmitt offered a neat formulation of the concept of sovereignty that mirrored Russell's reasoning. According to Schmitt, "the power to decide who is sovereign would signify a new sovereignty." See Carl Schmitt, *Roman Catholicism and Political Form*, trans. G. L. Ulmen (Westport, CT: Greenwood Press, 1996), 30.

97 See for example *Luther v. Sagor*, English High Court (King's Bench Division), December 21, 1920. On the public law nature of nationality legislation across interwar Europe, see Silving, "Nationality in Comparative Law." On the novel emphasis among British imperial officials on the international order as one of formally sovereign states, see Frank Trentmann, Philippa Levine, and Kevin Grant, eds., *Beyond Sovereignty: Britain, Empire and Transnationalism, 1880–1950* (New York: Palgrave, 2007); Susan Pedersen, "Getting Out of Iraq—in 1932: The League of Nations and the Road to Normative Statehood," *American Historical Review* 115, no. 4 (October 2010): 975–1000. On the general absence of the term *state* in British political thought, see Janet McLean, *Searching for the State in British Legal Thought: Competing Conceptions of the Public Sphere* (Cambridge: Cambridge University Press, 2012).

98 "Recent Cases," *Harvard Law Review* 35, no. 2 (1921–1922): 201–213.

99 "Ueber doppelte Staatsangehörigkeit und Staatenlosigkeit nach englischem Recht," *Deutsche Juristen Zeitung* 31, no. 6 (1926): 432–433.

100 *American Society of International Law Proceedings* 19, no. 78 (1925): 80–81. Weil, *Sovereign Citizen*, 81. Vivek Bald, *Bengali Harlem and the Lost Histories of South Asian America* (Cambridge, MA: Harvard University Press, 2013), 2. Between sixty and one hundred South Asians in the United States were deprived of naturalized US citizenship in the mid-1920s. Joan M. Jensen, *Passage from India: Asian Indian Immigrants in North America* (New Haven, CT: Yale University Press, 1988). On Das, see Tappan Mukherjee, *Taraknath Das: Life and Letters of a Revolutionary in Exile* (Calcutta: National Council of Education in Bengal, 1997). On Mary Das, see Nancy F. Cott, "Marriage and Women's Citizenship in the United States, 1830–1934," *American Historical Review* 103, no. 5 (1998): 1467. Second-class citizenship in US history has often turned into formal noncitizenship for women and minorities. See Kunal Parker, *Making Foreigners: Immigration and Citizenship Law in America, 1600–2000* (Cambridge: Cambridge University Press, 2015).

101 B. Traven, *The Death-Ship: The Story of an American Sailor*, trans. Eric Sutton (London: J. Cape, 1934). Compare John Torpey's analysis of *The Death Ship*. Torpey, "The Great War and the Birth of the Modern Passport System," in *Documenting Individual Identity: The Development of State Practices in the Modern World*, ed. Jane Caplan and John Torpey (Princeton, NJ: Princeton University Press, 2001), 256–270. On Traven's associations with the anarchist wing of the Munich Soviet in 1919 see George Woodcock, "Traven Identified," *London Review of Books* 2, no. 13 (1980): 9–11. E. E. Hale, *The Man without a Country* (Boston: Little, Brown, 1898), 448–479. In his study on international law from 1925, Sterling Edmunds quoted Oppenheim when he described the person with no nationality as "an individual who may be forced to tolerate an existence without hope of setting his foot upon land again." Edmunds, *The Lawless Law of Nations: An Exposition of Prevailing Arbitrary International Legal System in Relation to Its Influence upon Civil Liberty* (Washington, DC: J. Byrne, 1925), 248. In 1916, an American newspaper painted a particularly affecting portrait of Nathan Cohen, who "betrayed, insane, and speechless was tossed about the sea for 40,000 miles while every nation at whose door he knocked turned him away." The newspaper reported that this man, who remained on a boat of the Lamport and Holt shipping line for over a year, was a "brooding haggard specimen of a man, without speech and without memory." "Outcast Finds Home in Death," *New York Tribune*, March 6, 1916, 16.

102 Under the company name Concordia elektrizitats AG, Max Stoeck submitted a patent for "improvements in or relating to hand fire extinguishers" in 1927. UK Patent 288500-A, http://patent.ipexl.com/GB/288500ZZDASHZZA.html.

2. POSTIMPERIAL STATES OF STATELESSNESS

1 "Protest by M. Jakob Sinnwell against his expulsion from the Saar Territory," October 4, 1921, Société des Nations: Administrative Commission of the Saar Basin (R106), LNA.

2 F. M. Russell, "The Saar Basin Governing Commission," *Political Science Quarterly* 36, no. 2 (1921): 169–183. On plebiscites in the region, see generally, James Bjork et al., eds., *Creating Nationality in Central Europe, 1880–1950: Modernity, Violence and (Be)longing in Upper Silesia* (London: Routledge, 2016).

3 Susan Pedersen, *The Guardians: The League of Nations and the Crisis of Empire* (Oxford: Oxford University Press, 2015); Anthony Anghie, *Imperialism, Sovereignty, and the Making of International Law* (Cambridge: Cambridge University Press, 2007), 188.

4 On the many interwar experiments in politics and governance undertaken after World War I because tradition and dynastic legitimacy ceased to provide principles of public order, see J. W. Muller, *Contesting Democracy: Political Ideas in Twentieth Century Europe* (Princeton, NJ: Princeton University Press, 2011), 50. As Manu Goswami has argued, internationalisms prospered in the interwar era because "situated between empire and nation, internationalist intellectuals offered multiple visions of a nonimperial future." Goswami, "Colonial Internationalisms and Imaginary Futures," *American Historical Review* 117, no. 5 (2012): 1484.

5 W. E. B. Du Bois, "The African Roots of War," *The Atlantic Monthly* 115 (May 1915): 707–714.

6 For David Ben Gurion, who would later become the first prime minister of the State of Israel, one could only place bets on which empires would triumph. As of 1915 Ben-Gurion anticipated that the Ottomans would triumph over the British in the war and that Jewish autonomy would arise in the context of the Ottoman Empire. See Dmitry Shumsky, *Beyond the Nation-State: The Zionist Political Imagination from Pinsker to Ben-Gurion* (New Haven, CT: Yale University Press, 2018), 185–186.

7 Robert Gerwarth, *The Vanquished: Why the First World War Failed to End* (New York: Farrar, Straus and Giroux, 2016); Leonard Smith, *Sovereignty at the Paris Peace Conference of 1919* (Oxford: Oxford University Press, 2018); Volker Prott, *The Politics of Self-Determination: Remaking Territories and National Identities in Europe, 1917–1923* (Oxford: Oxford University Press, 2016).

8 Robert Lansing, *The Peace Negotiations—a Personal Narrative* (Boston: Houghton Mifflin, 1921), 97, cited in Erez Manela, *The Wilsonian Moment: Self-Determination and the International Origins of Anticolonial Nationalism* (Oxford: Oxford University Press, 2007), 42.

9 "Procès-Verbal of the First Meeting of the Council of the League of Nations, January 16, 1920," *League of Nations Official Journal* (February 1920); Stephen Wertheim, "The League that Wasn't: American Designs for a Legalist-Sanctionist League of Nations and the Intellectual Origins of International Organization, 1914–1920," *Diplomatic History* 35, no. 5 (2011): 797–836.

10 Joshua Keating, *Invisible Countries: Journeys to the Edge of Nationhood* (New Haven, CT: Yale University Press, 2018), 82.

11 On the expansion of mechanisms to enact popular sovereignty after World War I through the League, see Sarah Wambaugh, *The Doctrine of National Self-Determination: A Study of the Theory and Practice of Plebiscite, with a Collection of Official Documents* (London: Oxford University Press, 1919); Sarah Wambaugh, *La pratique des plébiscites internationaux* (Paris: Hachette, 1928); Nathaniel Berman, "Sovereignty in Abeyance: Self-Determination and International Law," *Wisconsin International Law Journal* 51, no. 7 (1988) 51–105.

12 See Pedersen, *Guardians.*

13 Though contested in Western states, women's suffrage was an important part of the interwar plebiscites. An international movement of women who sought emancipation in their home countries strategically used the associational zone created by international organizations to agitate for their cause. On Wambaugh, see Karen Knop, "Women and Self-Determination in Europe after World War I," in *Diversity and Self-Determination in International Law* (Cambridge: Cambridge University Press, 2004), 277–327. See also Nathaniel Berman, "'But the Alternative Is Despair': European Nationalism and the Renewal of International Law," *Harvard Law Review* 106, no. 1792 (1993): 1793–1808 (especially n316).

14 Carsten Stahn, *The Law and Practice of International Territorial Administration: Versailles to Iraq and Beyond* (Cambridge: Cambridge University Press, 2010). Compare

Anghie, *Imperialism, Sovereignty*, 188. As an innovative legal solution, the Saar Commission brought the untamable elements of international life into legible order. See Berman, "Sovereignty in Abeyance." Ann Laura Stoler, "On Degrees of Imperial Sovereignty," *Public Culture* 18, no. 1 (2006): 125–146.

15 "Question of Danzig," October 26, 1920, FO 893/8, TNA: PRO.

16 Patricia Clavin, *Securing the World Economy: The Reinvention of the League of Nations, 1920–1946* (Oxford: Oxford University Press, 2013), 14.

17 Mark Mazower, *Governing the World: The History of an Idea* (New York: Penguin, 2012), ch. 5 passim.; Patricia Clavin, "Interwar Internationalism: Conceptualizing Transnational Thought and Action, 1919–1939," in *International Reconfigured: Transnational Ideas and Movements between the World Wars*, ed. Daniel Laqua (London: I. B. Tauris, 2011), 1–15; Daniel Gorman, *The Emergence of International Society in the 1920s* (Cambridge: Cambridge University Press, 2012).

18 M. J. Landa, *The Man without a Country* (London: Herbert Joseph), 14. See Jeanne Morefield, *Covenants without Swords: Idealist Liberalism and the Spirit of Empire* (Princeton, NJ: Princeton University Press, 2005), 177. Carl Schmitt's *Verfassungslehre* from 1928 argued that much of the legal scholarship on the League of Nations failed to distinguish between "international" and "interstate" organization: "When one continues to confuse pacifism with a federation of people (in the vague sense of peace and understanding among peoples), on the one hand, one can easily draw imaginary consequences." Carl Schmitt, *Constitutional Theory*, trans. Jeffery Seitzer (Durham, NC: Duke University Press, 2008), 382.

19 Siegfried Weichlein, "Europe und der Foderalismus: Zur Begriffsgeschichte politischer Ordnungsmodelle," *Historische Jahrbuch* 125 (2005): 133–152; Barbara Stollberg-Rilinger, *The Emperor's Old Clothes: Constitutional History and the Symbolic Language of the Holy Roman Empire*, trans. Thomas Dunlap (New York: Berghahn Books, 2015).

20 Georg Jellinek, *Das Recht der Minoritäten* (Vienna: A. Hölder, 1898); Edmund Bernatzik, *Über nationale Matriken* (Vienna: Manz, 1910). The Czech nationalist movement of the nineteenth century, along with the Croatian and Slovenian national movements, the Ukrainian national movement in Galicia and Sub-Carpathian Russia, the Austro-Galician faction of the Polish national movement, the Romanian national movement in Hungarian Transylvania, fought for a *Staatsrecht* for the nation, which meant national territorial autonomy within the existing imperial framework—a United States of Great Austria. See Dmitry Shumsky, *Beyond the Nation-State*, 80.

21 In his 1899 essay "State and Nation," the Austrian socialist politician Karl Renner proposed internationalization and juridification as two solutions to the tension between national groups within the empire. Members of national groups would form personal associations with a distinctive legal status—like a corporation—that did not accord with any particular territorial jurisdiction. In areas that remained mixed, national minorities would receive protection from an imperial parliament possessing what amounted to sovereignty in international matters. International frontiers would define a multinational federation in which nations were constituted as peoples rather than states. A personal principle, in which individuals carry the legal rights of their

national status wherever they travel within the wider state, would replace a territorial one. For Renner, the modern state defined by its ultimate sovereignty over a territory and the subjects within it had led to a condition of endless social conflict. Rather than creating equal rights, different nationalities struggled over mastery of the state. Karl Renner, "State and Nation," in *National Cultural Autonomy and Its Contemporary Critics*, ed. Ephraim Nimni (London: Routledge, 2005), 15–47.

22 Janne Nijman, "Minorities and Majorities," in *Oxford Handbook of International Law*, ed. Bardo Fassbender and Anne Peters (Oxford: Oxford University Press, 2013), 116–117. On national claims for extraterritorial rights and authority at the turn of the century, see Simon Rabinovitch, *Jewish Rights, National Rites: Nationalism and Autonomy in Late Imperial and Revolutionary Russia* (Stanford, CA: Stanford University Press, 2014).

23 Pieter Judson, *The Habsburg Empire: A New History* (Cambridge, MA: Harvard University Press, 2016), 272; Brigitte Mazohl, "'Equality among the Nationalities' and the Peoples (Volksstämme) of the Habsburg Empire," in *Constitutionalism, Legitimacy, Power: Nineteenth Century Experiences*, ed. Kelly Grotke and Marcus Prutsch (Oxford: Oxford University Press, 2014), 107–127.

24 See Kelly Grotke and Marcus Prutsch, "Constitutionalism, Legitimacy, and Power: Nineteenth-Century Experience," in *Constitutionalism, Legitimacy, Power: Nineteenth Century Experiences*, ed. Kelly Grotke and Marcus Prutsch (Oxford: Oxford University Press, 2014), 3–23. On British analogues from this period, see Duncan Bell, *The Idea of Greater Britain: Empire and the Future of World Order, 1860–1900* (Princeton, NJ: Princeton University Press, 2008). On constitutionalism and its relation to democracy, see Richard Tuck, *The Sleeping Sovereign: The Invention of Modern Democracy* (Cambridge: Cambridge University Press, 2015).

25 In cooperation with the Allies, the Czechoslovak National Council was given the right to raise an army and to form a government in exile. See David Armitage, *The Declaration of Independence: A Global History* (Cambridge, MA: Harvard University Press, 2007), 132.

26 Cited in Andrew Barker, *Fictions from an Orphan State: Literary Reflections of Austria between Habsburg and Hitler* (Rochester, NY: Camden House, 2012), 5.

27 Mark Levene, *War, Jews, and the New Europe: The Diplomacy of Lucien Wolf, 1914–1919* (Oxford: Oxford University Press, 1992), 179.

28 Judson, *Habsburg Empire*, 266.

29 The rise of a "minority congress" indicated a shared sense of political interest and fate. The minorities section of the League secretariat fielded frequent complaints about its administrative structure when minority groups protested their exclusion from investigatory and reporting processes. Zara Steiner, *The Lights That Failed: European International History, 1919–1933* (Oxford: Oxford University Press, 2007), 363–365.

30 On the idea that the League's minority protection regime provided the foundation for the expansion of internationally guaranteed human rights after World War II, see A. W. Brian Simpson, *Human Rights and the End of Empire: Britain and the Genesis of the European Convention* (Oxford: Oxford University Press, 2001), chap. 3. On the

minorities of central Europe and the stateless as "cousins-germane" see Hannah Arendt, *The Origins of Totalitarianism*, 268.

31 Marc Raeff, *Russia Abroad: A Cultural History of the Russian Emigration, 1919–1939* (Oxford: Oxford University Press, 1990), 19.

32 On the concept of political stabilization, see Charles Maier, "The Two Postwar Eras and the Conditions for Stability," *American Historical Review* 86, no. 2 (1981): 327–352; Charles Maier, *Recasting Bourgeois Europe: Stabilization in France, Germany and Italy in the Decade after World War I* (Princeton, NJ: Princeton University Press, 1975). As Maier argued, a key strategy for stabilizing the European postwar order involved a careful delineation between matters defined as "political," which called for political contestation over the allocation of resources and the nature of rule, and those defined as "technical," dependent on procedures sequestered from political deliberation and conflict.

33 Steiner, *Lights That Failed*, 365–366.

34 The decree stated, "persons who left Russia after November 7, 1917, without the authorization of the Soviet authorities were to be deprived of the rights of Russian citizenship." Eric Lohr, *Russian Citizenship from Empire to Soviet Union* (Cambridge, MA: Harvard University Press, 2012), 151–152; Richard Flournoy and Manley Hudson, *A Collection of Nationality Laws of Various Countries as Contained in Constitutions, Statues, and Treaties* (Oxford: Oxford University Press, 1929), 511.

35 Andre Prudhomme, "La Révolution bolchevique et le statut juridique des russes," *Journal de Droit International* 51, no. 1 (1924): 5–7.

36 Landa, *Man without a Country*, 12.

37 Dzovinar Kévonian, *Réfugiés et diplomatie humanitaire: Les acteurs européens et la scène proche-orientale pendant l'entre deux-guerres* (Paris: Sorbonne, 2004), 388–391.

38 Peter Gatrell and Jo Laycock, "Armenia: The 'Nationalization,' Internationalization and Representation of the Refugee Crisis," in *Homelands: War, Population, and Statehood in Eastern Europe and Russia, 1918–1922*, ed. Nick Baron and Peter Gatrell (London: Anthem, 2004), 187.

39 "Report by Dr. Nansen, Repatriation of Prisoners of War," Volkerrecht, Ligen/Volkerbund, box 78, Archiv der Republik, Vienna.

40 Peter Gatrell and Nick Baron, *Homelands: War, Population, and Statehood in Eastern Europe and Russia, 1918–1922* (London: Anthem, 2004), 206.

41 M. Butler to Col. Amery, March 1921, "Russian Refugees: Origins of the Question of Assisting Them," R201/1, Correspondence on Russian Refugees 1920–1921, Series R (1921–1940), Archives of the International Labor Organization, Geneva.

42 Catherine Gousseff, *L'exil russe: La fabrique du réfugié apatride, 1920–1939* (Paris: CNRS, 2008), 22. By the end of 1921, about twelve thousand refugees had settled in Bulgaria, and in 1922 thirty thousand more joined their numbers. The Czechoslovak republic granted refuge to Cossacks and other peasant groups. Russian prisoners of war who had been concentrated in Poland and eastern Germany remained there. The largest group to escape from Soviet-controlled Russia was in the Manchurian town of Harbin.

43 Fridtjof Nansen, "The Suffering People of Europe," Nobel Lecture, 1922. See http://nobelprize.org/nobel_prizes/peace/laureates/1922/nansen-lecture.html.

44 Marit Fosse and John Fox, *Nansen: Explorer and Humanitarian* (Lanham, MD: Hamilton Books, 2016), 22–23.

45 W. E. Butler, "Russian International Lawyers in Emigration: The First Generation," *Journal of the History of International Law* 3, no. 1 (2001): 235–241.

46 Eric Lohr, *Nationalizing the Russian Empire: The Campaign against Enemy Aliens during World War I* (Cambridge, MA: Harvard University Press, 2003), 149.

47 In an essay from 1905, Max Weber cited the Zemstvo Congresses of the revolution as evidence that Russia had experienced a form of government more free than that found in a state with a more centralized bureaucracy. Weber, "On the Situation of Constitutional Democracy in Russia," in *Weber: Political Writings*, ed. Peter Lassman and Ronald Speirs (Cambridge: Cambridge University Press, 2002), 34.

48 Henri Reymond to T. F. Johnson, October 10, 1923, "Russian Attacks against the High Commissioner, 1921–1930," C1277, LNA. On the fascist faction among the diaspora community see Michael Kellogg, *The Russian Roots of Nazism: White Émigrés and the Making of National Socialism* (Cambridge: Cambridge University Press, 2005).

49 Lohr, *Russian Citizenship*, 142.

50 Marsha L. Rozenblit, *Reconstructing a National Identity: The Jews of Habsburg Austria during World War I* (Oxford: Oxford University Press, 2001), 66. Panikos Panayi and Pippa Virdee, eds., *Refugees and the End of Empire: Imperial Collapse and the Creation of Refugees in Twentieth Century Europe* (New York: Palgrave, 2011); Julie Thorpe, "Displacing Empire: Refugee Welfare, National Activism and State Legitimacy in Austria-Hungary in World War One," in Panayi and Virdee, *Refugees*, 102–127. Kévonian, *Réfugiés et Diplomatie Humanitaire*, 263; Peter Gatrell, *A Whole Empire Walking: Refugees in Russia during World War I* (Bloomington: Indiana University Press, 1999).

51 Maureen Healy, *Vienna and the Fall of the Habsburg Empire: Total War and Everyday Life in World War I* (Cambridge: Cambridge University Press, 2007), 164; Nicole Phelps, *U.S. Habsburg Relations from 1815 to the Paris Peace Conference: Sovereignty Transformed* (Cambridge: Cambridge University Press, 2015) 4.

52 Cited in Joshua Starr, "Jewish Citizenship in Rumania," *Jewish Social Studies* 3, no. 1 (1941): 67.

53 Joseph Reich, December 10, 1923, "Assistance judiciare au faveur des 'Heimatlose,'" R1287, LNA.

54 F. Levy to the Permanent Court at The Hague, November 15, 1923, "Assistance judiciare au faveur des 'Heimatlose,'" R1287, LNA.

55 Åke Hammarskjöld to Eric Drummond, November 19, 1923, "Assistance judiciare au faveur des 'Heimatlose,'" R1287, LNA. Hammarskjöld was a member of the secretariat of the League of Nations. He worked with the Committee of Jurists, which met in The Hague in 1920 to draft the statute of the Permanent Court of International Justice. See Manley Hudson, "In Memoriam: Ake Hammarskjold," *American Journal of International Law* 31, no. 4 (1937): 703–704.

56 "Case of Persons without Nationality," November 26, 1923, "Assistance judiciare en faveur des 'Heimatlos,'" R1287, LNA.

57 Eric Drummond added a handwritten note to the memo which simply read "minorities treaties" to suggest that the fledgling regime of international oversight might ameliorate the problem. Ibid.

58 "Addendum to Case of Persons without Nationality," November 26, 1923, "Assistance judiciare en faveur des 'Heimatlos,'" R1287, LNA. The memo also cited André Weiss, *Traité théorique et pratique de droit international privé* (Paris: L. Larose and Tenin, 1907).

59 Ralf Michaels, "Private Lawyer in Disguise: On the Absence of Private Law and Private International Law in Martti Koskenniemi's Work," *Temple International and Comparative Law Journal* 27, no. 2 (2012): 499–521. See Martin H. Geyer and Johannes Paulmann, eds. *The Mechanics of Internationalism: Culture, Society, and Politics from the 1840s to the First World War* (Oxford: Oxford University Press, 2001).

60 Norman Bentwich, "Nationality in Mandated Territories Detached from Turkey," *British Yearbook of International Law* 7, no. 1 (1926): 109.

61 Under the British mandate, Palestine did not develop clear rules about Palestinian nationality until 1925. Individuals over eighteen born in Palestine and with Ottoman nationality who had habitual residence abroad as of August 1, 1925, could opt for citizenship. This option had to be taken up within two years from the date of the order. To be naturalized, non-Ottoman citizens were required to have been resident since 1922 and had to surrender any passport or laissez-passer on receipt of citizenship. Nationality legislation in turn provoked further questions about national identification. See Lauren Banko, "Imperial Questions and Social Identities," *Revue des Mondes musulmans et de la Méditerranée* 137, no. 1 (2015): 95–114. The British government and Palestine administration adapted nationality laws in ways that distinguished between Arab and Jewish immigrants. Mutaz M. Quafisheh, *The International Law Foundations of Palestinian Nationality: A Legal Examination of Nationality in Palestine under Britain's Rule* (Leiden: Martinus Nijhoff, 2008).

62 Mark S. W. Hoyle, "The Mixed Courts of Egypt, 1926–1937," *Arab Law Quarterly* 2, no. 4 (1987): 357–389. On the League's active role in the transformation of the demographic and political make-up of the former Ottoman territories, see Umut Özsu, *Formalizing Displacement: International Law and Population Transfers* (Oxford: Oxford University Press, 2015), 72–73.

63 Manley O. Hudson, *Research in International Law: Harvard Law School* (Cambridge, MA: Harvard Law School, 1932).

64 Richard W. Flournoy Jr., "Suggestions Concerning an International Code on the Law of Nationality," *Yale Law Review* 35, no. 8 (1926): 939–955.

65 Gousseff, *L'exil russe*, 244. Hannah Arendt later referred to the Russian refugees, and the Armenian and Assyro-Chaldean refugees assimilated into their legal rubric, as the "aristocracy" of all European stateless people during the interwar period. Hannah Arendt, *The Origins of Totalitarianism* (New York: Schocken Books, 1951), 281. See also "Russian, Armenian, Assyrian, Assyro-Chaldean and Turkish Refugees: Execution of

the Recommendation of the Eleventh Assembly," *League of Nations—Official Journal* 12, no. 6 (1931): 1005.

66 Sixteen states signed the final accord certifying the Nansen passport in July 1922. By 1926, forty states recognized the passport. See Gousseff, *L'exil russe*, 56.

67 Austrian delegation to High Commissioner for Refugees, September 17, 1923, "Protection juridique et affaires judiciares," Delegation in Austria, C1282/44, LNA.

68 In 1921, the League of Nations stepped in to rescue Austria from hyperinflation and remained a key economic player until it formerly bowed out of national economic intervention in 1926. The League's financial assistance programs were creditor-imposed infringements on sovereignty, similar to earlier colonial precedents in Egypt. Newspapers reported on the dangers of Austrian dependence on foreign loans, which came with the threat of military intervention if the debts remained unpaid. See Nathan Marcus, *Austrian Reconstruction and the Collapse of Global Finance, 1921–1931* (Cambridge, MA: Harvard University Press, 2018).

69 "Protection juridique et affaires judiciares," C1282/44, LNA.

70 Red Cross to the League, "The 'Heimatlos' Problem," August 20, 1926, R1287, LNA.

71 Roger Picard, "Les 'sans-patrie' et la S.D.N," *La paix par le droit* 36, no. 2 (1926): 97–99.

72 "Rider A to Napier Report Nationality in the Succession States of Austria-Hungary," Refugees, Statelessness 1925–1935, International Federation League of Nations Societies, P98, LNA.

73 Ibid.

74 K. de Drachenfels, "La Comité International de la Croix-Rouge et le problème des 'Heimatlose,'" *Revue international de la Croix Rouge* 8, no. 95 (1926): 870–877.

75 Relief efforts on behalf of migrants reflected perceived differences between so-called Western and Eastern Jews. German Jewish philanthropic organizations like the Hilfsverein der deutschen Juden, for example, treated the refugees from the East in ways that prefigured later brutal methods—including transportation in sealed railroad cars and delousing. See Steven Aschheim, *Brothers and Strangers: The East European Jew in German and German Jewish Consciousness, 1800–1923* (Madison: University of Wisconsin Press, 1982), 32–58. On the emergence of Ottoman and Habsburg policy toward refugees, especially Muslim refugees as a result of the Balkan Wars beginning in 1878, see Jared Mansanek, "Protection, Repatriation and Categorization: Refugees and Empire at the End of the Nineteenth Century," *Journal of Refugee Studies* 30, no. 2 (2017): 301–317.

76 Lucien Wolf, "Notes on Staatenlose Question," 1928, ACC/3121/C11/ 3/5/2, London Municipal Archive.

77 Lucien Wolf to Eric Drummond, "La situation des 'Heimatlos,'" September 14, 1926, R1287, LNA. Wolf later described the Board of Deputies in Great Britain as the only Jewish body that took effective action on the statelessness question by working with the Red Cross to bring the problem before the League council. Lucien Wolf to N. Rabin, March 14, 1929, ACC 321/C/11/5/2, Board of Deputies, London Municipal Archives.

78   Dr. Heimroth to T. F. Johnson, "Extensions des measures en faveur des réfugiés russ-
     es at armeniens en faveur l'autre categories de réfugiés," November 2, 1926, 1282/44,
     LNA.

79   Red Cross to the League, "The 'Heimatlos' Problem."

80   B. S. Nicolas to the League, 1927, R59, LNA.

81   Response from December 28, 1927, R59, LNA.

82   Mackinnon Wood, Minute Sheet, R59, LNA.

83   Memo from Monsieur Catastini, December 7, 1927, R59, LNA.

84   Mandates section, re: Mr. Nicolas claim to Turkish nationality, December 15, 1927,
     R59, LNA. In a case brought before the Supreme Court of Poland, *Rajdberg v. Lewi*,
     in 1927, the Supreme Court of Poland held that "the plaintiff who has been deprived
     under Soviet law of Soviet nationality, could not be considered a Soviet national by
     other states, least of all by States (such as Poland) which had recognized de jure the
     Soviet republic." The court added, "The plaintiff's plea that he is a stateless person liv-
     ing in Berlin under the protection of the League of Nations could not be disregarded."
     See Paul Weis, *Nationality and Statelessness in International Law* (London: Stevens,
     1956), 121.

85   Sigismund Gargas, *Die Staatenlosen* (Leiden: Brill, 1928), 7.

86   "Homeless: Comité mondial pour la défense des interets des gens sans nationalité
     reconnu," July 15, 1928, Heimatlose 1925–1945, Series B CR 163, Archives of the Inter-
     national Committee of the Red Cross.

87   Romain Rolland, "Adresse aux 'Sans Etats' Réunis à Geneve," September 8, 1930, Situ-
     ation des Apatrides: Correspondence Diverse, R3589, LNA. On Gandhi and Rolland,
     see Ruth Harris, "Rolland, Gandhi and Madeleine Slade: Spiritual Politics, France
     and the Wider World," *French History* 27, no. 4 (2013): 579–599.

88   I. S. K. Soboleff, *Nansen Passport: Round the World on a Motorcycle* (London: G. Bell,
     1936), 89.

89   Anna Fries, *Memoirs of a Stateless Person* (Bloomington, IN: Authorhouse, 2013),
     17. See Mary D. Lewis, *Boundaries of the Republic: Migrant Rights and the Limits
     of Universalism in France, 1918–1940* (Stanford, CA: Stanford University Press,
     2007), 159.

90   Vladimir Nabokov, *Pnin* (Garden City, NY: Doubleday, 1957), 46, quoted in Tobias
     Brinkmann, "Permanent Transit: Jewish Migration during the Interwar Period," in
     1929: Mapping the Jewish World, ed. Hasia Diner and Gennady Estraikh (New York:
     New York University Press, 2013), 53–72. See also Anna Fries, *Memoirs of a Stateless
     Person* (Bloomington, IN: Authorhouse, 2013), 17.

91   Eileen Scully, *Bargaining with the State from Afar: American Citizenship in Treaty Port
     China, 1844–1942* (New York: Columbia University Press, 2001); Gousseff, *L'exil russe*,
     39; Manley Hudson, "The Rendition of the International Mixed Court at Shanghai,"
     American Journal of International Law 21, no. 3 (1927), 451–471; Par Kristoffer Cassel,
     *Grounds of Judgment: Extraterritoriality and Imperial Power in Nineteenth-Century Chi-
     na and Japan* (Oxford: Oxford University Press, 2012). Kon Balin, *Born Stateless: A
     Young Man's Story, 1923–1957* (Bloomington, IN: Authorhouse, 2009), 24.

92 M. K. Gandhi, "Without Nationality," *Young India*, February 14, 1929, in *The Collected Works of Mahatma Gandhi*, vol. 45 of 98 (New Delhi: Publication Division Government of India, 1999).

93 Ajay Skaria, "Gandhi's Politics: Liberalism and the Question of the Ashram," *South Atlantic Quarterly* 101, no. 4 (2002): 955–986; Shruti Kapila, "Self, Spender, and Swaraj: Nationalist Thought and Critiques of Liberalism, 1890–1920," in *An Intellectual History for India*, ed. Shruti Kapila (Cambridge: Cambridge University Press, 2010), 98–117.

94 Tara Zahra, *The Great Departure: Mass Migration from Eastern Europe and the Making of the Free World* (New York: W. W. Norton, 2016).

95 "Memorandum Presented by the Committee of Experts of Russian and Armenian Jurists on the Legal Status of Russian and Armenian Refugees," 1928, Extensions des mesures en faveur des réfugiés russes at armeniens en faveur l'autre categories de réfugiés, C1282/44, LNA.

96 On the importance placed in the League of Nations on the division between activities that qualified as "political" from those that were "technical," see Pittman B. Potter, "Note on the Distinction between Political and Technical Questions," *Political Science Quarterly* 50, no. 2 (1935): 264–271.

97 On Wolf's struggle with Jewish leaders who envisioned minority rights in terms of the rights of collectivities, rather than the rights of individuals as members of particular groups, see Carol Fink, *Defending the Rights of Others: The Great Powers, the Jews, and International Minority Protection, 1878–1938* (Cambridge: Cambridge University Press, 2004), chap. 5. Gabriella Safran and Steven J. Zipperstein, *The Worlds of S. Ansky: A Russian Jewish Intellectual at the Turn of the Century* (Stanford, CA: Stanford University Press, 2006), 454. Lucien Wolf, "Notes on Staatenlose Question," 1928, ACC/3121/C/11/ 3/5/2, Board of Deputies, London Municipal Archive.

98 Lucien Wolf, *Russo-Jewish Refugees in Eastern Europe: Report on the Fourth Meeting of the Advisory Committee of the High Commissioner for Russian Refugees of the League of Nations Held in Geneva on April 20, 1923* (London: Joint Foreign Committee, 1923); Nansen Office to Lucien Wolf, November 6, 1921, R201/26/2, Réfugiés Russes, Series R-Refugees (1921–1940), Archives of the International Labor Organization; Lucien Wolf, *Notes on the Diplomatic History of the Jewish Question: With Texts of Protocols, Treaty Stipulations, Public Acts and Official Documents* (London: Jewish Historical Society, 1919).

99 Lucien Wolf to Polish Foreign Ministry, December 9, 1926, Heimatlose 1925–1945, Series B CR 163, Archives of the International Committee of the Red Cross.

100 Cited in Gousseff, *L'exil russe*, 227. On Mirkine-Guetzevitch, see Dzovinar Kévonian, "Question des réfugiés, droits de l'homme: Eléments d'une convergence pendant l'entre deux-guerres," *Matériaux pour l'histoire de notre temps* 72 (2003): 40–49.

3. POSTIMPERIAL FOUNDATIONS OF POLITICAL ORDER

1 Mark Vishniak, "Le statut international des apatrides," *Recueil des Cours de l'Académie de la Haye* 43 (1933): 246. Robert Johnston, *"New Mecca, New Babylon": Paris and the*

Russian Exiles, 1920–1945 (Kingston, ON: McGill Queen's University Press, 1988), 20. Obituaries, "Mark Vishniak, Russian Expert," *New York Times*, September 3, 1976, 14.

2   I. G. Lipovano, *L'Apatridie* (Paris: Les Éditions Internationales, 1935), 27. On the idea that the invention of new terms such as *apatride* and *stateless* defined a new kind of mass vulnerability, compare Eric Hobsbawm, *Age of Extremes: A History of the World, 1914–1991* (New York: Vintage Books, 1996), 50.

3   Ibid., 2. The *Trésor de la Langue Française* affirms that "apatride" is a neologism dating to 1928. *Trésor de la Langue Française: Dictionnaire de la langue du XIXe et du XXe siè-cle (1789–1960)* vol. 3 (Paris: Éditions du Centre National de la Recherche Scientifique, 1974), 202. On the idea of the status of individuals in international law as the "question of questions," Lipovano cited Alfred de Lapradelle's introduction to Paul Gramain's *Les droits internationaux de l'homme* in reference to the Josef Kohler citation. See Alfred de Lapradelle, introduction to *Les droits internationaux de l'homme*, by Paul Gramain (Paris: Éditions Internationales, 1933), 11; Joseph Kohler, "International Law: A Treatise by Professor Oppenheimer," *Deutsche Juristen-Zeitung* 18 (1913): 117. Kohler (1849–1919) was a German legal philosopher associated with neo-Hegelianism and pacifism active in the period before World War I. Against the idea that only states represented the subjects of international law, Kohler defended the idea that private individuals and companies—railway companies, banks, international commissions—counted as legal agents within international society. See Kohler, Völkerrecht als Privatrechtstitel, *Zeitschrift für Völkerrecht* 2 (1908): 209–230. Also see Martti Koskenniemi, *The Gentle Civilizer of Nations: The Rise and Fall of International Law, 1870–1960* (Cambridge: Cambridge University Press, 2001), 211–215, 314–315.

4   Vishniak, "Le statut international des apatrides," 246.

5   Published as "Politik als Beruf," [1921] in *Gesammelte Politische Schriften* (Munich: Drei Masken, 1921), cited in H. H. Gerth and C. Wright Mills, *From Max Weber: Essays in Sociology* (New York: Oxford University Press, 1946), 77–128.

6   On Carl Schmitt's concept of the political as the condition for the modern state and how his account skirts the question of how political communities are constituted in the first place, see Samuel Moyn, "Concepts of the Political in Twentieth-Century European Thought," in *The Oxford Handbook of Carl Schmitt*, ed. Jens Meierhenrich and Oliver Simons (Oxford: Oxford University Press, 2016), 291–312.

7   M. Herbert Croly, "The Future of the State," *New Republic*, September 15, 1917, cited in Harold Laski, Introduction to *Law in the Modern State*, by Léon Duguit (New York: B. W. Huebsch, 1919), xxxi. On the "moral limitations of a purely national territorial state" in light of global war and the international consciousness around the League of Nations, see Radhakamal Mukerjee, *Democracies of the East: A Study in Comparative Politics* (London: P. S. King, 1923), v–vi, cited in Karuna Mantena, "On Gandhi's Critique of the State: Sources, Contexts, Conjunctures," *Modern Intellectual History* 9, no. 3 (2012): 535–563.

8   V. I. Lenin, *State and Revolution* (Chicago: Haymarket Books, 2014), 37. On the turn to Hobbes in European thought in the 1920s, see Richard Hönigswald, *Hobbes und die Staatsphilosophie* (Munich: Reinhardt, 1924); Ferdinand Tönnies, *Thomas Hobbes*

NOTES TO PAGES 87-90

Leben und Lehre (Stuttgart: Fromann, 1925); Werner Becker, *Die Politische Systematik der Staatslehre des Thomas Hobbes* (thesis, Rheinisches Friedrich Wilhelms Universität zu Bonn, 1928); Adolfo Levi, *La Filosofia di Tommaso Hobbes* (Milano: Societa editrice Dante Alighieri, 1929). John P. McCormick, "Fear, Technology, and the State: Carl Schmitt, Leo Strauss, and the Revival of Hobbes in Weimar and National Socialist Germany," *Political Theory* 22, no. 4 (1994): 619–652; David Armitage, "Hobbes and the Foundation of International Thought," in *Rethinking the Foundations of Modern Political Thought*, ed. Annabel Brett and James Tully (Cambridge: Cambridge University Press), 219–235; Brian Schmidt, *The Political Discourse of Anarchy: A Disciplinary History of International Relations* (Albany, NY: State University of New York Press, 1998).

9 Leo Strauss, "Notes on Carl Schmitt," in *The Concept of the Political*, trans. George Schwab (Chicago: University of Chicago Press, 2007), 99. See also Hugo Krabbe, *The Modern Idea of the State*, trans. George H. Sabine (New York: D. Appleton, 1922); Otto Hintze, *Wesen und Wandlung des Modernen Staates* (Berlin: de Gruyter, 1931). On the state as the basic concept of jurisprudence, see Herman Kantorowicz, "The Concept of the State," *Economica* 35 (1932): 1–21. On the prevalence of questions in the nineteenth century, see Holly Case, *The Age of Questions, or A First Attempt at an Aggregate History of the Eastern, Social, Woman, American, Jewish, Polish, Bullion, Tuberculosis, and Many Other Questions over the Nineteenth Century, and Beyond* (Princeton, NJ: Princeton University Press, 2018).

10 David Armitage, "The Fifty Year's Rift: Intellectual History and International Relations," *Modern Intellectual History* 1, no. 1 (2004): 87–109; Michael Goebel, *Anti-Imperial Metropolis: Interwar Paris and the Seeds of Third World Nationalism* (Cambridge: Cambridge University Press, 2015).

11 Jean Spiropoulos (1896–1972) was a professor of international law in Salonica. Jean Spiropoulos, "L'individu et le droit international," *Recueil des Cours* 30 (1929): 191–270.

12 Herbert Glücksmann, *Ausländer und Staatenlose als Kläger im Zivilprozess* (Breslau: Charlottenburg, 1930). See also Schulim Segal, *L'individu en droit international positif* (Paris: Librarie du Recueil Sirey, 1932), 163.

13 "Crises" dominated a range of intellectual fields from philosophy to literature in interwar Europe. Peter Gordon, *Continental Divide: Heidegger, Cassirer, Davos* (Cambridge MA: Harvard University Press, 2010), 43–52 passim. On the political role of international lawyers in the late nineteenth century, see Mark Mazower, *Governing the World: The History of an Idea* (New York: Penguin, 2012), 77–81. Aimee M. Genell, "The Well-Defended Domains: Eurocentric International Law and the Making of the Ottoman Office of Legal Counsel," *Journal of the Ottoman and Turkish Studies Association* 3, no. 2 (2016): 255–275. International lawyers trained in France had seen their scholarly output as a contribution to French constitutional thought and to shoring up state authority in the face of social and economic crisis. David Bates, "Political Unity and the Spirit of Law: Juridical Concepts of the State in the Late Third Republic," *French Historical Studies* 28, no. 1 (2005): 69–101.

14 Benjamin Coates, *Legalist Empire: International Law and American Foreign Relations* (New York: Oxford University Press, 2016); Stephen Wertheim, "The League of

Nations: A Retreat from International Law?" *Journal of Global History* 7, no. 2 (2012): 210–232. David Kennedy, *Of War and Law* (Princeton, NJ: Princeton University Press, 2006), 68–83; Koskenniemi, *Gentle Civilizer of Nations*, 237.

15 Mathias Schmoeckel, "Lassa Oppenheim and His Reaction to World War I," in *Peace Treaties and International Law in European History: From the Late Middle Ages to World War One*, ed. Randall Lesaffer (Cambridge: Cambridge University Press, 2004), 270–288.

16 Isabel Hull, *A Scrap of Paper: Breaking and Making International Law* (Ithaca, NY: Cornell University Press, 2014); James W. Garner, *International Law and the World War* (London: Longmans, Green, 1920); Mark Lewis, *The Birth of the New Justice: The Internationalization of Crime and Punishment, 1919–1950* (Oxford: Oxford University Press, 2014), 33.

17 On this point see Debora R. Coen, *Vienna in the Age of Uncertainty: Science, Liberalism, and Private Life* (Chicago: University of Chicago Press, 2007), 88–90. See generally James Gordley, *The Jurists: A Critical History* (Oxford: Oxford University Press, 2013).

18 On Ben Gurion's legal studies in Salonika, see Simon Rabinovitch, "Diaspora, Nation, and Messiah: An Introductory Essay," in *Jews and Diaspora Nationalism: Writings on Jewish Peoplehood in Europe and the United States*, ed. Simon Rabinovitch (Waltham, MA: Brandeis University Press, 2012), xxxi.

19 Piotr Wandycz, *The Lands of Partitioned Poland, 1795–1918* (Seattle: University of Washington Press, 1974), 350.

20 Philippe Sands, *East-West Street: On the Origins of "Genocide" and "Crimes against Humanity"* (New York: Knopf, 2016), 76–79.

21 Hersch Lauterpacht, *Private Law Sources and Analogies of International Law: With Special Reference to International Arbitration* (London: Longmans, Green, 1927), 82n2. On the idea that the legality of international legal order depends on the fact that its guardians are lawyers who "create certain categories of orderly behavior and state expectations," see Nicholas Onuf, "International Legal Order as an Idea," *American Journal of International Law* 73, no. 2 (1979): 266.

22 Philip Jessup to Edwin Borchard, October 5, 1926, box A4, Philip Jessup Papers, Library of Congress. See Mark Weston Janis, *America and the Law of Nations, 1776–1939* (Oxford: Oxford University Press, 2010), 206; Adam Tooze, *The Deluge: The Great War and the Remaking of Global Order, 1916–1931* (London: Penguin, 2015).

23 Quincy Wright, "Sovereignty of the Mandates," *American Journal of International Law* 17, no. 4 (1923): 691–703; Susan Pedersen, *The Guardians: The League of Nations and the Crisis of Empire* (Oxford: Oxford University Press, 2015), ch. 7, passim; James Garner, "Limitations on National Sovereignty in International Relations," *American Political Science Review* 19, no. 1 (1925): 1–24.

24 Quincy Wright, *Mandates under the League of Nations* (Chicago: University of Chicago Press, 1930), vii.

25 Segal, *L'individu*, 163–164.

26 M. Korowicz, "The Problem of the International Personality of Individuals," *American Journal of International Law* 50, no. 3 (1956): 533–562.

27 Edwin Borchard, "International Law," in *Encyclopedia of the Social Sciences* (London: Macmillan, 1932).

28 Clyde Eagleton to Manley Hudson, September 2, 1929, box 52, Manley O. Hudson Papers, Harvard University Law School Library.

29 Lassa Oppenheim, *The League of Nations and Its Problems: Three Lectures* (London: Longmans, Green, 1919), 75.

30 Hannah Arendt, *The Origins of Totalitarianism* (New York: Schocken Books, 1951), chap. 9; Quentin Skinner "The Sovereign State: A Genealogy," in *Sovereignty in Fragments: The Past, Present, and Future of a Contested Concept*, ed. Hent Kalmo and Quentin Skinner (Cambridge: Cambridge University Press, 2010), 26–47; see Janne Nijman, *The Concept of International Legal Personality: An Inquiry into the History and Theory of International Law* (The Hague: Asser Press, 2004).

31 The American Supreme Court justice John Marshall referred to the private corporation as a "mere creature of law, it possesses only those properties which the charter of its creation confers on it." *Trustees of Dartmouth College v. Woodward*, 17 U.S. 518 (1819). On the way that "the fictions of corporate personality and ship personification have strained to incorporate anthropocentric properties" see D. Lind, "The Pragmatic Value of Legal Fictions" in *Legal Fictions Theory and Practice*, ed. Maksmilian Del Mar and William Twining (Heidelberg: Spring, 2015), 99; Frederic Maitland, *Political Theories of the Middle Ages*, trans. Otto von Gierke (Cambridge: Cambridge University Press, 1913), xxx; David Runciman, *Pluralism and the Personality of the State* (Cambridge: Cambridge University Press, 1997), 52, 90.

32 See Jonathan Levy, "Accounting for Profit and the History of Capital," *Critical Historical Studies* 1, no. 2 (2014): 171–214; James Livingston, *Pragmatism and the Political Economy of Cultural Revolution, 1850–1940* (Chapel Hill: University of North Carolina Press, 1997).

33 Frederic Maitland, "Trust and Corporation," in *Maitland: State, Trust, and Corporation*, ed. David Runciman and Magnus Ryan (Cambridge: Cambridge University Press, 2003); Gregory S. Alexander, "The Transformation of Trust as a Legal Category, 1800–1914," *Law and History Review* 5 (1987): 303–350.

34 Maitland, "Trust and Corporation," 126.

35 Ibid. Theodor Herzl's *Der Judenstaat*, for example, from 1896 envisioned the state as a joint-stock communal partnership. Ulrich E. Bach, *Tropics of Vienna: Colonial Utopias of the Habsburg Empire* (New York: Berghahn Books, 2016). On the legal world of merchants and corporations, and the commodification of sovereignty in the era of high imperialism, see Steven Press, *Rogue Empires: Contracts and Conmen in Europe's Scramble for Africa* (Cambridge, MA: Harvard University Press, 2017).

36 Though compare Morton Horwitz on the direct relationship between natural entity theory, or the theory of the "real" personality of corporations and the legitimation of big business in the United States at the turn of the twentieth century. Morton J. Horwitz, *The Transformation of American Law, 1870–1960: The Crisis of Legal Orthodoxy* (Oxford: Oxford University Press, 1992), 72 and chap. 3. On the neglected significance of the pluralists for comprehending the contested nature of sovereignty in the twentieth

century, see Jeanne Morefield, "Political Theory as Historical Counterpoint: The Case of Schmitt and Sovereignty," *Theory and Event* 19, no. 1 (2016); Karuna Mantena, "On Gandhi's Critique of the State: Sources, Contexts, Conjunctures," *Modern Intellectual History* 9, no. 3 (2012): 535–563; Duncan Bell, "Beyond the Sovereign State: Isopolitan Citizenship, Race, and Anglo-American Union," *Political Studies* 62 (2014): 418–434.

37 David Runciman and Magnus Ryan, "Introduction," in *Maitland: State, Trust and Corporation*, ed. David Runciman and Magnus Ryan (Cambridge: Cambridge University Press, 2003), xxvi; Marc Stears, *Progressives, Pluralists, and the Problems of the State* (Oxford: Oxford University Press, 2002).

38 Josef Kohler, *Philosophy of Law*, trans. Adalbert Albrecht (Boston: Boston Book Company, 1914), 68.

39 P. W. Duff, "The Personality of an Idol," *The Cambridge Law Journal* 3, no. 1 (1927): 42–48; H. Rheinfelder, *Das Wort "Persona" Geschichte seiner Bedeutungen mit besonderer Berücksichtigung des frazösischen und italienischen Mitaelalters* (Halle: Niemeyer, 1928); Edwin DeWitt Dickinson, "The Analogy between Natural Persons and International Persons in the Law of Nations," *Yale Law Journal* 26, no. 7 (1916–17): 564–591; Hugo Krabbe, *The Modern Idea of the State*, trans. George H. Sabine (New York: D. Appleton, 1922).

40 John Dewey, "The Historic Background of Corporate Legal Personality" *Yale Law Journal* 35, no. 6 (1926): 655–673; W. M. Geldart, "Legal Personality," *Law Quarterly Review* 27 (1911): 90–109. The status of law and the legal state dominated political and legal debate in the United States as a growing number of administrative agencies began to take over the regulation and distribution of public services. See C. H. McIlwain, "Sovereignty Again," *Economica*, no. 18 (1926): 253–268.

41 Dewey, "Historic Background," 655. John Dewey, *The Public and Its Problems* (New York: Henry Holt, 1927), 6. See also Livingston, *Pragmatism and the Political Economy*, 197–200.

42 See Stuart Banner, *Who Owns the Sky? The Struggle to Control Air Space from the Wright Brothers On* (Cambridge, MA: Harvard University Press, 2008), 36–37; John Haffenden, *William Empson: Among the Mandarins* (Oxford: Oxford University Press, 2005), 47–48.

43 Max Radin, "The Endless Problem of Corporate Personality," *Columbia Law Review* 32, no. 4 (1932): 643–667; Robert E. Cushman, "Judicial Decisions on Public Law," *American Political Science Review* 11, no. 3 (1917): 545–555. In the American context, Adolf A. Berle and Gardiner C. Means argued that modern corporations had begun to compete with states as a result of their command of economic power. See Dalia Tsuk Mitchell, "From Pluralism to Individualism: Berle and Means and 20th Century American Legal Thought," *Law and Social Inquiry* 30, no. 179 (2005): 179.

44 Harold Laski, *The Foundations of Sovereignty and Other Essays* (New York: Harcourt, Brace and Company, 1921), 314. In their studies on corporate and state personality in the history of political thought, Quentin Skinner and David Runciman have both argued that the risk of losing sight of the philosophical question about what the state is, and where it comes from—what is distinctive about it as a particular kind of

human association—is that the loss of this perspective coincides with a more general disavowal of the idea that states are agents who bear important responsibilities for collective life. See Skinner, "The Sovereign State: A Genealogy"; Runciman, *Pluralism and the Personality of the State.*

45 Quoted in Peter C. Caldwell, "The Citizen and the Republic in Germany, 1918–1935," in *Citizenship and National Identity in Twentieth Century Germany*, ed. Geoff Eley and Jan Palmowski (Stanford, CA: Stanford University Press, 2008), 41. On Jellinek and state theory, see Duncan Kelly, "Revisiting the Rights of Man: Georg Jellinek on Rights and the State," *Law and History Review* 22, no. 3 (2004): 493–529.

46 Edward Borchard, "The Access of Individuals to International Courts," *American Journal of International Law* 24, no. 359 (1930): 359–365; Jasper Yeates Brinton, *The Mixed Courts of Egypt* (New Haven, CT: Yale University Press, 1930); Nathan J. Brown, "The Precarious Life and Slow Death of the Mixed Courts of Egypt," *International Journal of Middle East Studies* 25, no. 1 (1993): 33–52.

47 Catherine Gousseff, *L'exil russe: La fabrique du réfugié apatride, 1920–1939* (Paris: CNRS, 2008), 238.

48 Roger Picard, "Les 'Sans-Patrie' et la S.D.N.," *La Paix par le Droit* 37, no. 1 (1927): 97–99.

49 Ibid., 99. Politicians and publicists sympathetic to the plight of the stateless proposed international forms of protection that would likewise place the stateless in a tutelary role. Charles Evans Hughes, the American secretary of state from 1922 to 1925, argued that the Russian exiles would require "moral tutelage" as long as they were deprived of their "natural sovereignty." Quoted in Alexandre Gorovtsev, "La problème de la protection des 'Sans Patrie' par la S.D.N au point de vue juridique," *La Paix par le Droit* 37, no. 1 (1927): 113.

50 Giuseppe Nitti, *La situation juridique des émigrés italiens en France* (Paris: Pedone, 1929), 74; Giuseppe Nitti, "La situation juridique des émigrés italiens en France," *Revue generale de droit international public* 36 (1929): 742; Susan Treggiari, "Social Status and Social Legislation," in *The Cambridge Ancient History* (New York: Macmillan, 1996), 10:874.

51 Tristan S. Taylor, "Social Status, Legal Status, and Legal Privilege," in *The Oxford Handbook of Roman Law and Society*, ed. Clifford Ando, Paul J. du Plessis, and Kaius Tuori (Oxford: Oxford University Press, 2016), 349–362. For the idea that the descriptions of the world produced by jurists regulate social reality, and how law constructs reality by creating what it merely claims to describe, see Clifford Ando, *Law, Language, and Empire in the Roman Tradition* (Philadelphia: University of Pennsylvania Press, 2011).

52 J. G. A. Pocock, "The Ideal of Citizenship since Classical Times," *Queen's Quarterly* 99, no. 1 (1992): 33–55. On Karl Marx's rejection of law's mediation of social existence, see Donald Kelley, "The Metaphysics of Law: An Essay on the Very Young Marx," *American Historical Review* 83, no. 2 (1978): 350–367.

53 The article he submitted attempts to analyze the idea of "objective right" through an examination of the social phenomenology of possession. Alexandre Gorovtsev, "A

New Conception of the Right of Property as Considered from the Point of View of the 'Principiology of the Law.'" MS sent to Roscoe Pound, August 28, 1928, Roscoe Pound Papers, Harvard Law School Library.

54 Gorovtsev committed suicide in Paris in the Bois de Boulogne in 1933 after failing to find work in Paris or the United States. G. S. Starodubt͡sev, *Mezhdunarodno-pravovai͡a nauka rossii͡skoĭ ėmigrat͡sii: 1918–1939* (Moscow: Kniga i biznes, 2000). I'm grateful to Philippa Hetherington for identifying this source.

55 Gorovtsev, "La problème de la protection des Sans Patrie par la S.D.N au point de vue juridique," 115; Alexandre Gorovtsev, "La notion d'object en droit international en son role pour la constructions juridique de cette discipline," *Review de droit international et de la législation comparée* 6 (1925): 173–202. See also Anthony Pagano, "Personnalité juridique et représentation légale de l'incapable," *Revue internationale de la théorie du droit* 2 (1927/1928): 1–11.

56 Mark Vishniak, "In Two Worlds," in *The Russian Century: A Hundred Years of Russian Lives,* ed. George Pahomov and Nickolas Lupinin (Lanham, MD: University Press of America, 2008), 95–103.

57 Mark Vishniak, *La protection des droits des minorités dans les traités internationaux de 1919–1920* (Paris: J. Povolozky, 1920), 63–64.

58 The section of the League secretariat assigned to minority protection fielded frequent complaints about its administrative structure when minority groups protested their exclusion from investigatory and reporting processes. Zara Steiner, *The Lights That Failed: European International History, 1919–1933* (Oxford: Oxford University Press, 2007), 363–365.

59 Vishniak, "Le statut international des apatrides," 105.

60 Ibid., 121.

61 Record of conversation with Sir Willoughby Dickinson and Sir Walter Napier, "The 'Staatenlose' Problem," September 6, 1926, R1287, LNA.

62 "Rider A to Napier Report Nationality in the Succession States of Austria-Hungary," Refugees, Statelessness 1925–1935, International Federation League of Nations Societies, P98, LNA; also see Sir Walter John Napier, *Staatenlosigkeit: Being a Report of the Condition of Statelessness in Which the Subjects of the Former Austro-Hungarian Empire Are Left under the Peace Settlement* (Brussels: General Secretariat and Offices of the Federation, 1926).

63 "Nationality in the Succession States of Austria Hungary, Memorandum by Sir Walter Napier," November 12, 1925, Refugees, Statelessness 1925–1935, International Federation League of Nations Societies, P98, LNA.

64 Michael Marrus, *The Unwanted: European Refugees from the First World War to the Cold War* (Philadelphia: Temple University Press, 2002), 95.

65 Hans Kelsen, *Die Staatslehre des Dantes Alighieri* (Vienna: Franz Deuticke, 1906). On Strisower, see Mónica García-Salmones Rovira, *The Project of Positivism in International Law* (Oxford: Oxford University Press, 2013), 186.

66 Hans Kelsen, *Hauptprobleme der Staatsrechtslehre, entwickelt aus der Lehre vom Rechts-satze,* 2nd ed. (Tübingen: Mohr Siebeck, 2005).

67 Hans Kelsen, "Autobiographie," in *Hans Kelsen im Selbstzeugnis*, ed. Matthias Jestaedt (Tübingen: Mohr Siebeck, 2006), 49, 52.

68 According to John Boyer, the revolution in Austria in 1918 was characterized by the move to a democratically legitimate state, whose ethos was pluralistic and tried to remain above the ideological fray. John Boyer, *Culture and Political Crisis in Vienna: Christian Socialism in Power, 1897–1918* (Chicago: University of Chicago Press, 1995), 453. Robert Kann, cited in Boyer, *Culture and Political Crisis in Vienna*, 453.

69 Clemens Jabloner, "Kelsen and His Circle: The Viennese Years," *European Journal of International Law* 9, no. 2 (1998): 368–385; N. B. Ladavac, "Hans Kelsen: Biographical Note and Bibliography," *European Journal of International Law* 9, no. 1 (1998): 391–400.

70 Hans Kelsen, *Der soziologische und der juristiche Staatsbegriff: kritische Untersuchung des Verhaltnisses von Staat und Recht*, 2nd ed. (Tübingen: Mohr, 1928); Andrew Spadafora, "Georg Jellinek on Values and Objectivity in the Legal and Political Sciences," *Modern Intellectual History* 14, no. 3 (2015): 1–30.

71 Carl Schmitt, *Constitutional Theory*, trans. Jeffrey Seltzer (Durham, NC: Duke University Press, 2008).

72 Christopher Tomlins and John Comaroff, "'Law As . . .': Theory and Practice in Legal History," *UC Irvine Law Review* 1, no. 3 (2011): 1039–1079; Hermann Heller, *Die Souveränität: Ein Beitrag zur Theorie des Staats und Völkerrechtes* (Berlin: Walter de Gruyter, 1927).

73 Hans Kelsen, "Les rapports de système entre le droit interne et le droit international," *Recueil des Cours de l'Académie de Droit International* 14, no. 4 (1926): 227–331; Hans Kelsen, *Das Problem der Souveränität und die Theories des Völkerrechts: Beitrag zu einer Reinen Rechtslehre* (Tübingen: J. C. B. Mohr, 1928). See also Peter Langford and Ian Bryan, "Hans Kelsen's Legal Theory of Monism: A Critical Engagement with the Emerging Legal Order of the 1920s," *Journal of the History of International Law* 14, no. 1 (2012): 51–86.

74 Hans Kelsen, *Allgemeiner Staatslehre* (Berlin: Springer, 1925).

75 David Dyzenhaus, *Legality and Legitimacy: Carl Schmitt, Hans Kelsen, and Hermann Heller in Weimar* (Oxford: Oxford University Press, 1999), 155–156.

76 Eugen Ehrlich, *Fundamental Principles of the Sociology of Law*, trans. Walter Moll (Cambridge MA: Harvard University Press, 1936), 9. On finding law in communal practices, see Georg Gurvitch, *L'idée du droit social* (Paris: Recueil Sirey, 1932).

77 Ehrlich, *Fundamental Principles*; Bart Van Klink, "Facts and Norms: The Unfinished Debate between Eugen Ehrlich and Hans Kelsen," in *Living Law: Reconsidering Eugen Ehrlich*, ed. Marc Hertogh (Portland, OR: Hart Publishing, 2009), 127–156.

78 Allan Janik and Stephen Toulmin, *Wittgenstein's Vienna* (New York: Touchstone, 1973), 271.

79 On law's various sources of authority, see generally J. G. A. Pocock, *The Ancient Constitution and the Feudal Law: A Study of English Historical Thought in the Seventeenth Century* (Cambridge: Cambridge University Press, 1957).

80 Hans Kelsen, "Selbstdarstellung," in *Hans Kelsen im Sebstzeugnis*, ed. Matthias Jestaedt (Tübingen: Mohr Siebeck, 2006), 1927.

81 Coen, *Vienna*, 88–90.

82 William Johnston, *The Austrian Mind: An Intellectual and Social History, 1848–1938* (Berkeley: University of California Press, 1972), 97.

83 Johnston, *Austrian Mind*, 106; Karl Renner, "State and Nation (1899)," in *National Cultural Autonomy and Its Contemporary Critics*, ed. Ephraim Nimni (London: Routledge, 2005), 15–47.

84 Gerhard Stourzh, "The Multinational Empire Revisited," in *From Vienna to Chicago and Back: Essays on Intellectual History and Political Thought in Europe and America* (Chicago: University of Chicago Press, 2007), 145; John Deak, *Forging a Multinational State: State Making in Imperial Austria from the Enlightenment to the First World War* (Stanford, CA: Stanford University Press, 2015).

85 In a short autobiographical essay from 1927, Kelsen claimed that neo-Kantian philosophy had been "there for me from the beginning." Kelsen, "Selbstdarstellung," 23. On neo-Kantianism, see Gordon, *Continental Divide*, 52–69; Thomas Williey, *Back to Kant: The Revival of Kantianism in German Social and Historical Thought, 1860–1914* (Detroit, MI: Wayne State University Press, 1978).

86 Hans Kelsen, "On the Theory of Juridic Fictions: With Special Consideration of Vaihinger's Philosophy of the As-If," trans. Christophe Kletzer, in *Legal Fictions in Theory and Practice*, ed. Maksmilian Del Mar and William Twining (Heidelberg: Spring, 2015), 18.

87 Hans Kelsen, *Pure Theory of Law*, trans. Max Knight (Berkeley: University of California Press, 1967), 288. On the distinction between the juridical and the sociological, and its relation to the normativity of law, see Stephen P. Turner, *Explaining the Normative* (Cambridge, UK: Polity, 2010), ch. 3.

88 Hans Kelsen, "The Conception of the State and Social Psychology with Special Reference to Freud's Group Theory," *International Journal of Psycho-analysis* 5, no. 1 (1924): 1–38.

89 Ibid., 3.

90 Helen Silving-Ryu, *Helen Silving: Memoirs* (New York: Vantage, 1988), 75, 85. Also see Albert Ehrenzweig, "Preface," *California Law Review* 59, no. 3 (1971): 609–616.

91 Silving, *Memoirs*, 88. Egon Wellesz, Kelsen's neighbor and a student of the composer Arnold Schoenberg, recalled that in Vienna after World War I, "they did not like Kelsen, he abolished the state." Quoted in A. W. B. Simpson, *Reflections on the Concept of Law* (Oxford: Oxford University Press, 2011), 113.

92 Quoted in Fredrik Lindstrom, *Empire and Identity: Biographies of the Austrian State Problem in the Late Habsburg Empire* (West Lafayette, IN: Purdue University Press, 2008), 272. See also Josef Redlich, *Austrian War Government* (New Haven, CT: Yale University Press, 1929).

93 Gary B. Cohen, "Our Laws, Our Taxes, and Our Administration: Citizenship in Imperial Austria," in *Shatterzones of Empires: Coexistence and Violence in the German, Habsburg, Russian, and Ottoman Borderlands*, ed. Omar Bartov and Eric Weitz (Bloomington: Indiana University Press, 2013), 117.

94 Pieter Judson, *The Habsburg Empire: A New History* (Cambridge, MA: Harvard University Press, 2016), 387–388.

95 Hans Kelsen, "La naissance de l'état et la formation de sa nationalité: Les principes de leur application au cas de la Tchéchoslovaquie," *Revue de droit international* 4, no. 1 (1929): 612–641.

96 *Prager Tagblatt*, "Our Stateless," October 11, 1930, via "Situation des Apatrides: Correspondence Diverse," R3589, LNA.

97 "Wer keinem Staate als Bürger angehört, ist völkerrechtlich vogelfrei." Hans Kelsen, "Geleitwort," in *Die Staatenlosen*, by Heinrich Englander (Vienna: Schriften der österreichischen Liga für Menschenrechte, 1930), 6.

98 Hans Herz, "La problème de la naissance de l'état et la decision du Tribunal Arbitral Mixte germano-polonais du August 1929," *Revue de la droit international et de législation comparée* 3, no. 1 (1936): 1–27; Hans Herz, "Le sujet de droit en droit international public," *Revue international de la théorie du droit* 10, no. 2 (1936): 100–111. The Polish jurist Krystina Marek carried the Vienna School tradition forward in her 1954 treatise, *Identity and Continuity of States in Public International Law* (Geneva: Librairie E. Droz, 1954). See also James Crawford, "The Criteria for Statehood in International Law," *British Yearbook of International Law* 48, no. 1 (1976): 93–182. Mikulas Fabry, *Recognizing States: International Society and the Establishment of New States since 1776* (Oxford: Oxford University Press, 2010), chap. 4.

99 John Herz, "On Human Survival: How a View Emerged," box 2, John Herz Papers, German and Jewish Intellectual Émigré Collection, State University of New York at Albany.

100 Josef L. Kunz, *Die Völkerrechtliche Option* (Breslau: F. Hirt, 1926).

101 Rockefeller Foundation Archives, Record Group 10.2—Fellowship recorder cards, Discipline 5—Humanities, box 3, Rockefeller Archive Center, Sleepy Hollow, NY.

102 Josef L. Kunz, "The 'Vienna School' and International Law," *New York University Law Quarterly Review* 11, no. 3 (1934): 370–422. Among the well-known scholars who followed the Vienna School of Legal Theory were Adolf Merkel, Alfred Verdross, Felix Kaufmann, Fritzer Sander, Erich Voegelin, Alf Ross, Charles Eisenman, Franz Weyr, Leonidas Pitamic, Josef Laurenz Kunz, Rudolf Aladar Metall, Helen Silving-Ryu, Leo Gross, and John Herz. Jabloner, "Kelsen and His Circle." On Kelsen's theory, see Hans Kelsen, "Legal Formalism and the Pure Theory of Law," in *Weimar: A Jurisprudence of Crisis*, ed. Arthur J. Jacobson and Bernhard Schlink (Berkeley: University of California Press, 2000), 76–84, originally published as Kelsen, "Juristischer Formalismus und reine Rechtslehre," *Juristische Wochenschrift* 58, no. 23 (1929): 1723–1726. See also Kelsen, *Allgemeiner Staatslehre*, 1925; R. A. Métall, *Hans Kelsen: Leben und Werk* (Vienna: Deutike, 1969); Peter Caldwell, "Sovereignty, Constitutionalism, and the Myth of the State," in *The Weimar Moment: Liberalism, Political Theology, and Law*, ed. Leonard Kaplan and Rudy Koshar (Lanham, MD: Lexington Books, 2012), 345–371. Compare Josef L. Kunz, *Völkerrechtswissenschaft und reine Rechtslehre* (Leipzig: F. deutlicke, 1923); Michael Stolleis, *A History of Public Law in Germany, 1914–1945* (Oxford: Oxford University Press, 2004), 63.

103 Josef Kunz, Untitled Memoir, December 17, 1959, Hans Kelsen Institut Archive; Josef L. Kunz, *Bibliographie der Kriegsliteratur: Politik, Geschichte, Philosophie, Völkerrecht,*

Friedensfrage (Berlin: H. R. Engelmann, 1920); Josef L. Kunz, *Gaskrieg und Völkerrecht* (Vienna: Springer, 1927).

104 Kunz, Untitled Memoir, December 17, 1959, Hans Kelsen Institut, Vienna.

105 J. L. Kunz, "L'option de nationalité," *Hague Recueil* 31, no. 1 (1930): 1–31.

106 Karl F. Geiser, review of *Handbuch des Völkerrechts, II, 4: Die Staatenverbindungen*, by Josef L. Kunz, *American Journal of International Law* 24, no. 2 (1930): 417–418. See also Josef L. Kunz, *Die Anerkennung von Staaten und Regierungen im Völkerrecht* (Stuttgart: W. Wohlhammer, 1928).

107 Legal and administrative succession in Poland represented a particularly complex issue since the Polish state inherited its laws and bureaucracies from three distinct empires. On the reemergence of the Polish state in international law, see C. H. Alexandrowicz, "Recognition of New States in International Law," in *The Law of Nations in Global History*, by C. H. Alexandrowicz, ed. David Armitage and Jennifer Pitts (Oxford: Oxford University Press, 2017), 400.

108 Hersch Lauterpacht, "Sukcesja państw w odniesieniu do zobowiązań prywatno-prawnych" *Glos Prawa* 5, no. 6 (1928): 18–33, translated as "Succession of States with Respect to Private Law Obligations," in *International Law being the Collected Papers of Hersch Lauterpacht*, vol. 3, ed. Eli Lauterpacht (Cambridge: Cambridge University Press, 1977), 121–138.

109 This formulation borrowed directly from a 1910 decision of the administrative court in Vienna, determining that ethnic attribution in a local municipal dispute could rest on a municipality's assessment of the "tangible evidence" indicating the ethnicity of the individual in question. Gerald Stourzh, "Ethnic Attribution in Late Imperial Austria: Good Intentions, Evil Consequences," in *From Vienna to Chicago and Back: Essays on Intellectual History and Political Thought in Europe and America* (Chicago: University of Chicago Press, 2007), 169.

110 Benjamin Akzin, "Les sujets du droit international," *Revue de droit international* 3, no. 4 (1929): 451–489.

111 "Lyon Juridical Commission Meeting," June 27, 1924, International Federation League of Nations Societies Papers 1924–1927, P93, LNA.

112 "Commission Juridique Vienna," April 1924, International Federation League of Nations Societies Papers 1924–1927, P93, LNA.

113 Ibid.

114 Dzovinar Kévonian, "Les Juristes juifs russes en France et l'action internationale dans les années vingt," *Archives Juives* 34, no. 2 (2001): 72–94. On jurists and legalism in the late Russian Empire, see Peter Holquist, "Dilemmas of a Progressive Administrator: Baron Boris Nolde," *Kritika* 7, no. 2 (2006), 241–273. See generally Richard Wortman, *The Development of a Russian Legal Consciousness* (Chicago: University of Chicago Press, 1976).

115 As a Russian diplomat in Constantinople in the decade before World War I, Mandelstam proposed an internationalist solution to the so-called "Armenian question" in the Ottoman Empire, in which a single Armenian province in the empire would be administered by a governor-general who would be either an Ottoman citizen of the Christian

faith or a "European" nominated by the sultan. Later, during the war, Mandelstam was responsible for adjudicating the legal questions surrounding prisoners of war before he was promoted to principal legal advisor of the Ministry of Foreign Affairs after the liberal revolution in Russia in early 1917. Helmut Philipp Aust, "From Diplomat to Academic Activist: Andre Mandelstam and the History of Human Rights," *European Journal of International Law* 25, no. 4 (2015). Mandelstam began his study *Le Sort de L'Empire Ottoman* with the statement "This book is a work by a liberal Russian, a jurist who loves the law, and who has passed sixteen years in an Empire which has declared eternal war on law." *Le Sort de L'Empire Ottoman* (Paris: Payot, 1917).

116 Bruno Cabanes, *The Great War and the Origins of Humanitarianism* (Cambridge: Cambridge University Press, 2014), 168.

117 A. N. Mandelstam, "La protection international des droits de l'homme," *Recueil des Cours* 38, no. 4 (1931): 129–131.

118 A. N. Mandelstam, "La protection des droits de l'hommes," *Les minorités nationales* 5, no. 4 (1932): 65–75; A. N. Mandelstam, "La géneralisation de la protection internationale des droits de l'homme," *Revue droit international et de législation comparée* 11, no. 2 (1930): 297–326. On this group of émigré jurists, see Dzovinar Kévonian, "Exilés politiques et avènement du 'droit humain': La pensée juridique d'André Mandelstam (1869–1949)," *Revue d'histoire de la Shoah* 117–118 (2001): 245–273.

119 See Boris-Mirkine Guetzevitch, "Das Menschenrechte der Heimatlosen," *Die Freidens-Warte* 30, no. 7/8 (1930): 213–215. For a similar view, though with an emphasis on rights within the boundary of "civilization," see Paul Gramain, *Les droits internationaux de l'homme* (Paris: Éditions Internationales, 1933).

120 Vishniak, "Le statut international des apatrides," 165–166.

121 On Mandelstam as part of the "solidarist vogue" in France, see Dzovinar Kévonian, "La protection des minorities et l'internationalisation des droits de l'hommes," in *Revisiting the Origins of Human Rights*, ed. Pamela Slotte and Miia Halme-Tuomisaari (Cambridge: Cambridge University Press, 2015), 57–72.

122 Martti Koskenniemi, *From Apology to Utopia: The Structure of International Legal Argument* (Cambridge: Cambridge University Press, 2006), 201. Kelsen encouraged his students to compare him and Duguit in their dissertations. Silving-Ryu, *Memoirs*, 88.

123 For an analysis of the weakness of this approach in resisting fascism, see Nathaniel Berman, "'But the Alternative Is Despair': European Nationalism and the Renewal of International Law," *Harvard Law Review* 106, no. 1792 (1993): 1793–1808; Carl Schorske, *Fin de Siècle Vienna: Politics and Culture* (New York: Knopf, 1979). On this interpretation of Austrian liberalism, compare Coen, *Vienna*; Malachi Hacohen, *Karl Popper: The Formative Years, 1902–1945* (Cambridge: Cambridge University Press, 2000).

124 Silving-Ryu, *Memoirs*, 83.

125 There he discussed the future of the discipline with George Scelle, William Rappard, Paul Mantoux, Paul Guggenheim, and Hans Wehberg, among others. Yael Paz, *A Gateway between a Distant God and a Cruel World: The Contribution of Jewish German-Speaking Scholars to International Law* (Leiden: Martinus Nijhof, 2012), 182;

Rudolf Aladar Metall, *Hans Kelsen: Leben und Werk* (Wien: Franz Deuticke, 1969), 70–72.

126 Robert Musil, *The Man without Qualities*, vol. 1, trans. Sophie Wilkins (New York: Random House, 1995), 29. See also Marjorie Perloff, *Edge of Irony: Modernism in the Shadow of the Habsburg Empire* (Chicago: University of Chicago Press, 2016).

127 Johnston, *Austrian Mind*, 98. On the failure of the Habsburg constitution to confront social reality, see Janik and Toulmin, *Wittgenstein's Vienna*, 271–272. The French historian of science Georges Canguilhem described Kelsen's theory as "powerless to absorb political fact into juridical fact." *The Normal and the Pathological*, trans. Carolyn Fawcett (New York: Zone Books, 2007), 249. See also Steven Beller, *Vienna and the Jews, 1867–1938: A Cultural History* (Cambridge, Cambridge University Press, 1991), 236.

128 Michael Gubser, *Time's Visible Surface: Alois Riegl and the Discourse on History and Temporality in Fin-de-Siècle Vienna* (Detroit, MI: Wayne State Press, 2006). In Kelsen's own words, "considering the Austrian state which was made up of so many different racial, linguistic, religious and historical groups, theories that tried to found the unity of the state on some socio-psychological or socio-biological contexts of the persons legally belonging to a state clearly proved to be fictions. To the extent that this theory of state is an important part of the Pure Theory of Law, the Pure Theory of Law can be seen as a specifically Austrian theory." Hans Kelsen, "Autobiographie," in *Hans Kelsen im Selbstzeugnis*, ed. Matthias Jestaedt (Tübingen: Mohr Siebeck, 2006), 62. Judith Shklar, *Legalism: Law, Morals, and Political Trials* (Cambridge, MA: Harvard University Press, 1964), 41. See also Jabloner, "Kelsen and His Circle"; Beller, *Vienna and the Jews*, 211.

129 See for example Richard Falk, "Revisiting Westphalia, Discovering Post-Westphalia," *Journal of Ethics* 6, no. 4 (2002): 311–352. Casper Sylvest, "Realism and International Law: The Challenge of John H. Herz," *International Theory* 2, no. 3 (2010): 410–445; Nicolas Guilhot, *After the Enlightenment: Political Realism and International Relations in the Mid-Twentieth Century* (Cambridge: Cambridge University Press, 2017).

4. THE REAL BOUNDARIES OF MEMBERSHIP

1 Oskar Brandstaedter to the League, February 24, 1934, R5671, "Staatenlosen: Various Correspondence with Individuals and Organizations," LNA.

2 Oskar Brandstaedter to the League, October 4, 1935, R5671, LNA.

3 Claudena Skran, *Refugees in Inter-War Europe: The Emergence of a Regime* (Oxford: Clarendon, 1995), 48.

4 Karl Schlögel, *In Space We Read Time: On the History of Civilization and Geopolitics*, trans. Gerrit Jackson (Chicago: University of Chicago Press, 2016), 93–96. Discussed in Mark Mazower, "Endless Exodus: 3,000 Years of Fearing and Depending on Refugees," *Financial Times*, February 10, 2017.

5 Noël Vindry wrote his 1925 dissertation in France on *l'apatridie*. He went on in the 1930s to write a series of successful detective novels. Noël Vindry, *L'apatride* (Aix: Impremerie-Libraire A. Makaire, 1925). See Bruno Cabanes, *The Great War and the*

Origins of Humanitarianism, 1918–1924 (Cambridge: Cambridge University Press, 2014), 138.

6 Eric Ambler, *Epitaph for a Spy* (New York: Vintage, 2002), 22. See also Eric Ambler, *A Coffin for Dimitrios* (New York: Knopf, 1939).

7 John Maynard Keynes, "National Self-Sufficiency," *Yale Review* 22, no. 4 (June 1933): 755–769.

8 On asylum policy in the liberal state, see Frank Caestecker and Bob Moore, eds., *Refugees from Nazi Germany and the Liberal European States* (New York: Berghahn Books, 2012); Arieh Tartakower and Kurt Grossmann, *The Jewish Refugee* (New York: Institute of Jewish Affairs of the American Jewish Congress and World Jewish Congress, 1944); Tommie Sjöberg, *The Power and the Persecuted: The Refugee Problem and the Intergovernmental Committee on Refugees, 1938–1947* (Lund, Sweden: Lund University Press, 1991); Barbara McDonald Stewart, *United States Government Policy on Refuges from Nazism, 1933–1940* (New York: Garland, 1982); Vicky Caron, *Uneasy Asylum: France and the Jewish Refugee Crisis, 1933–1942* (Stanford, CA: Stanford University Press, 1999); Louis London, *Whitehall and the Jews, 1933–1948: British Immigration Policy, Jewish Refugees, and the Holocaust* (Cambridge: Cambridge University Press, 2000). On expulsion from democratic states, see Daniel A. Gordon, "The Back Door of the Nation-State: Expulsion of Foreigners and Continuity in Twentieth-Century France," *Past and Present* 186, no. 1 (2005): 201–232.

9 *Acts of the Conference for the Codification of International Law*, Issue 14, League of Nations, 1930.

10 Ibid., 15.

11 American minister to the Netherlands, Hague Conference, January 21–April 22, 1930, Herbert Hoover, 1929–1933, FRUS 1 (1945), 504.418A2/159.

12 David Hunter Miller, "Nationality and Other Problems Discussed at The Hague," *Foreign Affairs* 8, no. 4 (1930): 632–640. See Richard W. Flourney, ed., *A Collection of Nationality Laws of Various Countries, as Contained in Constitutions, Statutes, and Treaties* (New York: Oxford University Press, 1929).

13 Miller Telegram, Hague Conference, January 21–April 22, 1930, Herbert Hoover, 1929–1933, FRUS 1 (1945), 504.418A2/159.

14 Edwin M. Borchard, "The Hague Codification Conference," *The Nation* 131, no. 3394 (1930): 94–95.

15 Mackinnon-Wood to F. P. Walters, March 9, 1931, "Codification of International Law: Correspondence with the Faculty of the Harvard Law School," R2056, LNA.

16 The policy of contingent female citizenship first appeared in a statutory instrument of the Napoleonic Civil Code of 1804. The principle of conditional marital nationality captured in the code applied across Napoleonic Europe, and by the mid-nineteenth century it was followed in most of the world. Carol Miller, "Geneva—the Key to Equality: Interwar Feminists and the League of Nations," *Women's History Review* 3, no. 2 (1994) 219–245; John Witt, "Crystal Eastman and the Internationalist Beginnings of American Civil Liberties," *Duke Law Journal* 54, no. 3 (2004): 705–763; Helen Irving, *Citizenship, Alienage, and the Modern Constitutional State: A Gendered*

History (Cambridge: Cambridge University Press, 2016); Melissa Feinberg, *Elusive Equality: Gender, Citizenship, and the Limits of Democracy in Czechoslovakia, 1918–1950* (Pittsburgh: University of Pittsburgh Press, 2006), 74.

17 Candice Lewis Bredbenner, *A Nationality of Her Own: Women, Marriage, and the Law of Citizenship* (Berkeley: University of California Press, 1998), chap. 6.

18 Catherine Seckler-Hudson, *Statelessness, with Special Reference to the United States: A Study in Nationality and Conflict of Law* (Washington, DC: American University, 1934).

19 Patrick Weil, *The Sovereign Citizen: Denaturalization and the Origins of the American Republic* (Philadelphia: University of Pennsylvania Press, 2012), 90. On the expansion of federal authority to regulate internal migration and immigration in the 1930s, see Elisa Minoff, "Free to Move? The Law and Politics of Internal Migration in Twentieth-Century America" (PhD diss., Harvard University, 2013); Karen Tani, *States of Dependency: Welfare, Rights, and American Governance, 1935–1972* (Cambridge: Cambridge University Press, 2016).

20 Seckler-Hudson, *Statelessness*. Seckler-Hudson also reviewed Lipovano for the *American Journal of International Law*. Catherine Seckler-Hudson, "L'Apatridie, by I. G. Lipovano," *American Journal of International Law* 30, no. 4 (1936): 743–744. See also Waldo Emerson Waltz, *The Nationality of Married Women: A Study of Domestic Policies and International Legislation* (Urbana: University of Illinois Press, 1937).

21 "Notes on the Points Discussed," 1930, Nationality Law, DO 35 104/2, TNA: PRO.

22 Ibid.

23 See Arnulf Becker Lorca, *Mestizo International Law: A Global Intellectual History 1842–1933* (Cambridge: Cambridge University Press, 2014), chap. 9.

24 League of Nations Union to John Simon, April 6, 1934, Measures for Regulating Position of Stateless, League International Office for Refugees, HO 45/20528, TNA: PRO. Also see Jacques Scheftel, "L'apatridie des refugies russes," *Journal de Droit International* 61, no. 1 (1934): 36–69.

25 Unsigned memoranda, 1934, Measures for Regulating Position of Stateless, League International Office for Refugees, HO 45/20528, TNA: PRO.

26 Unsigned memoranda, 1934, Measures for Regulating Position of Stateless, TNA: PRO.

27 See Emma Haddad, *The Refugee in International Society: Between Sovereigns* (Cambridge: Cambridge University Press, 2008); Guy Goodwin-Gill and Jane McAdam, *The Refugee in International Law* (New York: Oxford University Press, 2007).

28 Gilbert Jaeger, "On the History of the International Protection of Refugees," *Review of the International Committee of the Red Cross* 83, no. 843 (2001): 727–737. Also see Michael Marrus, *The Unwanted: European Refugees from the First World War to the Cold War* (Philadelphia: Temple University Press, 2002), 161–164, 170–172.

29 See "Provisional Arrangement Concerning the Status of Refugees Coming from Germany, July 4, 1936" and "Convention Concerning the Status of Refugees Coming from Germany, February 10, 1938," cited in James C. Hathaway, *The Law of Refugee Status* (Toronto: Butterworths, 1991), 4.

30 League of Nations, Convention Concerning the Status of Refugees Coming from Germany, February 10, 1938, League of Nations Treaty Series, vol. 192, no. 4461, p. 59, http://www.refworld.org/docid/3dd8d12a4.html.

31 Hersch Lauterpacht, "The Nationality of Denationalized Persons," in *International Law, Being the Collected Papers of Hersch Lauterpacht*, vol. 3, ed. Eli Lauterpacht (Cambridge: Cambridge University Press, 1977), 392. Originally published as Lauterpacht, "The Nationality of Denationalized Persons," *Jewish Yearbook of International Law* 1, no. 1 (1949): 164–185. On the transformation of the basis for refugee status from the juridical to the social and finally to the individual fear of persecution, see J. C. Hathaway, "Evolution of Refugee Status in International Law, 1920–1950," *International and Comparative Law Quarterly* 33, no. 384 (1984): 348–380. Compare Jane McAdam, "Rethinking the Origins of 'Persecution' in Refugee Law," *International Journal of Refugee Law* 25, no. 4 (2013): 667–692.

32 Saul Friedlander, *Nazi Germany and the Jews*, vol. 1, *The Years of Persecution* (New York: HarperCollins, 1997), 146.

33 Durward V. Sandifer, "A Comparative Study of Laws Relating to Nationality at Birth and to Loss of Nationality," *American Journal of International Law* 29, no. 2 (1935): 248–279; John Wigmore, "Domicile, Double Allegiance, and World Citizenship," *Illinois Law Review* 21, no. 8 (1927): 761–770; Egidio Reale, "Passport," in *Encyclopedia of the Social Sciences* (New York: Macmillan, 1934), 12:13–16.

34 Bushe to Dowson, November 15, 1933, Nationality Law, DO 35 104/2, TNA: PRO.

35 Dowson to Bushe, November 17, 1933, Nationality Law, DO 35 104/2, TNA: PRO.

36 Claus von Stauffenberg, "Die Entziehung der Staatsangehörigkeit und das Volkerrecht, Eine Entgegnung," *Zeitschrift für ausländisches öffentliches Recht und Völkerrecht* 4 (1934): 261–276, cited in Detlev Vagts, "International Law in the Third Reich," *American Journal of International Law* 84, no. 3 (1990): 661–704. See also James Q. Whitman, *Hitler's American Model: The United States and the Making of Nazi Race Law* (Princeton, NJ: Princeton University Press, 2017).

37 Georges Scelle, "A propos de la Loi allemande du 14 juillet 1933 sur la déchéance de la nationalité," *Révue critique de droit international* 29, no. 1 (1934): 63–76; Stauffenberg, "Die Entziehung der Staatsangehörigkeit und das Völkerrecht, Eine Entgegnung," 261–276.

38 James W. Garner, "Recent German Nationality Legislation," *American Journal of International Law* 30, no. 1 (1936): 96–99.

39 Lawrence Preuss, "International Law and Deprivation of Nationality," *Georgetown Law Journal* 23, no. 2 (1935): 250–276. Also see Maximilien Philonenko, "Expulsion des Heimatlos," *Journal de droit international* 60 (1933): 1161–1187; John Fisher Williams, "Denationalization," *The British Yearbook of International Law* 8, no. 3 (1927): 45–62.

40 Preuss, "International Law," 250–276.

41 Todd Shepard, *The Invention of Decolonization: The Algerian War and the Remaking of France* (Ithaca, NY: Cornell University Press, 2006), 169–170.

42 Patrick Weil, *How to be French: Nationality in the Making since 1789* (Durham, NC: Duke University Press, 2008), 126–129.

43 Mark Mazower, "The Strange Triumph of Human Rights, 1933–1950," *Historical Journal* 47, no. 2 (2004): 388.

44 "Petition in Support of the Letter of Resignation of James G. McDonald and Concerning the Treatment of Jews and Non-Aryans by the German Government: Addressed to the XVIIth Plenary Assembly of the League of Nations," 1–2, Assistance International aux Réfugiés Allemandes, R5720, LNA. Hersch Lauterpacht, Neville Laski, and the London legal scholar Vladimir Idelson advised on the draft, along with two experts on the minority protection treaties, Oscar Janowsky and Melvin Fagin. See Monty Noam Penkower, "Honorable Failures against Nazi Germany: McDonald's Letter of Resignation and the Petition in Its Support," *Modern Judaism* 30, no. 3 (2010), 268; James G. McDonald, *Advocate for the Doomed: The Diaries and Papers of James G. McDonald, 1932–1935*, ed. Richard Breitman, Barbara McDonald Stewart, and Severin Hochberg (Bloomington: Indiana University Press, 2007), 57.

45 Compare Gary Bass, *Freedom's Battle: The Origins of Humanitarian Intervention* (New York: Knopf, 2008); Brendan Simms and D. J. B. Trim, eds., *Humanitarian Intervention: A History* (Cambridge: Cambridge University Press, 2011), 139–15; Davide Rodogno, *Against Massacre: Humanitarian Interventions in the Ottoman Empire, 1815–1914* (Princeton, NJ: Princeton University Press, 2012), ch. 2.

46 McDonald, *Advocate for the Doomed*, 104.

47 Lauterpacht to Laski, March 25, 1935, ACC/3121/C11/ 3/5/2, Board of Deputies, London Municipal Archives.

48 Seckler-Hudson, *Statelessness*. Seckler-Hudson also reviewed Lipovano for the *American Journal of International Law*. Seckler-Hudson, "L'Apatridie."

49 Cyrus Adler to Morris Waldman, April 11, 1935, ACC/3121/C11/ 3/5/2, Board of Deputies, London Municipal Archives.

50 See Alison Bashford, *Global Population: History, Geopolitics, and Life on Earth* (New York: Columbia University Press, 2014).

51 H. Donnedieu de Vabres, "Rapport sur le problème de l'expulsion des apatrides," *Travaux du Comité français de Droit International Privé* 1, no. 2 (1935): 64.

52 Arthur Kuhn, "International Measures for the Relief of Stateless Persons," *American Journal of International Law* 30, no. 3 (1936): 495–499.

53 Ibid., 498.

54 De Vabres, "Rapport sur le problème de l'expulsion des apatrides," 64.

55 Caron, *Uneasy Asylum*, 16. Also see Vicky Caron, "The Politics of Frustration: French Jewry and the Refugee Crisis," *Journal of Modern History* 65, no. 2 (1993): 311–356.

56 France sought to internationalize the refugee problem to reduce the pressure on its ability to absorb newcomers. Caron, *Uneasy Asylum*, 28.

57 J. L. Rubenstein, "The Refugee Problem," *International Affairs* 15, no. 5 (1936): 716–734. A similar sentiment animated Lawford Childs, "Refugees—a Permanent Problem in International Organization," in *War Is Not Inevitable, Problems of Peace* (London: International Labor Office, 1938). Louise Holborn publicized the definition of *refugees* promulgated by the Institut de Droit International at its Brussels session in 1936.

"Refugees" were those "who have left or been forced to leave their country for political reasons, who have been deprived of its diplomatic protection and have not acquired the nationality or diplomatic protection of any other state." See Louise W. Holborn, "The Legal Status of Political Refugees, 1920–1938," *American Journal of International Law* 32, no. 4 (1938): 680–703.

58 Sir Herbert Emerson, address to members of the Executive Committee of the Intergovernmental Committee dealing with refugee problems, Washington, DC, October 17, 1939. Printed as "Postwar Problems of Refugees," *Foreign Affairs* 21, no. 2 (January 1943): 211.

59 John Hope Simpson, *The Refugee Problem: Report of a Survey* (London: Oxford University Press, 1939), 2. Also see Dorothy Thompson, *Refugees: Anarchy or Organization?* (New York: Random House, 1938), 10–11; Holborn, "Legal Status of Political Refugees."

60 Marc Raeff, *Russia Abroad: A Cultural History of the Russian Emigration, 1919–1939* (Oxford: Oxford University Press, 1990), 24.

61 Simpson, *Refugee Problem*, 3–4.

62 Hans Morgenthau, *La réalité des normes, en particulier des normes du droit international* (Paris: Librarie Félix Allcan, 1934).

63 Paul Leon, "H. Morgenthau, *La réalité des normes*," *Archives de philosophie du droit et de sociologie juridique* 4 (1934): 271–273.

64 Jürgen Habermas, "Law and Morality," in *The Tanner Lectures on Human Values*, ed. S. McMurrin, trans. K. Baynes (Salt Lake City: Utah University Press, 1988), 8:217–279; David Rabban, *Law's History: American Legal Thought and the Transatlantic Turn to History* (New York: Cambridge University Press, 2013), 474. On the different trajectories of continental and American legal realism, see Katharina Schmidt, "Law, Modernity, Crisis: German Free Lawyers, American Legal Realists, and the Transatlantic Turn to 'Life,' 1903–1933," *German Studies Review* 39, no. 1 (2016): 121–140.

65 Felix S. Cohen, "Transcendental Nonsense and the Functional Approach," *Columbia Law Review* 35, no. 6 (1935): 809–849.

66 Wilhelm Grewe, "Gnade und Recht" (Hamburg: Hanseatische Verlagsanstalt, 1936), 5, cited in Bardo Fassbender, "Stories of War and Peace: On Writing the History of International Law in the 'Third Reich' and After," *European Journal of International Law* 13, no. 2 (2002): 488–489. On the discourse of "realism" in the 1930s, see Nathaniel Berman, "Beyond Colonialism and Nationalism? Ethiopia, Czechoslovakia, and 'Peaceful Change,'" *Nordic Journal of International Law* 65, no. 421 (1996): 421–479.

67 Peter C. Caldwell, "The Citizen and the Republic in Germany, 1918–1935," in *Citizenship and National Identity in Twentieth-Century Germany*, ed. Geoff Eley and Jan Palmowski (Stanford, CA: Stanford University Press, 2008), 40–57. Carl Schmitt organized a conference in October 1936 entitled "Jewry in German Law" in which Kelsen's formalism was attributed to his Jewish background. Quoted in Detlev Vagts, "Carl Schmitt in Context: Reflections on a Symposium," *Cardozo Law Review* 23, no. 6 (2002): 2157–2164.

68 Casper Sylvest, "Realism and International Law: The Challenge of John H. Herz," *International Theory* 2, no. 3 (2010), 410–445; Nicolas Guilhot, *After the Enlightenment:*

Political Realism and International Relations in the Mid-Twentieth Century (Cambridge: Cambridge University Press, 2017), 3–4. On Schmitt's influence on the development of postwar international relations realism, see Martti Koskenniemi, *The Gentle Civilizer of Nations: The Rise and Fall of International Law, 1870–1960* (Cambridge: Cambridge University Press, 2001), 459–474.

69 The field of international relations theory constituted itself in opposition to Kelsen's critique of sovereignty. William Scheuerman, "Professor Kelsen's Amazing Disappearing Act," in *Émigré Scholars and the Genesis of International Relations: A European Discipline in America?*, ed. Felix Rösch (London: Palgrave Macmillan, 2014), 81–103.

70 John Herz, "Expropriation of Alien Property: An Inquiry into the Sociology of International Law," *Social Research* 8, no. 1 (1941): 63–78; John Herz, "Einige Bemerkungen zur Grundlegung des Völkerrechts," *Internationale Zeitschrift für Theories des Rechts* 13, no. 1 (1939): 275–300.

71 Morgenthau, *La réalité des normes.*

72 William Scheuerman, *Morgenthau* (Cambridge: Polity, 2009), 12–14.

73 Alfred Zimmern, "The Decline of International Standards," *International Affairs* 17, no. 1 (1938): 3–31. On Zimmern, see Jeanne Morefield, *Covenants without Swords: Idealist Liberalism and the Spirit of Empire* (Princeton, NJ: Princeton University Press, 2005).

74 Max Radin, review of "The Personality Conception of the Legal Entity," by Alexander Nekam, *Harvard Law Review* 52, no. 4 (1938): 706–707. See also Cohen, "Transcendental Nonsense."

75 Hans Kelsen, *The Pure Theory of Law* (1934), 178.

76 Ibid., 191.

77 E. H. Carr, *The Twenty Years Crisis, 1919–1939: An Introduction to the Study of International Relations* (New York: Perennial, 1939). See Brian C. Schmidt, *The Political Discourse of Anarchy: A Disciplinary History of International Relations* (Albany: State University of New York Press, 1998). Mark Mazower, "An International Civilization? Empire, Internationalism, and the Crisis of the Mid-Twentieth Century," *International Affairs* 82, no. 3 (2006): 553–566.

78 Robert R. Wilson, "Gradations of Citizenship and International Reclamations," *American Journal of International Law* 33, no. 1 (1939): 146–148.

79 Oscar Janowsky and Melvin M. Fagen, *International Aspects of German Racial Policies* (New York: Oxford University Press, 1937).

80 H. W. Goering, "Decree Imposing Atonement Fine on Jewish Subjects (November 12, 1938)," in *The Jew in the Modern World: A Documentary History*, ed. Paul Mendes-Flohr and Yehuda Reinharz (Oxford: Oxford University Press, 1980), 653.

81 Martin Dean, "The Nazi Development and Implementation of Nazi Denaturalization and Confiscation Policy up to the Eleventh Decree to the Reich Citizenship Law," *Holocaust and Genocide Studies* 16, no. 2 (2002): 217–242.

82 Hans-Christian Jasch, "Civil Service Lawyers and the Holocaust: The Case of Wilhelm Stuckart," in *The Law in Nazi Germany: Ideology, Opportunism, and the Perversion of Justice*, ed. Alan Steinwies and Robert Rachlin (New York: Berghan, 2013), 49.

83 Judith Shklar, "A Life of Learning," in *Liberalism without Illusions: Essays on Liberal Theory and the Political Visions of Judith N. Shklar*, ed. B. Yack (Chicago: University of Chicago Press, 1996), 263–279.

84 Wilson, "Gradations of Citizenship."

85 The Rockefeller Foundation Archives, Record Group 10.2—Fellowship recorder cards, Discipline 5—Humanities, box 3, Rockefeller Archive Center, Sleepy Hollow, NY.

86 "The Problem of Statelessness (People Deprived of Nationality): Some Facts, Arguments, and Proposals Presented to the International Conference Called by the Women's International League for Peace and Freedom" (Geneva, September 1930); "Statenlosen: Correspondence with the Women's International League for Peace and Freedom," R3589/25612, LNA; Anna Askenazy, "The Problem of Statelessness," and Emma Cadbury, "The Problem of Statelessness from the Humanitarian Side," R3589/25612, LNA; Josef L. Kunz, *Die Völkerrechtliche Option* (Breslau: F. Hirt, 1926).

87 Josef Kunz, "The 'Vienna School' and International Law," *NYU Law Quarterly Review* 11, no. 3 (1933–1934): 370–422.

88 Koessler statement to the Social Science Research Council, January 1941, Philip Jessup Papers, Library of Congress.

89 Koessler to Lindsay Rogers, May 12, 1942, Philip Jessup Papers, Library of Congress.

90 Koessler noted that the US Nationality Act of 1940 distinguished between citizens and nationals. He also cited the German *Reichsbuergergesetz* from 1935 distinguishing between citizens and nationals. An examination of the special position of the "dediticii" under Roman law, who were subjects but not citizens of the Roman state, would also be a crucial part of his prospective study. Koessler statement to the Social Science Research Council, January 1941, Philip Jessup Papers, Library of Congress.

91 Koessler to Lindsay Rogers, May 12, 1942, Philip Jessup Papers, Library of Congress.

92 Koessler statement to the Social Science Research Council, January 1941, Philip Jessup Papers, Library of Congress.

5. A CONDITION OF WORLD ORDER

1 Grotius Society Committee for the Status of Stateless Persons, September 27, 1940, Paul Weis Papers, PW/PR/GRSO 1, Social Sciences Library, University of Oxford.

2 Martin Conway, "Legacies of Exile: The Exile Governments in London during the Second World War and the Politics of Post-War Europe," in *Europe in Exile: European Exile Communities in Britain, 1940–1945*, ed. Martin Conway and José Gotovitch (New York: Berghahn Books, 2001), 256.

3 For example, see Daniel G. Cohen, "The Holocaust and the 'Human Rights Revolution': A Reassessment," in *The Human Rights Revolution*, ed. Akira Iriye, Petra Goedde, and William I. Hitchcock (Oxford: Oxford University Press, 2012), 53–73; Ruti Teitel, *Humanity's Law* (New York: Oxford University Press, 2011); Elizabeth Borgwardt, *A New Deal for the World: America's Vision for Human Rights* (Cambridge, MA: Harvard University Press, 2005), 71; Dieter Grimm, *Sovereignty: The Origin and*

Future of a Political and Legal Concept (New York: Columbia University Press, 2015), 83–85.

4 Josef Kunz Memoir, draft, December 17, 1959, Hans Kelsen Archive.

5 Elihu Lauterpacht, *The Life of Hersch Lauterpacht* (Cambridge: Cambridge University Press, 2018), 115–118. Lauterpacht reported during his tour that in his lectures on the subject of the "Reality of International Law," "I attached importance to lecturing before law students and, occasionally, before wider audiences on these related aspects of international law at a time when it is assailed by many well-meaning but disappointed persons." Lauterpacht, *Life of Hersch Lauterpacht*, 117.

6 E. Lauterpacht, *Life of Hersch Lauterpacht*, 133; Manley Hudson memo to Philip Jessup, October 4, 1940, box 113, Manley Hudson Papers, Harvard Law School. Jessup was at that time promoting American neutrality. Philip C. Jessup, "The Monroe Doctrine in 1940," *American Journal of International Law* 34, no. 4 (1940): 704–711; E. Lauterpacht, *Life of Hersch Lauterpacht*, 106.

7 E. Lauterpacht, *Life of Hersch Lauterpacht*, 106.

8 "Mark Vishniak, Russian Expert," *New York Times*, September 3, 1976, 14.

9 Marc Vishniak, *The Legal Status of Stateless Persons* (New York: American Jewish Committee, 1945).

10 "Draft of the Legal Status of the Stateless," 1941–1945, Mark Vishniak Papers, box 18, Hoover Institution Archives. In his 1941 polemical study, Gerhart Niemeyer, a conservative German émigré political philosopher, asked, "What happened? Why should international law, which was vigorously surging upward only twenty years ago, have become almost a dead letter now?" Gerhart Niemeyer, *Law without Force: The Function of Politics in International Law* (Princeton, NJ: Princeton University Press, 1941), 14.

11 "Draft of the Legal Status of the Stateless," 1941–1945, Mark Vishniak Papers, box 18, Hoover Institution Archives.

12 *The Atlantic Charter: The Eight-Point Declaration of President Roosevelt and Prime Minister Churchill, August 14, 1941* (New York: Commission to Study the Organization of Peace, 1941). On the ideological origins and afterlife of the Atlantic Charter, see Borgwardt, *New Deal for the World*, 14–46.

13 *Atlantic Charter.*

14 Tamara Ehs and Miriam Gassner, "Hans Kelsen, Legal Scholar between Europe and the Americas," *Transatlantic Perspectives*, accessed June 29, 2018, http://www.transatlanticperspectives.org/entry.php?rec=132.

15 Published as Hans Kelsen, *Law and Peace in International Relations* (Cambridge, MA: Harvard University Press, 1948), 73.

16 Hans Kelsen, "Recognition in International Law: Theoretical Observations," *American Journal of International Law* 35, no. 605 (1941): 605–617.

17 See Jeremy D. A. Telman, "The Reception of Hans Kelsen's Legal Theory in the United States: A Sociological Model," *Law Faculty Publications* 7 (2008), http://scholar.valpo.edu/law_fac_pubs/7. On the tension between Austrian legal and political philosophy and the American intellectual environment, see Erich Hula, "Austrian Legal and Political Thought in the United States: Lecture at the Austrian Institute,

5 December 1958," box 2, Erich Hula Papers, German and Jewish Intellectual Émigré Collection, State University of New York at Albany. In his reflections on the foundation of an international organization based on the principle of sovereign equality, Kelsen argued that the meaningfulness of the concept of "sovereign equality" depended on submission to international law ("a body of slowly and steadily changing norms") because only international law could guarantee the coexistence of states as sovereign and equal communities. Logic, he argued, demanded it. Hans Kelsen, "The Principle of Sovereign Equality of States as a Basis for International Organization," *Yale Law Journal* 53, no. 2 (1944): 207–220.

18 Carl Friedrich, "The Deification of the State," *Review of Politics* 1, no. 1 (1939): 18–30. On Friedrich's Weberian view of the state and political responsibility, see Udi Greenberg, "Germany's Postwar Re-education and Its Weimar Intellectual Roots," *Journal of Contemporary History* 46, no. 1 (2011): 10–32; Greenberg, *The Weimar Century: German Émigrés and the Ideological Foundations of the Cold War* (Princeton, NJ: Princeton University Press, 2014).

19 Heinz H. F. Eulau, "The Depersonalization of the Concept of Sovereignty," *Review of Politics* 4, no. 1 (1942): 3–19.

20 On the revision of the relationship between democracy and legality among European émigrés intellectuals, see Anne Mira Kornhauser, *Debating the American State: Liberal Anxieties and the New Leviathan, 1930–1970* (Philadelphia: University of Pennsylvania Press, 2015).

21 Christian Fleck, *Transatlantic History of the Social Science: Robber Barons, the Third Reich and the Invention of Empirical Social Research* (London: Bloomsbury Academic, 2011), 59.

22 Erich Hula, "Sovereignty under Attack," unpublished paper, 1942, box 10, series 5, Erich Hula Papers, German and Jewish Intellectual Émigré Collection, State University of New York at Albany.

23 Erich Hula, "National Self-Determination Reconsidered," *Social Research* 10, no. 1 (1943): 1–21. Hula promoted a legalist vision of international order throughout his career and defended international law from its realist detractors such as Hans Morgenthau. Hans Morgenthau to Erich Hula, February 14, 1943, box 2, Correspondence, Erich Hula Papers, German and Jewish Intellectual Émigré Collection, State University of New York at Albany.

24 Otto Kirchheimer, "In Quest of Sovereignty," *Journal of Politics* 6, no. 2 (1944): 139.

25 James Minor Ludlow, "Postulates, Principles, Proposals for the International Law of the Future," January 1, 1943, James Minor Ludlow Papers, box 5, Hoover Institution Archives. In his 1933 essay, "Forms of Modern Imperialism in International Law," Carl Schmitt argued that the new age of American dominance would be characterized by the principle of the sovereign equality of states, with American power dictating the legal vocabularies that all states would be forced to speak. Carl Schmitt, "Forms of Modern Imperialism in International Law," (1933), trans. Matthew Hannah, in *Spaciality, Sovereignty and Carl Schmitt: Geographies of the Nomos*, ed. Stephen Legg (London: Routledge, 2011), 29–46. On the postwar invention of the "Westphalian" order

with its clear delineation between the domestic and the international and its presumption of equality rather than hierarchy among political entities, see Peter Stirk, "The
Westphalian Model and Sovereign Equality," *Review of International Studies* 38, no. 3
(2012): 641–660.

26 Grotius Society Committee for the Status of Stateless Persons, September 27,
1940.

27 Paul Weis curriculum vitae, 1967, PW/PR/HCR/BSN/14/38, Paul Weis Papers, Social Sciences Library, University of Oxford.

28 Paul Weis to W. R. Bisschop, December 30, 1941, Weis Papers, PW/PR/GRSO 1,
Social Sciences Library, University of Oxford.

29 Erwin Loewenfeld, "Status of Stateless Persons," *Transactions of the Grotius Society* 27,
no. 1 (1941): 59–112.

30 "Revised Draft of the Proposed Rules Regarding Nationality and the Prevention of
Statelessness," n.d., Grotius Society, Committee on Status of Stateless Persons, Weis
Papers, PW/PR/GRSO 1, Social Sciences Library, University of Oxford. See also
"Proposed Nationality Rules in Connection with Statelessness," *Transactions of the
Grotius Society* 28, no. 1 (1942): 157–158.

31 Eric G. M. Fletcher to W. R. Bischop, July 28, 1942, Weis Papers, PW/PR/GRSO 1,
Social Sciences Library, University of Oxford.

32 Memorandum by H. R. Pyke, Committee for the Status of Stateless Persons, Weis
Papers, PW/PR/GRSO 1, Social Sciences Library, University of Oxford.

33 Frederick Dunn and Alwyn V. Freeman, "The International Rights of Individuals,"
Proceedings of the American Society of International Law 35, no. 1 (April 24–26, 1941):
14–22; Frederick Dunn, *The Protection of Nationals: A Study in the Application of International Law* (Baltimore: Johns Hopkins University Press, 1932).

34 Hersch Lauterpacht, "The Subjects of International Law," in *International Law Being the Collected Papers of Hersch Lauterpacht*, vol. 1, ed. Eli Lauterpacht (Cambridge:
Cambridge University Press, 1970), 297.

35 The Grotius Society, Nationality (Draft Report), PW/PR/GRSO 1.

36 René Cassin, "La nouvelle conception du domicile dans le règlement des conflits de
lois," *Recueil des cours* 34 (1930): 659–663.

37 On the idea that Cassin's speech aimed primarily to desacralize state sovereignty,
compare Jay Winter, *Dreams of Peace and Freedom: Utopian Moments in the Twentieth
Century* (New Haven, CT: Yale University Press, 2008), 108.

38 Moria Paz, "A Most Inglorious Right: Rene Cassin, Freedom of Movement, Jews
and Palestinians," in *The Law of Strangers: Jewish Lawyering and International Legal
Thought*, ed. James Loeffler and Moria Paz (Cambridge: Cambridge University Press,
2019), 177–203.

39 Patrick Weil, *The Sovereign Citizen: Denaturalization and the Origins of the American
Republic* (Philadelphia: University of Pennsylvania Press, 2013), 128.

40 Patrick Weil, "The History and Memory of Discrimination in the Domain of French
Nationality: The Case of Jews and Algerian Muslims," *International Social Science Review* 6, no. 1 (2005): 56.

41 Commision pour l'étude des problèmes d'après-guerre d'ordre juridique et intellectual, sous-section des droits de l'homme, November 21, 1942, France Combattante, 382 AP 58, René Cassin Papers, National Archives of France.

42 The Beveridge Report circulated among the governments in exile in London and was parachuted into occupied Europe. Jay Winter and Antoine Prost, *René Cassin and Human Rights: From the Great War to the Universal Declaration* (Cambridge: Cambridge University Press), 143; Conway, "Legacies of Exile," 256; Commision pour l'étude des problèmes d'après-guerre d'ordre juridique et intellectual, section de la refome de l'etat, sous-section des droits de l'homme, March 9, 1943, 382 AP 58, René Cassin Papers, National Archives of France.

43 Vladimir Idelsen et al., "The Law of Nations and the Individual," *Transactions of the Grotius Society* 30, no. 1 (1944): 50–82; R. Graupner and P. Weis, *The Problem of Statelessness* (n.p.: World Jewry Congress Publications, 1944).

44 Idelsen et al., "Law of Nations."

45 See Duncan Bell, *The Idea of Greater Britain: Empire and the Future of World Order, 1860–1900* (Princeton, NJ: Princeton University Press, 2008), 267. On federation as a common solution offered in nineteenth-century Europe to resolve conflicting national political aspirations and the tension between nation and empire, see Holly Case, *The Age of Questions, or A First Attempt at an Aggregate History of the Eastern, Social, Woman, American, Jewish, Polish, Bullion, Tuberculosis, and Many Other Questions over the Nineteenth Century, and Beyond* (Princeton, NJ: Princeton University Press, 2018), chap. 4.

46 Mark Mazower, *Dark Continent: Europe's Twentieth Century* (New York: Vintage, 1999), 205.

47 Max M. Laserson, "On Universal and Regional Federalism," *Journal of Legal and Political Sociology* 2, no. 82 (1943): 82–93; J. O. Hertzler, "Some Basic Queries Respecting World Regionalism," *Social Forces* 22, no. 4 (1942–1943): 371–387. On the particular Central European context that fostered regionalist visions of world order, see Holly Case, *Between States: The Transylvanian Question and the European Idea during World War II* (Stanford, CA: Stanford University Press, 2009).

48 James A. Junker, *The Idea of World Government: From Ancient Times to the Twenty-First Century* (New York: Routledge, 2011), 50–52; Or Rosenboim, *The Emergence of Globalism: Visions of World Order in Britain and the United States, 1939–1950* (Princeton, NJ: Princeton University Press, 2017).

49 Wilfried Loth, "Sources of European Integration: The Meaning of Failed Interwar Politics and the Role of World War II," in *Crises in European Integration: Challenges and Responses, 1945–2005*, ed. Ludger Kühnhardt (New York: Berghahn Books, 2009), 24.

50 "Draft of the Legal Status of the Stateless," Mark Vishniak Papers, box 18, Hoover Institution Archives, 112. Rosika Schwimmer, a Hungarian Jewish feminist organizer, initiated the Campaign for World Federal Government in 1937, motivated by the European refugee crisis and by her own statelessness. Schwimmer lost her Hungarian citizenship after Bela Kun's communist revolution in Hungary. Stateless and in exile

in the United States, Schwimmer was denied American citizenship on the grounds of her pacifist affiliations and suspected socialism. See Glenda Sluga, *Internationalism in the Age of Nationalism* (Philadelphia: University of Pennsylvania Press, 2013), 76.

51 Omer Bartov and Eric D. Weitz, eds., *Shatterzone of Empires: Coexistence and Violence in the German, Habsburg, Russian, and Ottoman Borderlands* (Bloomington: Indiana University Press, 2013), 72.

52 Robinson to Vishniak, undated, Series C. Institute of Jewish Affairs, C95/13 Post War Planning 1941–1946, World Jewish Committee Collection, United States Holocaust Museum Memorial.

53 It was in the service of this question that a number of the émigré jurists, including Vishniak, worked together to produce the volume on the minorities treaties. See Jacob Robinson et al., *Were the Minorities Treaties a Failure?* (New York: Institute of Jewish Affairs, 1943).

54 Tara Zahra, "Going West," *East European Politics and Societies* 25, no. 4 (2011): 787.

55 On the preservation of European empires after World War II, see Mark Mazower, *No Enchanted Palace: The End of Empire and the Ideological Origins of the United Nations* (Princeton, NJ: Princeton University Press, 2009); William Roger Louis, *The British Empire in the Middle East, 1945–1951: Arab Nationalism, the United States, and Postwar Imperialism* (Oxford: Clarendon, 1984); Frederick Cooper, "Alternatives to Empire: France and Africa after World War II," in *The State of Sovereignty: Territories, Laws, Populations*, ed. Douglas Howland and Luis White (Bloomington: Indiana University Press, 2008), 94–124; Todd Shepard, *The Invention of Decolonization: The Algerian War and the Remaking of France* (Ithaca, NY: Cornell University Press, 2006).

56 Frederick Cooper, "Alternatives to Empire," 94–124; Shepard, *Invention of Decolonization.*

57 Frederick Cooper, "Reconstructing Empire in British and French Africa," *Past and Present* 210, suppl. 6 (2011): 196–210.

58 Jessica Reinisch, "Internationalism in Relief: The Birth and Death of UNRRA," *Past and Present* 210, suppl. 6 (2011): 258–289.

59 Michael Marrus, *The Unwanted: European Refugees from the First World War to the Cold War* (Philadelphia: Temple University Press, 2002), 297–298.

60 "Division of Duties between UNRRA and Existing Group Indicated in London," *New York Times*, November 22, 1943. See *UNRRA: Organization, Aims, Progress* (Washington, DC: United Nations Relief and Rehabilitation Administration, 1945); United Nations Relief and Rehabilitation Administration, *The Story of UNRRA* (Washington, DC: UNRRA Office of Public Information, 1948).

61 On the relation between the history of refugees and postwar reconstruction and nationalization, see David Feldman, Mark Mazower, and Jessica Reinisch, eds., *Post-War Reconstruction in Europe: International Perspectives, 1945–1949* (Oxford: Oxford University Press, 2011); Pamela Ballinger, "At the Borders of Force: Violence, Refugees, and the Reconfiguration of the Yugoslav and Italian States," *Past and Present*, suppl. 6 (2011): 158–176; Jessica Reinisch and Elizabeth White, eds., *The Disentanglement of Populations: Migration, Expulsion and Displacement in Postwar*

Europe, 1944–1949 (Basingstoke, UK: Palgrave Macmillan, 2011); Tara Zahra, "'A Human Treasure': Europe's Displaced Children between Nationalism and Internationalism," *Past and Present*, suppl. 6 (2011): 332–350; Zahra, *The Lost Children: Reconstructing Europe's Families after World War II* (Cambridge, MA: Harvard University Press, 2011).

62 Tara Zahra, "Prisoners of the Postwar: Expellees, Displaced Persons, and Jews in Austria after World War II," *Austrian History Yearbook* 41, no. 1 (2010): 191–215. On the nationalist ideals animating the refugee policies undertaken in the name of human rights, see Zahra, *Lost Children*.

63 Daniel G. Cohen, *In War's Wake: Europe's Displaced Persons in the Postwar Order* (Oxford: Oxford University Press, 2011), 20–21.

64 Note from Col. MG, May 29, 1945, DPs and Stateless Persons, FO 1052/278, TNA.

65 Ibid. "Stateless Displaced Persons Centers," June 7, 1945, DPs and Stateless Persons, FO 1052/278, TNA. On displaced persons in Germany, see Atina Grossman and Wolfgang Jacobmeyer, *Vom Zwangsarbeiter zum Heimatlosen Auslander: Die Displaced Persons in Westdeutschland, 1945–1951* (Gottingen: Vandenhoek and Ruprecht, 1985).

66 Stephen King-Hall, "A State for the Stateless," *National News-Letter*, and Harry Gregson, "Stateless," *Central European Observer*, cited in "The Postwar 'Stateless,'" *Social Science Review* 20, no. 3 (1946): 404.

67 Cited in "The Postwar 'Stateless,'" 403–406.

68 Andrei Matlos, "Apatrides," memo, July 17, 1946, NUOI 1944–1959, box 298, Archives du Ministère des Affaires Étrangères, La Courneuve.

69 Ibid.

70 Matlos, "Apatrides."

71 Maximilian Koessler, "'Subject,' 'Citizen,' 'National,' and 'Permanent Allegiance,'" *Yale Law Journal* 56, no. 1 (1946): 75–76.

72 Ibid.

73 Cited in A. W. B. Simpson, *Human Rights and the End of Empire: Britain and the Genesis of the European Convention* (Oxford: Oxford University Press, 2004), 141.

74 Kaeckenbeeck was a lawyer in the Belgian foreign ministry after World War I and a member of the legal section of the League of Nations secretariat from 1919 to 1922. Georges Kaeckenbeeck, *The International Experiment of Upper Silesia: A Study in the Workings of the Upper Silesian Settlement, 1922–1937* (Oxford: Oxford University Press, 1952).

75 Hersch Lauterpacht, "The Nationality of Denationalized Persons," *Jewish Yearbook of International Law* 1, no. 1 (1948): 179.

76 Ibid., 185.

77 Joseph P. Chamberlain to Martha Biehle, May 15, 1946, YIVO Archives, RG 278/23, Papers of Joseph P. Chamberlain, YIVO Institute for Jewish Research.

78 Sunil Khilnani, "Nehru's Judgment," in *Political Judgment: Essays for John Dunn*, ed. Richard Bourke and Raymond Geuss (Cambridge: Cambridge University Press, 2009), 254.

79 Karuna Mantena, "Popular Sovereignty and Anti-Colonialism," in *Popular Sovereignty in Historical Perspective*, ed. Richard Bourke and Quentin Skinner (Cambridge: Cambridge University Press, 2016), 316.

80 Samuel Moyn, *Christian Human Rights* (Philadelphia: University of Pennsylvania Press, 2015); Marco Duranti, *The Conservative Human Rights Revolution: European Identity, Transnational Politics, and the Origins of the European Convention* (Oxford: Oxford University Press, 2016).

81 Jacques Maritain, "Philosophical Examination of Human Rights," in *Human Rights: Comments and Interpretations, a Symposium Edited by UNESCO*, July 25, 1948.

82 Dunn and Freeman, "International Rights of Individuals," 14–22.

83 Hersch Lauterpacht, "The Grotian Tradition in International Law," *British Yearbook of International Law* 23, no. 1 (1946): 1–53.

84 "The Cassin Draft: Suggestions Submitted by the Representative of France for Articles of the International Declaration of Human Rights," in Mary Ann Glendon, *A World Made New: Eleanor Roosevelt and the Universal Declaration of Human Rights* (New York: Random House, 2001), app. 2, 278. Glendon does not examine the significance of Cassin's specific formulation, though she cites his departure from Humphrey's draft of the declaration. See Glendon, *World Made New*, 64. On the nationalist and welfarist premise of the 1948 Universal Declaration of Human Rights, see Samuel Moyn, *The Last Utopia: Human Rights in History* (Cambridge, MA: Belknap Press of Harvard University Press, 2010), chap. 2.

85 Johannes Morsink, *The Universal Declaration of Human Rights: Origins, Drafting, Intent* (Philadelphia: University of Pennsylvania Press, 2000), 80.

86 "UN Body Rejects Plan for Stateless," *New York Times*, June 5, 1948, 4.

87 H. F. Van Panhuys, *The Role of Nationality in International Law: An Outline* (Leiden: A. W. Sythoff, 1959), 221.

88 UN General Assembly, "Universal Declaration of Human Rights," December 10, 1948, 217, http://www.refworld.org/docid/3ae6b3712c.html.

89 Cited in Winter and Prost, *René Cassin and Human Rights*, 249.

90 Eduard Reut-Nicolussi, "Displaced Persons and International Law," *Recueil des cours* 73 (1948): 19–64, cited in Cohen, *In War's Wake*, 82.

91 Mark Greif, *The Age of the Crisis of Man: Thought and Fiction in America, 1933–1973* (Princeton, NJ: Princeton University Press, 2015), 79; Garry Davis, *The World Is My Country: The Autobiography of Garry Davis* (New York: Putnam, 1961). On world federalism, see Sluga, *Internationalism in the Age of Nationalism*; Rosenboim, *Emergence of Globalism*.

92 Giorgio Agamben, *Homo Sacer: Sovereign Power and Bare Life* (Stanford, CA: Zone Books, 1998).

93 Hersch Lauterpacht, "The Law of Nations and the Individual."

94 Hersch Lauterpacht, *An International Bill of the Rights of Man* (New York, 1945), 7; H. Lauterpacht, "Grotian Tradition"; H. Lauterpacht, *International Law and Human Rights* (New York, 1950), 347–348.

95 H. Lauterpacht, "Nationality of Denationalized Persons."

96 H. Lauterpacht, "Grotian Tradition"; H. Lauterpacht, *International Bill*, 7.

97 Philip C. Jessup, "The Subjects of a Modern Law of Nations," *Michigan Law Review* 45, no. 4 (1947): 383–408.

98 Ibid.

99 In January 1940, Hans Morgenthau had written to Jessup about the "disrepute" of international law and suggested that it would not have fallen into such dire straits "had not certain schools of thought imbued public opinion with illusions for which now public opinion takes international law as a whole to account." Morgenthau to Jessup, January 4, 1940, Philip Jessup Papers, Library of Congress.

100 His article had come out of a graduate seminar he taught at Columbia University in international law where students had written on "the equality of states as dogma and reality" and "the evolution of the equality of states in the inter-American system." Jessup, "Subjects of a Modern Law," 397n52.

101 Philip C. Jessup, *A Modern Law of Nations: An Introduction* (New York: Macmillan, 1948), 69.

102 In early 1948 in New York, Lauterpacht drafted a version of the Israeli Declaration of Independence with Shabtai Rosenne, the future legal advisor to the Israeli government after independence. The creation of the state of Israel proved, moreover, to be a special case for Lauterpacht, and he generally advised that if national sovereignty was to be a force in the postwar world, its birth should be dictated and carefully monitored by international institutions. When an Indian principality looking to assert its independence both from Britain and from independent India approached him for advice, Lauterpacht recommended that they seek recognition from the International Court of Justice. He advised the Jewish Agency in Palestine to avoid the international court. See James Loeffler, "The 'Natural Right of the Jewish People': Zionism, International Law, and the Paradox of Hersch Zvi Lauterpacht," in *The Law of Strangers: Jewish Lawyering and International Legal Thought*, ed. James Loeffler and Moria Paz (Cambridge: Cambridge University Press, 2019), 21–42. Lauterpacht produced a lengthy text entitled "Declaration of the Assumption of Power by the Provisional Governments of the Jewish Republic" in which he elaborated a legal argument for the recognition of the new state. Yoram Shachar, "Jefferson Goes East: The American Origins of the Israeli Declaration of Independence," *Theoretical Inquiries in Law* 10, no. 2 (2009): 589–618; E. Lauterpacht, *Life of Hersch Lauterpacht*, 305–306. Josef Kunz harshly criticized Lauterpacht for a 1948 treatise in which he argued that new states came into existence without the primary recognition of an international legal norm. Their debate turned on whether the creation of the independent state of Israel rested on the state's own declaration of its existence or on whether other states recognized it as such. Josef L. Kunz, "Critical Remarks on Lauterpacht's 'Recognition in International Law,'" *The American Journal of International Law* 44, no. 4 (1950): 713–719.

103 Elisabeth Young-Bruehl, *Hannah Arendt: For Love of the World* (New Haven, CT: Yale University Press, 1982), 107.

104 Hannah Arendt, "We Refugees," *Menorah Journal* 31, no. 1 (1943): 69–77; Arendt, "The Stateless People," *Contemporary Jewish Record* 8, no. 2 (1945): 137–153.

105 Lawrence Preuss, "International Law and Deprivation of Nationality," *Georgetown Law Journal* 23, no. 2 (1935): 250–276; Arendt papers, "Excerpts and Notes," Minority Statelessness, Hannah Arendt Papers, Library of Congress.

106 Karl Renner, "Die Nation: Mythos und Wirklichkeit," trans. S. Pierre-Caps and C. Tixador, in *La nation, mythe et réalité* (Nancy: Presses Universitaires de Nancy, 1998).

107 Koppel Pinson, "Simon Dubnow: Historian and Political Philosopher," in *Nationalism and History: Essays on Old and New Judaism*, ed. Koppel Pinson (Philadelphia: Jewish Publication Society, 1958).

108 Hannah Arendt, "Concerning Minorities," *Contemporary Jewish Record* 7, no. 4 (1944): 353–368.

109 Arendt, "Stateless People."

110 Arendt, "Stateless People"; Gil Rubin, "From Federalism to Binationalism: Hannah Arendt's Shifting Zionism," *Contemporary European History* 24, no. 3 (2015): 393–414; William Selinger, "The Politics of Arendtian Historiography: European Federation and the Origins of Totalitarianism," *Modern Intellectual History* 13, no. 2 (2014): 1–30; Douglas Klusmeyer, "Hannah Arendt's Case for Federalism," *Publius* 40, no. 1 (2010): 31–58; Wolfgang Heuer, "Europe and Its Refugees: Arendt on the Politicization of Minorities," *Social Research* 74, no. 4 (2007): 1159–1172. Compare Roy T. Tsao, "Arendt and the Modern State: Variations on Hegel in 'The Origins of Totalitarianism,'" *Review of Politics* 66, no. 1 (2004): 105–136. On the federalist imaginary, see Gary Wilder, *Freedom Time* (Durham, NC: Duke University Press, 2015); Adi Gordon, *Toward Nationalism's End: An Intellectual Biography of Hans Kohn* (Lebanon, NH: Brandeis University Press, 2017).

111 Hans Morgenthau reviewed the same work and arrived at the same conclusion. See Hans Morgenthau, review of *Nationalities and National Minorities*, by Oscar I. Janowsky, *Harvard Law Review* 59, no. 2 (1945): 301–304; Hannah Arendt, review of *Nationalities and National Minorities*, by Oscar I. Janowsky, *Jewish Social Studies* 8, no. 3 (1946): 204. See also Oscar Janowsky, *Nationalities and National Minorities (with Special Reference to East-Central Europe)* (New York: Macmillan, 1945); Janowsky, *The Jews and Minority Rights, 1898–1919* (New York: Columbia University Press, 1933).

112 Arendt, review of *Nationalities and National Minorities*.

113 Hannah Arendt, "The Nation," *Review of Politics* 8, no. 1 (1946): 138–141. See Istvan Hont, "The Permanent Crisis of a Divided Mankind," in *Jealousy of Trade: International Competition and the Nation-State in Historical Perspective* (Cambridge, MA: Harvard University Press, 2005), 498. On the affinities between Arendt and Hegel in *The Origins of Totalitarianism* on the role of the modern state, see Tsao, "Arendt and the Modern State." On the idea of an "enlightenment state" against nationalism, see Faisal Devji, *Muslim Zion: Pakistan as a Political Idea* (Cambridge, MA: Harvard University Press, 2013). See Ira Katznelson, *Desolation and Enlightenment: Political Knowledge after Total War, Totalitarianism, and the Holocaust* (New York: Columbia University Press, 2004). On the idea that the "state without qualities" served as the foundation for Cold War liberalism by providing the promise of value neutralism, see David Cieply,

"Why the State Was Dropped in the First Place: A Prequel to Skockpol's 'Bringing the State Back In,'" *Critical Review* 14, no. 2 (2000): 157–213.

114 Arendt to Broch, September 9, 1946, in *Hannah Arendt—Hermann Broch Briefwechsel, 1946–1951,* ed. Paul Michael Lützeler (Frankfurt: Jüdischer, 1996), 14. See also Elisabeth Gallas, "The Struggle for a Universal Human Rights Regime: Hannah Arendt and Hermann Broch on the Paradoxes of a Concept," *S.I.M.O.N* 4, no. 2 (2017): 123–130.

115 Note by Byron Dexter to Letter Mary Stevens, April 22, 1949, Correspondence, box 3, Hamilton Fish Papers, Mudd Library, Princeton University Library; Hannah Arendt, "The Rights of Man: What are They?," *Modern Review* 3, no. 1 (1949): 24–37. The essay appeared in *Modern Review,* perhaps because the managing editor at *Foreign Affairs,* Byron Dexter, suggested a number of substantive changes to the piece.

116 Arendt, "Rights of Man." The German translation retitled the piece to reflect the idea that the right to have rights amounted to the only meaningful human right. Hannah Arendt, "Es gibt nu rein einziges Menschenrecht," *Die Wandlung* 4 (1949): 754–770. The German title was suggested by Dolf Sternberger. See Christophe Menke, Birgit Kaiser, and Kathrin Thiele, "The 'Aporias of Human Rights' and the 'One Human Right': Regarding the Coherence of Arendt's Argument," *Social Research* 74, no. 3 (2007): 739–762; Justine Lacroix, "The 'Right to Have Rights' in French Political Philosophy: Conceptualizing a Cosmopolitan Citizenship with Arendt," *Constellations* 22, no. 1 (2015): 79–90.

117 Arendt, "Rights of Man." On the polemical nature of Arendt's singular appeal to the concept of rights within her wider oeuvre, see Samuel Moyn, "Arendt and the Right to Have Rights," in *The Right to Have Rights,* ed. Alastair Hunt et al. (London: Verson, 2017), 118–148.

118 Faisal Devji, *Muslim Zion: Pakistan as a Political Idea* (Cambridge, MA: Harvard University Press).

119 Hannah Arendt, *The Origins of Totalitarianism* (New York: Schocken Books, 1951), 128.

120 Ibid., 41.

121 Arendt, *Origins of Totalitarianism,* 292.

122 Arendt relied especially on Lawrence Preuss. See Arendt, *Origins of Totalitarianism,* 278; Preuss, "International Law." She also cited John Fischer Williams, "Denationalisation," *British Yearbook of International Law* 8, no. 3 (1927): 45–62. See Arendt, *Origins of Totalitarianism,* 284n36. In his study of the "man without a country" from 1946, the English journalist M. J. Landa wrote, "Until the end of the first world-war the term 'stateless' was unknown . . . it had not gained admission into the ordinary dictionaries. Even the lawyers could not say precisely what it meant, or implied, though it soon became patent to those who had to take cognizance of it that it referred to a new type of refugee, of lower degree, one of the 'lesser breeds without the law.'" M. Landa, *The Man without a Country* (London: Herbert Joseph, 1946), 8.

123 Arendt, *Origins of Totalitarianism,* 291–292. On Arendt's presumption of a disconnect between the Western political tradition and European imperialism and

pan-nationalism, see Dirk Moses, "Das römische Gespräch in a New Key: Hannah Arendt, Genocide, and the Defense of Republican Civilization," *Journal of Modern History* 85, no. 4 (2013): 867–913; Karuna Mantena "Genealogies of Catastrophe: Arendt on the Logic and Legacy of Imperialism," in *Politics in Dark Times: Encounters with Hannah Arendt*, ed. Seyla Benhabib, Roy T. Tsao, and Peter Verovsek (Cambridge: Cambridge University Press, 2010), 83. For criticism of Arendt's presentation of law in relation to the idea of humanity, see Samera Esmeir, *Juridical Humanity: A Colonial History* (Stanford, CA: Stanford University Press, 2012).

124 Arendt, *Origins of Totalitarianism*, ix.

125 Ibid.

126 Immanuel Kant, "Toward Perpetual Peace: A Philosophical Sketch," in *Toward Perpetual Peace and Other Writings on Politics, Peace, and History: Immanuel Kant*, ed. Pauline Kleingeld, trans. David Colclasure (New Haven, CT: Yale University Press, 2006), 82. Arendt quoted this in her 1970 lectures on Kant. Hannah Arendt, *Lectures on Kant's Political Philosophy*, ed. Ronald Beiner (Chicago: University of Chicago Press, 1992), 75.

127 On the role of the territorial state for the enforcement of rights in Kant's political thought, see Anna Stilz, "Nations, States, and Territory," *Ethics* 121, no. 3 (2011): 572–601.

6. NATIONALIZING INTERNATIONAL SOCIETY

1 Hélène Batresco to UN Secretary-General, October 21, 1960, SOA 261/41, United Nations Office at Geneva. For memoirs by stateless people, see Kon Balin, *Born Stateless: A Young Man's Story, 1923–1957* (Bloomington, IN: Authorhouse, 2009); Liliane Willens, *Stateless in Shanghai* (Hong Kong: Earnshaw Books, 2011); Victor Brombert, *Trains of Thought: Memories of a Stateless Youth* (New York: W. W. Norton, 2002); Anna Fries, *Memoirs of a Stateless Person* (Bloomington, IN: Authorhouse, 2013).

2 Hélène Batresco to UN Secretary-General, October 21, 1960, SOA 261/41, United Nations Organization Library.

3 Patrick Murphy Malin, "The Refugee, a Problem for International Organization," *International Organization* 1, no. 3 (1947): 443–459. A different study from the previous year drew attention to the technical difference between refugees and the stateless but emphasized statelessness as a broad category that should encompass both those without a formal connection to any state and those refugees who did not wish to return home. Jane Perry Clark Carey, "Some Aspects of Statelessness since World War I," *American Political Science Review* 40, no. 1 (1946): 113–123.

4 "Stateless Persons Win Inquiry by UN," *New York Times*, February 21, 1948, 4.

5 Economic and Social Council resolution 116 (6) D of March 1–2, 1948 (E/777).

6 United Nations, *Yearbook of the International Law Commission 1949: Summary Records and Documents of the First Session Including the Report to the General Assembly* (New York: United Nations, 1956), 281.

7 "Position Paper," June 10, 1949, box 3, RG59, General Records of the Department of State Bureau of International Organization Affairs, ECOSOC Special Subject Files

1945–1955, National Archives and Records Administration. On the resistance in the United States to asylum provisions, see Gil Loescher and John A. Scanlan, *Calculated Kindness: Refugees and America's Half-Open Door, 1945–Present* (New York: Free Press, 1986).

8 Laura Madokoro, *Elusive Refuge: Chinese Migrants in the Cold War* (Cambridge, MA: Harvard University Press, 2016).

9 R. Campbell to Ernst Bevin, May 27, 1949, Fraternity of Cypriots in Egypt and Stateless Persons of Cypriot Origin, FO 371/73669, TNA: PRO.

10 Confidential Memo Chancery Cairo Africa Department, August 7, 1949, Fraternity of Cypriots in Egypt and Stateless Persons of Cypriot Origin, FO 371/73669, TNA: PRO.

11 "Comments on the Disadvantages of Extending British Nationality to Stateless Persons of Cypriot Origin in Egypt," August 7, 1949, Fraternity of Cypriots in Egypt and Stateless Persons of Cypriot Origins, FO 371/73669, TNA: PRO.

12 United Nations Department of Social Affairs, *A Study of Statelessness* (Lake Success, NY: United Nations Department of Social Affairs, 1949).

13 Ibid., 11.

14 J. G. A. Pocock, "The Ideal of Citizenship since Classical Times," in *Theorizing Citizenship*, ed. Ronald Biener (Albany: State University of New York Press, 1995), 29–53.

15 Paul Weis to G. G. Kullman, January 19, 1950, Paul Weis Papers, PW/PR/IRO/6, Social Science Library, Oxford University.

16 Russian émigré jurists involved in advocating for the Russian stateless since the 1920s complained to Weis that the International Refugee Organization protected only those who became refugees after 1939 and that the new convention would exclude stateless refugees from before the war, including Russians and Armenian carriers of the Nansen passport. J. Rubenstein to P. Weis, February 3, 1950, Paul Weis Papers, PW/PR/IRO/6, Social Science Library, Oxford University.

17 P. Weis to G. G. Kullman, January 19, 1950, Paul Weis Papers, PW/PR/IRO/6, Social Science Library, Oxford University.

18 "Délégation française étude de la situations des apatrides," 1949, Apatrides, 1947–1959, box 298, Archives du Ministère des Affaires Étrangères, La Corneuve. On the turn to psychological explanations for the refugee experience in this period, see Tara Zahra, *The Lost Children: Reconstructing Europe's Families after World War II* (Cambridge, MA: Harvard University Press, 2011).

19 Ad Hoc Committee on Statelessness and Related Problems, "Status of Refugees and Stateless Persons—Memorandum by the Secretary General" (Statelessness Conference, January 3, 1950, www.unhcr.org/3ae68c280.html).

20 "Complete Rendering of Debates on 'Apatridie,'" box 298, Apatrides, 1947–1959, Archives du Ministère des Affaires Étrangères, La Corneuve.

21 "Ad Hoc Committee on Statelessness and Related Problems: Personal Summary Records of the Fourth Meeting," January 10, 1950, box 17, files of Durward V. Sandifer, Deputy Assistant Secretary of State for United Nations Affairs, 1944–1954, RG59, National Archives and Records Administration.

22 "Report of the Ad Hoc Committee on Statelessness—Position Paper," June 10, 1950, ECOSOC SD/E/448, box 3, RG59 General Records of the Department of State, National Archives and Records Administration.

23 Ibid.

24 UN General Assembly, "Convention Relating to the Status of Refugees," July 28, 1951, http://www.ohchr.org/EN/ProfessionalInterest/Pages/StatusOfRefugees.aspx.

25 On the distinction between asylum and *non-refoulement*, see James C. Hathaway, *The Rights of Refugees under International Law* (Cambridge: Cambridge University Press, 2005), 300–302.

26 On recent refugee historiography identifying a more insidious relationship between humanitarian actors and postwar national homogenization, see Pamela Ballinger, "Impossible Returns, Enduring Legacies: Recent Historiography of Displacement and the Reconstruction of Europe after World War II," *Contemporary European History* 22, no. 1 (2013): 127–138. Also see Mark Mazower, *Hitler's Empire: How the Nazis Ruled Europe* (New York: Penguin, 2008), 602–603.

27 "Is Statelessness an Evil? A Collection of Opinions, Statements, Declarations," box 4, Ivan S. Kerno Papers, Hoover Institution Archives. A lifelong international civil servant, Kerno began working at the Czechoslovak Foreign Service at the Paris Peace Conference and later became a member of the secretariat of the League of Nations. Before that, he studied law in Budapest and Paris. After the war, he became the assistant secretary-general for the UN Legal Department, and in this capacity he supervised the work of the International Law Commission. He drafted his legal reflections on statelessness at the same time that he faced the precariousness of his own status as a suspected communist who sought asylum in the United States. Kerno Travel Pass, box 2, Ivan S. Kerno Papers, Hoover Institution Archives. "Czech Ex Official of UN Says He Will Stay in US as an Exile," *Herald Tribune*, September 30, 1952, box 1, Ivan S. Kerno Papers, Hoover Institution Archives.

28 "Commentary on G. Scelle," Paul Weis Papers, PW/PR/IRO/6, Social Science Library, Oxford. On Lauterpacht's postwar faith in a transcendent international legal order, see Surabhi Ranganathan, "Between Philosophy and Anxiety: The Early International Law Commission, Treaty Conflict and the Project of International Law," *British Yearbook of International Law* 83, no. 1 (2013), 82–114.

29 Georges Scelle, "Le Problème de L'apatridue devant la Commission du Droit international de l'O.N.U.," *Die Friedens-Warte* 52 (1953/55): 142–153.

30 H. Lauterpacht to P. Weis, March 5, 1951, Paul Weis Papers, PW/WR/PUBL/9, Social Science Library, Oxford.

31 H. Lauterpacht to Cordova, September 17, 1953, Paul Weis Papers, PW/PR/IRO/6, Social Science Library, Oxford.

32 "Commentary on G. Scelle," Paul Weis Papers, PW/PR/IRO/6, Social Science Library, Oxford. Budislav Vukas, "International Instruments Dealing with the Status of Stateless Persons and of Refugees," *Revue Belge de Droit International* 8, no. 1 (1972): 142–144.

33 *1954 Convention Relating to the Status of Stateless Persons*, New York, September 28, 1954 (London: H. M. Stationery Office, 1960).

34 US State Department officials described the convention as one of "principal interest to European states." Durward V. Sandifer to M. Hickerson, January 16, 1950, Statelessness: Ad Hoc Convention, box 17, RG 59, General Records of the Department of State, National Archives and Records Administration.

35 See David Kennedy, *A World of Struggle: How Power, Law, and Expertise Shape Global Political Economy* (Princeton, NJ: Princeton University Press, 2016), 238. See generally, Max Weber, *Economy and Society: An Outline of Interpretive Sociology*, ed. Guenther Roth and Claus Wittich (Berkeley: University of California Press, 1968).

36 Ann Orford, "Constituting Order," in *Cambridge Companion to International Law*, ed. Martti Koskenniemi and James Crawford (Cambridge: Cambridge University Press, 2012), 286.

37 "Karl Marx and the Tradition of Western Political Thought," Christian Gauss Seminar in Criticism, Princeton University, Princeton, NJ, Speeches and Writings File, 1923–1975, Hannah Arendt Papers, Library of Congress. Aristide Zolberg, "The Formation of New States as a Refugee Generating Process," *Annals of the American Academy of Political and Social Science* 467, no. 1 (1983): 24–38.

38 Hannah Arendt, *Denktagebuch: 1950–1973*, bk. 17, ed. Ursula Lutz (Munich: Piper, 2002), 420.

39 On Arendt's response to American denationalization of suspected communists, see Elisabeth Young-Bruehl, *Hannah Arendt: For Love of the World* (New Haven, CT: Yale University Press, 1982), 274–275.

40 "UN Asked to Call Stateless Parley: Meeting of the Last Twenty Nations to Discuss Plight of Vast Group Sought," *New York Times*, October 17, 1954, 9. Excerpts and Notes, Minority statelessness, Speeches and Writings File, 1923–1975, Hannah Arendt Papers, Library of Congress.

41 Hannah Arendt, "Statelessness," lecture, 1955, Speeches and Writings File, 1923–1975, Hannah Arendt Papers, Library of Congress.

42 Ibid.

43 Ibid.

44 On Arendt's general aversion to legal formalism, see Christian Volk, "From Nomos to Lex: Hannah Arendt on Law, Politics, and Order," *Leiden Journal of International Law* 23, no. 4 (2010): 759–779.

45 On the postwar conflation of civil society, external security, and sovereignty, see Charles Maier, *Leviathan 2.0: Inventing Modern Statehood* (Cambridge, MA: Belknap Press, 2014). For the recent revisionist literature in American legal history criticizing the presumed opposition between state and civil society, see Jeremy Kessler, "The Struggle for Administrative Legitimacy," *Harvard Law Review* 129, no. 3 (2016): 718–783. On the creation of a bourgeois public space distinct from and in opposition to the state apparatus, and the reintegration of state and society in the welfare state, see Jürgen Habermas, *The Structural Transformation of the Public Sphere: An Inquiry into a Category of Bourgeois Society*, trans. Thomas Burger (Cambridge, MA: MIT Press, 1991).

46 The British theorist of the postwar welfare state T. H. Marshall developed the idea of "social citizenship," which likewise portrayed formal membership in a less favorable

light. T. H. Marshall, *Citizenship and Social Class, and Other Essays* (Cambridge: Cambridge University Press, 1950).

47 In a letter to her former mentor Karl Jaspers from December 1953, Arendt expressed her doubts on the durability of the American republic, worrying that it was being "dissolved from within by the democracy" and that "society is overwhelming the republic." Intellectuals, she wrote, were confused about these matters, and the blame for this confusion "lies with the sociologists and psychologists in whose conceptual swamp everything founders and sinks." Hannah Arendt to Karl Jaspers, December 21, 1953, in *Hannah Arendt / Karl Jaspers: Correspondence, 1926–1969*, ed. Lotte Kohler and Hans Saner (New York: Harcourt Brace Jovanovich, 1992), 236.

48 Hannah Arendt, *The Human Condition* (Chicago: University of Chicago Press, 1958); Dorothy Ross, "Changing Contours of the Social Science Disciplines," in *The Cambridge History of Science: The Modern Social Sciences*, vol. 7, ed. Dorothy Ross and Theodor Porter (Cambridge: Cambridge University Press, 2003), 205–238. Social scientists frequently came under attack in her writing for failing to comprehend the radically new understanding of human behavior required by the revelation of the concentration and extermination camps. See, for example, Arendt, "Social Science Technique and the Study of Concentration Camps," *Jewish Social Studies* 12, no. 1 (1950): 49–64.

49 See Angus Burgin, *The Great Persuasion: Reinventing Free Markets since the Depression* (Cambridge, MA: Harvard University Press, 2012). Arendt famously worried that the questions of redistribution at the heart of the welfare state could not sustain the realm of public citizenship. See Dana Villa, "Introduction: The Development of Arendt's Political Thought," in *The Cambridge Companion to Hannah Arendt* (Cambridge: Cambridge University Press, 2000), 1–25; Hanna Pitkin, *The Attack of the Blob: Hannah Arendt's Concept of the Social* (Chicago: University of Chicago Press, 1998); Steven Klein, "Fit to Enter the World: Hannah Arendt on Politics, Economics, and the Welfare State," *American Political Science Review* 108, no. 4 (2014): 856–869; Sheldon Wolin, *Politics and Vision: Continuity and Innovation in Western Political Thought* (Boston: Little, Brown, 1960).

50 Rogers Brubaker noted in his classic comparative study of citizenship in France and Germany that formal citizenship, the legal connection that binds individuals to particular states, has been largely neglected in the postwar social sciences. Brubaker, *Citizenship and Nationhood in France and Germany* (Cambridge, MA: Harvard University Press, 1992), 21–22. On this point also see Peter Sahlins, *Unnaturally French: Foreign Citizens in the Old Regime And After* (Ithaca, NY: Cornell University Press, 2004), xii.

51 Cited in Ayelet Shachar, "The Marketization of Citizenship in an Age of Restrictionism," *Ethics and International Affairs* 32, no. 1 (2018): 3–13.

52 Robert D. Sloane, "Breaking the Genuine Link: The Contemporary International Legal Regulation of Nations," *Harvard International Law Review* 50, no. 1 (2009): 4; Cindy G. Buys, "Nottebohm's Nightmare: Have We Exorcised the Ghosts of WWII Detention Programs or Do They Still Haunt Guantanamo?," *Chicago Kent Journal of International and Comparative Law* 11, no. 1 (2011): 1–76.

53 "Nottebohm Case (Second Phase)," I. C. J. Reports, 1955, http://www.icj-cij.org /docket/files/18/2676.pdf.

54 J. Mervyn Jones, "The Nottebohm Case," *The International and Comparative Law Quarterly* 5, no. 2 (1956): 244.

55 Legal scholars have described the ruling as part of a "romantic period of international relations" by affirming the principle that nationality should reflect a social fact of attachment. See Karen Knop, "Statehood, Territory, People, Government," in *The Cambridge Companion to International Law*, ed. James Crawford and Martti Koskenniemi (Cambridge: Cambridge University Press, 2012), 95–117. On decolonization generating an antiformalistic international law, see Umut Ozsu, "Determining New Selves: Mohammed Bedjaoui on Algeria, Western Sahara, and Post-Classical International Law," in *The Battle for International Law in the Decolonization Era*, ed. Jochen von Bernstorff and Philipp Dann (Oxford: Oxford University Press, 2019), 341–358.

56 "Nottebohm Case (Second Phase)," I. C. J. Reports, 1955.

57 On the creation of new states during decolonization through the recognition of international society, see Matthew Connelly, *A Diplomatic Revolution: Algeria's Fight for Independence and the Origins of the Post–Cold War Era* (Oxford: Oxford University Press, 2003).

58 *The Reminiscences of Sir Muhammad Zafrulla Khan*, interview conducted by Wayne Wilcox and Aisle T. Embree for Columbia University (Maple, Canada: Oriental, 2004), 188–190.

59 "American Department—Guatemala," January 6, 1953, FO 371/103358, TNA: PRO.

60 Annex to the memorandum from Mr. Schwelb to M. De Seynes of February 24, 1955, on the Right of Self-Determination, SOA 317/1/03 A.

61 "Nottebohm Case (*Liechtenstein v. Guatemala*) (Dissenting Opinion of Judge Guggenheim)," *International Court of Justice Reports of Judgments* 4, Advisory Opinions and Orders 1955, 59–60.

62 Elihu Lauterpacht, *The Life of Hersch Lauterpacht* (Cambridge: Cambridge University Press, 2010), 383.

63 Henry Franklin Butler et al., "The Draft Conventions on Statelessness of the International Law Commission," *Proceedings of the American Society of International Law at Its Annual Meeting*, 6th session (April 27, 1956), 173. On Soubbotich's interwar work on legal nationality, see Ivan Soubbotich, *Effets de la dissolution de l'Autriche-Hongrie sur la nationalité de ses ressortisants* (Paris: Rousseau, 1926).

64 Butler et al., "Draft Conventions," 175–176.

65 Paul Weis, *Nationality and Statelessness in International Law* (London: Stevens, 1956), 3.

66 Paul Weis, "The International Protection of Refugees," *American Journal of International Law* 48, no. 2 (1954): 193–221.

67 Weis, *Nationality and Statelessness*, 3.

68 Ibid., xvii. See also Nissim Bar-Yaacov, *Dual Nationality* (London: Stevens, 1961). Bar Yaacov's book is based on a dissertation supervised by Lauterpacht at Cambridge University and traces the principle of effective nationality back to court cases at the turn of the twentieth century.

69 "Denmark: Memorandum with Draft Convention on the Reduction of Statelessness," 1955, A/CONF.9/4, http://legal.un.org/diplomaticconferences/1959_statelessness /vol1.shtml.

70 See United Nations Conference on the Law of the Sea, Second Committee: Summary Records of Meetings and Annexes, February 24–April 27, 1958, 4, http://legal .un.org/diplomaticconferences/lawofthesea-1958/vol/english/2nd_Cttee_vol_IV_e .pdf. Under the guise of securing the sea as a "common heritage of mankind," the UN Convention licensed bringing 40 percent of the ocean's surface under national control. Martti Koskenniemi, "The Future of Statehood," *Harvard International Law Journal* 32, no. 2 (1991): 397–410. Debates over the boundaries of sovereignty in relation to airspace and outer space in this period likewise reflect the broader trend of nationalization. See Philip C. Jessup and Howard J. Taubenfeld, *Controls for Outer Space and the Antarctic Analogy* (New York: Columbia University Press, 1959); Stuart Banner, *Who Owns the Sky? The Struggle to Control Air Space from the Wright Brothers On* (Cambridge, MA: Harvard University Press, 2008), chap. 9. On the uniformity of migration law produced by postcolonial states from the 1940s to the 1970s as a crucial dimension of modern global convergence, see Alison Bashford, "Immigration Restriction: Rethinking Period and Place from Settler Colonies to Postcolonial Nations," *Journal of Global History* 9, no. 1 (2013): 26–48.

71 Josef L. Kunz, "The Nottebohm Judgment (Second Phase)," *American Journal of International Law* 54, no. 3 (1960): 536–571.

72 On the broader crisis of formalism in the international legal profession and in legal thought more generally, see Martti Koskenniemi, *The Gentle Civilizer of Nations: The Rise and Fall of International Law, 1870–1960* (Cambridge: Cambridge University Press, 2001); Judith Shklar, *Legalism: Law, Morals and Political Trials* (Cambridge, MA: Harvard University Press, 1964); David Kennedy, *The Dark Side of Virtue: Reassessing Modern Humanitarianism* (Princeton, NJ: Princeton University Press, 2005), 210–211; Kennedy, *World of Struggle*, 234; Rosalyn Higgins, *The Development of International Law through the Political Organs of the United Nations* (Oxford: Oxford University Press, 1963). Legal scholars from the global south endorsed the turn away from classical legal positivism as a way to empower non-European states. Umut Özsu, "'In the Interest of Mankind as a Whole': Mohammed Bedjaoui's New International Economic Order," *Humanity* 6, no. 1 (2015): 129–143.

73 Ian Brownlie, "The Relations of Nationality in Public International Law," *British Yearbook of International Law* 39, no. 284 (1963): 284–264.

74 Ian Brownlie, "The Individual before International Tribunals," *International and Comparative Law Quarterly* 11, no. 3 (1962): 701–720.

75 Josef Kunz, "The Distinctiveness of the International Legal System: Comparison and Contrast," *Ohio State Law Journal* 22, no. 3 (1961): 449. Marek St. Korowicz, a Polish scholar of international and constitutional law who had studied at the Jagiellonian University in Lviv before the Second World War, concluded that the proliferation of international and transnational legal instruments reflected the ultimate disintegration of international law into a dizzying number of branches from

maritime and air law to international crimes. Marek St. Korowicz, *Introduction to International Law: Present Conceptions of International Law in Theory and Practice* (The Hague: Martinus Nijhof, 1959), 21. Also see M. Korowicz, "The Problem of the International Personality of Individuals," *American Journal of International Law* 50, no. 3 (1956): 533–562.

76 Robert Kann, *The Habsburg Empire: A Study in Integration and Disintegration* (New York: Octagon, 1957). "National equality without the social basis of equal rights is a mere travesty that reduces supranational compromise to an empty formula." Robert A. Kann, "Die Habsburgermonarchie und das Problem des ubernationalen Staaten," in *Die Habsburger Monarchie, 1848–1918*, ed. Adam Wandruszka and Peter Urbanitsch, vol. 2 (Vienna: Austrian Academy of Science Press, 1975), 22, cited in Gerald Stourzh, "Multinational Empire Revisited," in *From Vienna to Chicago and Back: Essays on Intellectual History and Political Thought in Europe and America* (Chicago: University of Chicago Press, 2007), 135.

77 In his article on the legal aspects of the trial, Hans Baade registered the controversy over the *Nottebohm* decision, citing Josef Kunz's disagreement with the ruling. Hans W. Baade, "The Eichmann Trial: Some Legal Aspects," *Duke Law Journal* 1961, no. 3 (1961): 400–420.

78 Yosal Rogat, *The Eichmann Trial and the Rule of Law* (Santa Barbara, CA: Center for the Study of Democratic Institutions, 1961), 24; Book annotations, *The Eichmann Trial and the Rule of Law*, General, 1938–1976, Rogat, Yosal, Correspondence File, 1938–1976, Hannah Arendt Papers, Library of Congress.

79 Hannah Arendt, *Eichmann in Jerusalem: A Report on the Banality of Evil* (New York: Viking Press, 1963), 238. See Roy T. Tsao, "Arendt and the Modern State: Variations on Hegel in 'The Origins of Totalitarianism,'" *Review of Politics* 66, no. 1 (2004): 133.

80 Hannah Arendt, *On Revolution* (New York: Viking, 1963), 108–109. Arendt shared an interest in the mysteries of legal personality at this particular moment with Ernst Kantorowicz, the author of *The King's Two Bodies*, a work published in 1957 that developed out of an earlier reflection on the mystical medieval origins of sovereignty from a shorter essay written for a festschrift for Max Radin, a legal philosopher who developed some of the central twentieth-century legal writing on the subject of corporate legal personality. Kantorowicz argued that medieval corporation theory built on Roman legal conceptual foundations but acquired a deeper conception of the immortality of legal constructions like corporations, and later states, from its medieval ideas about the eternal life of angels and the doctrine of corpus Christi, entities that maintain their identity in spite of change. See Ernst Kantorowicz, *The King's Two Bodies: A Study in Medieval Political Theology* (Princeton, NJ: Princeton University Press, 1957). On the connection to Radin's writings, see Robert Lerner, *Ernst Kantorowicz: A Life* (Princeton, NJ: Princeton University Press, 2017), 344.

81 On the neoliberal conception of "Xenos Rights" originating in the post-Habsburg imperial setting, see Quinn Slobodian, *The Globalists: The End of Empire and the Birth of Neoliberalism* (Cambridge, MA: Harvard University Press, 2018). On Arendt's

criticism of "the social" and a comparison of her thought with that of Hayek, see Wendy Brown, *In the Ruins of Neoliberalism: The Rise of Antidemocratic Politics in the West* (New York: Columbia University Press, 2019). William Davies, *The Limits of Neoliberalism: Authority, Sovereignty, and the Logic of Competition* (Los Angeles, CA: Sage, 2017), 8.

82 On the postwar US cases, see Patrick Weil, *The Sovereign Citizen: Denaturalization and the Origins of the American Republic* (Philadelphia: University of Pennsylvania Press, 2013), chap. 11. See Sigal Ben-Porath and Rogers Smith, eds., *Varieties of Sovereignty and Citizenship* (Philadelphia: University of Pennsylvania Press, 2013).

83 *Trop v. Dulles*, 356 U.S. 86, 101 (1958); *Trop v. Dulles*, October Term 1957, box 104 folders 14–18 to box 105 folders 1–4, series 1, 20, reel 34, Felix Frankfurter Papers, Harvard Law School Library.

84 In his opinion, Warren cited the UN's *Study of Statelessness*, as well as works from the interwar era on the subject of statelessness written from a comparative and international legal perspective, including Edwin M. Borchard, *The Diplomatic Protection of Citizens Abroad* (New York.: Banks Law, 1915); Catherine Seckler-Hudson, *Statelessness, with Special Reference to the United States: A Study in Nationality and Conflict of Law* (Washington, DC: American University, 1934). An unsigned article by Stephan Pollack for the *Yale Law Review* on the Expatriation Act of 1954 first suggested the application of the Eighth Amendment to the expatriation cases. Pollack drew heavily on Arendt's discussion of statelessness. Weil, *Sovereign Citizen*, 160; "The Expatriation Act of 1954," *Yale Law Review* 64, no. 8 (1955): 1164–1200; *Trop v. Dulles*, October Term 1957, 104–14 to 105–4, series 1, 20, Felix Frankfurter Papers, Harvard Law School Library.

85 *Trop v. Dulles*, 356 U.S. 86, 125 (1958).

86 *Trop v. Dulles*, October Term 1957, 104–14 to 105–4, series 1, 20, Felix Frankfurter Papers, Harvard Law School Library.

87 *Trop v. Dulles*, 356 U.S. 86, 111–112 (1958).

88 Unlike the 1954 conference, which the United States did not participate in, the United States joined the 1959 proceedings and took a stronger interest in shaping the convention. M. Wilcox to M. Becker, January 29, 1959, UN Elimination and Reduction of Future Statelessness, box 365, A1 5536, National Archives and Records Administration. Stavropoulos to Liang, April 20, 1959, International Conference of Plenipotentiaries to Conclude a Convention on the Reduction or Elimination of Future Statelessness, SO 261/41, United Nations Office at Geneva. Nehemiah Robinson, July 1, 1960, box 96, file 5, World Jewish Committee Collection, United States Holocaust Museum Memorial; Nehemiah Robinson, *Convention Relating to the Status of Stateless Persons (A Magna Charta for Stateless Persons)* (New York: Institute of Jewish Affairs, World Jewish Congress, 1954).

89 Paul Weis, "The United Nations Convention on the Reduction of Statelessness, 1961," *International and Comparative Law Quarterly* 11, no. 4 (1962): 1073–1096; Alison Kesby, *The Right to Have Rights: Citizenship, Humanity, and International Law* (New York: Oxford University Press, 2012), 49. On the emphasis in the 1961 Convention on factual

connection and evidence of allegiance, and the influence of the Nottebohm decision, see Peter Mutharika, *The Regulation of Statelessness under International Law* (New York: Oceana, 1977), 120; Norman Bentwich, "Human Rights and the Reduction of Statelessness," *Contemporary Review* 201, no. 1153 (1962): 57–60; J. M. Ross, "English Nationality Law: Soli or Sanguinis?," in *Studies in the History of the Law of Nations*, ed. C. H. Alexandrowicz (Leiden: Martinus Nijhoff, 1970), 22.

90 Peter Gatrell, *The Making of the Modern Refugee* (Oxford: Oxford University Press, 2013).

91 See, for example, Vazira Fazila-Yaccobali Zamindar, *The Long Partition and the Making of Modern South Asia* (New York: Columbia University Press, 2007); Emma Haddad, *The Refugee in International Society: Between Sovereigns* (Cambridge: Cambridge University Press, 2008); Guy Goodwin-Gill and Jane McAdam, *The Refugee in International Law* (New York: Oxford University Press, 2007).

92 Frederick Cooper, *Citizenship between Empire and Nation: Remaking France and French Africa, 1945–1960* (Princeton, NJ: Princeton University Press, 2014).

93 In a 1966 essay Martin Wight, a British scholar of international relations, related that the "urgent problem of stateless persons" underscored the limits of the doctrine that only states had international legal personality. Martin Wight, "Western Values in International Relations," in *Diplomatic Investigations: Essays in the Theory of International Politics*, ed. Martin Wight and Herbert Butterfield (London: Allen and Unwin, 1966), 101; Rosalyn Higgins, "Conceptual Thinking about the Individual in International Law," *British Journal of International Studies* 4, no. 1 (1978): 1–19.

94 On the retention of the legal properties of statehood even under conditions of colonialism or occupation, see C. H. Alexandrowicz, "New and Original States: The Issue of Reversion to Sovereignty," in *The Law of Nations in Global History*, ed. David Armitage and Jennifer Pitts (Oxford: Oxford University Press, 2017), 375–384. Also see Matthew Craven, "The Problem of State Succession and the Identity of States under International Law," *European Journal of International Law* 9 (1998): 142–162.

95 For a survey of the populations that have become the object of the campaign to end statelessness, see Greg Constantine's website Nowhere People, http://www.nowhere people.org/.

   For the history of statelessness in Kenya, see Julie MacArthur, "Decolonizing Sovereignty: States of Exception along the Kenya-Somali Frontier," *American Historical Review* 124, no. 1 (2019): 108–143.

96 HO 213/2360, Sierra Leone: Commonwealth Citizenship to Reduce Statelessness, TNA: PRO.

97 HO 213/2345, Stateless in Zanzibar, 1964, Letter Solicitor Murgatroyd to O'Connor, Nationality and Consular department, July 8, 1965. People of Indian origin, who became registered as citizens of the United Kingdom and colonies when Zanzibar was still a protectorate, exchanged that citizenship for citizenship of Zanzibar when it became an independent commonwealth country in 1963, and were deprived of their citizenship by the revolutionary government in January 1964 so that they became stateless. On the fact that the United Kingdom continued to deploy complex legal

arrangements as the empire transferred sovereignty, see Steven Krasner, *Organized Hypocrisy* (Princeton, NJ: Princeton University Press, 1999), 230; Oliver Lissitzyn, "Territorial Entities Other than States in the Law of Treaties, vol. 125," in *Collected Courses of the Hague Academy of International Law* (1968); Vishnu D. Sharma, F. Wooldridge, "Some Legal Questions Arising from the Expulsion of the Ugandan Asians," *International and Comparative Law Quarterly* 23, no. 397 (1974): 397–425; HO 213/2360, Sierra Leone: Commonwealth Citizenship to Reduce Statelessness, TNA: PRO. Letter October 14, 1965.

98 Seth Anziska, *Preventing Palestine: A Political History from Camp David to Oslo* (Princeton, NJ: Princeton University Press, 2018); Paul Thomas Chamberlin, *The Global Offensive: The United States, The Palestine Liberation Organization, and the Making of the Post-Cold War Order* (Oxford: Oxford University Press, 2012); Lydia Walker, "Decolonization in the 1960s: On Legitimate and Illegitimate Nationalist Claims-Making," *Past and Present* 242, no. 1 (2019): 227–264.

99 Peter Mutharika, *The Regulation of Statelessness under International and National Law* (New York, 1977). The 1961 Convention on the Reduction of Statelessness took twelve years to secure the necessary ratifications, and now has only fifty-five state parties. For some exceptions to general scholarly neglect, see Myres McDougal, Harold Lasswell, and Lung-chu Chen, "Nationality and Human Rights: The Individual and External Arenas," *Yale Law Journal* 83 (1974): 900–998; Dorothy Jean Walker, "Statelessness: Violation or Conduit for Violation of Human Rights?," *Human Rights Quarterly* 3, no. 1 (1981): 106–123, cited in *The State of the World's Refugees*, http://www.unhcr.org/3eb7ba7d4.html; T. R. Subramanya, "Problem of Statelessness in International Law," *International Studies* 26, no. 337 (1989): 337–350.

CONCLUSION

1 Matthew Seet, "The Origins of the UNHCR's Global Mandate on Statelessness," *International Journal of Refugee Law* 28, no. 1 (2016): 7–24; Mark Manly and Santosh Persaud, "UNHCR and Responses to Statelessness," *Forced Migration Review* 32 (2009): 7; Andras Fehervary, "Citizenship, Statelessness and Human Rights: Recent Developments in the Baltic States," *International Journal of Refugee Law* 5, no. 3 (1993): 392–423.

2 Printed as J. G. A. Pocock, "The Politics of History: The Subaltern and the Subversive", in *Political Thought and History: Essays on Theory and Method*, ed. Pocock (Cambridge: Cambridge University Press, 2009), 256. On the normative tension between human rights and sovereign equality, see Jean Cohen, *Globalization and Sovereignty: Rethinking Legality, Legitimacy, and Constitutionalism* (Cambridge: Cambridge University Press, 2012). For an acute analysis of how the "globalization narrative" portrays a new era of globalization, transnational interaction, and privatization emerging in the 1970s that reconfigures borders, and generates new configurations of postnational membership and deterritorialized identities, see Adam Mckeown, *Melancholy Order: Asian Migration and the Globalization of Borders* (New York: Columbia University Press, 2008).

3 See for example Gidon Gottlieb, *Nation against State: A New Approach to Ethnic Conflicts and the Decline of Sovereignty* (New York: Council on Foreign Relations Press, 1993). For a critical perspective on these proposals, see Nathaniel Berman, "Legalizing Jerusalem or, Of Law, Fantasy, and Faith," *Catholic University Law Review* 45, no. 3 (1996): 823–836.

4 Miranda Johnson, *The Land Is Our History: Indigeneity, Law, and the Settler State* (Oxford: Oxford University Press, 2016); S. James Anaya, *Indigenous Peoples in International Law* (New York: Oxford University Press, 1996); Benedict Kingsbury, "Indigenous Peoples in International Law: A Constructivist Approach to the Asian Controversy," *American Journal of International Law* 92, no. 414 (1998).

5 See for example Quentin Skinner and Bo Strath, "Introduction," in *States and Citizens: History, Theory, Prospects*, ed. Skinner and Strath (Cambridge: Cambridge University Press, 2003), 2.

6 In the work of the Italian philosopher Giorgio Agamben, inspired by Arendt's writings on the stateless, the figure of the excluded person who is still subject to power is the essence of a previously concealed political sovereignty. Giorgio Agamben, *Homo Sacer: Sovereign Power and Bare Life* (Stanford, CA: Zone Books, 1998).

7 Lauren Benton, *Search for Sovereignty: Law and Geography in European Empires, 1400–1900* (Cambridge: Cambridge University Press, 2009), chap. 6.

8 See Atossa Abrahamian, *The Cosmopolites: The Coming of the Global Citizen* (New York: Columbia Global Reports, 2015).

9 Statement by António Guterres, United Nations High Commissioner for Refugees, Third Committee of the General Assembly, 68th Session, November 6, 2013, http://www.unhcr.org/52a83ce99.html. Brad Blitz and Caroline Sawyer provide a comprehensive overview of contemporary literature. See Caroline Sawyer and Brad K. Blitz, *Statelessness in the European Union: Displaced, Undocumented, Unwanted* (Cambridge: Cambridge University Press, 2011). Legal analysis interprets international agreements to overcome the protection gap through legal ingenuity and analysis—drawing on the UDHR, the ICCPR, The Convention on the Rights of the Child. See Carol Batchelor, "Stateless Persons: Some Gaps in International Protection," *International Journal of Refugee Law* 7, no. 2 (1995): 232–259; Batchelor, "Transforming International Legal Principle into National Law: The Right to a Nationality and the Avoidance of Statelessness," *Refugee Survey Quarterly* 25, no. 3 (2006): 8–25; Laura Van Waas, "Nationality Matters, 5 Years On: How Far Statelessness Has Travelled," November 28, 2013, http://statelessprog.blogspot.hu/2013/11/nationality-matters-5-years-on-how-far.html.

10 UNHCR, *The State of the World's Refugees: A Humanitarian Agenda* (1997), chap. 6 "Statelessness and Citizenship," http://www.unhcr.org/3eb7ba7d4.html. Also see Margaret Somers, *Genealogies of Citizenship: Markets, Statelessness and the Right to Have Rights* (Cambridge: Cambridge University Press, 2008); Jacqueline Bhabha, ed., *Children without a State: A Global Human Rights Challenge* (Cambridge, MA: MIT Press, 2011); Tendayi Bloom, Katherine Tonkiss, and Phillip Cole, eds., *Understanding Statelessness* (London: Routledge, 2017). According to James Hathaway, an expert on

international refugee law, "it is not enough . . . that the claimant carries a second passport from a nonpersecutory states if that state is not in fact willing to afford protection against return to the country of persecution." James Hathaway, *The Law of Refugee Status* (United Kingdom: Buttersworth Canada, 1991), 59.

11 See Guy Goodwin Gill on the potential for the Nottebohm case to have relevance beyond its limited context, https://www.ejiltalk.org/statelessness-is-back-not-that-it-ever-went-away/.

12 Hamsa Murthy, "Sovereignty and Its Alternatives: On the Terms of (Illegal) Alienage in US Law," in *Who Belongs? Immigration, Citizenship, and the Constitution of Legality,* ed. Austin Sarat (Bingley, UK: Emerald, 2013), 1–29; William E. Conklin, *Statelessness: The Enigma of an International Community* (Oxford: Bloomsbury, 2014); Eric Fripp, *Nationality and Statelessness in the International Law of Refugee Status* (Oxford: Bloomsbury, 2016); Linda Bosniak, "Being Here: Ethical Territoriality and the Rights of Immigrants," *Theoretical Inquiries in Law* 8, no. 2 (2007): 389–410.

13 Conklin, *Statelessness,* 223.

14 On the general neglect of the outward dimensions of citizenship and belonging in the social sciences and in political theory, see Linda Bosniak, *The Citizen and the Alien: Dilemmas of Contemporary Membership* (Princeton, NJ: Princeton University Press, 2006); Rogers Brubaker, *Citizenship and Nationhood in France and Germany* (Cambridge, MA: Harvard University Press, 1992). Though more recently, see Sarah Fine and Lea Ypi, eds., *Migration in Political Theory: The Ethics of Movement and Membership* (Oxford: Oxford University Press, 2016); Anna Stilz, *Territorial Sovereignty: A Philosophical Exploration* (Oxford: Oxford University Press, 2019). For an example of how the postwar agreements provide the basis for normative reflection on refugees and stateless persons, see for example David Owen, "On the Normative Basis of the Institution of Refugeehood," in *Migration in Political Theory: The Ethics of Movement and Membership,* ed. Fine and Ypi (Oxford: Oxford University Press, 2016); M. J. Gibney "The Rights of Non-Citizens to Membership," in *Statelessness in the European Union: Displaced, Undocumented, Unwanted,* ed. C. Sawyer and B. Blitz (Cambridge: Cambridge University Press, 2011), 45.

15 Melissa Lane, "Positivism: Reactions and Developments," in *The Cambridge History of Twentieth-Century Political Thought,* ed. Richard Bellamy and Terence Ball (Cambridge: Cambridge University Press, 2008), 321–342. On postwar liberal political philosophy, see Katrina Forrester, *In The Shadow of Justice: Postwar Liberalism and the Remaking of Political Philosophy* (Princeton, NJ: Princeton University Press, 2019).

16 Bruce Mazlish and Alfred Chandler, *Leviathans: Multinational Corporations and the New Global History* (Cambridge: Cambridge University Press, 2005); Kim Rubenstein and Daniel Adler, "International Citizenship: The Future of Nationality in a Globalized World," *Indiana Journal of Global Legal Studies* 7, no. 2 (2000): 519–548; Turkuler Isiksel, "The Rights of Man and the Rights of Man-Made," *Human Rights Quarterly* 38, no. 2 (2016): 308; Jose Alvarez, "Are Corporations 'Subjects' of International Law?," *Santa Clara Journal of International Law* 9, no. 1 (2011). It is moral personality that some hope to extend to nonnatural persons, based on the idea that trees

and landmarks, wilderness, corporations, states, and other artificial persons also have moral standing comparable to that of human beings. Christopher Stone, *Should Trees Have Standing? Law, Morality, and the Environment* (Oxford: Oxford University Press, 2010).

17 Charles Maier, *Once within Borders: Territories of Power, Wealth, and Belonging since 1500* (Cambridge, MA: Harvard University Press, 2017).

18 Marija Dobrić, "Rising Statelessness Due to Disappearing Island States: Does the Current Status of International Law Offer Sufficient Protection?," *Statelessness and Citizenship Review* 1, no. 1 (2019): 42–68; Heather Alexander and Jonathan Simon, "No Port, No Passport: Why Submerged States Can Have No Nationals," *Washington International Law Journal* 26, no. 2 (2017); Paulina Ochoa Espejo, "Taking Place Seriously: Territorial Presence and the Rights of Immigrants," *Journal of Political Philosophy* 24, no. 1 (2016): 67–87; Espejo, "People, Territory, and Legitimacy in Democratic States," *American Journal of Political Science* 58, no. 2 (2014): 466–478.

ACKNOWLEDGMENTS

It is a great pleasure to thank the teachers, mentors, friends, and family who have made this book possible.

This study took shape at Harvard University, where I was fortunate to develop the project under the guidance of David Armitage, Peter Gordon, Charles Maier, and Samuel Moyn. David Armitage believed in the book from early on in my research and encouraged me to range widely in my research and thinking across political philosophy, international history, and international legal theory. David has been a supremely generous advisor and teacher, as well as a steadfast source of encouragement, inspiration, and support.

At Harvard, I received guidance and vital instruction from Emma Rothschild, Alison Johnson, Mary Lewis, Erez Manela, and Jim Kloppenberg. I'm grateful to Charles Maier for many rich conversations that shaped my understanding and approach to international history. Peter Gordon challenged me to dig deeply into what it means to write the history of the category of statelessness and the moral and human implications of doing so. I'm grateful to Peter for his long-standing support and encouragement.

My time at Harvard was enriched through friendship and conversation with Phil Fileri, Jamie Martin, Erik Linstrum, Hannah Callaway, Philippa Hetherington, and Will Selinger. This project was supported financially by the Center for European Studies, the Graduate School of Arts and Sciences at Harvard, the Whiting Foundation Fellowship in the Humanities, the Edmond J. Safra Graduate Fellowship in Ethics, and the Cambridge University Centre for History and Economics.

The Princeton Society of Fellows provided an ideal community to test my ideas and expand my thinking as I transformed the dissertation into a book. I owe a great deal to Susanna Berger, Andrew Hamilton, Christophe Litwin, and Jonny Thakkar for making my years at Princeton so rich, meaningful, and lively. Mary Harper and Susan Stewart ensured that the Society of Fellows was a place of free exchange and intellectual creativity, and I'm very grateful for their incisive comments on the manuscript and for their advice and encouragement.

I'm grateful for Dirk Hartog's mentorship and guidance during my time at Princeton. Jeremy Adelman, Charles Beitz, David Bell, Dan Edelstein, Desmond Jagmohan, Harold James, Stanley Katz, Melissa Lane, David Minto, Phil Nord, Gyan Prakash, Anson Rabinbach, Daniel Rodgers, Maria Paula Saffon Sanin, Anna Stilz, and Jan Werner-Mueller were generous with their insights and comments.

For their feedback and suggestions as I revised the manuscript I'm grateful to Duncan Bell, Leora Bilsky, Nehal Bhuta, Rohit De, José Argueta Funes, Stefan-Ludwig Hoffman, Duncan Kelly, James Loeffler, Mark Mazower, Moria Paz, Jennifer Pitts, Sophie Smith, Phil Stern, and John Witt.

My thanks to audiences at the Davis Seminar at Princeton, the Legal History Forum at Yale Law School, the Planetary Futures seminar at UCL, and the Political Thought and Intellectual History Seminar at Cambridge.

I was fortunate to join a community of historians of political and legal thought at Queen Mary and to benefit from the expert advice of Richard Bourke, Joanna Cohen, Maksymilian Del Mar, Katrina Forrester, Maurizio Isabella, Aline-Florence Manent, Miri Rubin, Quentin Skinner, Gareth Stedman-Jones, Georgios Varouxakis. I'm particularly grateful to Richard for reading the complete manuscript. Julian Jackson, Maks Del Mar, Amanda Vickery, and Penny Green provided exceptional professional support under complex circumstances.

Richard Bourke has been an unfailing guide in my transition to London and now to Cambridge, and I'm grateful for his friendship and wisdom. In addition to his professional advice and steadfast support, Richard ensured that I was able to focus on my health when I needed to and helped me find my footing when I was able to return to work.

At Harvard University Press, Joyce Seltzer believed in the project long before I could imagine it as a book. I'm grateful for her guidance and her perspective on the moral and human stakes of the project. James Brandt helped me bring the book to completion, and I'm grateful for his advice and understanding. My thanks also to Mihaela Pacurer, Jamie Armstrong, Dave Prout, and the production team at Harvard.

Themes central to this study, particularly the networks and conditions that we rely on for security and safety, came into focus in a more personal way in the course of writing this book, and I've incurred many different kinds of debts to family and friends who sustained me spiritually and materially when I was compelled to put the book aside and concentrate on other things.

My friends who helped me get through a difficult period and who inspire me every day: Seth Anziska, Susana Berger, Katrina Forrester, Hana Landes, Jamie Martin, and Tehilla Sasson. Katrina and Jamie ensured that we felt welcomed and loved from the minute we arrived in London. Susana Berger has always known when to step in with clear-eyed advice and wisdom, and I hope she knows how much her friendship has meant to me. I cannot begin to express my gratitude for Katrina's friendship, and for the graceful way she has shared her insight, helped me clarify my thinking, and been there for me at crucial moments.

Samuel Moyn has been a constant source of inspiration since my first year as an undergraduate at Columbia. He has shaped this project in countless ways, read through the full manuscript, and continually nudged me toward new ideas and research directions. Sam has been a model of friendship, intellectual curiosity, and all-around *Menschlichkeit*, and I'm especially grateful for his support and grounded perspective when I needed it most.

It is difficult to properly thank my family, who I hope know how much their love and faith have meant to me, and who have done everything in their power to ensure my health and happiness in recent years. To Hannah and Brahna, for their incomparable love and understanding, and for being reliable sources of laughter and joy. To Warren, for generously furnishing a place to read and think in strange times. Ricky has shared the writing journey with me and provided sage advice at key junctures. Izabella, Eduard, and Gavriel Mullokandov welcomed me into their family—I'm extremely thankful for their love and generosity.

Asher has lived with this project as long as I have. He has patiently listened to me think aloud over the years since its inception, read drafts, and provided assurances and insight. Home is wherever he is, and his love makes everything possible.

I owe everything to my parents, Florence and Alan Siegelberg, my first and most important teachers, who have been unwavering with their loving encouragement. This book is dedicated to them, with all my love.

INDEX

Abrahamian, Atossa, 229–230
Adler, Cyrus, 143
Agamben, Giorgio, 182, 304n6
Akzin, Benjamin, 120–121
Algeria, 38, 141, 172, 212
Aliens Restrictions Bill (UK) (1914), 17
Alliance Israélite Universelle, 74
Ambler, Eric, 128–129
American Civil Liberties Union (ACLU), 41
American Indians: League of Nations and, 54
American Jewish Committee, 143
American Revolution, 190
American Society of International Law, 46, 167, 179, 213
apatrides, 73, 81, 83, 200, 263nn2–3; definitions of, 174–175; Lipovano on, 83–84; as quasi-state, 175; Vishniak on, 9, 83, 84, 158–159, 171, 214. *See also* stateless persons
apolitia, 206
Arendt, Hannah, 61, 185–192, 300n80; Aristotle and, 209; on citizenship, 207; on Eichmann, 218–219; Hayek and, 300n81; Hegel and, 291n110, 291n113; on federalism, 187–188; on human rights, 188–191; International Labor Organization and, 185–186; Jaspers and, 297n47; Kant and, 191–192; Kunz and, 216–217, 231–232; Lauterpacht and, 195; on legal personality, 192, 219; minimalist cosmopolitanism of, 190–192, 208–209; on natural rights, 95, 190; on refugees, 186, on revolution, 219, 219; on "right to have rights," 11, 189, 192; on statelessness, 157, 186–192, 205–209, 229; on "the social," 209
Aristotle, 209
Armenian refugees, 62, 73, 79; Cassin on, 169; Mandelstam on, 273n115
Askenazy, Anna, 282n86
Association de la Paix par le Droit (APD), 105–106

Atlantic Charter (1941), 160, 164
Augustine of Hippo, 185
Austria, 6, 59; citizenship laws of, 45, 59–60, 66–67, 107–109; Constitution of, 111, 124; Nansen passport and, 72; nationalities of, 275n128
Austrian League of Nations Society, 118
Austrian School of Economics, 220
Austro-Hungarian Empire. *See* Habsburg Empire

Baade, Hans W., 300n77
Baerwald, Eduard, 22–23
Bancroft Treaties, 246n52
Barker, Ernest, 99, 219
Bar-Yaacov, Nissim, 298n68
Batresco, Hélène, 193–195, 199, 201, 224
Bauer, Otto, 187
Ben Gurion, David, 92
Bentham, Jeremy, 162
Bentwich, Norman, 70, 143
Berle, Adolf A., 267n43
Berlin, Congress of (1878), 60
Bernatzik, Edmund, 109
Bernheim, Franz, 142
Beveridge, William, 169, 286n42
Bitcoin, 230
Bluntschli, Johann Kaspar, 34–35
Bolsheviks, 6, 53, 62–63, 141
Borchard, Edwin, 41, 93–95, 103, 132–133
Bourdieu, Pierre, 241n22
Brennan, William, 222–223
Bretton Woods Conference (1944), 172
Broch, Hermann, 188
Brownlie, Ian, 216, 218
Bulgaria, 6, 33, 61
Burke, Edmund, 25–26
Buzek, Jozef, 92

Campaign for World Federal Government, 286n50

311